The Minister's Annual Manual for Preaching and Worship Planning 1991-1992

Compiled and Edited by
Lois and Manfred Holck, Jr.

CHURCH MANAGEMENT, INC.
P.O. Box 162527, Austin, Texas 78716

3

This book has been typeset by
M & L Typesetting Service, Inc., of Austin, Texas
and printed by
Capital Printing Company of Austin, Texas

Scripture quotations in this publication are from the Revised Standard Version of the Bible, copyrighted 1946, 1952, 1971, 1973 by the Division of Christian Education of the National Council of Churches of Christ in the U.S.A. unless otherwise noted and are used by permission.

The *Hymn of the Day* for each worship experience has been prepared by Marilyn Stulken, who teaches organ and church music at Carthage College and organ at the University of Wisconsin, Parkside, Kenosha, Wisconsin. She is organist at St. Luke's Episcopal Church in Racine, Wisconsin and author of *Hymnal Companion to the Lutheran Book of Worship*.

The *Introductions to the Lessons* have been prepared by John R. Brokhoff, Professor Emeritus of Homiletics, Candler School of Theology, Emory University, Atlanta, Georgia.

ISBN: 0-9618891-5-2
ISSN: 0894-3966

CONTENTS

CHILDREN'S OBJECT TALKS

7

PART II   Other Worship Planning Resources

HOW TO USE THIS BOOK

This book is intended for use from August 1991 through July 1992 for your worship and preaching planning. This book is arranged to help ministers in their planning from summer to summer since many clergy find it convenient to plan a year of worship services and sermons in advance during vacation time.

Every minister, of course, develops his or her own style of preaching. The method, planning, study, writing and delivery of sermons is obviously unique to each preacher. How you preach is the result of your experiences over many years. Therefore, you will use this book in whatever ways will benefit your worship and sermon preparation most fully. Its usefulness is determined by your own style and manner of preparation.

Initially, in your planning, however, you may want to develop an overall thrust for the year, briefly detailing for each worship experience what you may plan to accomplish. Helpful suggestions to guide your thinking are included in this book for each Sunday as well as for several special worship events.

Then, once your initial planning is done, you may want to spend time several weeks in advance of a specific Sunday reviewing the texts for that day on your own. Subsequently, you may wish to review the materials in this book for that particular Sunday as you gather more information and ideas. You will certainly want to use the variety of prayers, the children's object talk and the sermon materials to develop your plan for each day.

Not all preachers use the lectionary lessons on a regular basis. If you don't use these texts for your preaching, these materials can still be extremely useful to you in providing sermon ideas and illustrations on specific texts appropriate for the time of year. On the other hand, if you are accustomed to using the lectionary lessons, you will find these materials especially suited to your preaching needs.

Since not all denominations use the same lectionary lesson listings during the entire year, this book notes the correct dates for use of the lessons for each Sunday for all major denominations. You should have no difficulty adapting these materials easily to your own church calendar.

Materials that are included for each Sunday are the following items:

Lessons as assigned for liturgical preaching.
Introduction to the Lessons brief explanation of all texts.
Theme of the day's materials.
Thought for the day to help set the tone for preaching.
Prayer of meditation prior to the worship experience.
Call to worship for the beginning of the service.
Prayer of adoration for beginning of worship.
Prayer of confession asking for forgiveness and blessing.
Prayer of dedication of gifts and self at the offering.
Hymn of the day description.
Sermon title for the day.
Announcements for next week for use in this week's bulletin.
Children's object talk for conversation with children.
The sermon including **hymns, scripture** and **sermon text.**

All of the preachers (most of whom are parish pastors) who have prepared these materials are listed in the appendix. You may wish to write any one of them to comment about their contribution to your sermon and worship planning.

You are encouraged to reprint in your Sunday bulletins the brief explanations to each of the lessons. This will be helpful to worshipers in grasping the background and context of the lessons being read.

You are also encouraged to use the announcements about the following week's worship in your bulletin. This will give your worshipers an opportunity to look forward with expectation to the next worship experience with some anticipation of subject matter.

The variety of prayers is presented to fit in with the theme for the day. Appropriate hymns are suggested, including a hymn for the day relating to the theme of the day. And the children's object talk is offered as a help to those ministers whose ministry in worship includes special attention to small children.

All texts, prayers, object talks and sermons are intended generally to follow the same theme throughout the materials for the day.

The appendices provide additional helps. Especially helpful to you can be the special article on "Resources for Preaching From the Common Lectionary". The suggestions for additional reading and study materials will provide significant helps in your sermon preparation on these many texts.

In addition, the appendices include a three-year church calendar; a 1991-1992 calendar for easy reference to dates, including all of the lectionary lessons for the year, names and addresses of all authors, and additional materials useful for sermon and worship planning.

Also included is a special listing of dedications, litanies and special services that will be useful to pastors and congregations anticipating special events, dedications, ground breakings, new buildings, etc.

For even more preaching planning helps, this book can be used in conjunction with *The Annual Planning Issue for 1991-1992* of *The Clergy Journal*. The annual planning issue of *The Clergy Journal* is an entirely different set of sermons, hymns, calls to worship and children's object talks than those included in this book. It is also published by Church Management, Inc. as the *1991 May/June* issue of *The Clergy Journal*.

Thus, preachers who use this book *and* also have a subscription to *The Clergy Journal* will have resources of unequaled value for preaching planning including:

1) three complete sets of sermons for every Sunday of the year,
2) two sets of object talks for children, plus
3) almost three dozen additional sermons, as well as
4) more hymn selections to match the texts,
5) handbook of dedication and litanies, and
6) more calls to worship and prayers.

The Minister's Annual Manual for Preaching and Worship Planning for 1991-1992 and the May/June planning issue of *The Clergy Journal* can both be helpful additions to your library of preaching resource materials.

Lois and Manfred Holck, Jr.

Spring 1991

PART I

Preaching and Worship
Resources 1991-1992

AUGUST 4, 1991

Lutheran: Eleventh Sunday after Pentecost
Roman Catholic: Eighteenth Sunday of the Year
Episcopalian: Proper 13
Pres/Meth/UCC: Eleventh Sunday after Pentecost

Lessons:

Lutheran:	Ex. 16:2-15	Eph. 4:17-24	John 6:24-35
Roman Catholic:	Ex. 16:2-4, 12-15	Eph. 4:17,20-24	John 6:24-35
Episcopal:	Ex. 16:2-4, 9-15	Eph. 4:17-25	John 6:24-35
Pres/Meth/UCC:	2 Sam. 12:15b-24	Eph. 4:1-6	John 6:24-35

Introductions to the Lessons

Lesson 1

(1) *Exodus 16:2-15* (**Lutheran**); *Exodus 16:2-4, 9-15* (**Episcopal**). The Israelites escaped from Egyptian captivity and began their wilderness wanderings. In just a few weeks the people complained that they were about to die of hunger and accused Moses of bringing them out of Egypt in order to kill them. Yahweh comes to Moses' rescue by sending quail each evening and manna each morning.

(2) *II Samuel 12:15b-24* (**Pres/Meth/UCC**). The child of David and Bathsheba, conceived out of wedlock, became seriously ill. In the hope of his recovery, David fasted, prayed, and prostrated himself. When the child died seven days later, David arose, washed, ate, and worshiped. When asked why he did not mourn, he explained that his fasting could not bring his son back to life, but some day he would go to him.

Lesson 2

(1) *Ephesians 4:17-24* (**Lutheran**); *4:17-25* (**Episcopal**). Paul contrasts the lifestyle of the Christian and the nonChristian. Before his readers became Christians, they were alienated from God and practiced every form of wickedness. This is no way for Christians to live, for Christ taught them to put away the old self for a new self that indulged in holy living.

(2) *Ephesians 4:1-6* (**Pres/Meth/UCC**). Chapter 4 begins the practical half of Ephesians. Paul appeals for unity in the church. This unity results from humility, patience, and love. Christian unity is seen in the fact that there is one Spirit, one Lord, one faith, one baptism, and one God who permeates all.

Gospel

John 6:24-35 (**Luth/Epis/Pres/UCC**). This is the second of five selections from John 6. Jesus had just fed 5000 people with a boy's lunch. The next day Jesus and his disciples go to the other side of the Sea of Galilee. The crowd follows them. Jesus tells them they came for more bread and not for his miracles. He urges them not to work for perishable but for eternal food. When they ask for this kind of bread, he reveals himself as the Bread of Life.

Theme: Only Jesus can feed a hungry heart.

Thought for the day: There is a natural hunger for God in the human heart, but our taste for the Bread of Life is only acquired through a discipleship which has been fed at the Lord's Table.

Prayer of meditation: Holy One, may we feel the stirrings of hunger this morning. May there be a rumbling in the center of our lives. Remind us that we need to have a hunger which only you can feed. Give us this day our daily bread so that we may continue to hunger for righteousness. We ask this in the name of Jesus, who is our Bread of Life.

Call to worship: O give thanks to the Lord, who is good, whose steadfast love endures for ever! Let us thank the Lord for such steadfast love, for wonderful works to all humankind. For the Lord satisfies all who are thirsty, and fills the hungry with good things. (based on Psalm 107:1, 8-9)

Prayer of adoration: O God, you are our God, we seek you, our hearts long for you, as in a dry and weary land. We have looked for your presence in the sanctuary, glimpsing your power and glory. Because your steadfast love is better than life, our lips will praise you. We will bless you as long as we live; we will lift up our hands and call on your name. (based on Psalm 63:1-4)

Prayer of confession: Hear our prayer, O Lord. Let our sighs become sounds of prayer. Our days drift away like smoke. Sin has left its scorch marks on us. Love has withered like summer grass. We are too wasted to care. Feed us with the Bread of Life. Remove the bitter taste of our mistakes with the cup of forgiveness. Restore our appetite for truth and enable us to return to the work of inviting others to your table.

Prayer of dedication of gifts and self: O Lord, our creator and redeemer, bless and empower these gifts. May they feed both the hungry and the hungry of heart. Bless those who have given with a full measure of your grace which nurtures life, body and soul, and in the life to come heals with eternal life. Amen.

Sermon title: The Way to Any One's Heart.

Sermon thesis: The miracle of communion is that the feeding of the heart by the love of God in Jesus removes the bitterness of life.

Hymn for the day: *"You satisfy the hungry heart."* Selected from among more than 200 entries, this hymn was the official hymn of the 41st International Eucharistic Congress, held in Philadelphia in 1976. The author, Omer Westendorf (b. 1916) studied at the College-Conservatory of Music of the University of Cincinnati and at age twenty began a forty-year tenure as organist-choirmaster of St. Bonaventure Church. His St. Bonaventure Choir was heard frequently on radio and television and appears on a dozen recordings of religious music. In 1950 he founded the World Library of Sacred Music and seven years later, the World Library Publications. He has written over three dozen hymns and compiled four successive hymnbooks, culminating in the *People's Mass Book.* The hymn ties closely with the sermon with its theme: "Only Jesus can feed a hungry heart."

Announcements for next week:

Sermon title: Beyond the Next Meal.

Sermon theme: The living bread of Christ's love gives our lives meaning.

Sermon summary: The ability to love and be loved that is imparted to us through communion with Christ offers a crucial dimension of meaning to our lives that no amount of material riches can provide.

Children's object talk:

God's Favorite Food

Objects: Pink mints for every child

Lesson: Sharing food is what makes a meal happy and holy.

Outline: 1. Share an example of a favorite food of yours.
2. Food is a way that we are cared for by those who love us.
3. If we love others, we will share our favorite food with them.
4. God's favorite food is any food which we share with others who are hungry.

SUNDAY MORNINGS, just about now, I get hungry for my favorite food. For some people that means hamburgers, for some people that means rice, for some people that means tacos. What that means for me is candy! Not every kind of candy, though. My favorite food isn't Mars Bars, or Milky Ways, or even M & M's. My favorite food is mints. Not every kind of mint, mind you. Just pink ones. These are my favorite kind of food, at least when I'm in church. When

17

I was your size, I used to sit behind a nice lady with silver hair in church. When I'd start to wiggle because I was hungry, or tired, she would turn around and give me a smile and this kind of pink mint. The smile made me feel as good as the mint. She was sharing with me, and that made these mints into my favorite food.

One way we know somebody loves us is that they feed us when we're hungry. Jesus fed people who came to be near him when they were hungry. One way we show that we are friends of Jesus is feeding people who are hungry today. To show we love them, we share our favorite foods, and some not so favorite ones like *spinach* so that they can have healthy, happy lives.

Sharing food makes it into happy meal. A happy meal is not something you can buy. A happy meal is something you make when you share it with someone else. Your favorite food can become somebody else's favorite food if you share it with a smile. And the most important thing to remember is that God's favorite food is any kind of food that you share with somebody who's hungry. Have a happy meal for Jesus this week.

The sermon:

The Way To Anyone's Heart

Hymns:
Beginning of worship: Come, Christians, Join to Sing
Sermon hymn: O the Depths of Love Divine
End of worship: O Thou Eternal Christ of God

Scripture: John 6:24-35

Sermon Text: *"I am the bread of life; he who comes to me shall not hunger."* v. 35

I HATE CHICKEN SOUP. I need chicken soup. My grandmother fed me chicken soup. The problem with my relation to chicken soup is that it does only what it does, not what it's supposed to do. When I was ill, either in truth or fiction, my grandmother would invariably prepare me a bowl of this foul liquid. She would place it under my nose with the comment, "This will cure all that ails you." Then she would confidently hover over me until I had finished the whole bowl and ask, "Don't you feel better now?"

This would always raise the dilemma whether I would rather break the commandments by lying or break them by telling her the truth and thereby refusing to honor my father and mother's mother so that my days may be long upon the earth. The chicken soup dilemma was this. If I admitted that my body felt better, despite the fact that I was sure I was going to die, then the physician would never be called and I would be packed off to school. If I said that I didn't feel better, then another bowl was forthcoming. It took me a long time to learn that the right answer is: chicken soup is a cure for a cold heart not a cold. Though I was taught that chicken soup was medicine for body and soul, I finally learned that it was my hunger for love and comfort that was met in my grandmother's communion. I must confess though that the sight of a can of Campbell's soup still produces a slightly queasy sensation.

Grandmother's holy chicken soup contains the ingredients for the interpretation of the text for today. There is a physical hunger and a spiritual hunger, a hunger for bread and a hunger for the Bread of Life. The mistake of the multitudes is to confuse one hunger for another. In their confusion they collapse one hunger into another.

This is not a new confusion. The multitude in the time of Moses mistook manna for a free offering on the celestial menu. Rather than experiencing it as a gift of grace they thought it was guaranteed. The multitude of Capernaum remembered the meals in the desert and wanted a similar sign from Jesus. They wanted to be fed, again and again, day by day, by the bread blessed, broken, and multiplied by Jesus. But Jesus knows that they have followed his trail of crumbs not from a hunger for righteousness but because they were hungry. They wanted to be fed, they wanted only their daily bread, not the will of God. The bitter taste of discipleship, the broken body of Christ, the cup of forgiveness was and is an acquired taste.

We can satisfy simple hunger with bread, but if we wish to satisfy a hunger for life itself then we need to feed on Christ in our hearts. We need to look beyond the life we receive from the bread to the Creator of life itself. In this way Grandmother was perhaps a profound theologian. Like all theologians she said more than she meant, and much less than the simplest mystery of grace. Her simple serving of soup was offered to cure not all that ails us but what ails us the most. A heart so hungry that it consumes itself has been fed on mere bread. Throughout the Gospel of John the mystery of the Eucharist meals is repeatedly offered in the words of Christ: "For the bread of God is that which comes down from heaven and gives life to the world."

What is the difference between the hungry multitude then and us fast food addicts today? They wanted holy food for ever and we want it right now. The multitude would have been satisfied with bread as sign of a God. We want it our way. The multitudes did not suffer from a cynical separation between sign and the thing signified. We are different, though. We think that bread is only bread, that chicken soup cannot be holy, that love is not stronger than death, and we fail to find in a simple communion the taste of a mystery. How then is it possible for us to find the connection between bread that gives life and the "bread of life," "the food which endures to eternal life"?

The miracle of communion is that it is the feeding of the heart by the love of God in Jesus that removes the bitter taste of life. This was not always clear to me. I remember though when I first learned this simple lesson. I was working my way through graduate school by waiting tables in the evening in a local restaurant. The hours were long, when there was work. After a time I became somewhat bitter at having to struggle to make ends meet by waiting upon customers who, while spending a week's pay on a dinner for two, demanded much and gave little in return. I was caught though; I needed the days for school, so I worked nights. Finally, during one summer slow season, I was so broke that I had only enough money for my next meal and no idea how I would buy my books. That day I left my apartment to return with only nine cents and in debt for a cup of coffee. I was so tired and in so much despair that the dirt of the road was about as far as I could see. But as I made the turn on the way home I discovered a package of cookies on the ground. It was one of those raisin cookie packages that are sold in the best stores. Seeing it I thought, "How strange, I want bread and I get cake." But not to be ungrateful for a little luck, I stooped to pick it up. While kneeling I happened to look up the road and I discovered to my surprise a trail of bread, cake, cookies, fruit pies, cheese danish, and all different kinds of rolls, spread from my feet all the way up the road. This was so strange that I looked around, suspecting that I was on candid camera. But there was no one around so one by one I began to pick up the packages. One by one I balanced them in my arms, and when I reached for the last package it was all I could do to pick it up and walk up the steps to my apartment without dropping the entire pile. In the couple of weeks that followed I ate the best cookies, rolls and danish that I could possibly imagine. Each time I took bread, though, in the strange communion of cookies and milk, I was struck by the mystery and a need to account for the presence of these gifts. Most probably a bread truck had forgotten to lock its back door, hit a bump and spilled the contents of a couple of trays while it turned my corner. This is an explanation. But it did not account for how good this bread tasted, even as it reached its expiration date. I expect that the bread tasted good because it fed my hunger. I felt better. But, in addition, what was good for my body was also good for my spirit. This bread was a gift, and my gratitude for this gift fed a deeper hunger, a hunger that needed a sign that life would be good whether I ate stale cookies or expensive chateaubriand. All I know is that when I was called back to work it was easier to serve and to receive. I was not so bitter, so hungry, whatever life served up. Later, when I was more a part of the communion of faith, I realized that my hunger was then and there, whether I knew it or not, being met by Jesus, who said "I am the bread of life; he who comes to me shall not hunger, and he who believes in me shall never thirst." For these gifts I am grateful.

Heather Murray Elkins
William Wesley Elkins
Bernardsville United Methodist Church
Bernardsville, New Jersey

AUGUST 11, 1991

Lutheran: Twelfth Sunday after Pentecost
Roman Catholic: Nineteenth Sunday of the Year
Episcopalian: Proper 14
Pres/Meth/UCC: Twelfth Sunday after Pentecost

Lessons

Lutheran:	1 Kings 19:4-8	Eph. 4:30-5:2	John 6:41-51
Roman Catholic:	1 Kings 19:4-8	Eph. 4:30-5:2	John 6:41-52
Episcopal:	Deut. 8:1-10	Eph. 4:(25-29) 30-5:2	John 6:37-51
Pres/Meth/UCC:	2 Sam. 18:1, 5, 9-15	Eph. 4:25-5:2	John 6:35, 41-51

Introductions to the Lessons

Lesson 1

(1) *I Kings 19:4-8* (**Lutheran**). On Mt. Carmel the prophet, Elijah, in the 9th century B.C. had a dramatic victory over the 450 prophets of Baal whom he executed. When King Ahab told his wife Jezebel what Elijah had done to her prophets, she sent word to him that she would have him dead by the next day. He flees for his life into a wilderness where an angel twice awakens and feeds him for his journey to Mt. Sinai.

(2) *Deuteronomy 8:1-10* (**Episcopal**). The Israelites are poised to enter the promised land. Before they enter, Moses gives them final admonitions. He reminds them how Yahweh led them successfully for forty years through the wilderness. They are now to enter a good land with all kinds of natural resources. In this new land he charges them to keep God's commands.

(3) *II Samuel 18:1, 5, 9-15* (**Pres/Meth/UCC**). David had a rebellious son, Absalom, who raised an army and went out to defeat his father's forces. The battle took place in a forest. Absalom's men were being routed and Absalom in fleeing had caught his head in an oak branch. His mule went on and he was left hanging in mid-air. General Joab drove three spears into the heart of Absalom.

Lesson 2

Ephesians 4:30-5:2 (**Lutheran/Episcopal**); *4:25-5:2* (**Pres/Meth/UCC**). Paul continues to give moral directives to his church: don't lie, steal, or talk evil. By so doing you grieve the Holy Spirit who is the seal of your redemption. In the place of evil, a Christian is to be kind, tenderhearted, and forgiving. By so doing we imitate God and love as Christ loves us.

22

Gospel

John 6:41-51 (**Lutheran**); *6:37-51* (**Episcopal**); *6:35, 41-51* (**Pres/Meth/UCC**). The series from John 6 continues. The Jews take issue with Jesus' claim that he is the bread of life from heaven. They question that he came from heaven because they know his parents. Jesus repeats that he is the bread of life. Their forefathers in Moses' day ate the manna from heaven and died. Believers who eat the Bread of Life will never die.

Theme: The living bread of Christ's love gives our lives meaning.

Thought for the day: Our lives do not get their meaning from solitary living and material wealth, but through loving and being loved within a community of thanksgiving. We do not live by bread alone but by communion with the love of Christ, which gives a center of meaning to our lives lived in communion with all God's children.

Prayer of meditation: O Lord of the Universe, sometimes the complexity of our lives overwhelms us. It is so easy to get lost and frantic in the daily tasks of running a household. We wonder where the meaning is and where we are going. Sometimes when we are successful and don't have to worry about mortgage payments, we can feel lost and empty, wondering what is really important. Guide us, O God. Be our center. Help us know what is real. Give us grace to see you and those around us through the eyes of Christ, whose look of love gives us new life always. Amen.

Call to worship: Jesus said, "I am the bread of life." Let us be drawn by God to this miracle of Christ's love. Jesus said, "I am the living bread." Let us worship the One who shows us the wonder of God's self-giving. Let us worship in song, praise and thanksgiving!

Prayer of adoration: O God of compassion and incarnation, we give thanks that the wonder of your love lifts us into a new day. We rejoice that the gift of your love is the gift of yourself. We offer ourselves in grateful obedience to your loving service, which fills our cup to overflowing with all that is meaningful and worthwhile. Amen.

Prayer of confession: O God, who draws us toward the living bread of Christ's unending love, we confess before you and each other that we resist your pull, like our brothers and sisters before us. We too question this Jesus. Is he not merely the son of a carpenter, Joseph? We murmur within when we hear him claim his kinship with heaven. We chafe at the thought of letting him feed and lead us. . . (Pause for reflection). . . Give us grace, O God, never to ignore your message because of the humbleness of your messenger. Help us to surrender our willful pride. Enable us to offer our willingness to be fed by Christ through common elements and relationships, that he not remain a distant curiosity for debate, but become for us the living knowledge of your unlimited, unconditional love, which gives life and light to all our days. For in the spirit of Christ's self-giving love we pray. Amen.

Prayer of dedication of gifts and self: O God of infinite and perfect love, that your love through Christ can transform us into willing and happy servants, who celebrate your love in everyday life, we give thanks. Accept now these gifts as our offering of thanks, and use them for your service in Christ's name. Amen.

Sermon title: Beyond the Next Meal

Sermon thesis: The ability to love and be loved that is imparted to us through communion with Christ offers a crucial dimension of meaning to our lives that no amount of material riches can provide.

Hymn for the day: *"O Living Bread from Heaven."* Johann Rist was a highly respected author and poet of his day. Prior to his ordination as a Lutheran pastor he studied mathematics and medicine, and in his parish near Hamburg, Germany, he ministered to the physical as well as the spiritual needs of his people. This hymn, published in 1651, was one of some 680 hymns he wrote during his lifetime. In today's sermon we are reminded that "communion with Christ offers a crucial dimension of meaning to our lives that no amount of material riches can provide." That thought is echoed in the hymn: "For you have freely given What earth could never buy."

Announcements for next week:
   Sermon title: The Bread of Life is Ours
   Sermon theme: Jesus is our bread of life.
   Sermon summary: Jesus offered himself to others by his caring, his teachings, and his self giving. He also provided the experience of the Lord's Supper for those who do not live in the first century. Christ is truly present, offering himself to us when we partake with faith.

Children's object talk:

What Do I Really Want?

Objects: If available, an expensive solitary game a child could play alongside different, cheaper games that are meant to be played with others.
Lesson: God made us for each other.
Outline: 1. Material things alone don't make us happy.

2. God made us to be happy living with others.
3. Jesus teaches us about living with others.

I WOULD LIKE to talk to you about a choice between two things and have you tell me which one you would like and why. Maybe you would like both choices and you can say why you would like each one. The choice is a pretend one. Imagine that I could give you a nice two week vacation time. One choice is that you could go alone on the vacation and have some neat toys to play with alone like an Nintendo and some video games. The other choice is that you could take along some wonderful friends, but you would only have some balls and card games and board games to play with together? Which choice would you make?

(Time for discussion, listening, acknowledging)

(Points to underline in the discussion or summary) Yes, the Nintendo would be neat, but it gets lonely and boring after awhile being by ourselves too long. We need friends to play with to be happy. God didn't make us to live alone. God made us for each other. Sometimes it is hard to live with others because we fight. We are happiest in life when we have people to love and enjoy and who love and enjoy us. Jesus came to teach us how to love and enjoy each other the way God wants.

The sermon:

Living Beyond The Next Meal

Hymns:

Beginning of worship: All Praise to Thee, for Thou, O King Divine
Sermon hymn: Jesus, Thou Joy of Loving Hearts
End of worship: Awake, Awake to Love and Work

Scripture: John 6:41-51

Sermon Text: *"I am the living bread which came down from heaven: if any one eats of this bread, he will live for ever. . ."* v. 51

IF THERE IS ONE THING I love, it is the thought of material security. I realize it is an illusory thought on one level, but on another level it would be great not to feel two paychecks or one medical catastrophe away being homeless and on the street, not to feel the oppression of being strung out on credit and up to my ears in debt so that it feels like the necessity of my work life is predetermined for the foreseeable future. Economic stress is the greatest stressor of my marriage, which puts me in with the majority. The pressure evokes dreams of winning the lottery.

What often pulls me out of such self-absorbed ruminations is coming in contact with the misery of people who have material security and couldn't be unhappier, in spite of their possessions. It's not that is it better to be in poverty than to be well-to-do, but the lack of meaning that riches in themselves do not supply is striking. When I experience the emptiness of some people who do not have to worry about finances on a survival level, I instantly affirm that I begrudge none of my debts when I realize that they have been in the service of supporting loving relationships, important causes, and education for a career with a sense of calling and vocation to it. I realize the richness of the meaning in my life that I would not trade for any amount of money. I wish I could more easily pass on these riches to some of my materially secure, spiritually searching friends who would entertain with horror the thought of living eternally in their present circumstances.

It was a similar confusion of two levels of living that is interwoven throughout John 6. Jesus feeds the five thousand. People get excited on a material level. Having one's daily bread was a real issue then. Here was Jesus performing a miracle of feeding like Moses providing manna in the wilderness, like Elisha multiplying the barley loaves (2 Kings 4:42-44).

Jesus wouldn't have provided physical food if he didn't acknowledge it as important, but he calls the people to a different level of living. He says, look, "Your fathers ate the manna in the wilderness, and they died." (v.49). I want to tell you about "the bread that comes down from heaven, that a man may eat of it and not die." (v. 50) I want to talk to you about a different kind of sustenance for the journey than just the physical.

Here Jesus actually gets the people's attention. There is a part of all of us that is drawn toward the sacred dimension of meaning. But when Jesus goes on to say things like, "I am the living bread which came down from heaven; if any one eats of this bread, he will live for ever; and the bread which I shall give for the life of the world is my flesh," (v. 51) the people revert back to the material level. They say, who is this guy anyway? "Isn't this Jesus, the son of Joseph, whose father and mother we know?" (v. 42). As biblical scholar William Barclay says, they resist being drawn by God to

Jesus through despising the message coming from such a humble messenger. But such is God's way, who from the beginning chose Abraham and others, not because they were the greatest of people, but precisely because they were the least.

The church, of course, from the luxury of looking back on such scenes from the other side, understands Jesus' reference to himself as living bread as a eucharistic reference, a reference to the bread and wine of Holy Communion. So who does the church think this Jesus is? According to John he is the Son of God who participates in the glory of God. What or who is God? God is love. What is God's glory? It is the glory of the cross of Jesus Christ. It is the glory of passionate, seeking, suffering, saving love. What are the bread and wine of the Eucharist? They are a gift, God's love through Christ made visible. They are, as Professor of Worship James White puts it, an expression of God's self-giving. "God loved the world so much that he gave." (John 3:16)

Giving can never be an abstraction. It must always take tangible form. Life is relational. We need both to be given to and to have others to whom we can give. This is the drama and unity of eucharistic worship. We hear the offer of God's life and love given to us through Christ. We thankfully offer our lives in return through presenting the bread and wine at the altar, both creations of human industry. Through the power of God's Spirit the broken bread and poured out wine become Christ's body and blood. The gift and giver become one and by Christ we are given back to ourselves whole. We are empowered to go out of the sanctuary to a life of loving service in the world God loved so much. We follow the Supreme Lover in offering the loving gift of ourselves to those around us, especially the poor, the strangers, and the enemies.

So, it is once again the old, old story. God is love. Christ is love. We, made in the image of God, are love. Love is eternal. It never dies. When we walk in love we walk in God. There is sustenance for the journey. When we walk in God we love those around us. Eucharistic worship reminds us, brings to living remembrance for us, what is real, what is true. It empowers us to love through the knowledge that we have first been loved.

As always, of course, it is easier to say all these things in the abstract than to live them out in the passionate, concrete, historical circumstances of our lives. It is hard for us to bring together the material and spiritual levels of living so that there is unity of meaning in our lives, so there is both bread and life beyond bread.

In his book, *Teach Only Love* (New York: Bantam Books, 1983) Gerry Jampolsky, a physician who works with children who have catastrophic illnesses, records the story of a nurse name Sharon Tennison who lived out the reality we are talking about.

Sharon begins her story by saying it was a mid-December day. She was affluent enough that Christmas presents were already taken care of, and her family did not need to worry about where their next meal was coming from. Her kids were busy this particular day. So, she called in to one of the area hospitals to see if they needed her on the evening shift, which they usually did. On the way to the hospital, as was her custom, her heart put out a prayer that she be placed where she could be most useful or where her mind or soul could learn something she needed, and then dropped the matter, assuming it would be so.

The hospital assigned her to a medical wing in which, she was informed, that there was a very irascible forty-four-year-old man in room 322 who was in end-stage alcoholic disease. He needed to be restrained, kept to himself, never had visitors, hurled verbal abuse when bothered, and got back at the world though such anti-social acts as not asking for bedpans, thus constantly requiring the staff to change linens. When Sharon had opportunity to check on him, she found all this to be true.

She was impressed with how offensive the air was as she approached his room; a mix of formaldehyde, human excrement, and paraldehyde, a powerful injected medicine he was taking for delirium tremens. She was also impressed, as she contrasted his shriveled-up body rolled up in a fetal position with her own healthy body, with how such devastation could have come to a man who was her same age. Her mind puzzled and wondered if there was any way to reach this withdrawn soul. Her heart told her that the only thing he could probably register would be loving, gentle service. At dinner he actually allowed her to feed him a few spoonfuls of jello, though without ever saying anything, before disappearing beneath his covers again.

When she returned later with his prescribed syringes of paraldehyde, she smelled the evidence that he had fought back again. She stood there silently beside the curtained bed. She remembered Dr. Jampolsky saying that the most offensive people were the ones in the most need of love, that we need to let go of judgment and extend love to these others as we sense them as true brothers and sisters. Knowing the needs of the ward were covered for the moment, she allowed her love to silently extend and create a sphere which included her and this little restrained man whose days were numbered. As she did so a realization welled up within her that he had probably never been touched in a kind way in his entire forty-four years. A vision came to her of a poor Mexican boy, from a large family, growing up poor and without support, who turned to the bottle for consolation.

She didn't know if the visions were in her own mind or were sensitive intuitions of the truth, but it didn't matter. She put the syringes aside, sat down on the bed, and let her heart lead her in brushing the black hair from his eyes and silently giving gentle, comforting touch to the small boy she envisioned in her mind. Some time later she found herself saying something to him in a more loving tone than she normally used. He responded. He began to tell her his story, a story of drinking as a teenager to drown the misery he felt growing up in a harsh border town in Texas. He wouldn't choose to drink again if he had his life to live over, but he knew he would go back to it if he lived to get out of the hospital.

Sharon felt that all of her training to support a fight for life and the conquest of disease was not useful here. She thought to herself that "my heart just loves this little man. Whether he can quit alcohol or not is not material to me. He is precious, and by some quirk of fate, I have been allowed to see into him and love him somewhere deep where alcohol doesn't touch." (p. 86) She held his hand and acknowledged with him the pain and predicament of his life. She let him know his specialness to her. She sensed his soul might soon leave his crippled body and realized that what was important was that he go into eternity knowing that he had been loved and accepted. Later he was untied, no longer combative. His bed was changed. He apologized for the extra work. There was a new feeling in the room.

As for Sharon, she went away from the room exclaiming to herself, "Oh, Jesus, this is how you must feel – about all the children of Earth – as we get caught in the webs of limitations, and get lost. You see beyond all this into the core of our very being. *So this is how unconditional love feels.* It is my first experience at this depth, and I feel lifted into another dimension by being allowed to share in this oneness." (pp. 86-7).

Sharon shared in a communion of love which healed her as well as the man. She shared in an eternal moment of giving and receiving which can never die, an eternity that gave both her and the man sustenance for their journeys. She had followed Jesus in making her gift and herself one. She had an increased sense of meaning from participating in a living bread that transcended and infused the material level of her life. So may it be with us.

Gregory J. Johnson
Delaware Valley United Methodist Church
Branchville, New Jersey

AUGUST 18, 1991

Lutheran: Thirteenth Sunday after Pentecost
Roman Catholic: Twentieth Sunday of the Year
Episcopalian: Proper 15
Pres/Meth/UCC: Thirteenth Sunday after Pentecost

Lessons

Lutheran:	Prov. 9:1-6	Eph. 5:15-20	John 6:51-58
Roman Catholic:	Prov. 9:1-6	Eph. 5:15-20	John 6:51-58
Episcopal:	Prov. 9:1-6	Eph. 5:15-20	John 6:53-59
Pres/Meth/UCC:	2 Sam. 18:24-33	Eph. 5:15-20	John 6:51-58

Introductions to the Lessons

Lesson 1

(1) *Proverbs 9:1-6* (**Lutheran/Episcopal**). Wisdom is personified as a woman who has prepared a feast for the simple and immature. She built her house on earth and sent her servant girls to invite those who would live and have insight.

(2) *II Samuel 18:24-33* (**Pres/Meth/UCC**). The story of David and Absalom continues. Absalom, David's son, was killed in battle. Two messengers, Ahimaaz and a Cushite, were sent to David to give him the news of Absalom's death and defeat. Ahimaaz did not have the courage to tell David about Absalom. When David learned that fact from the Cushite, he went to his room and wept.

Lesson 2

Ephesians 5:15-20 (**Lutheran/Episcopal/Pres/Meth/UCC**). Paul continues with ethical admonitions. Be wise and live like Christians. Stupid people live wickedly. Get drunk with God's Spirit and you will sing and thank God always for everything. A wise person will make the most of these evil days and will understand what is God's will.

Gospel

John 6:51-58 (**Lutheran/Episcopal/Pres/Meth/UCC**). The first verse of today's gospel lesson was the last verse of last Sunday's gospel. Jesus continues to speak of himself as the Bread of Life. His reference to eating his flesh and drinking his blood causes the Jews to ask how one can eat his flesh. While teaching in the synagogue at Capernaum, Jesus explains that eating his flesh and drinking his blood results in eternal life.

31

Theme: Jesus is our bread of life.

Thought for the day: Certain fish may starve in the midst of plenty; we can starve spiritually if we do not feed on Jesus Christ continually.

Prayer of meditation: Dear Lord, the summer has been busy with family, refreshing recreation, and concern for absent members and friends of the church. Help me to put aside the anxiety and care I have experienced and bask in the strength of your renewing Spirit. Help me to look forward to the coming weeks as an opportunity for serving you. Fill me with hope, love, and enduring grace. In the name of Christ. Amen.

Call to worship: Thou, O Lord, are enthroned for ever;
thy name endures to all generations.
      Psalm 102:12

Prayer of adoration: Lord, we praise and glorify your name. You bless us with the beauty of your world, the love we experience among family and friends, the comfort of your holy people, and the communion of saints. May your name be blessed throughout all creation. Amen.

Prayer of confession: Forgive us our failures to partake of the bread of heaven. Jesus came to bring life, and we have preferred death. Jesus came to bring hope, and we have chosen despair. Jesus came to bring love, and we have lived in hate and anger. We have failed to be his holy people even when we wanted to do all things for your sake.
    But, we know that we are forgiven by you, O Lord. So we come with boldness, seeking that bread which brings life, hope, and love for all humanity through us. In the name of our Lord, we pray. Amen.

Prayer of dedication of gifts and self: Here are our gifts, O Lord, responses to your love and grace. Yet, these gifts are not all we give. We offer to you our time, our talent, our hearts, our minds, our body and our spirit; in fact, we offer all we are and have. May this one act of devotion become the daily pattern for our lives. In the name and for the sake of Christ Jesus we pray. Amen.

Sermon title: The Bread of Life is Ours.

Sermon thesis: Jesus offered himself to others by his caring, his teachings, and his self giving. He also provided the experience of the Lord's Supper for those who do not live in the first century. Christ is truly present, offering himself to us when we partake with faith.

Hymn for the day: *"Deck thyself, my soul/Soul adorn yourself with gladness."* The German lawyer, Johann Franck (1618-1677), ranks second only to Paul Gerhardt as one of the writers who marked the transition from objective German hymnology to a more personal and mystical kind of poetry. His hymns were finished in form and of earnest faith and simplicity. This hymn was first published in 1649 in Johann Cruger's *Geistliche Kirchen Melodien*, Berlin. Cruger, who wrote the music to which this hymn is universally sung, was a composer of first-rate hymn tunes who published a number of hymn collections in his lifetime.

Announcements for next week:
Sermon title: Where Else Can We Go?
Sermon theme: Only Jesus Christ can provide real life for all.
Sermon summary: To search for meaning only in ourselves is fruitless. To search for strength in the past is hopeless. To seek meaning in humans alone is frustrating. Only through Jesus Christ can anyone find that exceptionally real life.

Children's object talk:

Enjoying the Good Bread

Objects: A loaf of bread
Lesson: Finding food for our lives.
Outline: 1. Bread is good for us.
2. Many people have made this bread possible.
3. Jesus provided bread that gives us strength.

SOMETIMES WHEN I AM HUNGRY, I like to reach into the loaf of bread, take out a slice of bread, and eat it. The only thing that could make it any better might be some butter and jelly, but I like it just the way it is—fresh, tasty—don't you?

Many persons helped make this bread. Farmers grew the grain. People harvested the wheat, and merchants sold it to the flour mills. The millers ground up wheat and made flour. The baker mixed the flour and other ingredients and baked the bread. Some delivery person brought the bread to my store. The people at the store helped to put it on the shelf where I could buy it.

In our church we sometimes have bread as a part of our worship, when we observe the Lord's Supper or the Holy Communion. That bread reminds us that Jesus gives strength to us, helps us, fills us, just as this bread fills us when we are hungry. Jesus said that he was the bread of life. He was and is the bread that helps us to live the Christian life.

The sermon:

The Bread of Life is Ours

Hymns:
Beginning of worship: Jesus United By Thy Grace
Sermon hymn: Lord, I Want To Be A Christian
End of worship: Spirit of Faith, Come Down

Scripture: John 6:51-58

Sermon Text: *"I am the living bread which came down from heaven; if any one eats of this bread, he will live forever; and the bread which I shall give for the life of the world is my flesh."* v. 51

USUALLY WE PREACH about the Lord's Supper and its meaning on those Sundays when we provide that sacrament for the congregation. Today is not normally a Communion Sunday for us, but the Scripture text which we have read today is filled with images which remind us of communion, of the Lord's Supper.

It is proper that we should make such associations. Almost every scholar who has written on the gospel of John points to those images and symbols, noting the obvious ties which the words of Jesus in John's gospel have with the institution of the Lord's Supper in the other three gospels.

In the gospel of John, there is no story of that Upper Room experience during the last week of Jesus' earthly life. We really do not know why. But, we do know that the Lord's Supper is obviously important in the community for whom John has written the story of Jesus. That same sacrament is vitally important to us, so today we will closely examine those words of Jesus.

Note the source of the bread which is eaten. "This bread," says Jesus, "came down from heaven." It is God who is the source of this bread, this gift. The God who sent Jesus into the world is a God of compassion. John began his gospel with the phrase, "God so loved the world."

Bishop James Armstrong, who teaches preaching at Iliff Seminary in Denver tells of an experience that illustrates this truth. His father, a minister, was warmhearted, volatile, lovable, and a most remarkable man. Years before when James was a college student, they were walking through a park in a desert town in Southern California. A woman approached from the other direction. As she passed, the father went to her and said, "You are in trouble. Can I help?" The woman slumped on a park bench and began to cry. She and her husband, traveling from a distant state, were driving through a mountain pass. A boy darted from behind a rock into the road. Their car had struck and killed the boy. Her husband was with the boy's family. She was alone and terrified. What had the father seen? What was it about him that responded so quickly and so compassionately?

God is like that. Always looking into the depths of our being and seeing our pain and hurt. God then comes to comfort and to console us, to strengthen us and to equip us for the rest of our journey. The gift of Christ through the bread and the cup of the Supper is another way that God has given for us to be in fellowship with him.

Note the results of this bread. Unlike the fathers of old who ate the manna in the wilderness, those who eat this bread will not die, but will live. Jesus had said earlier that eating his flesh and drinking his blood provides eternal life now and life everlasting in the future as well.

We humans do fear death. We fear as deeply that life will not have any meaning, any significance. So much of what we do is an attempt to escape the reality of death and the futility of senseless living. The gift of God is the gift of eternal life, meaning for today, and significance for tomorrow.

Note the time of the eating. It is not a past event, but a present one. The tense of the language of the new Testament is present tense. He who EATS. Eats it now. Today, the gift of Christ is as valid as ever. And we have his presence among us and in us, transforming and sustaining us.

The past surrounds us in the present. John Steinbeck tells the story of the migration of people from the dust bowl of the midwest to California. Someone in the novel, *The Grapes of Wrath,* tells the family not to worry about packing pictures, the reminders of the past, for they are going to a new land. One of the characters in the novel responds, "How we know who we are if we cannot remember the past?"

Vital as the past may be, we do live in the present. Christ is here not as a memory of long ago and far away. Christ is present to us through his Supper, not as a future hope but a present reality.

Around the Table of the Lord, we discover anew his love for us. And it is a love which sends us out to love others as Christ has loved us. At the table of the Lord, we discover hope and strength. It is a hope and strength which allows us to strengthen others in Christ and for Christ. Through that holy meal, Christ gives us life, that we might be sparks which enliven all of life. We discover a new light, a light which can lighten the world in which we live. This is truly our bread and our cup, not just for our enjoyment, but for our ministry. Christ gives himself to us that we might give ourselves for others.

Harold C. Perdue
The United Methodist Church
Round Rock, Texas

AUGUST 25, 1991

Lutheran: Fourteenth Sunday after Pentecost
Roman Catholic: Twenty-first Sunday of the Year
Episcopalian: Proper 16
Pres/Meth/UCC: Fourteenth Sunday after Pentecost

Lessons

Lutheran:	Josh. 24:1-2a, 14-18	Eph. 5:21-31	John 6:60-69
Roman Catholic:	Josh. 24:1-2a, 15-17, 18b	Eph. 5:21-32	John 6:60-69
Episcopal:	Josh. 24:1-2a, 14-25	Eph. 5:21-33	John 6:60-69
Pres/Meth//UCC:	2 Sam. 23:1-7	Eph. 5:21-33	John 6:55-69

Introductions to the Lessons

Lesson 1

(1) *Joshua 24:1-2a, 14-18* (**Lutheran**); *24:1-2a, 14-25* (**Episcopal**). As the final act of his leadership, Joshua, Moses' successor, calls a meeting of all the Israelites at Shechem. He offers them a choice to choose either the gods of Egypt and Canaan or Yahweh. He and his family will serve Yahweh who brought them out of slavery, through the wilderness, and to the promised land. The people decide to serve the Lord. As a result of this decision, the covenant with Yahweh is renewed.

(2) *II Samuel 23:1-7* (**Pres/Meth/UCC**). David ends his words with a song in praise to his God who exalted and anointed him. In this song he testifies that God speaks through him and causes him to rule in the fear of God. In his covenant with God, he prospered while the godless perished.

Lesson 2

Ephesians 5:21-31 (**Lutheran**); *5:21-33* (**Epis/Pres/Meth/UCC**). Today's pericope deals with the Christian home. It is characterized by husband and wife's mutual subjection in love to each other. The model for their love is Christ's love for the church for which he died. The relationship of husband and wife is the relationship between Christ and the church. The two are one.

Gospel

John 6:60-69 (**Lutheran/Episcopal**; *6:55-69* (**Pres/Meth/UCC**). The series from John 6 comes to a close. Jesus has been saying that he came from heaven and that he is the Bread of Life. To eat his flesh and drink his blood gives eternal life. This was too much for many of his disciples (not apostles) to accept. They deserted him. This caused Jesus to ask the Twelve if they, too, wanted to leave. As the spokesman, Peter vows that they will continue to follow because only he has the words of eternal life.

Theme: Only Jesus Christ can provide real life for all.

Thought for the day: "How hard it is to be a Christian."
— Robert Browning

Prayer of meditation: Dear God, your expectations of me are great, and I am small. Your dreams are eternal, but my own are finite. Your desire is love, while my desire is self-love. Give me a new spirit, a new vision, a new hope. For in your gifts I find what I truly desire but have not discovered apart from you. Guide me this day in serving you more fully. In the name of Christ. Amen.

Call to worship: "God has blessed us.
Let all the ends of the earth fear him!
    (Psalms 67:7)

Prayer of adoration: Gracious Father, your love is perfect. Your grace is complete. Your will is effective. In the presence of such greatness, how can we do anything other than give you praise? In the presence of such perfection, how can we do anything but adore you? In the name of the Lord Jesus Christ, we pray. Amen.

Prayer of confession: We confess our slowness of heart, our fear of the demands of discipleship, our anxiety about failure. No matter how clearly you have spoken, we misunderstand as often as we understand. Sometimes, we have not listened to you. At other times, we have been so preoccupied that we have not concentrated on your words.

You have expected faithful deeds from us and we have disappointed you. You focused your expectations of us, and we were filled with fear. You want so much, expect so much, from us.

You have offered to us the possibility of magnificent acts for your sake, and we have been satisfied with ones of little consequence. We have chosen to do small things exceedingly well rather than to attempt great things and not succeed. We do not want you to be disappointed with us and have disappointed you just the same.

Forgive us all our sins. In the name of Christ. Amen.

Prayer of dedication of gifts and self: Accept these gifts, O Lord, as a sign of our love and dedication. We have received all things from you, and all our lives and all our possessions are yours. We dedicate today all we give, all we are, all we have, in the name and through the strength of your grace in Jesus Christ. Amen.

Sermon title: Where Else Can We Go?

Sermon thesis: To search for meaning only in ourselves is fruitless. To search for strength in the past is hopeless. To seek meaning in humans alone is frustrating. Only through Jesus Christ can anyone find that exceptionally real life.

Hymn for the day: *"O Jesus, I have promised."* A native of St. Pancras, England, John Ernest Bode (1816-1874) attended Oxford and was ordained in 1841. He was rector of Westwell, Oxfordshire, for thirteen years and of Castle Camps, Cambridgeshire, for fourteen. This hymn was written in 1866 for the confirmation of Bode's daughter and two sons. It especially reflects the Old Testament (Joshua) lesson, *"We will serve the Lord."*

Announcements for next week:

Sermon title: Having a Clean Heart

Sermon theme: The inner condition of the heart is more important than outward acts of piety.

Sermon summary: God is constantly moving toward people with an offer of gracious acceptance. When people accept that free offer of God's grace they usually respond by simply being thankful. But, for some reason, the temptation is to turn thankfulness into a rigid obedience to religious rituals or some other compulsive behavior.

Children's object talk:

I Can, I Can

Objects: Swim trunks
Lesson: We can be helped to do what we think is too hard.
Outline: 1. I tried to swim but became frightened.
2. Another person helped me to trust the water.
3. We can be helped to follow Jesus.

DO YOU REMEMBER THE FIRST TIME YOU WENT SWIMMING? I do. Was it fun? It wasn't fun for me. It frightened me and I was not a good swimmer.

It was a long time ago for me. I went into the water like all young people do. Then I sank beneath the water, and I panicked rather than relaxing. I got water in my nose, and opening my mouth too soon, I got water in my throat. I began to sputter and beat the water. When I got out I wanted to forget about swimming. I knew it would be too hard for me ever to swim.

For a long time, I did not try to swim. But I grew bigger. Everyone else could swim, but not me. I didn't want to go into the water. A friend came along that I trusted, and he taught me to trust the water. I began to float, to let the water hold me up. Then I learned to move my arms just right and tilt my head and breathe at the right time. Before you knew it, I was swimming and enjoying it. It wasn't too hard for me. It was fun!

Sometimes we are afraid to follow Jesus. He expects so much of us, we just know that we couldn't do it. But we can trust him, let him support us, hold us up. And when we do, we find we can do all those wonderful things Jesus expects us to do. To tell others about him, to love people who have not loved us first, and help persons who need so much. And what fun it is!

The sermon:

Where Else Can We Go?

Hymns:
Beginning of worship: All Hail the Power of Jesus' Name
Sermon hymn: Be Thou My Vision
End of worship: O How I Love Jesus

Scripture: John 6:60-69

Sermon Text: *"Simon Peter answered him, 'Lord, to whom shall we go? You have the words of eternal life. . .'"* (v. 68)

MANY OF THE MOST FAMILIAR REMEMBRANCES about the story of Jesus are not to be found in the Gospel of John. We remember the stories of the birth of Jesus, but John tells the coming of Christ in a different set of images. We remember the baptism at the River Jordan, but John tells it in a way that is difficult to merge with the other accounts. We do not understand all of the reasons, few of the reasons, why John wrote such a different gospel. But, we do know that it not like the others.

In the other gospels there is a story about Jesus and his disciples at Caesarea Philippi. Jesus asks the disciples what others are saying about him. After the reports from the disciples, Jesus asks what they think of him. Peter replies and confesses Jesus as the Messiah, the Son of God.

The Gospel of John has presented this same reality in a different setting, with a different wording, but with the same final understanding. The teachings of Jesus are becoming more personal, more difficult for the traditional Jewish person to believe. The crowds are deserting Jesus; they're going back home. When Jesus confronts his disciples about their possible desertion, Peter replies with our text.

The fact is that being a follower of Jesus is not easy. Robert Browning summed up that truth in the beginning of one of his poems, Easter Day, where he wrote:

How hard it is to be a Christian!

As hard as it may be, where else can we find meaning and purpose in life?

We know that we cannot find that meaning in ourselves.

We do in fact live east of Eden, where we are a part of fallen humanity. We are a mixture of good and evil. Like Paul, the good that we would want to do is not what we do. We tell the truth. But, we also tell lies. Sometimes they are not big ones or significant ones; but we do stretch the truth and put ourselves in the best light. We are involved in the struggle with demons and demonic forces. The light in us is often turned down to dim.

The meaning we seek is not to be found in ourselves. We may attempt to find that meaning in other human beings, but it is not there either. All humanity is trapped in the reality of hoping and trying, but not having the strength to accomplish. Sometimes a church will look to its pastor as a tower of strength. The pastor may encourage that view. Yet, at some point, the members discover that the pastor is less than perfect. His faith is not as strong as they had believed, and the anger spills over throughout the church.

The same experience happens in the family. A child may believe that parents are perfect. When their imperfections are finally seen, the child struggles with those disillusions.

Meaning for life cannot be found in ourselves or others like ourselves.

We know that we cannot find that meaning in the past.

In 1225, the builders at Beauvais began to erect a cathedral that would out-soar every other cathedral in Europe. Fifty years later the choir vault was completed. The cathedral stood for twelve years, then it fell. Finally, we cannot find the answer to our lives in the past, for the past is filled with failures.

We may honor our Christian heritage, but we must also acknowledge the Inquisition, the Crusades, the immorality of church leaders in the Middle Ages, even in our own time. Tradition will not suffice for us. As important as the past is, we cannot build our life upon that past. It is not adequate.

We know that we cannot find that meaning in human wisdom.

We have done so many things in our times because of our human skill. Make a list of the inventions of our century. We have designed the automobile, the airplane, the radio, the television. Human wisdom has created much. We have captured the power of the atom, making not only bombs, but also nuclear power. We have made one advance after another in medicine, often as a result of our travels in space and the technology of science.

But, we have failed to find meaning in that. All of us know about persons who come to the end of highly successful careers in their chosen vocations, only to struggle at retirement with the meaning of their lives. As much as they know, as much as they have contributed, they begin to talk about golf and fishing, travel and hobbies, as a substitute for what has given meaning to their lives for so long.

Peter was and is correct. We don't have anywhere else to go. Where will we find life? Where can we discover meaning and purpose? Only in Jesus Christ!

Harold C. Perdue
The United Methodist Church
Round Rock, Texas

September 1, 1991

Lutheran: Fifteenth Sunday after Pentecost
Roman Catholic: Twenty-second Sunday of the Year
Episcopalian: Proper 17
Pres/Meth/UCC: Fifteenth Sunday after Pentecost

Lessons:

Lutheran:	Deut. 4:1-2, 6-8	Eph. 6:10-20	Mark 7:1-8, 14-15, 21-23
Roman Catholic:	Deut. 4:1-2, 6-8	James 1:17-18, 21b-22, 27	Mark 7:1-8, 14-15, 21-23
Episcopal:	Deut. 4:1-9	Eph. 6:10-20	Mark 7:1-8, 14-15, 21-23
Pres/Meth/UCC:	1 Kings 2:1-4, 10-13	Eph. 6:10-21	Mark 7:1-8, 14-15, 21-23

Introductions to the Lessons:

Lesson 1

(1) *Deuteronomy 4:1-2, 6-8* (**Lutheran**); *4:1-9* (**Episcopal**). The Israelites are about to enter the Promised Land which Moses is allowed to see from Mt. Pisgah but not enter. Moses charges his people to keep the laws he taught them. If they do, they will live in the new land and other nations will admire them as a great nation.

(2) *I Kings 2:1-4, 10-13* (**Pres/Meth/UCC**). The long series dealing with David and his times comes to an end today. David, realizing he was dying, calls in his successor, his son Solomon, and charges him to keep the Lord's commandments that his reign might never end. After a reign of forty years, David "slept with his ancestors."

Lesson 2

Ephesians 6:10-20 (**Luth/Epis**); *6:10-21* (**Pres/Meth/UCC**). Today we close the readings from the book of Ephesians. According to tradition Paul wrote this letter while he was in prison where he daily was in contact with a military person. He used the figure of a soldier's equipment to describe a Christian's armor. Christians are soldiers fighting a war against Satan and his powers of wickedness. Like every soldier, a Christian needs appropriate armor in terms of truth, righteousness, peace, faith, salvation, and the Word of God.

Gospel

Mark 7:1-8, 14-15, 21-23 (**Luth/Epis/Pres/Meth/UCC**). After 5 weeks with John 6, we resume our survey of Mark beginning with chapter 7. A group of Pharisees and scribes find fault with Jesus for allowing his disciples to eat with unwashed hands. He defended them by teaching that what defiles a person is not what enters but what leaves a person. The source of wickedness is the heart. Out of a dirty heart come various vices.

Theme: The inner condition of the heart is more important than outward acts of piety.

Thought for the day: How often it is that we, like the Pharisees, are tempted to judge other people's "cleanness" or social acceptability on the basis of outward appearance, rather than the inner condition of their heart.

Prayer of meditation: Almighty God, who sees into our hearts and knows the secrets of our thoughts and feelings, save us from addictions to rituals which have as their aim to justify us in other people's eyes. Grant to us in this hour of worship an experience of the presence of God which works in us doing God's good pleasure. May the mind and heart of Christ our Lord be found in us this day, as we confess our powerlessness over the forces of evil which wage war against the chambers of our hearts. Give us all gathered here enough spiritual insight to see the importance of the spiritual health of our hearts. Amen.

Call to worship:

Leader: Who may ascend the hill of the Lord? Who may stand in his holy place?

People: He who has clean hands and a pure heart, who does not lift up his soul to an idol or swear by what is false.

Leader: I will praise the Lord for giving me a pure and upright heart.

People: I will honor God who has caused me to desire to love others even as he has shown me his love in Christ Jesus.

Leader: The Lord's name be praised.

People: Let us worship God!

Prayer of adoration: Who is like the Lord? Who sees into the human heart knowing us better than we know ourselves? You keep ever before us the law of love. In your presence we have a lamp for our eyes, and a light for our path. You have called us to journey with you in life. Your Spirit guides our worship and shines like a light into the darkness and unknown corners of our hearts. In Jesus Christ we have come to know your overwhelming gracious nature. We can hardly fathom the depth of your love which reached us in our lost condition. You have saved us to witness to your faithfulness and to reflect to others the love and acceptance of Jesus Christ. We praise you for being the one and only God who forgives, renews, and creates the heart and mind of Christ in his worshipers. For all that you have done, are doing and ever will do, we offer you our praise, with hearts that look to the future with expectation and hope. Amen.

Prayer of confession: We confess, O God, that we often come to you striving for just the right thing to say, as if the effectiveness of confession depended upon us. We confess that we have been striving and fruitlessly grasping after you, when it is you who searches and knows our hearts. In this moment of confession deliver us from the temptation to think our heart's health is in our hands. Restore broken hearts which have made a habit of saying one thing and doing another. By your grace, grant us each integrity and unity of heart and mind. Apply our hearts to wisdom. In honesty we confess to you that we are powerless over sin. We confess that we have struggled along in our own power. In the stillness of this moment, reveal yourself to ones who have come to worship you in spirit and in truth. Search us. And teach us to confess the truth about ourselves, in order that we may know and be known. Amen.

Prayer of dedication of gifts and self: Of all things we offer to you, the thing you most desire from us is simply our humble, thankful hearts. We bring to you our gifts. But they do not have their genesis with us. They are ours because you gave them to us in the first place. So then, we offer to you what is already yours. For we are yours. We are your servants.

Some of us bring organizational ability. Stimulate us as to how we might organize people and resources to meet the real needs of real people. Some of us are gifted by you with a special ability to listen to the hurts, pains, and joys of others. We offer ourselves to you. May your Spirit empower us, and then move us to reach out with the love of Christ to others. Some of us bring the ability to be an encouragement to others. We dedicate this gift to you. Some of us are blessed with extra faith, courage and vision. Help us to find our rightful place and use of our gift in the Body of Christ for its betterment. Some of us you have given the gift of hospitality.

We warmly open our homes to people longing for a sense of belonging. For the sake of your church multiply this gift in our midst. Some of us can communicate the gospel in such a way that others respond with faith in Christ. We pray that you might strengthen this part of your Body. Others make clear those spiritual truths that most miss. May a blessing of peace and joy rest upon our teachers. Others of us are in the autumn of our years and think that our usefulness is over. Let not that attitude take its hold on your church. Say to each of us this day that we are important members of Christ's Body. By your Spirit stimulate your people to pray for and with each other.

We dedicate our hearts to you, which are righteous because you have made them that way. Free us to choose to do what we sense you are leading us to do. And with this spirit of adventure may we face the week ahead of us. Go with us, O God, or we go in vain. Amen.

Sermon title: Having a Clean Heart

Sermon thesis: God is constantly moving toward people with an offer of gracious acceptance. When people accept that free offer of God's grace they usually respond by simply being thankful in their hearts to God. But, for some reason, the temptation is to turn thankfulness into a rigid obedience to religious rituals or some other compulsive behavior.

Hymn of the day: *"We sing the praise of him who died"* Thomas Kelly (1769-1855) was the author of over 750 hymns, some of which rank among the finest hymns of the English language. After studying law for a time, he studied for the priesthood and was ordained in the Church of Ireland. He later left the Church of Ireland and became an independent preacher. A generous and humble man, he became a friend of the poor in Dublin and was especially helpful during the Irish famine in the 1840s. The hymn is one of gratitude for Christ's sacrifice on the cross and his forgiveness of sins.

Announcements for next week:

Sermon title: Hearing and Speaking the Truth

Sermon theme: Something tells us when we are hearing the truth, and something tells others when we are speaking it.

Sermon summary: There is more to speaking than merely talking, and there is more to listening than just hearing.

Children's object talk:

You Are More Than What You Eat

Objects: A vegetable, fruit, cookie, etc.

Lesson: Just as we are careful about what we would put in our mouth, we can be careful not to put meanness into our heart.

Outline: 1. You wash of fruit and vegetables before eating them.
2. You wash your hands before eating.
3. It is just as important to keep our spirit and mind healthy, as it is to keep our bodies clean.

WHAT DO YOU DO before you eat an apple? That's right, you wash it. What do you do before you eat a carrot? The same thing. You wash it. Why is it important to wash the things we eat? Sometimes chemicals are used to preserve the things we eat, but they are not good for us to eat. So we wash our food.

What else do we wash before we eat? That's right, your Mom and Dad tell you to go wash your hands with soap and water before eating. Why? You may have touched something that was dirty and not good for your body. By keeping germs out of our bodies we stay healthy. So, it makes good sense to wash our hands before eating, doesn't it?

We wash our food and we wash our hands because we care about our bodies. Jesus tells us that it is important to keep our hearts clean too. Now, when Jesus uses the word "heart" he is talking about the place deep inside us. Our hearts can be loving. Or our hearts could let mean thoughts stay inside, and then our hearts would become unclean. An unclean heart may be jealous, greedy, or desire to see someone else hurt.

Just as you would not put something dirty in your mouth, the wise person does not allow an evil thought or desire to grow in his or her heart. God is the one who keeps our hearts clean. Let us pray. God clean our hearts and keep them healthy, in order that we might have more love in our hearts. Amen.

47

The sermon:

Having a Clean Heart

Hymns:
Beginning of worship: Where Cross the Crowded Ways of Life
Sermon hymn: O for a Heart to Praise my God.
End of worship: O, God, Our Help in Ages Past

Scripture: Mark 7:1-8, 14-15, 21-23

Sermon text: *"Why don't your disciples live according to the tradition of the elders instead of eating their food with 'unclean' hands?"* v. 5

IN A CONVERSATION with one of the world's most insightful New Testament scholars, Dr. Kenneth Bailey, head of the New Testament Department, Jerusalem, Israel, Dr. Bailey mentioned that the highest compliment that could be given to a man in the Middle East would be that he is a keeper of the traditions of the elders. The collective wisdom of ages is handed down in the traditions. Any self-respecting teacher would never consider changing one of the traditions or teaching others not to follow the tradition's path. The Jewish book of traditions, the Mishnah, lists over 600 traditions that any conscientious Pharisee would have dutifully kept. One of these traditions was not unlike a similar tradition that we may have heard growing up. "Always wash your hands before eating. Never eat with dirty hands."

Knowing that much about the importance of traditions, let us consider the indictment put in the form of a question which the Pharisees asked of Jesus. "Why don't your disciples live according to the tradition of the elders instead of eating their food with 'unclean' hands?" Jesus is accused of breaking the traditions of the elders. This is no small offense. If he is able to defend his behavior, then he will be able to preserve his honor and his standing in the eyes of the people. If not, then no doubt he will bring shame on himself, his ministry and he will probably not be seriously listened to by the people.

His defense is not so much a rationalization of his behavior as it is an attack on the Pharisee's behavior. Jesus points out that Isaiah spoke of these hypocritical Pharisees when he wrote:

"These people honor me with their lips, but their hearts are far from me.

They worship me in vain; their teachings are but rules taught
    by men."
These words would have to be interpreted as nothing less than a
slap in the face. We might well imagine shame and the rage that
welled up inside of the Pharisees at this point. Then Jesus summarizes
their behavior by saying that they have let go of the teachings of
God and are holding onto the traditions of men.

There is a shift in the subject of the conversation. The teachers
of the law were concerned with the condition of the hands during
eating. By the way, Mothers and Fathers, the point of this lesson
is not that we should make a practice of eating with dirty hands
every chance we get, or teach our children to do the same. The point
is that a clean heart is more important than clean hands. If hands
are important, how much more important is a clean heart?

It was Soren Kierkegaard who wrote a little book entitled, *Purity
of Heart is to Will One Thing.* It is so easy to get caught up in traditions and forget about the really important commands of God. Jesus
said that there is one thing that is important. What is the condition
of our heart? Does it will one thing? Does it will God's will? Is it
committed to loving people above all else? Is it fooled by outward
appearances? Or does it look on the hearts of others as God lov-
ingly looks at us?

The condition of the heart is so important to God that the word
"heart" is mentioned nearly 1,000 times in the Bible. Ben Johnson
in his little book, *To Will God's Will,* tells the story about a seminary
student who was going through all the proper religious activities,
yet he was very troubled. He prayed. He read his Bible. He attended
groups in his church. Yet something was not quite right with his
inner condition. Ben asked the young man if he had decided to will
God's will. "What do you mean?" the student asked. God's will is
that we should love the Lord with all our heart, soul and mind, and
our neighbor as ourselves. Have you decided to do that? Or better
yet, have you really decided to allow God to do that through you?
Ah, what does it profit a man if he gains the whole world, but loses
his heart, his soul, his ability to love?

I do not know how many heart diseases there are. But I would
guess fairly safely that if any of us could, we would live in such
a way as to avoid getting a heart disease. Our physical hearts are
very important to us. Our lives depend on our hearts. Doesn't it
stand to reason that we should be just as interested in avoiding the

diseases of the spiritual heart? What are they? Jesus said evil thoughts, sexual immorality, theft, murder, adultery, greed, malice, deceit, lewdness, envy, slander, arrogance and folly are diseases of the heart.

If we make room for these things in our hearts they find a home there. In his book, *Habits of the Heart*, Robert Bellah portrays four characters who are motivated by various drives that are very common in our culture. What comes out of the very center of our being, our heart, is what makes us either clean or unclean. What or who is on the throne of our hearts?

It is not by force that we change the inner condition of our heart. But by the discipline of inviting Christ to be Lord, and by the habit of willing God's loving will, God resides with us and does his work in us. If there is any goodness in us, it is God's doing.

The clean heart is free to worship God joyfully, for it is thankful for God's presence. A thankful person wrote, "Now thank we all our God with heart and hands and voices, Who wondrous things hath done, In whom his world rejoices." Henry van Dyke, with a clean heart wrote, "Joyful, joyful, we adore thee, God of glory, Lord of love; Hearts unfold like flowers before thee, Opening to the sun above. Melt the clouds of sin and sadness, drive the dark of doubt away; Giver of immortal gladness, fill us with the light of day." When our hearts are clean and healthy, then we with the songwriter sing a heartfelt new song, "When morning gilds the skies, my heart awaking cries, May Jesus Christ be praised."

Keeping human traditions is no substitute for a clean heart. The key to having and keeping a clean heart is by admitting that our hearts, without Christ's loving presence, are unclean and in need of repair. So, remember, always wash your hands before dinner. And draw near to God. Ask Jesus for a clean heart and it will be yours. It is Christ who saves and keeps us.

Let us pray. God, who touches earth with beauty, make my heart anew; With thy spirit recreate me, pure and strong and true.

Thomas N. Gard
The Presbyterian Church of Watertown
Watertown, South Dakota

September 8, 1991

Lutheran: Sixteenth Sunday after Pentecost
Roman Catholic: Twenty-third Sunday of the Year
Episcopalian: Proper 18
Pres/Meth/UCC: Sixteenth Sunday after Pentecost

Lessons:

Lutheran:	Is. 35:4-7a	James 1:17-22, (23-25) 26-27	Mark 7:31-37
Roman Catholic:	Is. 35:4-7a	James 1:2-5	Mark 7:31-37
Episcopal:	Is. 35:4-7a	James 2:17-27	Mark 7:31-37
Pres/Meth/UCC:	Prov. 2:1-8	James 1:17-27	Mark 7:31-37

Introductions to the Lessons:

Lesson 1

(1) *Isaiah 35:4-7a* (**Lutheran/Episcopal**). According to Biblical scholars, this lesson was written during the Babylonian exile. The people are promised that Yahweh will come and save them from their bondage. When he comes, the handicapped will be healed and the desert will have water.

(2) *Proverbs 2:1-8* (**Pres/Meth/UCC**). If a person seeks wisdom and understanding like material treasure, God will give the person wisdom. Wisdom comes from God, because he is wisdom. To have wisdom is to know God and to understand the fear of the Lord.

Lesson 2

James 1:17-27 (**Luth/Epis/Pres/Meth/UCC**). For the second lesson the lectionary turns to the book of James for the next four Sundays. In this passage James emphasizes the practical nature of the Christian religion. True faith is expressed in good deeds, and pure religion is evidenced in personal purity and social welfare.

Gospel

Mark 7:31-37 (**Luth/Epis/Pres/Meth/UCC**). Jesus has been to the seacoast town of Tyre and was on his way back to the Sea of Galilee. On the way people brought to him a deaf man with a speech handicap. It was a private healing. Jesus used touch as a method of healing, for he touched both the man's ears and tongue. When Jesus said, "Be opened," the man immediately had his hearing and he could speak plainly.

51

Theme: Something tells us when we are hearing the truth, and something tells others when we are speaking it.

Thought for the day: In one of Paul Simon's songs he penned the words, "A man hears what he wants to hear and disregards the rest." This may be a poetic way of talking about selective listening or just a simple observation. In our lesson for today we are told about a deaf man who heard for the first time. In one sense, we have all heard nothing until we have heard the good news of God's love for us in Jesus Christ. Jesus also caused the man to speak. And in a way, we begin to really speak when our words are seasoned with the characteristics of grace, wisdom and truth.

Prayer of meditation: Our Lord and God, in this hour of worship our hearts are in need of hearing words which heal and inspire. We open ourselves before you. We meditate on your faithfulness and our hearts are strengthened. For the babbling brook and the singing bird that speak to our ears a message of your sovereignty, we thank you. For reeds, brass, strings and percussion that lift the weariness from our shoulders, our hearts say thanks be to God. If our ears do not hear the joys of life, then perhaps we are growing deaf. Draw near to us, O God, and by your presence minister to our ears that have grown tired of hearing. If our tongues have lost their graciousness toward others, then perhaps we are no better off than the mute. Loosen our tongues to be instruments of your grace, love and truth. Together we come into your presence aware that you are the source of life's quality. Amen.

Call to worship:
Leader: He opened the ears of the deaf man. We make ready to hear the news.
People: Jesus is the Lord of glory.
Leader: He gave speech to the speechless. We are ready to speak as you have spoken to us in Christ.
People: With the Father and the Holy Spirit, Jesus is worshiped and glorified.
Leader: Let us worship our Creator, Redeemer and Sustainer.

Prayer of adoration: Who is like the Lord? Creation says that God has done everything well. The stars above us fill our hearts with childlike awe and wonder. The mountain peaks renew the weary. The vast prairie speaks to us in its silence. The mountain stream teaches us to dance. The clear lake calms the restless. Truly Lord, you have done everything well. In your teachings and through your ministry we have light for our path. Who is like Jesus? We confess that you are Lord. Like a hound of heaven the Spirit of God sought out each of us. We were lost, but now we are found. We were faithless, but now God has given us faith. Our inner condition was nothing to brag about, but through the Spirit's work we have the fruit of God's labor in us. Our hearts say that God has done everything well.

Prayer of confession: We confess to you our energy draining tendencies. In moments of silence you speak to us. A problem or struggle is revealed to us, and we sometimes fail to see you at work in us. Rather than naming the persistent feeling we push it back down below the conscious level. We confess that we are for some reason afraid of knowing ourselves. We spend so much energy avoiding who we are and what is really going on inside of us. Therefore, Lord, grant to us a secure confidence that we are lovable. Grant us courage and honesty in our journey of knowing you and knowing ourselves. Take away our need of pretense. Free us that our energies may be used productively in your kingdom. We confess that we need you and we need what each other can offer for spiritual growth to happen. Give us ears to hear and mouths to speak the truth to you and to ourselves. Amen.

Prayer of dedication of gifts and self: You are at work in us to do your good pleasure. It pleases you that we glorify you and enjoy you forever. Truly, without you we can do nothing of redemptive value. Yet, we can do all things through Christ who strengthens us. We dedicate ourselves to you. Yet, we do not consecrate ourselves to you through the power of our own wills. We do not worship our will power. The power of our will as revealed in determination and persistence can do most anything in the external world. Yet, there is a greater power at work in our inner world. We dedicate the gracious spiritual gifts that you have given us to service in the world and for the building up of the Body of Christ. We submit ourselves to your Lordship and dedicate the power at work within us to the common good. Use us as you will for your kingdom's sake. Amen.

Sermon title: Hearing and Speaking the Truth

Sermon thesis: There is more to speaking than merely talking, and there is more to listening than just hearing.

Hymn of the day: *"O Son of God, in Galilee."* Anna Bernardine Dorothy Hoppe was born in 1889 in Milwaukee of German immigrants. She received an eighth-grade education and throughout her life was employed as a stenographer in various business offices. She began writing poetry as a child and wrote spiritual poetry from age 24. Published in the *Northwest Lutheran,* a periodical of the Wisconsin Synod, some of her work came to the attention of Dr. Adolf Hult of Augustana Seminary, who influenced her to write her *Songs for the Church Year,* 1928. Several hymnals subsequently contained her work. The hymn is based very specifically on the Gospel lesson for today.

Announcements for next week:

Sermon title: The Good Life Through Self Abandonment

Sermon theme: Our life does not find its meaning through preoccupation with self.

Sermon summary: When our ultimate goal is to preserve life, we lose it. When our goal is to follow Christ, we find our real self and live a life worth remembering. There is no place for a policy of safety first in the Christian life.

Children's object talk:
Listening and Speaking

Objects: Walkman radio and the microphone
Lesson: What we hear has an effect on what we say.
Outline: 1. What we hear has an effect on the way we feel inside.
    2. How we feel inside has an effect on what we say.
    3. What are some things that we need to hear from each other?
    4. What are some things that we need to hear from our parents?
    5. What are some things that others need to hear from us?

HOW MANY OF YOU like to listen to the radio? How many of you like to listen to the TV? How many of you like to listen to the birds singing? to the train blowing its horn when it goes by? to the school bell ring? What we hear has an effect on what we say. For example, if I hear my doorbell ring I might say, "Who is there?" Different sounds give us different feelings inside, don't they? If I hear thunder I might feel a little nervous, right? Then, how I feel might cause me to say how I feel inside. Would one of you like to put on the radio earphones and listen to the music? How does the music make you feel? There's happy music, sad music, funny music, etc. You'll remember that King David when he was a boy would play music to soothe King Saul. What we listen to has an effect on us, doesn't it?

What are some things that we need to hear from our friends? We need to hear that they want to play with us. We need to know that we'll always be friends, no matter what. We need to know that we are lovable and likable, don't we?

What do we need to know from our parents? We need to know what our limits are, that is, what we can and can not do. What we hear is important, isn't it? What we feel is important, too, isn't it? Our words are important, too. They can either build other people up, or they can tear them down. If we tear other people down, that means that we don't feel good about ourselves. If we build other people up, then that means we like ourselves. Let us pray. God guide us in what we say and help us to be good listeners. Amen.

The sermon:

Hearing and Speaking the Truth

Hymns:
  Beginning of worship: We Have Heard the Joyful Sound
  Sermon hymn: Come to the Saviour Now
  End of worship: Blest Be the Tie that Binds

Scripture: Mark 7:31-37

Sermon text: *"He looked up to heaven and with a deep sigh said to him, 'Be opened'!"* v. 34

ONCE THERE WAS A YOUNG MAN, we'll call him Burt, who expected everyone to like him. Of course his expectations did not pan out. So, one day his wife said to him, "Don't you think that it is unreasonable that you should expect everyone to like you?" Burt agreed, but the message did not sink in. He took his problem to a counselor who listened to him explain his problem with needing everyone to like him. After listening carefully and thoughtfully, the counselor offered an insight. "Why should it be important to you to try to control everyone by making them like you? Don't you think that is an unreasonable expectation to lay on yourself?" "That's it," Burt exclaimed. "That is the answer to my problem. Thanks Doc." Burt finally heard what his wife was telling him all along. Isn't that the way it is? There is more to speaking than merely talking, and there is more to listening than just hearing.

In our scripture lesson for today, Jesus has just heals a man who cannot hear or speak. We are not told the name of the man who was healed or the city where the miracle occurred. It does not seem pivotal in terms of the gospel narrative.

However, if we reflect on the story, and listen carefully, we may hear more than the first time we listened. We are told that some people brought a man to him who was deaf and could hardly talk, and they begged him to place his hand on the man. This story reminds us of a similar story when friends brought a lame man to Jesus; they could not gain access to him, so they lowered him through the roof. Both stories give us a picture of a community of people who had a great deal of concern for the lame and the deaf. We are told that they begged Jesus to heal the man.

What does that little observation have to say to us today? Might that caring community be a picture of the church? They were truthful about their feelings for the deaf man. Their actions revealed a deep compassion for one who could not hear them and could not talk to them. Why this compassion and concern for one who had been reduced by his handicap to a useless position in his society? Subtly, doesn't the story say to us that all life is valuable? Is it possible that we, like our imaginary character "Burt", are hearing something that we did not hear the first time through?

The story also says to us that the man did not bring himself. He was brought. Being deaf, he had no clue as to who Jesus was. The man did not seek and finally find Jesus. Rather, the caring community was instrumental in the man coming to Jesus and being healed. It is like the story of the lost sheep. The sheep did not seek out the shepherd. No, it was the good shepherd who sought out the lost sheep, found it, put it on his shoulders and carried it home rejoicing. We may be sure that the deaf man was glad that Jesus found him and changed his life.

The story tells us about a community who cared enough to bring to Jesus a man whom the rest of society may have considered worthless. The story also gives us a special glimpse of Jesus as he sighs, looking up into heaven, and says to the man's ears, "Be open." The delightful thing about Jesus' ministry is that he went to ordinary people. He went to the Jews. He ministered to the Greeks and Romans. He showed the love of God to people that the Jews hated. Truly, in Jesus Christ we learn that God is not partial to any particular people. How can we best follow in his footsteps? Oddly enough, it is the little nondescript stories about our Lord's life that, when reflected on, when listened to so that we hear them, stimulate us to similar forms of ministry. There is more to speaking than merely talking, and there is more to listening than just hearing.

The man began to speak. The village rejoiced. The man listened to family members he had never heard before. He rejoiced. The village was in an uproar as we might imagine. And then, Jesus says something that carried absolutely no weight with the excited crowd. He commanded them not to tell anyone about the healing. And the more he tried to convince them to keep quiet, the more they kept talking. Is there some humor here that we have missed before? Did we not hear it the first time through? Maybe we are a bit too somber in the way we read the gospel stories. Visualize the scene with me for a moment. Jesus is trying to hush the crowd and not let the proverbial cat out of the bag, and the crowd completely ignores his pleading. The crowd was in a pitch of excitement and there was nothing that Jesus could say that would make them be quiet. I would liken Jesus' predicament to anyone trying to hush the crowd after Kirby Puckett has hit a home run. Let's face it, they wouldn't listen.

Hear the crowd speaking the truth about what has happened. Part of interpreting a passage involves interpreting the feeling of the characters in the story. Hear the crowd responding to God with thankful hearts. Even Jesus cannot silence them. The story ends in a peak of emotion and thanksgiving. It is like a worshipful experience, wrapped in a little humor.

Let me end by saying that I do not have the slightest idea why Jesus asked the crowd to be quiet after he healed the deaf man. Was he trying to keep his identity a secret? Was he only joking with them? He must have known that he could not hush their thankful response.

Now, let us go from here, and go straight home. Do not talk to anyone. Do not show any excitement or joy. Remain controlled and inhibited at all costs.

For some reason I expect you are not going to listen to me.

Thomas N. Gard
The Presbyterian Church of Watertown
Watertown, South Dakota

September 15, 1991

Lutheran: Seventeenth Sunday after Pentecost
Roman Catholic: Twenty-fourth Sunday of the Year
Episcopalian: Proper 19
Pres/Meth/UCC: Seventeenth Sunday after Pentecost

Lessons:

Lutheran:	Is. 50:4-10	James 2:1-5, 8-10 14-18	Mark 8:27-35
Roman Catholic:	Is. 50:5-9a	James 2:14-18	Mark 8:27-35
Episcopal:	Is. 50:4-9	James 2:1-5, 8-10, 14-18	Mark 8:27-38
Pres/Meth/UCC:	Prov. 22:1-2, 8-9	James 2:1-5, 8-10, 14-17	Mark 8:27-38

Introductions to the Lessons:

Lesson 1

(1) *Isaiah 50:4-10* (**Lutheran**); *50:4-9* (**Episcopal**). This passage written during the Babylonian exile is considered a "Servant Song." Christians interpret the Servant to be the coming Christ. The Servant is portrayed as one taught by Yahweh, but one who has to suffer at the hands of humankind. However, the Servant is vindicated by the help of Yahweh.

(2) *Proverbs 22:1-2,8-9* (**Pres/Meth/UCC**). There is something more valuable than riches. It is a good name. The people who are rich in this world's goods are blessed if and when they share their wealth with the poor.

Lesson 2

James 2:1-5, 8-10, 14-18 (**Luth/Epis/Pres/Meth/UCC**). James says that showing favoritism to the rich is a sin. Love of one's neighbor eliminates partiality based upon being rich or poor. Moreover, true faith will express itself in love for the neighbor in want and need.

Gospel

Mark 8:27-35 (**Lutheran**); *8:27-38* (**Epis/Pres/Meth/UCC**). Jesus is approaching the end of his public ministry. Before doing so, he needs to know if his disciples understand who he is. At Caesarea Philippi he asks them who they think he is. On behalf of his fellow-disciples, Peter declares that Jesus is the Messiah. Then Jesus announces his coming death in Jerusalem. Peter objects to this, but Jesus interprets his objection as the voice of Satan. As he must suffer and die, Jesus warns his followers that they must do the same for the sake of the Gospel.

Theme: Our life does not find its meaning through preoccupation with self.

Thought for the day: Our life is saved through the discipline of being willing to lose it for a cause greater than ourself. I want you to think about this. Our culture teaches us that the quality of life is improved the more we pamper it. There is a philosophy of life which wars against community, cooperation and partnership. One focus is on me. The other is on the common good. Into the tension of this situation comes the observation that the greatest people have always been service minded. They have found their lives by losing them in service to God and to others.

Prayer of meditation: Our Lord and God, you have made us so that from whatever height we climb we see you far above us, and thus being dissatisfied, we realize that what we ought to be outreaches what we are. Instill in us this divine discontent. From all complacency, from all forgetfulness of the spirit and from the slothful contentment which embraces living mediocre lives we pray for continued deliverance. We acknowledge our temptation to measure our lives by the standards of the crowd and to excuse ourselves by pointing to the common practices of others. Grant to us an independence of mind and will which lives according to our best conscience, without fear or need for favor from the crowd. Lord, have mercy on us and grant us this blessing. Amen.

Call to worship:
Leader: We have heard the imperative of your call to pick up our cross and follow you.
People: In a grateful response of joyous celebration we lay down our old life and pick up our new life in Christ.
Leader: The wants and intentions of our hearts are easily deceived.
People: And we are powerless over the unseen forces that wage war against the church.
Leader: Therefore, with the heart and mind of Christ, let us worship God, in whom is our strength and power.

Prayer of adoration: Our loving God and Creator, we bow ourselves before you, for you are worthy of our praise. Our minds cannot comprehend your greatness. Your willingness to humbly assume the cross on our behalf shatters any notion of a distant and uncaring God. By your cross we are healed. By your cross our pride is confronted with the love of God which sets us free. We give thanks to you for being a light in our darkness. Your gospel message is a light for our eyes. What you have said gives us something to say. What you have done gives us courage to bear a message to others. We stand amazed and awestruck at your loving intent to forgive those who crucified you. At your cross the hostilities of the world are absorbed and a people are redeemed. Praise be to the Father, Son and Holy Spirit, in whom we move, live and have our being. Amen.

Prayer of confession: We confess that many times we find it hard to understand the paradoxes of life. We do not easily understand how the last shall be the first and how the meek shall inherit the earth. We confess that it is our nature to grasp and try to hold, rather than to receive. Our senses are shocked when we hear that we really find life by losing it. We confess our need of a guide on our spiritual journey. Draw near to us in this hour, Lord, instilling confidence in us that the work you have done on the cross was complete, and that your grace can be sufficient for us. Lift up our hearts by the power of your pardon to higher levels of love and trust in you and each other. In the name of Christ, we pray. Amen.

Prayer of dedication of gifts and self: We have reflected this day on our actions of this week. We have opened ourselves to the searching and examination of your Spirit. In this hour we would not hide ourselves from you or from ourselves. May this hour be for us an hour of honesty, of truth, of submission to your Lordship and of spiritual growth. We simply present ourselves before you and invoke your life-changing presence. Rekindle in our hearts Christlike feelings, thoughts, attitudes and actions toward our fellow humans. We believe in your power to redeem, restore and renew. We resolve to offer the spiritual gifts you have given us to do your good pleasure. Draw near to us and make of us partners in reconciling the world to God. In Christ's name we pray. Amen.

Sermon title: The Good Life Through Self Abandonment

Sermon thesis: When our ultimate goal is to preserve life we lose it. When our goal is to follow Christ we find our real self and live a life worth remembering. There is no place for a policy of safety first in the Christian life.

Hymn of the day: *"O God, thou/my faithful God."* Johann Heermann (1585-1647), who gave us the beautiful Holy Week text, "Ah, holy Jesus," also gave us this fine hymn of Christian commitment. Heermann was a Lutheran pastor who lived in Germany during the time of the Thirty Years War and the pestilence. This hymn seems to have been written between 1623 and 1630, during the time of Heermann's greatest suffering.

Announcements for next week:

Sermon title: Greatness Through Welcoming the Least Great

Sermon theme: Spiritually great people are close to, not distant from, the rest of humanity.

Sermon summary: Our quest for greatness, the desire to leave our mark on the sands of history, can sometimes cause us to relate with others in such a way as to make that quest less likely.

Children's object talk:

Many Things Are Possible When You Think You Can Do It

Objects: A small child's bicycle.

Lesson: Overcoming fears is like learning to ride a bicycle.

Outline: 1. It is not easy to learn to ride a bicycle.
2. The person who always tries to protect himself or herself from ever getting hurt loses out on life.
3. The person who is brave enough to follow Jesus, finds life as exciting as the one who is brave enough to learn to ride a bicycle.

HOW OLD WERE YOU when you started to ride a bicycle? At first it seems like it will take forever to learn how, doesn't it? Did you believe that you could learn how? You probably saw other kids riding their bikes. Did any of you ever fall off? Did it hurt? Did you get right back on, or wait a little while, think about it, and then get back on? Are you glad you know how to ride a bicycle? They are great fun, aren't they? I'm proud of you all for being brave enough to get back on your bicycles.

Riding a bike can be risky. And we have to be careful when riding our bicycles so that we don't get hurt too badly. So, we follow all the safety rules.

Jesus said that the person who tries to save his life will lose it. And then he said that the person who loses his life for Jesus and the gospel will save it. The person who tries to save his life is like the kid who never gets back on the bicycle because he wants to save himself from being hurt. He is afraid. The person who loses his life for Jesus, is like the kid who gets back on the bicycle. In the end she gets more out of life, because she was willing to learn. Let us pray. Lord give us courage to risk doing big things for you and for others. Amen.

The sermon:

The Good Life Through Self Abandonment

Hymns:
Beginning of worship: I Love to Tell the Story
Sermon hymn: Jesus, Saviour, Pilot Me
End of worship: O For a Closer Walk with God

Scripture: Mark 8:27-35

Sermon text: *"For whoever wants to save his life will lose it, but whoever loses his life for me and for the gospel will save it."* v. 35

CONSIDER A FEW ILLUSTRATIONS OF PEOPLE WHO WERE WILLING TO RISK THEIR LIVES FOR something in which they believed. Socrates pursued truth. His pursuit of truth brought him into trouble with the keepers of rigid traditions. As most of us know, his method of arriving at truth by questioning another person in order to elicit from the person a clear expression of something supposed to be implicity known by all thinking people led to his death sentence. Epictetus says of Socrates: "Dying, he was saved, because he did not flee."

Later in history, another man who saved his life by losing it was John Bunyan. He was ordered to attend public worship and stop holding and preaching at private worship services of his own design. In his day, he championed the idea of freedom of speech. His journals indicate that he questioned within himself whether to flee to safety or to stand by his principles and suffer the consequences. He suffered the consequences. Had he chosen otherwise, the world may have retained a tinker, but lost a thinker.

Thomas Jefferson deliberated as to whether he should pursue the peaceful life of a farmer and architect; or should he put to use his literary and political skills in framing together the principles by which we live in this country? One of his biographies tells us that he was one of the least hot-headed of the early revolutionaries, and adept at not stirring up reactionary responses from the British. Trouble came, nonetheless. He stood his ground. He risked his peaceful and genteel life for a much higher calling. For that reason history remembers him. His life was not lost.

These examples of people like Socrates, Bunyan, and Jefferson illustrate for us pioneers of new ideas. They all met resistance. They all faced choices as to whether to save their lives, or to lose them in the pursuit of a higher calling. They were pioneers of thought and action. They were risk takers. The sincerity of their beliefs was tested and they proved themselves true to the test.

In the 1960s a weary black woman sat down in the white section of a bus and refused to give up her seat to a white person. Rosa Parks decided to live out the meaning of the principles in our constitution. In part because of her courage, a new era in American life began as an idea took shape in her action.

In 1942, Clarence Jordan, a pecan farmer and Biblical scholar, founded a cooperative Christian community named Koinonia Farm. The farm served as a springboard for his belief that Christianity requires a social conscience as well as a spiritual dimension. His belief that race does not divide people in God's kingdom made Koinonia a target of violence. Local town people cut down his trees, burned fields and shot holes in Koinonia houses. Jordan's life was not long, but it was significant.

In 1976, a young man who was greatly influenced by Clarence Jordan began Habitat for Humanity. Since then, Habitat has built thousands of homes for God's people in need. To date, there are over 330 towns in the U.S. and Canada where the affluent and the needy minister together building and remodeling homes. In just fourteen short years Habitat is building homes for Third World people in twenty-six different countries.

The point can again be illustrated by considering a child on a bike. When he or she falls off, the child reasons, "Hey, riding a bike is risky business." Then, the child either decides to get back on the bike or to stay off. There is a great lesson in riding a bike.

My point is this. Our life does not find its meaning through our preoccupation with self. Rather, our life is saved through the discipline of being willing to lose it for a cause greater than ourself.

Think about this. Our culture teaches us that the quality of our life is improved the more we pamper it. There is a philosophy of life which wars against community, cooperation and partnership. One focus is on me. The other is on the common good. Into the tension of this situation comes the observation that the greatest people have always been service minded. They have found their lives by losing them in service to God and to others.

My aim is that our Lord's words, and my few footnotes, will persuade us all to accept and live by the truth in the passage: "Whoever wants to save his life will lose it, but whoever loses his life for me and for the gospel will save it."

The story line of our passage is quite brief. Jesus tries to prepare his disciples for the events ahead by explaining to them that all religious leaders will reject him and the gospel, he will be put to death, but later God would bring him back to life. Peter responds to Jesus' words by rebuking him. At this point the dialogue thickens. Jesus rebukes Peter and to our surprise calls Peter, "Satan." Jesus continues his rebuke by telling Peter that he does not have in his mind the things of God, but of men. Then, Jesus employs a rather different disciple recruitment strategy. He offers his followers a life of self-denial and the all-too-well understood symbol of death — the cross. We are not told, but we may assume that neither of these offers were the fulfillment of the disciples' dreams. Then in verse 35, Jesus speaks to his listeners by using a "chiasm." The characteristic of a chiasm is that the ideas are switched around in the second line. Jesus used a chiasm in Mark 2:27 when he said, "The Sabbath was made for man, not man for the Sabbath." Here he says:

"Whoever wants to save his life will lose it,
but whoever loses his life for me and for the gospel will save it."

Jesus continues his dialogue by adding, "What is the good gaining the world, but losing one's life?" And, "What can a person give in exchange for one's life?"

What effect did these words have on the first listeners? The words elicit a response on the deepest level of commitment. Jesus is asking his followers to make the ultimate sacrifice. Perhaps that is why the passage grabs us the way it does.

It was William Barclay, the Scottish theologian from Glasgow, who said, "Knowledge only becomes relevant when it is translated into action. Theology must become life. Theory must become practice." Jesus' words are just as action oriented. "If anyone wants to be my disciple, he must deny himself and take up his cross and follow me." The implications are obvious. A Christian will have to sacrifice her will, for no Christian can ever again do what she likes; she must do what Christ likes.

We in the church are in the spiritual company of a list of people who have grasped this truth and lived by it. Life does not find its meaning through preoccupation with self. Rather, our life is saved through the discipline of being willing to lose it for a cause greater than ourself. Abraham, the father of our faith, left all the land he had and set out for a promised land. Ruth, remembered for her kindness and loyalty, risked it all by following Naomi back to Judah. Daniel, under orders not to pray to his God, proved true to himself and to God.

When our ultimate goal is to preserve life we lose it. When our goal is to follow Christ we find our real self and live a life worth remembering. There is no place for a policy of safety first in the Christian life. A person can hoard life, if one wishes to do so. But that way one will lose all that makes life valuable to others and worth living for oneself. The way to true happiness is to spend life, for only thus will we find life, here and hereafter.

In the Presbyterian Book of Order there is a brief statement that responds to Christ's invitation to take up the cross. It says, "The church is called to tell the good news of salvation by the grace of God through faith in Jesus Christ as the only Savior and Lord. The church is called to undertake this mission even at the risk of losing its life, trusting in God alone as the author and giver of life."

And so you see, Presbyterians believe, as do other Christians, that the good life is found through self abandonment.

Thomas N. Gard
The Presbyterian Church of Watertown
Watertown, South Dakota

September 22, 1991

Lutheran: Eighteenth Sunday after Pentecost
Roman Catholic: Twenty-fifth Sunday of the Year
Episcopalian: Proper 20
Pres/Meth/UCC: Eighteenth Sunday after Pentecost

Lessons:

Lutheran:	Jer. 11:18-20	James 3:16-4:6	Mark 9:30-37
Roman Catholic:	Wisd. 2:12, 17-20	James 3:16-4:3	Mark 9:30-37
Episcopal:	Wisd. 1:16-2:1, (6-11) 12-22	James 3:16-4:6	Mark 9:30-37
Pres/Meth/UCC:	Job. 28:20-28	James 3:13-18	Mark 9:30-37

Introductions to the Lessons:

Lesson 1

(1) *Jeremiah 11:18-20* (**Lutheran**). The enemies of Jeremiah are out to kill him for his pointed preaching of doom and destruction for the nation. Yahweh revealed to him their schemes to get rid of him. He saw himself as a lamb led to the slaughter. He cries to God for protection and for divine vengeance on his enemies.

(2) *Wisdom 1:16-2:1, 12-22* (**Episcopal**). Ungodly people consider death to be a friend. However, the ungodly have no love for the godly. They resent the opposition of the godly. They decide to put godly persons to a test by insult and torture. They want to see how the godly will take death. But, the ungodly are unsound in their reasoning, for they forget the purposes of God in behalf of the righteous.

(3) *Job 28:20-28* (**Pres/Meth/UCC**). Where can wisdom be found? This is the question that Job discusses. Nature, people, and even death do not know the answer. Only God knows wisdom and its source. God revealed the nature and source of wisdom. The fear of the Lord and righteous living constitute wisdom.

Lesson 2

(1) *James 3:16-4:6* (**Luth/Epis**). Why are we humans plagued with conflicts and disputes? James says these conflicts result from getting what we want in wrong ways: wars, murders, and disputes. Rather, we should go to prayer for what we want. However, our problem is that we do not ask for the right things. We should ask for the things of God and not things of the world.

(2) *James 3:13-18* (**Pres/Meth/UCC**). There are two kinds of wisdom: earthly and heavenly. Earthly wisdom leads to things wicked and devilish. Heavenly wisdom is characterized by mercy and good works.

Gospel

Mark 9:30-37 (**Luth/Epis/Pres/Meth/UCC**). For the last time Jesus is on his way to Jerusalem. Again he advises his disciples that he must go to Jerusalem to die and rise again. When they arrive in their house at Capernaum, Jesus asked them what they were discussing while on the way. They were embarrassed to answer, for they were arguing who was the greatest. However, Jesus knew what they were talking about and gave the answer to true greatness: service.

Theme: Spiritually great people are close to, not distant from, the rest of humanity.

Thought for the day: Have you ever noticed how people who compete for positions of greatness may lose popularity in the public eye if they do not display an ability to be approachable as a person? Sometimes, the quest for greatness, the desire to leave our mark on the sands of history, can cause us to relate in such a way as to make that quest less likely. Our agenda is not to be hooked by a desire to present ourselves as greater than others. Jesus offers another of his paradoxes as a means to greatness. If we want to be truly great we must make it our practice to put our need for affirmation last. And if we make it our agenda to build other people up, to express warm affection and acceptance of those who are not highly esteemed, then we have the affirmation that really counts. We will have God's affirmation and true greatness.

Prayer of meditation: Out of another week of challenge and opportunities your people come to make themselves available to you, O God. We have come to worship you and witness to your faithfulness. We want to be imitators of Christ. It is our desire that our knowledge of his words and his actions might take root in us, causing us to put into practice the relational greatness of Christ, our Lord. Open our hearts and minds, as you move toward us, to higher aspirations and more faithful demonstrations of the love of Christ. Amen.

Call to worship:
Leader: Into your presence we come together to offer ourselves for spiritual renewal.
People: We turn to Christ who makes us into his image.
Leader: As we forget our striving for affirmation, let us focus on the needs of others first.
People: We come to the one who embraced the little child.
Leader: May we feel the love of Jesus embrace us as we worship God together.

Prayer of adoration: Great God, who for our sake and for the quality of life we might live, taught us the meaning of greatness, we worship you. Look upon your servants gathered here who are bombarded with messages that war against real greatness. In the Lord who was servant we find greatness. In the shepherd who sought the lost we find your nature. Truly, in Christ you have been made known to us. We focus our minds, therefore, upon you. We empty ourselves of self concern and worry, fear and doubt. If our prayer of adoration is to become a life of adoration you must come near to us and by your presence work your life-changing way in us. To this purpose we offer ourselves to you in worship. Free our hearts to glorify you. You are worthy, O Lord, of our worship. And your life and teaching are worthy of our meditation. Amen.

Prayer of confession: (unison): We turn to you from the complexities of daily life, and pray for relief from misguided thoughts and unfounded fears. Wearied by the world's confusion, we lose sight of stability and calm. We are tempted by the desire to achieve greatness through pointing out everyone else's weakness, all the while remaining blind to our own shortcomings. O deliver us from such misguided attempts at greatness which only make us small. Restore to your servants the sanity and courage which we sorely need. We confess that we have distanced ourselves from those we could have helped. By our admission of our powerlessness over the enticements of various quests for personal transcendence, free us from dependency on public opinion. We turn away from attempting to overcome evil through our own power, and in faith, believing in your power to win a shining victory, we turn our lives over to you. Amen.

Prayer of dedication of gifts and self: Our Lord and God, in response to your grace and goodness we dedicate ourselves to you. As your presence becomes a living reality in us may we mirror that connection to other people. We dedicate ourselves to the quest of being your servants. Because we are thus committed, assist us to take our minds off of ourselves and instead, focus our attention on the duties of service. Teacher of what it means to be great, let none of us miss the meaning of what we have learned today. We dedicate ourselves to embracing children. We offer our ears to show that we care enough to understand them. And we offer them our eye contact to show that we have faith in them. Help us to grow in our relational skills and in the attitudes of our hearts toward one another, to the end that we might be builders of the Body of Christ. In our Lord's name we pray. Amen.

Sermon title: Greatness Through Welcoming the Least Great

Sermon thesis: Spiritually great people are close to, not distant from, the rest of humanity.

Hymn of the day: *"Lord, whose love in/through humble service"*. This hymn was one of *Seven New Social Welfare Hymns* published by the Hymn Society of America for the Second National Conference on Churches and Social Welfare, 1961. Albert F. Bayly (1901-1984), a Congregational minister, served a number of churches in England between 1928 and 1972. He wrote his first hymn in 1945 and thereafter published four volumes of hymnody. He was made an honorary fellow of Westminster Choir College in 1968 and ten years later was honored at a special service in Westminster Abbey.

Announcements for next week:

Sermon title: Proof's in the . . .

Sermon theme: Faith that is true must take feet.

Sermon summary: We dare not get caught up in the argument of correct doctrine versus right actions. Christ cuts through that divisiveness that can paralyze, and calls his people to recognize God's goodness and claims, and to respond, to be wise in understanding God's ways and committed in following his will.

Children's object talk:

Who Is The Greatest?

Objects: A trophy

Lesson: A person's greatness is measured by his/her ability to love other people.

Outline: 1. We measure a person's greatness by how well he/she can do something.

2. We can also measure a person's spiritual greatness by how willing he/she is to be a friend to others.

3. It is good to be great at *doing* something. It is even better to be great at *being* a loving person.

WHAT DO I HAVE IN MY HAND? Why do people receive trophies? Well, it's because they are very good at doing something, isn't it? Who are some of the greatest people you know of? (pause). Who is the greatest quarterback in football? Joe Montana perhaps? Who is the greatest basketball player? Michael Jordan perhaps? Who is the greatest bicycle rider? Perhaps Greg LaMond? Who is the greatest tennis player? It's probably Martina Navratilova. Who is the greatest golfer? Maybe Jack Nicklaus. Who is the best actor? Is it Michael J. Fox or Big Bird? Who is the greatest singer? Is it Barbra Streisand or Mr. Rogers? Who is the greatest comedian? Is it Bill Cosby? Who is the greatest cook? You'll be glad if you say it is Mom or Dad.

We measure a person's greatness by how well they do something. We can also measure a person's spiritual greatness by how willing he or she is to be a friend to others. What good would it do us to be the best quarterback in football and not have a friend? A friend knows how to help other people feel good about themselves.

So, it is good to be great at doing something. And it is fun to compete with each other. But, it is even better to be great at being a loving person.

The sermon:

Greatness Through Welcoming the Least Great

Hymns:

Beginning of worship: My Hope is Built on Nothing Less
Sermon hymn: Jesus Keep Me Near the Cross
End of worship: More About Jesus Would I Know

Scripture: Mark 9:30-37

Sermon text: *"He took a little child and had him stand among them. Taking him in his arms, he said to them, 'Whoever welcomes one of these little children in my name welcomes me'. . ."*

THEY CAME BACK TO THEIR HEADQUARTERS IN CAPERNAUM. The fishing village was a cultural melting pot compared to isolated Jewish villages to the south. Here, Romans, Greeks, Arabs and Jews traveled and traded. Situated on the north shore of Lake Galilee, Capernaum served well as a central location for their mission trips to various other towns and villages. They came to the house which served as their headquarters. They entered the courtyard of the home and a few extra followers accompanied them.

The boy was probably only six years old. And although he was the son of established parents, since he was just a child, his status was the same as a servant. People began to greet one another. Those with a lower social standing greeted the men with a kiss on the hand.

71

Servants approached the owner of the house and kissed his feet and waited for instructions for entertaining and refreshing Jesus and his followers. The boy too, was careful to obey the cultural expectations. He greeted his superiors with a bow to the earth and a gesture of kissing their feet. Above all else, an atmosphere of proper honor and respect would be maintained. Such customs of greeting let everyone know who was the greatest and who was not so great.

The boy took a station of less honor by positioning himself along the wall of the courtyard. He sat and waited with his friends, like curious people about to read a newspaper, for they came to learn of the news from the other towns. To be up to date on the news, people always gathered around travelers. As he waited with his ears wide open, Jesus turned to his followers and asked them what they had been arguing about as they traveled the road. There was silence. In response to this silence, Jesus made a gesture which indicated to everyone to listen very carefully. He calmly moved to the center of the courtyard and sat down. As a teacher he had just indicated that he had something important to say.

"If anyone wants to be first, he must be the very last, and the servant of all." Men of honor opened their mouths and looked surprised. Heads were turning this way and that asking one another what Jesus could possibly mean. Servants lifted their heads as if they had just received a gift of dignity.

The boy questioned to himself what this could possibly mean. To do as Jesus instructed was not the way to hold first place in honor in everyone else's eyes. What was he trying to teach his disciples? As he thought to himself and looked at Jesus to read his face, their eyes met and Jesus beckoned him to come to him. In obedience, he quickly presented himself to Jesus face down at his feet. But Jesus gave him permission to stand among his superiors. And then, in an action that conveyed as much honor on the boy as the owner of the house, Jesus greeted the boy by giving him a warm hug. Suddenly, the six-year-old boy was given as much honor and respect as an honorable man in the community. Jesus' action spoke louder than words and sent ripples of surprise through the crowd. While still holding the boy, Jesus taught his disciples a lesson on the habit of welcoming people. He said to them, "Whoever welcomes one of these little children in my name welcomes me; and whoever welcomes me does not welcome me but the one who sent me."

The boy thought to himself as he heard these words. "If I want to be great I must be the very last and servant of all. What this means is that inasmuch as I receive the person of lowest social standing I receive Christ, and in receiving Christ I receive God. This must mean that my relationship with God is directly connected with how I relate with other people. They are inseparable. Who would have thought that a warm and genuine hug would have so much meaning?"

There was a populist rather than an elitist tendency in what Jesus had said. His words were significant because they encouraged his followers to do just the opposite of what one would expect a great person to do. His teaching, if followed, would change not only how his disciples thought, but also how they would relate to other people regardless of status. In order to follow Jesus' instructions a person would have to give up the desire to lord it over others.

Those who heard his words raised objections in their minds. "I was no better off than a servant when I was a child. I received no expression of respect until I became an adult. Jesus, do you expect me to let go of my position in my community? Shall I become a child again, who greets superiors by kissing their feet? Do you want me to hug these children as if they were my equals, instead of having them kiss my feet? You are asking me to act differently than everyone else. How will I explain my behavior? If I do as you say, more than likely I will lose the respect of my peers. And what is worse, the children will not respect or obey me. What might happen to the sense of order and control we have in our communities if we actually did what you tell us to do?"

The disciples thought to themselves that if they continued in their old way of relating, the cycle of one generation oppressing another, rather than blessing them, would not be broken. Children would not be affirmed and valued. They would grow up to be hungry for affirmation and do all kinds of crazy things to try to meet their need for affirmation. They reasoned that if they did not change they would simply pass on their shame from one generation to another. If we do not change then we will continue to fear our superiors but we will feel no love for them. Jesus wants us to break this cycle of poor relational skills by being willing to lay aside our pride and to welcome those of low estate.

A disciple closed his eyes and envisioned Jesus hugging him and putting him in a place of honor. He had a feeling that he might be able to do what Jesus had asked them to do. The boy caught a glimpse of what a change this simple behavior would make in his society. He imagined what it would be like if all the adults treated children like Jesus treated him. He prayed that they would find the courage to follow Jesus' words. The boy wanted the adults to recognize their pursuits for greatness that do not lead them to greatness. He thought of Joseph who hugged his brothers who had sold him as a slave into Egypt. What a healing effect that hug had on them all. He thought of Jacob and Esau who embraced each other after years of division. And the boy thought of the story that Jesus told of a prodigal son who was embraced by his father. What grace there is in an embrace. What power there is in a hug.

"I can," the boy exclaimed. "I can imitate Christ." The thought occurred to him that we start to be great when we let go of our need to be great in other people's eyes. Our action of putting ourselves last sets us free from trying to make sure that everyone else respects us. We are no longer bound by the need to meet our own need for greatness. "I'm free," the boy said to himself. "I'm free to be of service."

Thomas N. Gard
The Presbyterian Church of Watertown
Watertown, South Dakota

September 29, 1991

Lutheran: Nineteenth Sunday after Pentecost
Roman Catholic: Twenty-sixth Sunday of the Year
Episcopalian: Proper 21
Pres/Meth/UCC: Nineteenth Sunday after Pentecost

Lessons:

Lutheran:	Num. 11:4-6, 10-16, 24-29	James 4:7-12 (13-5:6)	Mark 9:38-50
Roman Catholic:	Num. 11:25-29	James 5:1-6	Mark 9:38-43, 45, 47-48
Episcopal:	Num. 11:4-6, 10-16, 24-29	James 4:7-12 (13-5:6)	Mark 9:38-43, 45, 47-48
Pres/Meth/UCC:	Job 42:1-6	James 4:13-17, 5:7-11	Mark 9:38-50

Introductions to the Lessons:

Lesson 1

(1) *Numbers 11:4-6, 10-16, 24-29* (**Luth/Epis**). While in the wilderness the Israelites grew tired of manna as their only food. They came to Moses and demanded that he give them meat. 600,000 were protesting and crying, "Give us meat." Moses, disappointed and frustrated, took the complaint to Yahweh and asked him to kill him, for the task of leadership was too heavy. Yahweh ordered Moses to bring seventy elders together, and God gave them some of Moses' spirit that they might share the burden. It was reported that two who did not come to the meeting were preaching among the people. Joshua urged Moses to stop them, but Moses wished all the people would prophesy.

(2) *Job 42:1-6* (**Pres/Meth/UCC**). The book of Job closes with this account of Job's surrender to God. He did not get an answer to his question why a righteous person suffers. Job confesses that he spoke without understanding, but now he has a personal knowledge of God. Heretofore he only heard about God but now he sees him. This causes Job to repent.

Lesson 2

(1) *James 4:7-12* (**Luth/Epis**). James continues to give moral directions. We are to draw close to God and at the same time resist the devil. If we humble ourselves, God will exalt us. James goes on to warn us against judging each other.

75

(2) *James 4:13-17* (**Pres/Meth/UCC**). One never knows what tomorrow will bring. In our arrogance we say what we will do tomorrow. But, life is like a mist, here today and gone tomorrow. We should say, God willing, we will do this or go there.

Gospel

Mark 9:38-50 (**Luth/Epis/Pres/Meth/UCC**). Today's gospel begins with the very next verse after what we read last Sunday. The disciple John tells Jesus that he forbade a non-follower from casting out demons in Jesus' name. However, Jesus encouraged the man to cast out demons, for anyone not against Jesus is for him. Then Jesus goes on to say that it would be better to sacrifice a sin than to cause the whole person to go to hell.

Theme: Faith that is true must take feet.

Thought for the day: Our God calls us to be his people. He gifts us with compassion, acceptance and purpose, and then he empowers us to share those gifts in a world that desperately longs for them.

Prayer of meditation: Dear Heavenly Father, in this day in which we are pulled and pushed by our busy-ness and so many choices to be made, please keep our lives focused, know that you are God and we are your people. In Christ's name we pray. Amen.

Call to worship: "Great is the Lord, and greatly to be praised. . . His compassion is unsearchable. Enter into his presence humbly and hopefully."

Prayer of adoration: Almighty Lord, all good spills from the graciousness of your love. For the hope in children's eyes, for the friendship of well known smiles, for rest that is free of anxiety, for work that tires us, and challenges that develop us, thank you. Allow us to grow more grateful. Amen.

Prayer of confession: Dear Father, your arms are always open to us. But yet we, as your children, too often stray away. We have not been the family you call us to be. We have been too concerned for ourselves rather than for our brothers and sisters. We have sought after our own selfish desires, rather than listen to your loving guidance. We have not acted for the good of your family when we could have. Father forgive us, sensitize us, empower us and help us to be the children you created us to be. Amen.

Prayer of dedication of gifts and self: Almighty God, we are your people: strengthen us in our efforts to serve you. Draw our hearts to you, guide our minds, fill our imaginations, and control our wills, so that we may be wholly yours. Use us as you will, always to your glory and the welfare of your people. Amen.

Sermon title: Proof's in the. . .

Sermon thesis: We dare not get caught up in the argument of correct doctrine versus right actions. Christ cuts through that divisiveness that can paralyze, and calls his people to recognize God's goodness and claims, and to respond. . . to be wise in understanding God's ways and committed in following his will.

Hymn of the day: *"Eternal Ruler of the ceaseless round".* "We would be one" is the prayer of this hymn by John White Chadwick. It was written during the Civil War for the author's graduation from Harvard Divinity School. Chadwick served for 40 years as minister of the Second Unitarian Church in Brooklyn, New York.

Announcements for next week:

Sermon title: We Wouldn't Have A Chance. . . But

Sermon theme: We fall far short, yet God's love gives us hope.

Sermon summary: Some things make us very uncomfortable. They really bother us. Today's Gospel is one of those occasions in which we have a look at something very bothersome. We fail to live as God longs for us to live. All of us fall short. And yet, the cross makes it possible to live with hope and to take risks at being God's children.

Children's object talk:

Actions Speak Louder Than Words

Objects: A sack full of M & M's
Lesson: We can say anything, but our actions show what is real.
Outline: 1. Eat in front of the young people.
2. Tell them how important it is to share.
3. Let them talk about the discrepancy.
4. Let them know that God longs for us to show his love to others.

I LOVE EATING M & M's, don't you? They really are good. You know what else? I believe it is very important to share. (Eat a few M & M's) Can anyone tell us what it means to share? (Let them explain while you keep eating the M & M's) That's right, sharing means that you give to others what you have. You make sure that no one is left out. You know that God wants us to share, don't you? It is very important to him, because people get hurt when others don't share. (Keep eating) You agree, don't you?

Say what's wrong? Some of you are looking at me like something's not right. (Let them voice their disappointment in you that you are not sharing. Talk through how they felt.) I shouldn't just say I believe in sharing, should I? I should show it by sharing. (Share the M & M's)

You know, God loves us very much. He cares for us. And he wants us to share with others his care. But we can't just say it, we need to do it. You know how you felt when I said sharing was important, but yet I didn't do it. We know God wants us to love others, but we can't just talk about it, we need and want to do it. Make sure that our faith isn't just talk, but that we do and live it!

The sermon:

Proof's in the. . .

Hymns:
Beginning of worship: Open Now Thy Gates of Beauty
Sermon hymn: O Jesus, I Have Promised
End of worship: Stand Up, Stand Up for Jesus

Scripture: Mark 9:38-50

Sermon text: *"For no one who does a mighty work in my name will be able soon after to speak evil to me. For he that is not against us is for us. For truly I say to you, whoever gives you a cup of water to drink because you bear the name of Christ, will by no means lose his reward."* vs. 39-41

AN OLD EASTERN FABLE is told about a man who possessed a ring set with a wonderful opal. Whoever wore the ring became so sweet and true in character that all the people loved him. You see, the ring was a charm. Always it was passed down from father to son and always it did its work. . . or magic.

Now as time went on, it came to a father who had three sons whom he loved with an equal love. What was he to do when the time came to pass on the ring?

The father made a decision. He had two other rings made that were precisely the same, so that no one could tell the difference. On his death bed, he called each of his sons in, spoke some words of love to each, and without telling the others, gave a ring . . . telling them to allow it to work its magic in their lives.

When the three sons discovered that each had a ring, a great dispute arose as to which was the true ring that could do so much for its owner. The case was taken to a wise judge. He examined the rings and then spoke: "I cannot tell which is the magical ring," he said, "But you yourselves can prove it." "Us?" asked the astonished sons, "How can we?"

"If the true ring gives sweetness and leadership to the character of the man who wears it, then I and all the people of the city will know the one who possesses the true ring by the goodness of his life. So go your ways, and be kind, be truthful, be brave, be just in your dealings, and he who does these things will be the owner of the true ring."

I like that old story because I believe it points in the same direction as our Gospel lesson for today. This morning, we heard about a time in which the disciples were concerned about which was more important: 1) believing the right things or 2) doing the right things. Or as the fable put it: having the true ring or leading the charmed life. Which is more important: having true faith or doing good works?

The disciple John came to Jesus with the problem encased in a specific situation: "Teacher," he said, "we saw a man casting out demons in your name — doing good works — but we told him to quit because he was not following us . . . he was not one of your true followers. Is that right?"

And Jesus responded with a double-edged statement: "If he's doing good work in *my* name . . . that's good." You see, Christ didn't get caught in the game of which is more important — to believe right or to do right. But rather, he put the two together in a way which proves they cannot be separated. The two *must* be together in order for either one to be real and good and true. And that's what I want to focus on for these brief moments together this morning.

I want to make two statements that as Christians we can base our lives. First, *what you believe is of critical importance!* What you believe makes all the difference in your world. What you believe dictates how you perceive your world . . . how you understand your life . . . how you reckon with the past . . . and how you hope for the future. If you believe life is a test or a trial, as some do, there will be no joy in your life. If you believe life is meant only to be an effort to feel good — search for parties — you'll spend more time disappointed and empty than not. If you believe life is an obstacle course in which survival of the fittest is the key — every person for themselves – your life will be burdened by that selfishness and its consequences.

I recently read a story in which some boys were looking for crabs, and as each crab was caught, it was placed into a basket. A man walking by warned: "You'd better cover the basket, otherwise the crabs will climb out and escape." "That won't happen," replied one of the boys, "If one crabs tries to climb up, the others will pull him back down."

I am afraid that "survival" instinct in each of us – afraid to let others get ahead – pulls us all down in individual situations and in corporate institutions. If we think this world was created just for us, to be for all our wants and whims, that selfishness keeps all of us from caring and sharing . . . from having a world where all are important and whole. What you believe is of critical importance.

Much has been made recently about the increase in Satanic cults in our society. I do think that is frightening. That some folks are being sucked into the grasp of evil as enticing and something worth pursuing is horrible. But, I honestly don't fear that as much as I fear those whose faith is pure indifference or whose faith is a matter of accident of birth or parentage. "Oh, I was born a Christian . . . my mother was faithful."

You see, without the struggle to seek God and his will, to be active in recognizing our Creator's purpose for us, we fail to live. When faith is just a label, but not a relationship, it is nothing! I'm more concerned for those who don't have time to be bothered about considering their faith, who think all's well, but refuse to hear any upward calling or any prioritizing to life. Christ himself said, "I'd rather you were cold or hot concerning me, but to be lukewarm, I spit that out."

What we believe causes our life to go in certain directions. If we truly understand God's love for us and his care, given freely as a gift – unearned – we feel differently about ourselves. Our self-esteem does not always have to worry if we are getting a fair shake.

If we truly recognize that Christ gave his life for that person we don't like, we treat them differently. Our Lord died for her or him too. If we truly understand that there is a purpose to our living, we have meaning and direction. Then discouragement is not allowed to become despair. What we believe is of critical importance!

The second statement: *our faith must cause action!* Our belief must grow feet. For faith without action will soon die, just as good works without faith is hollow and empty and eventually fades away.

The second part of our Gospel *is* harsh and heavy with the theme of condemnation — for actions can be harmful. "Whoever causes one of these little ones who believe in me to sin, it would be better for him if a great millstone were hung round his neck and he were thrown into the sea . . . and if your hand causes you to sin, cut it off."

God doesn't take our actions lightly, as though it really doesn't matter. It does! We need to heed that, to recognize that there are consequences to sin, and not make light of that.

And, we also need to hear how Christ concluded these statements: "Have salt in yourselves." That means live life fully, add flavoring, good flavoring to the world. Christ doesn't want to rob us of the enjoyment of living; rather he desires to protect us from those things which drain life out of the soul and erode the energy and efficiency of abundant living in his Spirit.

He calls us to live out our faith. If we believe we have received love, then share it! If we believe God forgives us, then we are given the power to forgive others. If we believe our life is precious and purposeful, then we will recognize that truth in our neighbor as well.

I was always taught as a kid that talk was cheap. In our home, if ever any great claims were made, we were told: "The proof's in the pudding." If it is true, it will show. I believe that is at the core of our Christian lives. If our faith is true, if it is of God, our actions will follow. They have to . . . and they will be good and right.

In 1988, at the Olympics, Greg Louganis, the great American diver, won, but under great adversity. Then 28 years old, he hit his head on the board on his next to last dive. On his final effort, he needed a near perfect dive to win. Afterward, a sportscaster asked him how he reassured himself to even try the dive. Louganis stated: "I kept telling myself, 'No matter how I do, my mother still loves me'." He nailed that dive!

No matter how our efforts turn out, God still loves us. Now go do the best you can. Right theology, good faith, God's grace . . . now be confident, hear God's call and respond . . . act . . . do!

David deFreese
Immanuel Lutheran Church
Bellevue, Nebraska

Pre-publication Advance Order Form

THE MINISTER'S ANNUAL MANUAL
FOR
PREACHING AND WORSHIP PLANNING
1992-1993

60 complete sermon and
worship planning helps
beginning August 2, 1992
through July 31, 1993

(Available by June 1, 1992)

$19.90

CLIP AND SEND NAME/ADDRESS WITH PAYMENT TO:

CHURCH MANAGEMENT, INC., P.O. Box 162527, Austin, TX 78716.
My check for $19.90, payable to CHURCH MANAGEMENT, INC. is enclosed for
one copy of *The Minister's Annual Manual for Preaching and Worship Planning
1992-1993*

Name _____

Address _____

City/State/Zip _____

OCTOBER 6, 1991

Lutheran: Twentieth Sunday after Pentecost
Roman Catholic: Twenty-seventh Sunday of the Year
Episcopalian: Proper 22
Pres/Meth/UCC: Twentieth Sunday after Pentecost

Lessons:

Lutheran:	Gen. 2:18-24	Heb. 2:9-11 (12-18)	Mark 10:2-16
Roman Catholic:	Gen. 2:18-24	Heb. 2:9-11	Mark 10:2-16
Episcopal:	Gen. 2:18-24	Heb. 2:(1-8) 9-18	Mark 10:2-9
Pres/Meth/UCC:	Gen. 2:18-24	Heb. 1:1-4, 2:9-11	Mark 10:2-16

Introductions to the Lessons

Lesson 1

Genesis 2:18-24 (**Luth/Epis/Pres/Meth/UCC**) How did woman come into existence? The answer is given in the second creation account, our first lesson today. All was created except woman, but none of the rest of creation filled Adam's need. Accordingly, God took a rib from Adam and made Eve. She was created to be his helper and companion. At once Adam recognized her as a part of his being. This justifies a son to leave parents to take a wife.

Lesson 2

Hebrews 2:9-11 (**Lutheran**); *2:9-18* **Episcopal**); *1:1-4, 2:9-11* (**Pres/Meth/UCC**) Today we begin a series of seven lessons from the book of Hebrews. It was written at a time when Christians were persecuted and faith was waning. The book begins by declaring that God's last Word was Jesus. Now we see Jesus, who was made superior to the angels, as a human who suffered death as an atonement for our sins.

Gospel

Mark 10:2-16 (**Luth/Pres/Meth/UCC**); *10:2-9* (**Episcopal**) Today's gospel lesson deals with marriage and children. While on his way to Jerusalem, a large crowd gathered around Jesus and he addressed them. Pharisees brought up the question of divorce. Jesus explained that divorce is not in the plan of God, for what he joins should not be separated. In the crowd were children who were brought to Jesus for his blessing. With little children in his arms, he declared that to enter God's Kingdom one must be like a child.

Theme: We fall far short, yet God's love gives us hope!

Thought for the day: Most of the time, we don't like to see how far we miss the mark of God's calling. But when we do, and when we realize that God still loves us and has hope for us, we are empowered to strive to be the people he sees in us.

Prayer of meditation: Dear Heavenly Father, thank you for loving us despite our failings, our self-centeredness, our evil. Thank you for giving us hope and the guidance and power to live lives that are worthwhile. Keep us focused. Keep us grateful, and keep us always. Amen.

Call to worship: Bless the Lord, Oh my soul, and all that is within me bless his holy name. Bless the Lord, Oh my soul, and forget not all his benefits.

Prayer of adoration: Giver of all good gifts, teach us to recognize your activity in our lives and in our world. Stimulate within us a sensitivity to your love and presence, and grant us truly grateful hearts which are aware that all we have and are is a gift from you. Amen.

Prayer of confession: Heavenly Father, make us discontented with things the way they are in the world and in our lives. Teach us to blush again for our tawdry deals: the arrogant but courteous prejudice; our selfish use of the rights and privileges others are unfairly denied. Make us notice the stains when people get spilled on . . . stains of our insensitivity, our self-centeredness, our smallness, our lack of concern. Amen.

Prayer of dedication of gifts and self: O God, our Father, by the cross of your Son, you reconciled the whole world to yourself, enabling us to live in love and harmony. We thank and praise you for this precious gift. And we dedicate our living to your call, to your desire that we be your people. Help us to forgive each other and to establish justice and concord in our lives. Amen.

Sermon title: We wouldn't have a chance . . . but.

Sermon thesis: Some things make us very uncomfortable. They really bother us. Today's gospel is one of those occasions in which we have to look at something very bothersome. We fail to live as God longs for us to live. All of us fall short. And yet, the cross makes it possible to live with hope and to take risks at being God's children.

Hymn for the day: *"O Christ, our hope."* This Latin hymn dating from the seventh or eighth century, was translated by John Chandler (1806-1876), a priest of the Church of England, and included in his *Hymns of the Primitive Church,* 1837. The hymn is a celebration of Christ's redemption.

Announcements for next week:

> **Sermon title:** First Thing
> **Sermon theme:** God calls us to trust him and to put him above all else.
> **Sermon summary:** God calls us to keep our priorities straight, to trust him above all else. We fail by putting our security in things and places that are only temporary. God demands to be God, and he gives us the faith and power to allow him to be God in our living.

Children's object talk:

God Lifts Us

Objects: An egg, a tall, clear glass filled ¾ with water, and a lot of table salt
Lesson: We feel down sometimes, but God's love can lift us.
Outline: 1. Discuss that we sometimes don't feel good about ourselves.
2. Show how the salt lifts the egg in the glass.
3. Talk about how God loves us no matter how we feel about ourselves . . . and that should help us.

DO YOU EVER FEEL BAD about yourself? I do sometimes. Maybe when I've said something mean, or I didn't do something right. Sometimes I don't like me. Do you always like you? . . . Maybe not.

Watch this egg go to the bottom of this glass. That's how we feel sometimes when we're not happy about ourselves . . . down! But God's love is ours. God loves us no matter how we feel about ourselves. God loves you more than you can even love yourself. God loves you. Watch. God's love is like this salt that comes and lifts us . . . just like this egg is lifted to the top of the glass. Pretty amazing, isn't it? But that's nothing like the amazing love of God that lifts us. Even when we feel bad, God loves us!

The sermon:

We Wouldn't Have a Chance . . . But

Hymns:

> Beginning of worship: Joyful, Joyful, We Adore You

Sermon hymn: Lord Jesus, Think on Me
End of worship: Rejoice, O Pilgrim Throng

Scripture: Mark 10:2-16

Sermon Text: *"He said to them, 'Whoever divorces his wife and marries another commits adultery against her, and if she divorces her husband and marries another, she commits adultery . . . Let the children come to me; do not stop them; for it is to such as these that the kingdom of God belongs. Truly I tell you, whoever does not receive the kingdom of God as a little child will never enter it.' "*
Mark 10:11, 12, 14b, 15

HENRI NOUWEN TELLS THE STORY of a family he knew in Paraguay. The father was a doctor who spoke out against the oppressive government there and its human rights abuses. The local police took their revenge on him by arresting his teenage son and torturing him to death. It was a brutal and senseless murder. The father responded with the most powerful protest imaginable. At the funeral, the father did not have the son's body embalmed and restored to an attractive memory. Rather, he displayed his son's body as he found it in the jail—naked, scarred and twisted from the electrical shocks, open sores from the beatings, and burns from cigarettes. All the villagers filed past the grotesque corpse, which lay not in a coffin, but on the blood-soaked mattress from the prison. It's a horrid story. But the reality of evil was not covered up.

You and I gather again to worship under the cross. That is another horrid story in which the reality of evil was and is not covered up. And yet, our God, out of incredible love, has turned it for our good. We rejoice in the power of mercy and compassion that defeats evil, and the cross gives us hope!

When something is bothersome, I like getting it off my chest as quickly as possible, and that's what I want to do right now. Out of all the passages in St. Mark's strong gospel, all the stories and verses, I can honestly say that today's first verses are the last ones I would like to preach on. I don't even like to read them. Did you hear what they say?

The passage begins with those ever persistent Pharisees trying to trap our Lord. They want to know what he thinks of divorce. They want to know because several in the crowd had practiced this easy way of dismissing the spouse. All it took back then was a written statement from the man declaring that they were no longer married, and the statement, "I divorce you" repeated three times. You see, the woman was seen much more as a possession than a partner in marriage. The Pharisees knew this Jesus of Nazareth seemed to lift women to a higher level of relationship. He respected them. They also knew that Jesus might lose some of his following among the men if he responded too kindly to the women, or he would lose some followers among the women if he took the "good ol' boy" path. The trap was well laid.

But Jesus amazes them all. He answers with a harshness that no one was ready to hear. He went beyond Moses' law to a deeper, more exacting law. He claims that God has a higher calling for his creation made in his image. Jesus said that God longs for the marriage to be a lifelong union, one that obviously takes commitment and work. We are not told how the crowd responded. Their silence would not be a surprise.

Later the disciples asked Jesus to explain what he meant, and the strongest statement on the subject follows: "Whoever divorces his wife and marries another commits adultery against her; and if she divorces her husband and marries another, she commits adultery."

That makes me gulp . . . doesn't it you? Who among us hasn't been affected by divorce in our lives? In our own lives or the lives of loved ones. With the current statistics telling us that half of the marriages today end in divorce, we had better gulp! We know adultery to be a sin. It is one of God's ten commandments. Yet, if we take Jesus at his word today, that particular sin is much more rampant then we are willing to admit.

You know what amazes me? In the midst of this kind of reading, I just announced this passage as the Gospel of our Lord, which means the "Good News" of our Lord. Good news? . . . and none of you questioned it . . . at least out loud.

Tell me, how is this good news? Is this crazy talk? We hear of heavy expectations and then serious judgment, and we call it good news? But it is!

You see, God *honors* us by believing we can live on such a high level. He envisions us being strong enough, disciplined enough to be the right kind of people. God hates evil, that which gets in the way of living harmoniously with him and with each other. He hates it. And he invites us to rise above it, to do better than just to do right, but to be right. God honors us by requesting that we be that kind of people.

A cartoon in a national magazine showed Moses with two tablets under his arm coming down the mountain. "I've got good news and bad news," he said. "The good news is that I got him down to ten. The bad news is adultery is still in there."

You see, God calls us to a higher standard, a deeper level of living. He calls us to be fully human — made in his image — and to live that way. Theologian Soren Kierkegaard once said: "Most people believe that the Christian commandments are intentionally a little too severe — like setting a clock a half hour ahead to make sure of not being late in the morning." But they're not! They are God's straightforward expectations of us. He believes we should live that way. He expects it of his children . . . always.

In my experience, I have never known anyone who has gone through a divorce who was flippant about it. It hurts terribly. It causes feelings of failure and tremendous disappointment. It is the death of hopes and dreams. It ravages self-esteem. It hurts. And God hates it, because it does hurt us so badly.

And yet we do fail. Marriages end. Divorce happens. People hurt.

And that leads us to the Good News of God's Gospel. We don't make it. Period. We don't live on that high level that God calls us to. We don't even have a chance. We are all damned because we fall far short. We don't have a chance of getting to heaven if left to our own devises.

We can't and we won't, except when our righteousness is transformed by the cross of Christ. On our own, we are in trouble; but Christ took on our failings and selfishness, he bore a cross on which all our unrighteousness was nailed. Our righteousness is enhanced and acceptable because Christ offers us the freshness of forgiveness, the cleansing of the cross.

How can we make it into the kingdom? Jesus says only if we accept the gift of his grace. Only if we are like little children, who know that they can't earn, but so readily receive.

That first story I told of the hateful murder in Paraguay is a good understanding of the evil in our world . . . and so is the cross of Christ, but it is more. The cross also points to a new beginning, of acceptance and love that powerfully overcame evil. That's where our righteousness comes from. It is our only hope! Mother Teresa has said it well: "You will never know that Jesus is all you need, until Jesus is all you've got!"

That's the good news today. God calls us to live life in a great and grand way, and when we can't, when we know how far we miss it, his love draws us to him. He lifts us with his compassion and guides us and bolsters us to keep trying. That's good news!

David deFreese
Immanuel Lutheran Church
Bellevue, Nebraska

OCTOBER 13, 1991

Lutheran: Twenty-first Sunday after Pentecost
Roman Catholic: Twenty-eighth Sunday of the Year
Episcopalian: Proper 23
Pres/Meth/UCC: Twenty-first Sunday after Pentecost

Lessons:

Lutheran:	Amos 5:6-7, 10-15	Heb. 3:1-6	Mark 10:17-27 (28-30)
Roman Catholic:	Wisd. 7:7-11	Heb. 4:12-13	Mark 10:17-30
Episcopal:	Amos 5:6-7, 10-15	Heb. 3:1-6	Mark 10:17-27 (28-31)
Pres/Meth/UCC:	Gen. 3:8-19	Heb. 4:1-3, 9-13	Mark 10:17-30

Introductions to the Lessons

Lesson 1

(1) *Amos 5:6-7, 10-15* (**Luth/Epis**) Amos laments the gross sins of Israel: the poor are trampled, bribes are taken, and truth is abhorred. Through Amos God calls upon the people to seek him, to seek the good, and hate the evil. If they will repent, God will be gracious and will be with them.

(2) *Genesis 3:8-19* (**Pres/Meth/UCC**) Adam and Eve ate the forbidden fruit. One evening Yahweh comes to them and asks for an accounting. Adam blames Eve, and Eve blames the serpent. Nevertheless, all three receive punishment for their sins.

Lesson 2

(1) *Hebrews 3:1-6* (**Luth/Epis**) As Jesus is superior to the angels, he is also greater than Moses, whom the Jews consider the greatest prophet. Jesus is greater than Moses just as a builder is more important than the house. In God's house Moses was a servant but Jesus was the son.

(2) *Hebrews 4:1-3, 9-13* (**Pres/Meth/UCC**) For 40 years the Israelites had no rest as they wandered in the wilderness. They were promised rest when they came to the Promised Land. However, because of disobedience, only Caleb and Joshua got to Palestine. The author of Hebrews reminds Christians that God has promised them also rest into which they will enter if they are faithful and obedient.

Gospel

Mark 10:17-30 (**Luth/Epis/Pres/Meth/UCC**) Can a rich person enter heaven? The question was raised when a rich man asked Jesus how he could inherit eternal life. The price was to sell all his goods, and give the proceeds to the poor, and follow Jesus. Unwilling to pay the price, the man walks away. This causes Jesus to say to his disciples how difficult it is for a rich person to enter God's Kingdom. In response to Peter's reminder that they gave up all to follow him, Jesus assures them of eternal life.

Theme: God calls us to trust him and to put him above all else.

Thought for the day: We seek security in so many things that will rust and die. Today God reminds us that he alone is true security. He longs for us to live fully as his children, dependent on him and trusting in his care.

Call to worship: "For the Lord is good; his steadfast love endures for ever and his faithfulness to all generations."

Prayer of meditation: Dear Heavenly Father, this morning we come to you with questions; questions of eternal life and how we gain it. Hear us, answer us, and strengthen us courageously to accept your will and follow it. Amen.

Prayer of adoration: Dear Lord, for all who offer themselves in your name, we give thanks. Give them the joy of service and your constant care and guidance. Help us all to be both willing servants and thankful recipients of your love, that your name may be glorified, your people may grow in grace, and your will may be done. Amen.

Prayer of confession: Loving Lord, your light shines in darkness, but yet we cower in the corners. In shadows of excuses and self-justification, we have hidden ourselves. Your love exposes our accommodations to evil. Your brightness lays bare our murky indifference. Your beauty unveils the drabness which we have made our peace. Forgive us, O Christ, and by your Spirit make of us a people who have nothing to fear in being seen for who we are. Amen.

Prayer of dedication of gifts and self: Almighty God, you have shown us in the life and teaching of Christ the true way of blessedness. You have also shown us in his suffering and death that the path of love may lead to a cross and the reward of faithfulness may be a crown of thorns. Give us the grace to learn these hard lessons and the courage to answer your call. Empower us as we dedicate ourselves to you. Amen.

Sermon title: First Thing

Sermon thesis: God calls us to keep our priorities straight, to trust him above all else. We fail by putting our security in things and places that are only temporary. God demands to be God, and he gives us the faith and power to allow him to be God in our living.

Hymn for the day: *"Son of God, eternal Savior."* This hymn reminds us that "the wealth of land and sea" belongs to God and prays that we may live for others. Written in 1893 the hymn was published two years later in the *Christian Social Union Hymn Book*. Somerset Thomas Corry Lowry (1855-1932) was born in Ireland and studied at Trinity Hall, Cambridge. He was ordained a priest of the Church of England. He was the author of a number of books as well as of hymns.

Announcements for next week:

Sermon title: Best Seats

Sermon theme: God understands us and loves us.

Sermon summary: We, like the disciples, too often fail to realize what it means to be God's people. We get caught up in the selfishness of our own lives, missing God's gift of abundant life. Yet, God still cares for us, understands us, because he came to us as one of us. The incarnation of God enables us to see what life is truly meant to be.

Children's object talk:

Let God be God

Objects: A beautiful painting and a paint brush.

Lesson: We are silly when we fail to see God as God, the source of all good.

Outline: 1. Admire painting and desire to thank who is responsible.

2. Paint brush didn't do, even if we thank it.

3. God is behind all that is good.

ISN'T THIS A BEAUTIFUL PAINTING? Just look at all the colors and the shapes that we can see. It is beautiful. I like just looking at it. It makes me feel good and happy. Doesn't it make you feel that way? You know what, it would surely be a good idea to thank whoever's responsible for this beautiful painting . . . to let them know how much we like it. Would you like to do that? (reach inside your bag and pull out the paint brush.) This is what's responsible for the beautiful painting. Do you want to say thank you to it? Let's all do that together: THANK YOU.

What's the matter? Some of you are looking at me like I'm silly. Tell me what you are thinking. (Elicit the oddness off thanking a paint brush.) This is silly, isn't it? We don't thank a "thing" which was just a tool to making this beautiful painting. We should thank the person who made it, the artist.

You know what? Sometimes we are that silly in forgetting to thank God. God is the one who gives us all good things, our homes and families, our food and health. God is God. And we can trust him to be God. You know, he wants us to say thank you to him so that we can show how much we love him. I hope we don't forget to say thanks to God and to trust him. That would be as silly as thanking a paint brush.

The sermon:

First Thing

Hymns:
Beginning of worship: Awake My Soul
Sermon hymn: Where Cross the Crowded Ways of Life
End of worship: Praise to the Lord, the Almighty

Scripture: Mark 10:17-30

Sermon Text: *"As Jesus was setting out on his journey, a man ran up and knelt before him and asked him, 'Good teacher, what must I do to inherit eternal life?' Jesus answered him"* . . . *and later we're told, "They were exceedingly astonished, and said to him, 'Then who can be saved?'* . . . *Jesus looked at them and said, 'With men it is impossible, but not with God; for all things are possible with God."*

PHILADELPHIA FREE PRESS . . . April 14, 1877 . . . The story is told of a woman at the spring doing her week's washing. Suddenly she looked up from her washboard to see her home engulfed in flames. She dropped her washing, hurried into the house and brought out an armful of quilts. Back she went to drag out some pillows, next she lugged out a mattress and frame. Then the house reeled, staggered, and crashed into ruins. But louder than the crash of the falling building was the wail of the woman, as she realized too late, her little child was asleep in the house.

It was surely no harm for this woman to have saved her quilts, pillows, and bed. But for her to become so absorbed in such tasks as to forget her child was sheer tragedy! Sadly, that story is the sorrow of mistaken priorities . . . stupid, fatal priorities.

And so is the story in our Gospel today. One of the Bible's best known stories, is re-told in two other Gospels and is one which has a wealth of insight wrapped in it!

A rich, young ruler, who raced up to Jesus one day had eternal life on his mind, but he carried with him the false thought that perhaps the insurance policy for heaven could be purchased with good deeds. So he asked Jesus, "What must I do to inherit eternal life?" Jesus listed some of the Ten Commandments and the young fellow interrupted him, saying, "Teacher, all these I have observed from my youth."

There was no question about the fact that this man was a decent, civilized, respectable person. Jesus liked him and saw powerful potential in him. But Jesus also knew that the fellow was so tied to his possessions that it would be difficult for him to let go and take a leap of faith into headlong loyalty to Christ.

You see, Jesus asked him to re-align his priorities, to shift what was important to him to what was truly important eternally. To sell all that he had, give it to the poor, and follow Christ. That takes quite a shift. A tremendous effort and change, and Jesus challenged him to do it.

This young man was a good prospect for the kingdom, but Christ offered no bargains. Christ did not conceal the cross nor disguise the cost. He never tried to recruit folks saying it would be easy to follow him, nor that it would even feel good. Jesus always called for a loyalty that spoke of a committed priority. God is to be above all else . . . all else!!

And the rich young ruler turned and went away sorrowful. He wanted only a few more regulations to keep. He did not want to be swept off his feet by a new relationship, nor such total commitment. He couldn't cut it. He wasn't going to shift his priorities so completely, so radically, so fanatically.

We understand that and this story bothers us . . . genuinely grinds at us, if we listen seriously to it. You see, this story hits us with a Christian truth that is never comfortable. That truth is that RESPECTABILITY is *not* enough.

Jesus quoted the commandments which were the basis of a decent life. Without hesitation, the young ruler said he kept them all. You need to note, with one exception, all the commandments Jesus asked about were negative ones—do not steal, do not kill, do not . . . In effect, the young ruler was saying, "I never in my life did anyone any harm," and that was probably true.

But the question is: Have you trusted God to use you, to serve. What good have you done? Do you hear the priority again?

Jesus asks, "With all your possessions, with your youth and wealth, what positive good have you done for others?" Has God used you? How much have you gone out of your way to help and comfort and strengthen others as you know God would have you? Sadly, respectability often consists in *not* doing things. Christianity consists of doing things! And that's precisely where this rich young ruler — like many of us — failed. Christ challenged him to get out of his comfortable, respectable settled life into the adventure of following God's calling . . . of being a Christian!

The road to heaven is not paved with conventional moralism: "He's a good person . . . She never hurt anyone." Rather, the road is made by a relationship with Jesus Christ, who is the WAY . . . a faith and setting of priorities that calls for complete trust in God! For the rich young ruler, the one thing that was missing was the willingness to surrender his life to God . . . to love God and put him above all else. The young man was too engrossed in his own business pursuits to discover the real business of living as a child of God. Christ put a finger on life's priority and he side-stepped it. Sadly, he had a problem with his wealth: it owned him. He couldn't let go of it and what it meant to him, therefore God couldn't be God to him either.

And again, we're uncomfortable with that. We know what that feels like. There are many of us, if we were asked, who would say, "Oh yes, I trust God," but in our heart of hearts we know that we are much more concerned with the value of our IRAs, our pension, our property, and our investments. Jesus tells us not to be anxious about life, that God will provide; and he encourages us to be wise about future plans, but never consumed.

I like that old story about the good Baptist who was about to be immersed, and a friend hollered out, "Let me hold your wallet." To which he replied, "My billfold needs baptizing most of all!" You see, God is to be trusted above all — to be God! And that should not be just a pious little saying that we repeat, but honest and lived!

The story is told of some preachers who came from all parts of the country to a seminar on preaching. One of the main speakers was forced at the last minute to cancel out. He was suppose to preach right after lunch that day and they had no speaker. So the Bishop in charge went to a young pastor and asked him to fill in. The young preacher asked, "How can I do that? I didn't bring any sermons with me. How could I possibly get up there to deliver a sermon to this gathering?" The Bishop replied, "Son, just trust the Lord. Trust the Lord."

The pastor was horrified. In his despair, he saw the Bishop's Bible near, and he started thumbing through it trying to find a text. Inside the Bible, he found a sermon the Bishop was to give that very night. The young man was desperate, so when the time came for the afternoon service, he took the Bishop's notes and preached that sermon. The response was great. Everyone expressed their appreciation for his insight and proclamation. It was exciting for the young pastor, until the Bishop got to him. He was furious. "Young man, what have you done? You preached the sermon I was going to give tonight. What am I going to do now?" And the young pastor, with a twinkle in his eye, stated, "Trust the Lord, Bishop, trust the Lord!"

You know how glibly we often say, "Just trust" when we really mean we're going to trust our own devices. Yet there needs to come that time when we settle the issue once and for all. What is the source of our ultimate security? Is it our bank accounts, our status, or do we trust in the love and wisdom of our God?

And you see, that's the Good News today. You and I know we aren't capable of garnering up enough faith and trust on our own. We don't have what it takes by ourselves to place God in the priority he should have. We're too selfish and scared . . . and we know it! So did the disciples. "They were exceedingly astonished, and said to Jesus, 'Then who can be saved?' " No one they thought. We can't do it.

But Christ again puts the focus where it should be, not on us, but on God. "With men it is impossible, but not with God; for all things are possible with God." God can help us overcome our passion for worldly security which is so fleeting. God can guide us to put him first, above all else. God can teach us to trust. He gives the power and strength and courage of such faith. We need only try, and receive and respond. And that is the Good News!

We began with the sad account of the woman who carried pillows and quilts out of her burning house, while her treasured child was forgotten and died. I didn't believe that story at first. How could a mother really overlook her own child? How could a person have their priorities so confused? It's ridiculous!

Yet, each one of us understands the rich young ruler. God was demanding too much, we say. God says, "I am the treasure — that which should be first and foremost, above all else." God wants to be God. I pray for us that we are never found being concerned about pillows and quilts, while our lives are being lived and possibly consumed like fire, and that we forget the living and loving treasure who is God. It's just as ridiculous! But the Good News is that God is with us to give us the power to trust him, to have the right priorities, to be his people. "For all things are possible with God!"

David deFreese
Immanuel Lutheran Church
Bellevue, Nebraska

OCTOBER 20, 1991

Lutheran: Twenty-second Sunday after Pentecost
Roman Catholic: Twenty-ninth Sunday of the Year
Episcopalian: Proper 24
Pres/Meth/UCC: Twenty-second Sunday after Pentecost

Lessons:

Lutheran:	Is. 53:10-12	Heb. 4:9-16	Mark 10:35-45
Roman Catholic:	Is. 53:10-11	Heb. 4:14-16	Mark 10:35-45
Episcopal:	Is. 53:4-12	Heb. 4:12-16	Mark 10:35-45
Pres/Meth/UCC:	Is. 53:7-12	Heb. 4:14-16	Mark 10:35-45

Introductions to the Lessons

Isaiah 53:10-12 (**Luth**); *53:4-12* (**Epis**); *53:7-12* (**Pres/Meth/UCC**) Isaiah 53 is one of the Servant poems in Deutero-Isaiah. Various opinions are held as to the identity of the Servant. Christians see the Servant as Jesus. It is a beautiful and meaningful description of the cross and its benefits.

Lesson 2

Hebrews 4:9-16 (**Luth**); *4:12-16* (**Epis**); *4:14-16* (**Pres/Meth/UCC**) The author of Hebrews exhorts us to seek God's rest. Disobedience can cause us to lose that rest. To help us we have the Word of God and Jesus as our high priest who, though tempted as we are, did not sin. In and through him we can receive mercy and grace in our time of need.

Gospel

Mark 10:35-45 (**Luth/Epis/Pres/Meth/UCC**) Who are the greatest in God's kingdom? The question was raised when James and John asked Jesus to give them the chief seats in his Kingdom. They claimed they were able to pay the price, but Jesus told them it was not his privilege to hand out these honors. When the other disciples heard of John's and James' request, they were angry. So Jesus called them together and told them that the greatest is one who serves, even as he came not to be served but to serve.

Theme: God understands us and loves us.

Thought for the day: Even though we disappoint God; we fail to understand what it means to be his people; he keeps caring for us and loving us. Even though we make selfish and arrogant demands, God still forgives by the power of the cross.

Prayer of meditation: Dear Heavenly Father, thank you, thank you. Thank you for loving us even when we're dull, when we don't even come close to understanding your will and your ways. Thank you for hanging in there with us. Please continue to call us, to teach us, and to help us be the people you see we can be. Humbly in Christ's name we pray. Amen.

Call to worship: "O give thanks to the Lord, for he is good, for his steadfast love endures forever." Enter his gates with praise and his courts with thanksgiving.

Prayer of adoration: Gracious God, we praise and glorify your marvelous coming to us in many ways, and especially that you do not force our allegiance, but seek out our response of love and trust. May we, with your help, have you alone as the master of our lives and in all our doings, recognize your greatness. You alone are God! Amen.

Prayer of confession: Loving Lord, we who are so easily led to put ourselves in the center of all things, and to consider our importance . . . help us to be humble before you. Stand with us, enabling us to resist temptation. Forgive our dullness to recognize creature from Creator. Make our faith strong and keep us growing in our realization that you are God. Grant us loyalty through suffering time, and bring us joy in your promises.

Prayer of dedication of gifts and self: O Lord our God, we need your guidance for all that we do. Use your wisdom to counsel us, your hand to lead us, and your arm to support us. Conform us to your image and make our service acceptable to you and worthwhile in our troubled world. As we dedicate ourselves to you, bless us and use us. Amen.

Sermon title: Best Seats

Sermon thesis: We, like the disciples, too often fail to realize what it means to be God's people. We get caught up in the selfishness of our own lives, missing God's gift of abundant life. Yet, God still cares for us, understands us, because he came to us as one of us. The incarnation of God enables us to see what life is truly meant to be.

Hymn for the day: *"Once he came in blessing."* "Once he came in blessing . . . in likeness lowly. Still he comes within us . . ." This hymn by Johann Horn was first published in Nurnberg in 1544. The author (c. 1490-1547) was a priest of the Bohemian Brethren. In 1522 he went with Michael Weisse to Wittenberg to discuss the views of the Brethren with Martin Luther. His Czech hymn book published in Prague in 1541 far surpassed any other songbook of its time in size, containing 481 hymns with 300 melodies. A tune by Horn, GAUDEAMUS PARITER, can be found in a number of American hymnals.

Announcements for next week:

Sermon title: Grace-full Interruption

Sermon theme: When interruptions are grace-full.

Sermon summary: Many of us see the annual pledge drive as an interruption of our spiritual life, like the interruption of Jesus' trip to Jerusalem by the blind beggar Bartimaeus. However, it may become an opportunity for us to understand and experience commitment as a response to grace.

Children's object talk:

Tools for God

Objects: A variety of different tools, i.e. hammer, pliers, screwdriver, etc.

Lesson: God longs to use us for his purposes.

Outline: 1. What are tools?

2. We are God's tools to do his will.

TODAY I WANT TO TALK ABOUT some things that are very important. What are these? (Hold up the individual tools and get their names.) What are these for or how do you use them? (Let the children go into detail on how they work or where they have experienced them in use.) Why do you think these are so important? (Try to elicit explanations that state that we couldn't get some things made or done without the proper tools.) That's right, these are very important to make things and to get things to work right. Can you imagine what it would be like to build a house without these? Couldn't be done.

You know what? You are a tool for God. That's right, a tool for God. Now what do you think that means? (See if they can make the connection) God wants others to know that he loves them and cares for them. How do you think he can let them know that? That's right, he wants you to tell them. You see, you are a tool for God. He uses you to get his work done, to let others know how much he cares. When you share, when you help someone, when you are kind to others, God is using you as his tool.

I hope it feels good to you to know how important you are to God, and I hope you try to be the best "tool" in helping God care for others.

The sermon:

Best Seats

Hymns:
Beginning of worship: Praise and Thanks and Adoration
Sermon hymn: Lord, Whose Love
End of worship: The Church's One Foundation

Scripture: Mark 10:35-45

Sermon Text: *"Teacher, we want you to do for us whatever we ask of you"* . . . *"What do you want me to do for you?"* . . . *"Grant us to sit in your glory."* . . . *"You don't know what you're asking . . . Whoever would be great among you must be your servant, and whoever would be first among you must be slave of all."*

THE STORY IS TOLD of the woman who went to her pastor for counseling concerning her marriage. After a few preliminaries, the pastor said he had a few questions that would help identify the problems if she would answer his questions as openly as possible. She agreed, and he began: "Do you have any grounds?" She replied, "Why yes we do, we have about ten acres north of town." "No ma'am," the pastor said, "that's not what I meant. What I mean is do you have a grudge?" "Oh no," she responded, "but we do have a nice little car-port." "No." said the pastor, "What I mean is, does you husband beat you up?" "Beat me up? Oh no, I get up before he does just about every morning." In complete exasperation, the pastor said, "Lady, you're not listening to me. Why are you having trouble with your husband?" "Well," she said, "the man just doesn't know how to communicate!"

How important communication is, and how frustrating it is when it is lacking. How very difficult. God communicates with his people as clearly and concisely as he can, and yet we still don't get it!

Today, we are given an image of the dullness and insensitivity of Jesus' disciples. A group who tried to follow and understand, but yet so often are found lacking . . . very much like you and me.

The scene for today's Gospel has the disciples, who have been with Jesus for quite some time now, making demands, arrogant and selfish demands. They have witnessed his humility following great miracles. They have heard Jesus teaching on the importance of being servants — the last being the first. They have heard his parables of compassion, of not needing to be the greatest. But yet they still don't understand.

Here James and John, trying to get Jesus to promise them a share in God's glory and power, want a position greater than the other disciples. In effect, they are trying to reduce Jesus' promise of the coming Kingdom to the level of a political spoil system, and they want a guarantee of moving into the top spots in exchange for their loyal support. They want the best seats. When all is said and done, the promise of "glory" sells well, and they want it!

And too often, so do we. We want the glory of what God can offer, not the challenge nor the demands. We don't want to be servants, let alone slaves. We too want the best seats in glory land!

Now usually, I suspect a sermon preached on this text deals with our need to respond to God's call, to quit being so self-centered and go out to be the servants God wants us to be. Heaven knows we need those kinds of sermons, probably at least once a week.

But this morning I want to do something different. Rather than focusing on us and what we are to do, I want to concentrate your thinking and your faith on God, and what he does: on our God who is beyond our deepest understanding.

Again, the scene is set. God's people just aren't getting the hang of what God wants them to be . . . servants. But yet, he keeps trying. He keeps trying to communicate to them what he desires — on their level. Our second lesson for today states it as beautifully as it can be said: "Since then we have a great high priest who has passed through the heavens, Jesus, the Son of God, let us hold fast our confession. For we have not a high priest who is unable to sympathize with our weaknesses, but one who in every respect has been tempted as we are, yet without sin."

Did you hear what God has done? He came down as one of us, to live among us and show us how he wants us to live. Jesus of Nazareth, our Christ, he understands us, our feelings, thoughts, and temptations.

A while back, there was an up-rising at Gallaudet University in Washington, D.C. It seems that the students at this university were defying the administration and the college president. Now that hasn't been unusual in our society over the past three decades. But this president was finally removed for a very unusual reason. She was *not* deaf, and Gallaudet University serves 21,000 deaf students. It was interesting to read about the first meeting between I. King Jordan, the 46 year old president who was chosen in the aftermath of that controversy, the student body president, and the chairperson of the Board of Trustees. They met to talk about the future of the school. When they came out of that meeting, the president of the student body turned to the new president of the university and said with tears in his eyes: "There was no interpreter." And that was true, because the new president, I. King Jordan, is as deaf as the students he was chosen to serve.

We can appreciate the need of these young people to have someone leading their school who was like them, who shared their struggle. You see, that is what our God has done for us. We have a great high priest who has passed through the heavens and come down to us to be like us and with us. "For we have not a high priest who is unable to sympathize with our weakness, but one who in every respect has been tempted as we are . . . yet without sin." He understands.

As you heard the Gospel for today, James and John selfishly want the best seats in Christ's glory. Don't you wonder why Jesus doesn't explode at them? Why he doesn't get mad? He's been teaching them by word and actions that the last will be the first. He said it several times. Yet they still ask him for glory and he's not angry. Why?

Because he understands them. He knows what they feel and what they're thinking. He has empathy and sympathy. He's probably hurt and frustrated that they still don't get it. But he doesn't walk away from the relationship. He still cares. He understands and he keeps trying and teaching. Our God forgives us, our mistakes, our selfishness, our short-comings. The Old Testament lesson for today has three lines that tell us about our Christ, the Messiah, God's suffering servant: "He makes himself an offering for sin. He bore the sin of many, and made intercession for the transgressors." Christ died on the cross to kill our sin! God never makes light of sin or our responsibility for sin, but he handles it through his gracious forgiveness. We have one who sympathizes with us in our hurts, who understands our weaknesses, and can get past them.

There is a story about two little boys who were fighting as kids will do. One of them yelled at the other, "I'll never speak to you again." They went to their own homes, but the next day they were back out playing, as if nothing had happened. One of the little boys' mother asked him why they were speaking to each other now. He responded, "Me and Johnny are good forgetters."

God is a good forgetter. Christ has experienced what it is to be human, and he conquered sin. He has made it possible for us to experience God's grace. He walked where we walk. He has fought the battle that we fight. He has revealed the Father's love to us and for us.

That's what our Gospel is about today: God's ability to relate to us and to forgive us. But we dare not *just* selfishly receive this care and love. Christ calls us to respond, to serve, to act out of the wealth of love we have received. "Whoever would be great among you . . . must be your servant."

David deFreese
Immanuel Lutheran Church
Bellevue, Nebraska

OCTOBER 27, 1991

Reformation Sunday

Lessons:

Lutheran:	Jer. 31:31-34	Rom. 3:19-28	John 8:31-36
Pres/Meth/UCC:	Hab. 2:1-4	Rom. 3:21-28	John 8:31-36

Introductions to the Lessons

Lesson 1

(1) *Jeremiah 31:31-34* (**Luth**). A new covenant is promised for Israel. The old Mosaic covenant was broken by Israel's faithlessness. This new covenant will be different. The law will be an internal possession as well as a personal possession. Through this covenant the people will receive forgiveness. Christians believe that Jesus is the mediator of this new covenant.

(2) *Habakkuk 2:1-4* (**Pres/Meth/UCC**). The prophet, Habakkuk, complains that apparently God does nothing to stop the invading army of the Chaldeans. Why does he permit the violence and destruction? The prophet waits for an answer. The answer comes: "The righteous live by their faith."

Lesson 2

Romans 3:19-28 (**Luth**); *3:21-28* (**Pres/Meth/UCC**). How does a person get right with God? By law? By works? Paul is emphatic when he writes that we are made right only by faith in Christ who died for our sins. By grace are we saved through faith in Christ.

Gospel

John 8:31-36 (**Luth/Pres/Meth/UCC**). As long as we remain in the truth of the word of Christ, we will be his disciples. As disciples we will know the truth. This truth will set us free. Therefore, faith in Christ makes us free to embrace the truth and to love and serve.

Theme: The Word of God reforms our understanding of freedom.

Thought for the day: Most of our expressions of freedom center around freedom *from* things that confine us, limit us, or exclude us; but the Gospel of Jesus Christ is a liberating Word of God which frees us *for* new possibilities in our life.

Prayer of meditation: Open my eyes, Lord, to see the freedoms I enjoy. Open my ears, Lord, to hear the sounds of freedom in my every day life. Open my heart, Lord, as I come to hear your Word of freedom, see your Word of grace and taste your Word of love; Through Jesus Christ, who sets me free. Amen.

Call to worship: "Come behold the works of the Lord . . . Be still, and know that I am God! I am exalted among the nations, I am exalted in the earth. The Lord of hosts is with us; the God of Jacob is our refuge." Psalm 46:8, 10, 11 (NRSV)

Prayer of adoration: Almighty God, creator of the universe, you have given us life, you have placed us in this world, and you have given us the grand opportunity that this new day brings. We come together to adore and praise you. We offer our life as a testimony of your grace. Give our worship together this day your joyful presence that we may proclaim your praise for all the world to hear; through Christ, our Lord. Amen.

Prayer of confession: Eternal God, you have given us the gift of freedom as you created humankind, and we have given ourselves to the slavery of sin and self-centeredness. You have given us the freedom of forgiveness and new life through our Baptism, and we continue daily to give ourselves to the slavery of sin. Hear our confession of our failure to live as free persons, forgive our bondage to our selfish desires, and set us free once again, for life as your people; through Christ, our Lord. Amen.

Prayer of dedication of gifts and self: Father we bring our representatives of our freedom to you: our tithes, our offerings, and ourselves. Use these thankofferings for your purposes, and bless us with your power and direction so that all our money, all our resources, and all our lives freely show forth your grace, and fulfill your purpose; through Jesus Christ our Lord, who freely gave himself for us. Amen.

Sermon title: Re-forming Freedom

Sermon thesis: The Word of God (Jesus) reforms the world. The Word of God reshapes our understanding of freedom, moving us from "freedom from" to "freedom for." It reforms daily life from the treadmill approach to discipleship to a truly liberated life in Christ. It moves us from the gospel life as product to the gospel life as process.

Hymn for the day: *"Salvation unto us has come."* This text, together with its tune, appeared in *Etlich Christlich lider,* 1523/1524, the earliest Lutheran hymnal. The text was written by Paul Speratus (1484-1551) who assisted Luther in the preparation of the hymnal. Speratus, who was ordained a priest, was one of the first priests to dare to marry. After experiencing many difficulties, including imprisonment, for his Protestant leanings, he became a Lutheran pastor in 1524. The opening lines clearly reflect Luther's conviction: we are saved by grace, not by works.

Announcements for next week: (All Saints Sunday)

Sermon title: Being Blessed

Sermon theme: In the Beatitudes Jesus calls us to a new understanding of being blessed.

Sermon summary: The Beatitudes are Jesus' announcement of a radical new understanding of blessing: blessings come in the midst of problems and needs of the world, causing us to implement positive changes.

Children's object talk:

Freedom Is Discipleship

Objects: Goldfish in a bowl
Lesson: The limits of discipleship give us freedom to live.
Outline: 1. Goldfish in bowl is confined.
2. Taking goldfish out of bowl with unlimited freedom means death!
3. Discipleship — following Jesus — gives us the the structure in which we are free to live, just as the bowl and water give the fish the structure to live.

TODAY, MY FRIENDS, I brought a new friend for us to enjoy here at church. I'll keep him in my office and you all can come and see him, and help me feed him. (Hold up a gold fish in a small aquarium). At another time we'll give him a name, but today I want to talk about his environment. What do you think about living in this aquarium filled with water? It seems like a pretty small world to live in, doesn't it? Our friend the fish doesn't seem to have much freedom, does he? Or does he? What would happen if we set him free? What would happen if we take him out of the bowl and let him go free here on the church floor? That is too much freedom for him to handle. He can't live with that kind of freedom. He will die!

Some people think being a follower of Jesus is like living in a small fish bowl. It doesn't seem like much freedom. In today's Gospel, our Lord Jesus talks about freedom — the freedom of discipleship. Now take a look at our friend, the fish. In his bowl he is free to swim, and grow, and eat and sleep, and play. As followers of Jesus we are free to live as God created us to be. We are free to grow up, to love, to play, to learn and eat, and sleep. We are free to know God and to love others. May God bless you as you grow in your faith in Jesus.

The sermon:

Re-forming Freedom

Hymns:
> Beginning of worship: A Mighty Fortress is Our God
> Sermon hymn: God's Word is our Great Heritage
> Closing hymn: Lord, Keep us Steadfast in your Word.

Scripture: John 8:31-36

Sermon Text: *"If you continue in my word, you are truly my disciples; and you will know the truth and the truth will make you free."* John 8:31-32

THE REFORMATION of the sixteenth century began with a concern for reforming the spiritual dimension of life out of the personal spiritual experience of Dr. Martin Luther. Its effect touched every dimension of life, not only in the sixteenth century, but ever since that time. One dimension of the Reformation which both encouraged the spiritual dimension and was enhanced by it was the whole area of music.

J.S. Bach and G.F. Handel are examples of the liberating effect of the Reformation in their music. Under their creative genius church music moved from the simple tones of the plain chant to the elegance of the Baroque Chorale. In plain chant, the music was a single note with no beat of its own used to convey the words of the text.

A simple tone carried the words. In the Reformation era music took on the freedom and great variety of its composers, giving sensual dimensions to the words of the texts that enriched and enhanced their messages. The centerpiece of the Reformation and of the great music in the Christian faith is the Word of God. By the Word of God, the world was created. By the Word of God, our world is re-formed as God wills it to be. The Word of God is carried in the great variety of the Reformation themes. Each theme, like the rich music of Bach and Handel, moves the simple message of God's gracious salvation into the very fabric of our lives. The Word of God re-forms our understanding of freedom itself. Today we shall consider some of the Reformation themes which the Gospel for today touches.

The Word of God moves us from "freedom from . . ." to "freedom for . . ." While seniors in seminary, we were often sent to preach in nearby congregations that had no pastor, or whose pastor was on vacation. Usually some kind family would invite the visiting student preacher home for Sunday dinner. It was on one of those occasions I was confronted by a strange understanding of freedom. It seems that the congregation was in the process of building a new building, so our table discussion quite naturally turned to the plans for the new church building. My host was explaining the new building and told me that the first set of plans for the inside of the building were rejected.

I asked why, and he said because the architect had pictured the altar rail with a closed gate in front of the altar itself. He quickly then went on to say that "we Lutherans," because of the Reformation, can go directly to God, and a closed gate did not show our freedom! I didn't understand why that would be so controversial, but I felt the emotion of the moment and understood the importance of the concept of freedom in the theology of lay people! I have reflected on that and other similar emotions I have encountered regarding the Reformation. It seems that many folks think of the Reformation as a defiant process declaring what we don't believe, and what we don't do. But today's Gospel talks about the truth setting us free, and it seems that freedom from tyrannical theology would merely make us non-believers! But, if the truth makes us free, then we are free to confess what we believe about God, ourselves, the world and our salvation. We are free to live out our forgiveness. The Word of God is a Gospel word that comes into our life and sets us free for life in Christ, and for rich relationships with everyone who shares that Good News with us!

The Word of God also moves us from sin (which is a form of bondage) to the source of life (which is discipleship). Often we see daily life as a treadmill. Day in and day out, life is sameness. Routines, schedules, repeated actions and demands of others, are all the usual of life that make it boring and deadening. On the other hand, discipline and the discipline of daily life sets us free to experience even more. The discipline of daily piano practice frees us to play and even create all kinds of musical patterns. The discipline of daily exercise and healthy eating habits frees us for more comfortable and perhaps longer and less painful life. The discipline of study frees us to be able to put concepts together abstractly in such a way that we "discover" new dimensions of life.

The Word of God moves us from regarding the Christian faith as a product to understanding the Christian faith as a life process or style. Christian faith as product ultimately means laws, rules, specific patterns to which we must conform in order to be saved. It concentrates on past orientation and future orientation. The Word of God in freedom says to us as we confront life at the present moment that by God's grace we are able to meet the challenge of the present, and we have the potential to handle it as God has created us to do so, from the power of Christ at work within us.

The text for today proclaims to us the freedom which God gives in Jesus, the Christ. But even in the text there are attempts to see it as "freedom from," instead of "freedom for . . ." Examples:

"If you continue in my word, you are truly my disciples; and you will know the truth and the truth will make you free." NRSV
In contrast to that here are some other common translations:

"You are truly my disciples if you live as I tell you" TLB
"If you dwell within the revelation I have brought you" NEB
"If you are faithful to what I have said . . ." JBP
"If you hold to my teachings . . ." NIV

To dwell in the Word of God is radically different from following the rules or doing what we are told. It is living in the presence of the most High God. It is walking and talking and knowing and sharing the presence of Christ on a daily basis — the Living Christ. It is being constantly re-formed by God's intent for each moment.

It is re-forming the world, because we are re-formed by God's Word. It is a whole new freedom for life and living, by the power of Jesus, the Christ, who is the truth and who makes us free indeed every day!

Dale I. Gregoriew
Christ the Servant Lutheran Church
Allen, Texas

OCTOBER 27, 1991

Lutheran: Twenty-third Sunday after Pentecost
Roman Catholic: Thirtieth Sunday of the Year
Episcopalian: Proper 25
Pres/Meth.UCC: Twenty-third Sunday after Pentecost

Lessons:

Lutheran:	Jer. 31:7-9	Heb. 5:1-10	Mark 10:46-52
Roman Catholic:	Jer. 31:7-9	Heb. 5:1-6	Mark 10:46-52
Episcopal:	Is. 59:(1-4) 9-19	Heb. 5:12-6:1, 9-12	Mark 10:46-52
Pres/Meth/UCC:	Jer. 31:7-9	Heb. 5:1-6	Mark 10:46-52

Introductions to the Lessons

Lesson 1

(1) *Jeremiah 31:7-9* (**Luth/Pres/Meth/UCC**). Jeremiah sees beyond the Babylonian captivity to Israel's return. Because of Yahweh's everlasting love and faithfulness as the father of Israel, the exiles will be brought back to their homeland with great rejoicing.

(2) *Isaiah 59:9-19* (**Epis**). God looks upon his people and sees the terrible state of affairs caused by sin: injustice and lack of truth. He is so displeased over the condition that he clothes himself with righteousness and salvation and executes vengeance upon his enemies. As a result the people everywhere fear his name and see his glory.

Lesson 2

(1) *Hebrews 5:1-10* (**Luth**); *5:1-6* (**Pres/Meth/UCC**). Jesus was greater than any high priest because he was after the order of Melchizedek. As our high priest he prays for us with tears. Through his suffering he learned obedience and earned our salvation.

(2) *Hebrews 5:12-6:1, 9-12* (**Epis**). In this passage the author of Hebrews is encouraging his people to remain faithful to Christ. To be loyal they need to drink the milk of truth, to go on to perfection, and to know that their good works are not overlooked by God.

Gospel

Mark 10:46-52 (**Luth/Epis/Pres/Meth/UCC**). Jesus is passing through Jericho on his way to Jerusalem. A blind beggar, Bartimaeus, hears the commotion of the crowd and calls repeatedly to Jesus for mercy. Jesus has him come and grants him his eyesight. So grateful was the beggar that he follows Jesus to Jerusalem.

111

Theme: When interruptions are grace-full.

Thought for the day: Most of the time an interruption is a negative experience, or at least we think of it that way. However, have you ever considered that most interruptions are opportunities for grace, such as God's breaking into the world in the Incarnation!

Prayer of meditation: Interrupt me, Lord, with the hurts and joys of other persons so that I may share your gracious love with them. Interrupt my worship today, Lord, with the awesomeness of your grace so that I may sense it anew today as we sing and pray and hear your Word, and give ourselves to your will. Interrupt me, Lord, so that I may meet my Lord Jesus anew today. Amen.

Call to worship: "I sought the Lord, and he answered me, and delivered me from all my fears. Look to him, and be radiant; so your faces shall never be ashamed." (Psalm 34:4-5 NRSV)

Prayer of adoration: Holy God, we come before your throne of grace today with praise and adoration on our lips and in our hearts. You have graciously given us life and this new day, and we offer ourselves anew to you that our lives may be examples of your love as we gather for worship, through Jesus Christ our Lord. Amen.

Prayer of confession: Almighty God, we have filled our lives with busyness and things of our own making so that we no longer have time for those along life's way who are in need. We confess our blindness to those around us in need, and our impatience with those in need whom we consider to be an interruption. We ask your forgiveness and the gift of your healing Spirit, that we may become instruments of your grace for those in need; through Jesus Christ our Lord. Amen.

Prayer of dedication of gifts and self: Accept our gifts, our pledges, our offerings, O Lord, as a portion of our total commitment of all we are and have. Bless them with your power, O Lord, and use them as instruments of your grace; through Jesus Christ our Lord. Amen.

Sermon title: Grace-full Interruption

Sermon thesis: Many of us see the annual pledge drive as an interruption of our spiritual life, like the interruption of Jesus' trip to Jerusalem by the blind beggar Bartimaeus. However, it may become an opportunity for us to understand and experience commitment as a response to grace.

Hymn for the day: *"O for a thousand tongues to sing."* This hymn was written by Charles Wesley on May 21, 1738, the first anniversary of his great spiritual change. Charles Wesley (1707-1788), one of the first group of "Oxford Methodists," was ordained to the Church of England. After spending some time in America as a missionary in Georgia, he returned to England and spent many years as an itinerant preacher, and later as a minister to Methodist Societies in London. One of the great hymnwriters of all ages, he composed some 6000 hymns.

Announcements for next week: (Pentecost 24)

Sermon title: Will the Real Christian Stand Up?

Sermon theme: Seeking our real motivations for being Christian.

Sermon summary: Because we come together as Christians for a variety of reasons, today's Gospel confronts us with a challenge and affirmation of our motivations that opens the way for us to know the Kingdom of God.

Children's object talk:

Interruptions

Objects: A person who interrupts the children's sermon
Lesson: Sometimes interruptions are necessary, and can be good.
Outline: 1. Begin talking about Jesus' trip to Jerusalem.
2. Worship interrupted by someone who needs to talk with pastor.
3. Interruptions can sometimes be a means of grace.

FRIENDS, THE GOSPEL LESSON for today is more about Jesus' trip to Jerusalem. You may remember that Jesus and his disciples were walking to Jerusalem, and passing through many towns and cities on the way. Today, Jesus and his disciples were just leaving Jericho when . . . (Suddenly someone comes walking down the aisle speaking to the pastor:) Excuse me, Pastor! Pastor! I need to tell you something important . . . (Pastor stands up and speaks:) Yes, can it wait just a moment? I am talking with my friends right now.

"Excuse me, Pastor, but this is important! You forgot something!" (Pastor:) "Please, can it wait a moment? I don't want to interrupt my time with my young friends here."

"No, it can't wait. Pastor, you forgot to make the announcement that after worship there are special treats for all children in the parish hall." (Pastor:) "Thank you. Yes, I did forget. I was thinking about what I was going to say to my young friends here."

(Pastor turns back to children:) Most of us have interrupted adults at one time or another. Most often we are told not to interrupt.

In today's Gospel story, a man named Bartimaeus, interrupted Jesus. Jesus turned that interruption into an example of God's love. The crowd was so busy that they didn't want Jesus to be bothered by the blind man. They wanted to ignore him. But Jesus said no. Jesus tells us that Bartimaeus is important. That people with special needs are important. He also shows us that God cares for everyone. Sometimes it is best not to interrupt others. And sometimes it is necessary. I arranged for the special treats, and the interruption to show you that God cares for you and has time for you, too! I'll see you in the parish hall after worship. God bless you!

The sermon:

Grace-Full Interruption

Hymns:
    Beginning of worship: You Servants of God, Your Master Proclaim
    Sermon hymn: Come to the Water
    End of worship: Help, O Lord the Thrown Away

Scripture: Mark 10:46-52

Sermon Text: *". . . But he cried out all the more, 'Son of David, have mercy on me!' "*

TODAY'S GOSPEL IS LIKE TURNING on your TV set and seeing the middle of an inaugural parade in Washington, D.C. The well groomed speaking voice says as you see the president's limousine with its retinue of secret service agents, motorcycle escort, etc,: "The president's car is approaching the treasury building where it will turn left and head for the White House." Today's Gospel begins: "They came to Jericho, and as (Jesus) was leaving Jericho with his disciples and a great multitude . . ." Jesus had reached the farthest point in his ministry/journey at Caesarea-Philippi. It was from Caesarea-Philippi that he "set his face toward Jerusalem." As you read the account of Jesus' journey from the confession of Peter at Caesarea-Philippi to the triumphal entry into Jerusalem you become caught up in the movement. Jesus and his followers walk and talk. It is filled with incidents of dialogue. It is foreboding in its prediction

114

of what will befall Jesus in the Holy City. Nevertheless the story is a story of a movement. It is more than a travelogue, or even the report of a parade. As you read you become caught up in the momentum of the events. The promise is coming to fulfillment. Jesus, at long last, is on his way to Jerusalem; and he is followed by his disciples and a great multitude of followers. There is direction and purpose for this journey.

Suddenly from the side of the road as the crowd left the historic city of Jericho, there is a disturbance. A blind man heard that Jesus of Nazareth was passing by, and no amount of effort by his companions would keep him quiet. "JESUS, SON OF DAVID, HAVE MERCY ON ME!" "And Jesus stopped . . ." The movement is interrupted by a blind man screaming for mercy.

I have often wondered why Mark put this story of blind Bartimaeus here. The followers of Jesus are finally seeing some hints of messianic action. Jesus is going to Jerusalem to establish his kingdom. But look carefully at the crowd. The disciples who have spent much time with Jesus still are blind to his real purpose. The Pharisees are blind to Jesus' purpose. The great multitude are following a miracle worker — it is as if the crowds have tunnel vision. Even James and John, Jesus's closest followers, have just asked for special privileges. Those who can see Jesus are blind to his purpose. And Mark has blind Bartimaeus, who cannot see Jesus, call to him with a messianic title, "Jesus, Son of David."

Dr. Fred Craddock once suggested that by including the interruption of the movement to Jerusalem by the story of Bartimaeus, Mark may be offering a critical judgment of the early church. The church goes parading after Jesus with no real notion or acceptance of the cross that lies ahead, or the cost of discipleship. The church refuses to be interrupted by the world around it. It is unwilling to include the disqualified, the unwanted, and the uncertain people of the world. The church tries to quiet the blind beggar, who is after all the only one really qualified to follow Jesus. He alone trusts. He alone can see!

Now, my brothers and sisters, we need to interrupt this sermon and talk with you about your pledge for the coming year. We are in the midst of our annual pledge drive. Today we need to talk about money. Money is very important to all of us. We work for it. We spend great amounts of energy earning it. spending it, saving it, and worrying about our lack of it. Money is a substitute for us. It represents us in kind. It goes where we cannot go. Money is a spiritual matter: Our Lord Jesus made it very clear in Matthew 6:21 "For where your treasure is, there your heart will be also." (NRSV) As productive and creative persons, one of our great needs is to give.

Your pledge to your church is a means for applying your spiritual relationship with God to your everyday life. Such a pledge is one that calls us to re-orient our life. Nationally, church members give about two or three per cent of their income to their church. For most of us this is a very comfortable level of giving. What would it mean for you to increase your church pledge by one percent of your income? What would it mean for you to double your giving to the Church? What would it mean for you to tithe? (That is, to set aside one-tenth of your income for the work of Christ?) Would you consider that a significant interruption of your life to get your attention? Meanwhile, back in the Gospel story, the movement of Jesus and his followers to Jerusalem has been interrupted by a blind man just outside the walls of Jericho. The disciples followed Jesus throughout the countryside. They enjoyed his presence and his power. But they did not grasp his mission. All along the way Jesus was confronted again and again by Pharisees. They were always disturbed by Jesus, but they were intrigued enough to keep coming back. But they could not accept his mission to bring in the Kingdom of God. The general crowd, like most of the world, went along for the excitement, the big show, looking for the latest hero. Blind Bartimaeus was the most unqualified of all: no abilities; no pride (he was a beggar); nothing to offer; no calculation ahead of time. We are interrupted by his unabashed pleading: "Jesus, son of David, have mercy on me!" And Mark the Gospel writer, sets the stage for us to witness the power and the transformation of life that is given by God's grace. Did Bartimaeus know that Jesus would heal him? Or did he go beyond knowledge, and react to Jesus by faith alone?

As you prepare to make your pledge, think about Bartimaeus. How does your household budget, and all that you spend, reflect your faith in Christ? As you make your pledge for next year, will it take the power of Christ working in you every day to keep it? Is it really a pledge of faith? Are you willing to test it, by making next Sunday's offering equal to your weekly pledge for next year? Will it make any difference in your life?

"And Jesus said to the blind man, "What do you want me do to for you?"

"Master, let me receive my sight."
"Go your way, your faith has made you well."
And immediately he received his sight and followed him on the way."

Dale I. Gregoriew
Christ the Servant Church
Allen, Texas

NOVEMBER 3, 1991

Lutheran: Twenty-fourth Sunday after Pentecost
Roman Catholic: Thirty-first Sunday of the Year
Episcopalian: Proper 26
Pres/Meth/UCC: Twenty-fourth Sunday after Pentecost

Lessons:

Lutheran:	Deut. 6:1-9	Heb. 7:23-28	Mark 12:28-34 (35-37)
Roman Catholic:	Duet. 6:2-6	Heb. 7:23-28	Mark 12:28b-34
Episcopal:	Duet. 6:1-9	Heb. 7:23-28	Mark 12:28-34
Pres/Meth/UCC:	Deut. 6:1-9	Heb. 7:23-28	Mark 12:28-34

Introductions to the Lessons

Lesson 1

Deuteronomy 6:1-9 (**Luth/Epis/Pres/Meth/UCC**). In his farewell address to the Israelites before they enter the Promised Land, Moses urges the people to fear the Lord by obeying the commandments. The laws are summed up in one: love God with your whole being. With this greatest commandment is the shema, the basic creed of the Jews: "The Lord our God is one Lord." This law is to be taught to children generation after generation, and ever to be remembered.

Lesson 2

Hebrews 7:23-28 (**Luth/Epis/Pres/Meth/UCC**). The author of Hebrews continues to explain the superiority of Jesus as high priest. All other priests die and are replaced, but Jesus has his priesthood permanently. Other priests had to make sacrifices for their sins as well as for others, but Jesus made one perfect and eternal sacrifice, not for his but for the world's sins.

Gospel

Mark 12:28-34 (**Luth/Epis/Pres/Meth/UCC**). Jesus is now in Jerusalem for the last week of his life. Jesus is having discussions with the religious leaders. One of the group, a scribe, asks Jesus which of all the laws is the greatest. He repeats the command given by Moses to love God completely and then adds love of neighbor. The scribe agrees with the answer and Jesus tells him he is not far from the kingdom.

Theme: Seeking our real motivations for being Christian.

Thought for the day: In most of life we have mixed reasons for our actions and attitudes. Jesus confronts us with the call to examine our motives and see behind them to our needs; and he does this ever so gently in today's Gospel.

Prayer of meditation: O God, I come to you today with many thoughts and reasons. Come to me, Lord, in every aspect of our worship. Come to me, Lord, through your Word. Help me see myself as I am, and help me accept your grace which transforms me from who I am into the likeness of my Savior, Jesus Christ. Amen.

Call to worship: "Happy are those whose way is blameless, who walk in the law of the Lord. Happy are those who keep his decrees, who seek him with their whole heart, who also do no wrong, but walk in his ways." (Psalm 119:1-2 NRSV) Come, let us learn to walk in the ways of the Lord.

Prayer of adoration: O God, our Creator, as the morning sun brings light and new life to the world, so we come to you with our praise and adoration. We come because your grace is so rich we cannot stay away. We come because your love is so powerful we do not want to live without it. We come because you have given us life and show us how to walk in your ways. We come today to acclaim you, our God; through Jesus Christ our Lord. Amen.

Prayer of confession: O God, Redeemer of the world, you have come into our world to touch us with your love and bring us back to you. We confess that we have followed other gods, and we have given you lip service only. We confess that we have tried to follow your ways for our own self-centered reasons. We have failed to be your people. Forgive us, renew us, and set our lives on the course of faithful discipleship once again, through Jesus Christ, our Lord. Amen.

Prayer of dedication of gifts and self: O God, you alone can make all things holy; we offer to you the first fruits of our hands: our pledges for the work of your church, our offerings for those in need, our gifts in thankfulness for your grace, and most of all ourselves to be your faithful people once again. Take all that we bring and use it for your purpose, that these offerings may be a means for you to bless your whole creation; through Jesus Christ, our Lord. Amen.

Sermon title: Will the Real Christian Stand Up?

119

Sermon thesis: Because we come together as Christians for a variety of reasons, today's Gospel confronts us with a challenge and an affirmation of our motivations that opens the way for us to know the Kingdom of God.

Announcements for next week:

Sermon title: Real Giving Is . . .

Sermon theme: A poor widow teaches the whole world how to give.

Sermon summary: When Jesus praised the widow for her gift of two small coins, he taught us that real giving must be sacrificial, real giving is sometimes even reckless, and real giving is not just a matter of the gift's size. Have you done any real giving?

Hymn for the day: *"Spirit of God, descend upon my heart."* George Croly (1780-1860) was first a minister of the Church of Ireland. After moving to London, where for 25 years he was a very successful author, poet, and playwright, he returned to the ministry, serving a united parish in England. This hymn prays that the Spirit strengthen our love for God.

Children's object talk:

What Do We Really Want?

Objects: A large glass jar filled with tootsie rolls

Lesson: Learning to ask for what you really want.

Outline: 1. How many ways to talk about the jar of candy?

2. What do we really want?

3. Jesus teaches us to be honest with our needs.

4. Wanting something and getting it are not the same.

(Before worship a large glass jar of tootsie rolls is placed in an obvious place near the place of the children's sermon)

GOOD MORNING FRIENDS! Today Jesus wants us to talk about something inside us. It's not something we can see, or hold in our hand. We call them desires — the things we want. Oh, by the way, did anyone notice something unusual here at the altar this morning? (Let them respond and when someone points out the tootsie rolls, acknowledge it.)

Yes. We have a large jar of tootsie rolls here. Now tell me, what did you think about when you saw those tootsie rolls? Did you think: I hope pastor gives those out during the children's sermon. I wonder if I'll get two or three. I wish I could have the whole jar!

As most of you know, that jar is usually in my office. It is fun to watch people who come there, when they discover it. Some just keep looking at it. Sometimes some of my friends say: "What are the tootsie rolls for?" Or they look longingly at them and say: "I sure do like tootsie rolls." Some even say, "May I have a tootsie roll?"

In the Gospel story for today, Jesus asks his followers to think about what they really want. And he tells them it is O.K. to ask for it. He wants us to be honest with ourselves. Now, there's one more part of the story: Sometimes, when people ask for a tootsie roll, I can say "Certainly, help yourself." Sometimes when someone says I wish I could have a whole handful, I say, "That would be nice, but everybody who comes here gets only one, so there will be another for the next time you come, and for everyone else who comes." And sometimes I have to say: "I'm sorry, there are only ten left, and I have ten friends coming later this morning and I need one for each of them."

Isn't it great that we can be so honest with each other? That's what Jesus calls us to be all the time! Oh yes, each of you may have a tootsie roll now! God bless you.

The sermon:

Will the Real Christian Stand Up?

Hymns:
    Beginning of worship: Jesus Calls Us
    Sermon hymn: Let Us Ever Walk with Jesus
    End of worship: O That the Lord would guide my Ways

Scripture: Mark 12:28-34

Sermon Text: *"Which commandment is first of all?"* v. 28 (NSV)

WHY DOES AN ATTRACTIVE, intelligent person like yourself belong to, and give time, money and talents to a congregation like this one?

I'll repeat the question. Why does an attractive, intelligent person like yourself belong to, and give time, talents and money to a congregation like this one?

If you were to visit any congregation and ask that question you would hear just about every conceivable answer possible for that question. People identify with congregations for a great variety of reasons. When I was a young pastor, serving my first congregation, a seasoned pastor from a neighboring congregation helped me understand a variety of motives with this story. The congregations in that part of the country were known for their annual dinners; and each one had a specialty: turkey, ham, roast beef, etc.

My pastor-friend and his wife were having dinner one evening in a restaurant when they were approached by a very friendly woman who greeted them by name. The pastor responded, but said, "I'm sorry, but I am having difficulty remembering your name." "Oh, Pastor Jones, I come to your church all the time," the woman replied. "You do?" said the pastor, "I must be getting forgetful. I'm sorry." "Oh yes," said the woman, "I come to every ham dinner your church has!"

People identify with a congregation, and claim a relationship with the church for a variety of reasons. Today, let's explore some of those reasons.

A very common reason for younger families to claim a congregation is "for the children." Children need to learn about God, just as we do. They need a good foundation. And furthermore that thesis is supported and affirmed by our culture. When the children's choir sings, attendance is always higher than usual. A special event put on by the Sunday School classes, Vacation Church School or the week-day pre-school will always attract a crowd. Take a look at *"Who's Who"* in the public library and read about a few famous people. A solid Church and Sunday School foundation is found in a majority of people.

Another common reason for people belonging to a church is that it's good for life and health and the community. In western culture it has become a part of the fabric of our society. The American way of life, and positive general morality presume affiliation with a religious community. Some recent medical research has been published that indicates that persons who are regularly religious in their activities are less prone to stress, have fewer heart attacks, and risk less chance of a stroke.

A third common reason is that persons have grown up in the church. They have never known life any other way. It is the thing to do in their family. It is part of the fabric of their concept of family. "We go to church."

I am discovering among my friends in many different congregations another group of people with a common reason. They say it this way, rather frankly to me: "We are members of our congregation (usually saying the name of the church.) We don't come very often. We are not looking for another congregation. This is our congregation. We are just not motivated right now." Sometimes these folks are burned out, or weary, or have had a painful experience. Sometimes they are just plain bored. But they are members and would not think of changing their membership; and would be offended if the pastor suggested it!

There is also a group of folks, both local and who have moved away years ago, who are not involved, but want to keep their names on the church roll. Somewhere deep in the corner recesses of their life God and the church have touched their life and they do not want to cut themselves off from that experience.

Yet another group of members are these: "My Lord, my church and my faith are the center of my life. Here, I share my faith with others. Here, I am nourished by Word and Sacraments. Here, I am comforted, challenged, and commissioned for my daily Christian life."

Why does an attractive, intelligent person like yourself, belong to this congregation?

As you can see there are many answers. All the reasons I mentioned are positive. All are good and valid reasons for the individual. In every one there is hope, and direction, and room for growth.

In Jesus' day rabbinical method of teaching was through question and answer. There are many variations on this method. For example, Mark the gospel writer makes a drama out of the teaching situation in today's text. The Jews were in Jerusalem for a holy day. The air seemed thick with tension and excitement. In previous scenes the drama has unfolded like this:

When Jesus was in the Temple some of the Temple leaders came to him and said, "By what authority do you do these things?"

In another scene it is obvious that messengers are sent to Jesus asking, "Is it lawful to pay taxes to Caesar?"

Then a group of Jews who did not believe in resurrection came to him and asked' "If a woman has seven husbands, all who have died, whose wife will she be in the resurrection?"

In today's text, Jesus is in the Temple teaching Temple leaders. In the three previous scenes those asking the questions were Temple leaders, messengers and a group of religious fanatics. Now comes the ultimate authority: rabbi and disciple. "Teacher, tell us, what is the greatest commandment?" This is the great question. Every person knew it. It was the question in great and serious debates. It was casual table conversation. To answer the question one had to take a side. What is the one thing necessary above all else? And the responses to that question are very much like the variety of reasons persons belong to a congregation! Jesus is the one who gives the answer. He begins with the Shema, recited by every faithful Jew at least three times each day. "Love God with all that is in you!" and the second is just as important: "Love your neighbor as yourself!"

The scribe from the Temple then clinches Jesus' authority: "Teacher, you are right! . . . This is even more important than the offerings and the sacrifice."

Jesus then turns to the scribe, with the eyes of all around him riveted on the two men:" You are not far from the kingdom of God!" The scribe has the context for faith. For one reason or another he knows God. But knowing takes doing to make it real in our life. And that is the call to us today: we know. We have our own reasons for our being here. And our Lord Jesus comes to us and says to us, "You are not far from the Kingdom. Come follow me."

Dale I. Gregoriew
Christ the Servant Lutheran Church
Allen, Texas

NOVEMBER 3, 1991

All Saints Sunday

Lessons:

Lutheran:	Is. 26:1-4, 8-9, 12-13, 19-21	Rev. 21:9-11, 22-27 (22:1-5)	Matt. 5:1-12
Roman Catholic:	Rev. 7:2-4, 9-14	I John 3:1-3	Matt. 5:1-12a
Episcopal:	Eccles. 44:1-10, 13-14	Rev. 7:2-4, 9-17	Matt. 5:1-12
Pres/Meth/UCC	Rev. 21:1-6a	Col. 1:9-14	John 11:32-44

Introductions to the Lessons

Lesson 1

(1) *Isaiah 26:1-4, 12-13, 19-21* (**Luth**). Isaiah gives us a picture of the city of God, a strong city of salvation. In this city dwell the righteous who long for God and trust in him. God's people will be safe in this city while the earth receives God's judgment.

(2) *Ecclesiasticus 44:1-10, 13-14* (**Epis**). Famous ancestors who contributed great things to humanity are to be praised. These godly people will never be forgotten. Their children will always exist, and their names will live on generation after generation.

(3) *Revelation 21:1-6a* (**Pres/Meth/UCC**). John sees a new heaven and a new earth. A new Jerusalem comes out of heaven. In this eternal city God dwells with his people and there is no more sorrow or death. Christ makes all things new.

Lesson 2

(1) *Revelation 21:9-11, 22-27* (**Luth**). Heaven is described as the new Jerusalem that came from God. The city has the glory of God, for God is in it. Because of this, there is no light in it nor a temple. The gates of this glorious city are always open, but nothing unclean may enter it. The citizens of this city are those whose names appear in the book of life.

(2) *Revelation 7:2-4, 9-17* (**Epis**). Heaven consists of a multitude of people of every race and nation. They stand before God's throne praising him. They are people who have cleansed their souls in the blood of Christ. Now they lack nothing, have no sorrow, and continually worship God.

(3) *Colossians 1:9-14* (**Pres/Meth/UCC**). In his prayer for the church Paul refers to their sharing the inheritance of the saints in heaven. Because of their faith in Christ, they have been transferred from the kingdom of darkness to the Kingdom of Christ in whom they have forgiveness.

Gospel

(1) *Matthew 5:1-12* (**Luth/Epis**). Jesus begins the Sermon on the Mount with the Beatitudes. They say how and why believers are happy. They describe the condition and qualities of those in heaven.

(2) *John 11:32-44* (**Pres/Meth/UCC**). Lazarus, whom Jesus loved as a friend, died. Jesus went to the grave and wept. Though the man was dead for four days, Jesus called him forth from the tomb. It was a demonstration of Jesus' power over death.

Theme: In the Beatitudes Jesus calls us to a new understanding of being blessed.

Thought for the day: In a world where being blessed means having a special talent; or children who don't get in trouble; or driving a Mercedes; or being physically fit and attractive; when Jesus calls us to be blessed; it is a call to a radically different life-style.

Prayer of meditation: O God, you have called persons in all ages to be your people, and you have made them saints before our eyes. Help me to hear your call, to know your blessing and to know that I, too, belong to the communion of saints; through Jesus Christ, my Lord. Amen

Call to worship: "I sought the Lord, and he answered me, and delivered me from all my fears. Look to him, and be radiant; . . . O taste and see that the Lord is good; happy are those who take refuge in him." Psalm 34: 4, 5, 8 (NRSV)

Prayer of adoration: Almighty and Eternal God, we come today to join our praises to the praises of all generations; we join with cherubim and seraphim, angels and archangels, apostles and prophets, disciples and martyrs and all your saints of every age to sing Holy, Holy, Holy, the whole earth is full of your glory; through Jesus Christ, our Lord. Amen.

Prayer of confession: O God of our fathers and mothers, you have given us life in this creation and you have called us to new life by your grace; we confess that we have failed to heed your call, and we have chosen to walk in our own ways. Forgive our sinful desires and our sins, and give us the renewing call of your love that will transform us into your faithful saints; through Jesus Christ, our Lord. Amen.

Prayer of dedication of gifts and self: Accept these offerings O God, as a sign of our renewed commitment to you. Consecrate our money gifts as they are used for the work of your church. Sanctify our skills and talents as they are used to be the healing touch of Jesus in our world. Bless our lives, as your Holy Spirit directs them to be visible evidence of your kingdom in this world; through the power of Christ. Amen.

Sermon title: Being Blessed

Sermon thesis: The Beatitudes are Jesus' announcement of a radical new understanding of blessing: Blessings come in the midst of problems and needs of the world, causing us to implement positive changes.

Hymn for the day: *"Jerusalem, my happy home."* This hymn seems to be based on *Liber Meditationum,* published in Venice in 1553. Two English poems dating from the late sixteenth century—one 26 stanzas long and one 44. The 26-stanza version is attributed to F.B.P., whose identity is unknown, although some have suggested it might have been Francis Baker, Pater (priest), who was for a time imprisoned at the Tower of London.

Announcements for next week:

Sermon title: Real Giving Is. . .

Sermon theme: A poor widow teaches the whole world how to give.

Sermon summary: When Jesus praised the widow for her gift of two small coins, he taught us that real giving must be sacrificial, real giving is sometimes even reckless, and real giving is not just a matter of the gift's size. Have you done any real giving?

Children's object talk:

What Is A Saint?

Objects: A picture of someone who influenced my life
Lesson: We all are saints, as God's children.
Outline: 1. What is a saint?
2. An example of a saint for me.
3. You too are a saint.

TODAY IS ALL SAINTS SUNDAY. Do you know what a saint is? Is a saint a holy person who lived a long time ago? Is a saint someone who has died? Is a saint a holy person who is still alive? Is a saint someone you know?

I have here a picture of a person who was very special to me. When I was about 12 years old, I went to see him, and ask him about a project I was working on. He helped, he became my friend, and he showed me that God loves me. His kindness to me changed

127

my life. There have been lots of people who have done the same thing for me. I think the man in this picture is a saint.

Have you ever had someone who made you feel special, and who changed your life? Those persons are saints. Why do we think those persons are saints? What do they do that is different? They are kind. They care about us. They show us that God loves us. Because we learn from them that God loves us, they change our lives. They can do that because they know that God loves them. They are special because they know that God loves them. They are saints because they are God's children. Have you ever been kind to someone? Do you know that God loves you? Are you one of God's children? So am I.

That makes us saints too, doesn't it? Wow! All Saints day is pretty neat. Today we can join with all God's people from every time and place and celebrate his love, for all the saints, including you and me.

The sermon:

Being Blessed

Hymns:
   Opening hymn: For All the Saints
   Sermon hymn: Blest Be the Tie that Binds
   Closing hymn: Who is this Host Arrayed in White

Scripture: Matthew 5:1-12

Sermon Text: *The Beatitudes*

THE FAINT SMELL of flowers comes to you as you open the door. You tell the woman who opened the door who you have come to see, and she politely says "Follow me." There is hushed conversation among the others in the large entry way, and when you enter the room you are aware of at least four generations of one family gathered. You have come to share your feelings and concerns with the family, and to say your farewell to a special friend. Her living brothers and sisters, her children and grandchildren are all there. Her great grandchildren are too small to realize what has happened, but her love and her life will be told to them. Pinned on her favorite dress is a corsage from the great-grandchildren. You feel a deep sense of loss, yet a great sense of peace as you leave that funeral home.

This dear friend, who died with the sign of faith, was indeed blessed. For the next few days you reflect on the truly blessed life of your friend. But, as you see real and "made for TV" violence; or you recall the sudden tragic death of a middle aged pastor-friend; or the teenage suicide you wonder if you will ever be so blessed as your friend. When you think of all the pain and anguish in the world; violence in homes and families; hunger in our town as well as around the world; households and families torn apart by greed and lust and ego; employees and employers set against each other; you wonder if anyone can be blessed today.

Our common understanding of "blessed" is related to a reward — something good given or received for an accomplishment. Sometimes we think of being blessed as having a special talent or being "privileged." Thus, for most of us, being blessed is usually out of reach. Others may be blessed, but for us it is usually out of reach.

The Beatitudes, which are today's Gospel lesson, tell us that Jesus calls us to a whole new understanding of being blessed. Beatitudes are a common literary form in the world of the Bible and in every era of humankind. Furthermore, they frequently reinforce our common understanding of being blessed. They seem to be conditional phrases: "Blessed are you, if. . ." or "Blessed are you because. . ." The Beatitudes of Jesus are radically different from any others. The literary phrases, the subjects, and the emotional impact represent a whole new order. One commentator describes Jesus' announcement of blessed as "a concept of human blessedness which reverses all values of any social order that ever existed. . ."[1]

The Beatitudes can be divided into two groups. The first group describes people in need. The poor in spirit are the humblehearted, those who have experienced the bankruptcy of the world's values. Those who mourn are those for whom a cross is the cruel reality of their world. The meek are those who know limitations of all sorts. Those who hunger and thirst for righteousness are those for whom life is an endless search for justice, for peace, for identity, for God.

The second group of Beatitudes describe the implementation of blessedness. The merciful, when confronted with human need, never pause to ask, "Should I?", but instead, ask, "When do we start?" The pure in heart are not the goody two-shoes that you may know, but

1. Beare, Frank W. *The Earliest Records of Jesus.* Abingdon, Nashville, 1962. p. 55

they are those who know and are nourished on the Word and Sacraments. When Jesus talks about peacemakers, he is not referring to career diplomats, but to those people who routinely treat all others as persons in their daily life. Jesus makes it clear that the peacemakers, in their positive regard for all other persons, are truly blessed. The persecuted are those who will not waiver from their values; who will not be seduced into prostituting themselves for anything. These new definitions of being blessed sound very much like all the rest, until you grasp the tense of the verbs in the Beatitudes.

Note the difference: "Blessed *are* the poor in Spirit. . . Blessed *are* the peacemakers." These are present tense verbs. Furthermore the conjunction is not "if" or "because" but "when. . ." Jesus proclaims blessings for people now, in the present tense. The blessings come in the midst of the problems and needs of the world. The blessings are there, causing us to implement positive actions in our world.

To be blessed is to know God in Jesus;
    not a reward for good deeds.
To be blessed is to have the handles of faith
    that give us comfort and confidence every day.
To be blessed is to live in a new order
    which transforms our whole life.
To be blessed is to know the grace of God
    as we journey through life in this world.
To be blessed is to see ourselves in the Beatitudes right now,
    and not to see them as someone else's
    or for someday in our life — maybe.
To be blessed is to live this life, facing real pain and joy,
    real comfort and struggle,
    real problems and solutions,
    real love and injustice,
    with the confidence that Jesus has called us
    to be his own people.
Blessed are you as you hear God's word.

Dale I. Gregoriew
Christ the Servant Lutheran Church
Allen, Texas

NOVEMBER 10, 1991

Lutheran: Twenty-fifth Sunday after Pentecost
Roman Catholic: Thirty-second Sunday of the Year
Episcopalian: Proper 27
Pres/Meth/UCC: Twenty-fifth Sunday after Pentecost

Lessons:

Lutheran:	I Kings 17:8-16	Heb. 9:24-28	Mark 12:41-44
Roman Catholic:	I Kings 17:10-16	Heb. 9:24-28	Mark 12:38-44
Episcopal:	I Kings 17:8-16	Heb. 9:24-28	Mark 12:38-44
Pres/Meth/UCC:	I Kings 17:8-16	Heb. 9:24-28	Mark 12:38-44

Introductions to the Lessons

Lesson 1

I Kings 17:8-16 (**Luth/Epis/Pres/Meth/UCC**). Because of King Ahab's wickedness, Elijah the prophet calls for a drought that lasts three years. Elijah was caught up in the famine caused by the drought. Yahweh directs Elijah to a widow in Zarephath for food. She tells him that she and her son are down to their last meal. Regardless, he orders her to feed him. God promised that the food supply would not fail until the rain came. And so it was.

Lesson 2

Hebrews 9:24-28 (**Luth/Epis/Pres/Meth/UCC**). Unlike a human priest, Jesus entered the holy of holies, the sanctuary of heaven. A human high priest enters once every year to make atonement for sins, but Christ offered his blood for atonement once and for all time.

Gospel

Mark 12:38-44 (**Epis/Pres/Meth/UCC**); *12:41-44* (**Luth**). Jesus is at the Temple in Jerusalem. He observes the hypocritical behavior of the scribes and warns his disciples to beware of them. Also, he notices the gifts put in the Temple treasury. A poor widow gave a sacrificial gift worth a penny. He pointed out that she gave the largest gift because it came out of her poverty while the other gifts came out of affluence.

Theme: A poor widow teaches the whole world how to give.

Thought for the day: When the poor widow gave her two mites to the Temple treasury that day, little did she know that her act would

131

be noticed or that it would become an example of giving that would instruct millions of Christians the world over. Would we give differently if we thought Jesus might want to use our giving as an example for others?

Prayer of meditation: O Lord, through baptism you have made me your child, and through the efforts of many I have come to know what that means. Help me also to grow in giving to your work so that the widow of long ago may no longer put me to shame. Lord, whoever said the pocketbook is the last part of a person to be converted knew whereof he spoke. Help me to find the joy in giving that you have promised those who trust you. Amen.

Call to worship: Come, let us praise God with all our being. Let us thank him for life and health, friends and family, and most of all for the privilege of knowing Jesus as our Savior and Lord, to whom with the Father and the Holy Spirit we offer our praises, both now and forever. Amen.

Prayer of adoration: Creating and sustaining God and Father of our Lord Jesus Christ, we praise you for your boundless mercy. Seeing all our deeds, yet you love us. Knowing even our inmost thoughts, still you forgive us. Open our hearts to praise you, and give us grace to act more and more often in ways, like that of the widow, that you can praise, so that when others too see our good works, they do not focus on us but give the glory to you, our Heavenly Father, and seeking the source of our actions, discover our Lord Jesus Christ to be their Lord as well. In his name we pray. Amen.

Prayer of confession: God and Father of us all, you have called me to be your special child, giving me all that I have, especially Jesus my Savior. And while I am grateful, I have often acted ungratefully, particularly in my use and sharing of the things I have from you. Teach me to join the widow in giving all I have to you, and help me to use even that which you give back in ways that will further your kingdom, both here and abroad. Amen.

Prayer of dedication of gifts and self: O Lord, we return to you now a small part of what you have first given us. Receive these gifts and use them for your purposes, considering them a symbol of our rededicating our lives to you as well. In Jesus' name we pray. Amen.

Sermon title: Real Giving Is. . .

Sermon thesis: When Jesus praised the widow for her gift of two small coins, he taught us that real giving must be sacrificial, real giving is sometimes even reckless, and real giving is not just a matter of the gift's size. Have you done any real giving?

Hymn for the day: *"God, whose giving knows no ending"* (LBW 408). This hymn, written for a Hymn Society of America competition for stewardship hymns, speaks of our response to God's endless love. Robert Lansing Edwards, born in Auburn, New York, in 1915, studied at Princeton University and Harvard University. After serving from 1941 to 1946 as a captain of intelligence for the Army, he continued his education at Union Theological Seminary and was ordained to the Congregational ministry in 1949. In addition to his pastorates he has held a number of other positions, including delegate to the International Congregational Council and delegate of the United Church of Christ to the World Council of Churches Assembly in Upsala, Sweden in 1968.

Announcements for next week:

Sermon title: Through Good Times and Bad
Sermon theme: The Christian's calling is life-long, "to the end."
Sermon summary: When Jesus taught his disciples about what it would be like to be a Christian before his return, he painted a picture that seems quite different from our reality. Or is it? In what ways do we "answer" for our faith, and how can we at last be found faithful?

Children's object talk:

Learning to Love God

Objects: A Lepton (a coin from Jesus' time) and some pennies
Lesson: We can give freely to God, because God knows our heart.
Outline: 1. When we love God, we want to give him gifts.

    2. The gift's size isn't as important as the love.

    3. God, knowing our heart, accepts every loving gift.

GOOD MORNING, KIDS. TODAY I have something very special to show you. It's a coin that is about 2,000 years old, and may have been one of the very coins mentioned in our Gospel lesson today. It is called a Lepton. On one side it shows some wheat, and on the other are some words, but you can't see much detail. A lepton in Jesus' day was much like a penny today. Actually, the Bible says it was like half a penny. What can you buy with half a penny? (Get some answers.)

I guess we would all agree that we can't buy much with a penny and it wasn't much different in Jesus' time. When Jesus was in the Temple one day, he noticed a woman putting two leptons in the offering. Those two coins were hardly worth anything, but they may have been all the woman had. Yet, what did Jesus say about them? "This poor widow has put in more than all those who are contributing to the treasury. . . she out of her poverty has given everything she had." By saying that, Jesus is telling us that he is just as happy with a small gift from a poor person as with a large gift from a rich person. What matters to him is not the gift's size, but whether or not we love him. So we may bring him loving gifts, small or large, knowing he sees our hearts and is happy with our gifts.

The sermon:

Real Giving Is. . .

Hymns:
　Beginning of worship: When Morning Gilds the Skies
　Sermon hymn: Take My Life, That I May Be
　End of worship: O Jesus, I Have Promised

Scripture: Mark 12:41-44

Sermon Text: *". . . she out of her poverty has put in everything she had, her whole living."* v. 44

ARE YOU A TITHER? I mean, are you one of those committed, dedicated Christians who regularly and faithfully gives 10% or more of all your income to the Lord's work through your local church? If you are, permit me to thank you for your commitment even as I invite you to struggle with Jesus' words for us this morning — words which may be directed at "tithers" especially, as we run the risk of smugness and self-satisfaction leading to complacency about our actions in behalf of the Lord.

Among the many stories about tithing that I have heard, the one that is my favorite has a successful man complaining to his pastor about a problem that has developed in his life as a tither. "When I was a young Christian," the story goes, "I promised God that I would tithe a tenth of all my income, which was at that time $100 a month. I kept that promise, and soon my income had grown to where it was $100 a week — $400 a month, and I was still tithing."

"That seems to be no problem," interrupted the Pastor, not sure where this story was headed. "Oh, but pastor, that's just the beginning of my story," continued the man. "As time went on, my income grew until I was making $50 a day, then $100, and the tithe just kept going up and up and up. It's gotten so that now I make $100 per hour at what I do, I have to turn away work, and my tithe is simply tremendous. Yet, I don't know what to do, because I promised God that I would tithe, and I'm a man of my word."

The pastor sat for awhile in silence. Finally he asked the man to join him in prayer. "Dear Lord," he began, "ever since Joe began tithing, you've blessed him more and more each year until now his promise to give a tithe of his income has become a burden. Please adjust Joe's income until the tithe is no longer such a problem. For Jesus' sake, Amen."

Obviously, nobody would want to have their pastor pray such a prayer in their behalf. After all, each time "Joe" had to increase his tithe, he still had nine times that increase available for his own use. Who would forego ninety cents in order to save a dime? Certainly, not Joe. Still, the humor in this story is an opportunity to think again about giving, just as is the poignancy in the story of the woman who gave all she had. What would move someone to give that much? How much she must have loved and been loved by God! Her action leads us to realize that true giving to God is a matter of sacrifice, of recklessness, and of generosity.

True giving is a matter of sacrifice. For the widow, that meant putting in "her whole living," and while very few of us do that, the very act of giving a significant percentage of our income is a sacrifice. Imagine doubling or even tripling the offering you planned for today. Where would you get the money? Most of us would have to rearrange priorities to make such a sudden change in our giving patterns, yet statisticians tell us that the "average" Christian would have to triple her or his giving to approach giving 10%.

Let us suppose, however, that someone were willing to make the sacrifice and move upward in giving to a significant percent of their income. Such a move would not only be sacrificial, but also reckless. It would follow the example of the widow who gave all she had without going to the degree she achieved. If I made the adjustment to triple my giving without finding new income to cover the difference, I might be recklessly planning to spend more than I make. And you would, too, if you are spending about all you take in right now.

But recklessness may be what it would take for us to discover what it's like to depend on God; to say to God that we really do trust him more then we trust our budgeting skills or our own ability to make ends meet. Reckless trust of God means knowing that, with the lilies of the field and the birds of the air, God will take care of us, whatever happens.

Finally, the giving this widow models for us is a giving that is generous. And here we must be careful. We can know that this widow's giving was generous and her gift was to be praised, because Jesus did so. However, we must be careful not to use his omniscient example as a model for our own praise of people and their gifts today. It seems to me that television preachers are particularly guilty of this, but maybe they are simply more public in their excesses. There can be many motives other than generosity for a person to give. But truly giving as a response to God's prior love for us is a wonderful opportunity to experience generosity in one's giving.

There's one more remarkable thing about this story. The widow who has become our example did not have the incredible reason for giving that each of us has. She didn't know Jesus as her God and Savior. She didn't know Jesus as the embodiment of God's love for her — love that died so she might live, love that lived so she need never die. That is our privilege. That is our blessing. That, ultimately, is our reason for practicing real giving — giving that is sacrificial, that is reckless, and that is generous beyond comprehension, other than that it flows from the love of God who first gave all for us.

Walter H. Mees, Jr.
Palisades Lutheran Church
Culver City, California

NOVEMBER 17, 1991

Lutheran: Twenty-sixth Sunday after Pentecost
Roman Catholic: Thirty-third Sunday of the Year
Episcopalian: Proper 28
Pres/Meth/UCC: Twenty-sixth Sunday after Pentecost

Lessons:

Lutheran:	Daniel 12:1-3	Heb. 10:11-18	Mark 13:1-13
Roman Catholic:	Daniel 7:9-14	Heb. 10:11-18	Mark 13:24-32
Episcopal:	Daniel 12:1-4a (5-13)	Heb. 10:31-39	Mark 13:14-23
Pres/Meth/UCC:	Daniel 7:9-14	Heb. 10:11-18	Mark 13:24-32

Introductions to the Lessons

(1) *Daniel 12:1-3* (**Luth**); *12:1-4a* (**Epis**). The oldest book in the Old Testament tells us of the end of the world. It will be a time of great trouble, but the guardian angel of Israel, Michael, will deliver those whose names are in God's book of life. There will be a resurrection of the dead and a judgment resulting in some going to everlasting life and others to hell.

(2) *Daniel 7:9-14* (**Pres/Meth/UCC**). We have here a description of the final judgment. God the Father sits on his throne for judgment. The beast, Satan, was destroyed by fire. God the Son was presented to the Father and was given a universal and eternal dominion.

Lesson 2

(1) *Hebrews 10:11-18* (**Luth/Pres/Meth/UCC**). A priest repeatedly offer sacrifices that cannot remove sin. By contrast, Jesus made one perfect sacrifice of himself for the sin of the world. Then he sat down in authority and glory at the right hand of God waiting until all enemies are defeated. His sacrifice effected a new covenant in which there is forgiveness.

(2) *Hebrews 10:31-39* (**Epis**). The writer of Hebrews refers to the sufferings of church people: persecution and loss of property. Nevertheless they continued to have compassion on others who were mistreated. He encourages them to endure in their faith so that they may be among the saved.

Gospel

(1) *Mark 13:1-13* (**Luth**). Mark 13 is known as the "Little Apocalypse," the last lengthy discourse of Jesus. It deals with end times. The disciples marvel at the Temple buildings but Jesus predicts that they will be destroyed. But when, the disciples want to know. There will be false prophets, natural disasters, and wars, but these will only be the prelude of the end. Before the end comes, the Gospel must be preached to all nations.

(2) *Mark 13:14-23* (**Epis**). According to this passage, the end of time will come when the desolating sacrilege is set up. This is a reference to desecrating the holy of holies in the Temple. For the Jews nothing worse could happen. When this day comes, the people need to flee. Jesus' advice is "Be alert."

(3) *Mark 13:24-32* (**Pres/Meth/UCC**). The universe some day is going to collapse. Then Christ will return and the faithful will be gathered. How will we know when the end is upon us? Jesus uses the fig tree to explain. Just as we know summer is near when a fig tree produces leaves, we will know the apocalypse is here. However, though the universe will end, Jesus' words will remain forever.

Theme: The Christian's calling is life-long, "to the end."

Thought for the day: When Jesus wanted to tell his disciples what to expect from life as his followers, it was a mixed message both of hard times and of ultimate victory. The promise that was to keep them going, and is still valid for us, is that he will one day return. The circumstances of his return may be debatable, but its certainty is not. Therefore, we pray, "Come quickly, Lord Jesus!"

Prayer of meditation: O Lord, when you told your disciples what would be in store for them as Christians, you were also letting me know that a Christian's life is not necessarily easy. Help me, even in this great free country, so to guard myself and my family against those who would take away our faith that we might always remain faithful to you, even being found faithful to the end of our lives. In Jesus' name I pray. Amen.

Call to worship: Come, let us praise God with all our being. Let us praise him with our voices, even in the presence of those who do not believe in him. Let us praise God with our lives, even when others would have us live lives contrary to the Gospel. Let us praise God every day of our life. Come, let us praise God!

Prayer of adoration: "Father, we adore you, lay our lives before you. How we love you." As we think, O heavenly Father, of all the blessings you have showered upon us your children, blessings of faith and family, privilege and possessions, we cannot help praising you and giving glory to your name. But of all the reasons we have for praising you, Father, the most important one is our Lord Jesus Christ, the manifestation of your love, through whose life, death and resurrection we have obtained all the good things that our lives contain, both now and forever more. Amen.

Prayer of confession: God and Father of us all, you have called me to be your special child, giving me all that I have, especially Jesus my Savior. And while I am grateful, I also suffer bouts of doubts, times of fear, seasons of insufficient faith in you and your loving care both of myself and of your other people. Forgive my doubt, wipe away all my sins, blot out all my transgressions, for Jesus' sake. Amen.

Prayer of dedication of gifts and self: Mighty God, Gracious Lord, we bring to your altar gifts which are merely a return of what you first gave us. We offer them to you for use in your kingdom work, and as signs of our gratitude for all you have done for us, particularly for the gift of your Son Jesus, our Lord, in whose name and for whose sake we pray. Amen.

Sermon title: Through good times and bad. . .

Sermon thesis: When Jesus taught his disciples about what it would be like to be a Christian before his return, he painted a picture that seems quite different from our reality. Or is it? In what ways do we "answer" for our faith, and how can we at last be found faithful?

Hymn for the day: *"Through the night of doubt and sorrow"* ("Singing songs of expectation"). This Danish hymn has, through its translation by Sabine Baring-Gould, come into widespread use in English-speaking churches. The author of the Danish hymn, Severin Ingemann (1789-1862), was much admired for his poetry and was sent by his government to study for two years abroad—in Germany, France, Italy, and Switzerland. For twenty years he was professor of literature at the academy at Soro on the Island of Sjaelland, and for seven years thereafter he was director of the academy. The hymn speaks of God's guidance through fearsome times, and also of Christian unity.

Announcements for next week:

Sermon title: Encountering the Truth
Sermon theme: Like Pilate, we all must face Jesus sometime.
Sermon summary: Pilate encountered the truth on the day he sat in judgment over Jesus, and found himself to be on trial. By his refusal to treat Jesus fairly, he failed himself miserably. How often do we do the same, as we too ignore God's truth and instead do what the world or our own desires lead us to? Show yourself to be a person who is "of the truth." Hear, and heed, Jesus.

Children's object talk:

Reading the Signs

Objects: Signs such as a stop sign, no parking, restroom, etc.
Lesson: Reading the signs Jesus promised tells us to be ready for him to come back at any time.
Outline: 1. We know how to read many signs every day.
2. Jesus told us to watch for signs of his return.
3. Watching for those signs keeps us ready for him.

GOOD MORNING, KIDS. TODAY I'd like you to look at some signs I have and tell me what you think they mean. (Show the signs and have the kids shout out the meanings.) In today's lesson, Jesus gave us some signs — some things that will happen before he returns. Some are that people will come claiming to be Jesus who aren't. There will also be wars we know about and wars we only hear about. Then there will be earthquakes and famines, and Christians will suffer for their faith. Have you heard of any of those things ever happening? You have? So have I.

Does that mean that Jesus is coming soon? What do you think? Well, let's look at it this way. Those things have happened all along, ever since Jesus said them. Yes they have. Now, does that mean that Jesus is a lousy prophet? I don't think so. It means that Jesus could come at any minute. Or he might not. It's our job not to worry about when he will return, but to be ready for him whenever he does come. So watch the signs that remind us that Jesus will come. Keep trusting in him and thanking him for loving you, and you'll be ready. And by all means, don't worry!

The sermon:

Through Good Times and Bad

Hymns:
Beginning of worship: O Word of God Incarnate
Sermon hymn: Trust and Obey
End of worship: Standing on the Promises

Scripture: Mark 13:1-13

Sermon Text: *"But he who endures to the end will be saved."* v. 13

AS THIS SERMON IS BEING WRITTEN, Iraq has taken over Kuwait, U.S. troops are gathering in Saudi Arabia, Arab nations have finally agreed to condemn the actions of Iraq's leader, and the public is once again interested in those Christian leaders some call Restorationists—those who have seen the rebirth of Israel as fulfillment of prophecy leading to the Second Coming of Christ, and are interpreting daily events as steps in their "Scripture-revealed" countdown toward the end of this present age.

Knowing all this is going on, someone might say that writing a sermon which won't even be read until a year or more from now is a waste of time, since the Lord will probably return before this book will even be in print. Some might say that, but they are not people who take seriously our text for this day. This text, you see, is an answer to the question asked by the disciples: "When are these things all to be accomplished?" The answer is both that it could happen any day, and that it may not happen for quite a while. But while you are waiting for that day to come, there will be plenty for each Christian to do, and God, the Holy Spirit will be with us, in the doing.

The catalog of events in our text, being the first part of Jesus' answer to the disciples' question, is remarkable for its unremarkability. The Temple which he referred to in verse 2 was destroyed only a few decades after he spoke. Wars are commonplace in history— so common that the number of years in which there was nobody at war on the whole earth can probably be counted on one hand.

Those who have come claiming to be Christ have also been many, and one of them was recently convicted of tax evasion in our own country. Could it be earthquakes or famines that are so rare as to be a clue about the imminent return of Christ? Not by any stretch of the imagination. What, then, was Jesus' point in answering his disciples' question in this way? It is simply this: the events he recounted occur with great regularity, and as such serve as a constant reminder to us to be ready for his return.

Let us remember that this is the same Jesus who told the story of the wise and foolish virgins waiting for the bridegroom. The point is not to have a warning about the nearness of the end, but to live in a constant state of readiness for its arrival at any moment. But Jesus' answer continues.

Don't worry about the end, says Jesus. See that you are ready for what is to come. You will be hauled into court, accused of following me, and asked to explain yourselves. When that happens, you may trust me for the words to use, but it will be a terrible time when you can't even trust members of your own family not to betray you, because they will.

William Barclay reminds us of what that must be like by telling a story about Hitler's Germany, where ". . . a man was arrested because he stood for freedom. He endured imprisonment and torture with stoic and uncomplaining fortitude. Finally, with spirit still unbroken, he was released. Some short time afterwards he committed suicide. Many wondered why. Those who knew him well knew the reason — he had discovered that his own son was the one who had informed against him. The treachery of his own broke him in a way that the cruelty of his enemies was unable to achieve." (Barclay, William, *The Daily Study Bible: The Gospel of Mark,* revised edition, 1975, p. 313)

Such dynamics are part of the tragedy of Judas' betrayal of Jesus, and in our own lives whenever someone we love returns that love with an act of betrayal. Yet, says Jesus, these things will happen, time and time again, until he returns. And this leads us to our final point — that of our purpose in the interim. There are two clues about that purpose, and they are more than clues, really.

The first comes in verse 10: "And the gospel must first be preached to all nations." What is this but one more reminder of the church's task and the Christian's purpose to proclaim Jesus to those who don't know him? Ask Jesus about the end, and he tells you that it won't come until the Great Commission is fulfilled. While it may be easy to get 20th century Christians off the subject of evangelism and onto issues like abortion, euthanasia, capital punishment and the rest, Jesus is not so easily side-tracked. You want the end to come? Get busy and do your job and it will. But there's a second answer that is not a reminder so much as a promise.

"But whoever endures to the end will be saved." Everything that happens will fall short of forcing us to give up our faith. It will be terrible. It will be disappointing. It may even hurt, the things the world will do to Christians. But it won't be overwhelming. It not only will be possible to endure it all, but for those who do remain faithful, they will have God's best. But the endurance must be to the end. And with the Holy Spirit's help, we all will endure.

During the '60s there was a slogan that appeared here and there. It is appropriate as we look at signs that may lead us to believe that the end is near. Whether it is or isn't near is not nearly as important as this tiny bit of advice: whatever the future brings, you can trust Jesus to see you through it. Therefore, KEEP THE FAITH, BABY! It's a faith worth keeping.

Walter H. Mees, Jr.
Palisades Lutheran Church
Culver City, California

NOVEMBER 24, 1991

Last Sunday after Pentecost, Christ the King

Lessons:

Lutheran:	Dan. 7:13-14	Rev. 1:4b-8	John 18:33-37
Roman Catholic:	Dan. 7:13-14	Rev. 1:5-8	John 18:33b-37
Episcopal:	Dan. 7:9-14	Rev. 1:1-8	John 18:33-37
Pres/Meth/UCC:	Jer. 23:1-6	Rev. 1:4b-8	John 18:33-37

Introductions to the Lessons

(1) *Daniel 7:9-14* (**Epis**); *7:13-14* (**Luth**). God, the "Ancient of Days," sat on his throne for judgment of the nations. Satan, the beast, was put to death. At this time there came one "like a son of man," interpreted by Christians as God's Son. To him was given an eternal kingship.

(2) *Jeremiah 23:1-6* (**Pres/Meth/UCC**). Through Jeremiah the Lord accuses the shepherds of his people of scattering his sheep. He also promises to gather his sheep and give them a shepherd-king, a son of David. This son will be known as "The Lord is our righteousness."

Lesson 2

Revelation 1:1-8 (**Epis**); *1:4b-8* (**Luth/Pres/Meth/UCC**). An angel gives John a revelation of end times. In his opening greeting to the seven churches in Asia, Christ is referred to as the king of kings; and by the cross he made us a kingdom of priests to serve God.

Gospel

John 18:33-37 (**Luth/Epis/Pres/Meth/UCC**). Jesus stands before Pilate for a private interview. The Jews are calling for the death sentence but Pilate is not sure this should be the verdict. He asks Jesus whether he is the king of the Jews and what he has done that he should have been arrested. Jesus explains that his kingship is not of the world and that he came to the world to witness to the truth.

Theme: Like Pilate, we all must face Jesus sometime.

Thought for the day: Pilate did all he could to avoid facing Jesus. He sent Jesus to Herod, sought to give him back to the Jews, wanted to trade him for Barabbas. But it was all to no avail. Finally, he had to face Jesus. Like Pilate, every human who ever lives will one

144

day also face Jesus. May our "day of trial," unlike that of Pilate, be a wonderful audience with our Lord and King!

Prayer of meditation: Lord Jesus, you came to be our King, and to inaugurate a kingdom in the hearts of your people that would never end. On some days, I know myself to be part of that kingdom. On others, I feel more like Pilate, wondering aloud what truth is, looking for ways to avoid the confrontation you set before me. Help me have more days like the former, fewer like the latter, so that at the end, I might be found faithful to you. Amen.

Call to worship: I was glad when they said unto me, "Let us go into the house of the Lord." Let us come before his presence with thanksgiving for the greatness of his love for us. For our God is a great God; and a great King above all gods. He speaks, and all the earth obeys. Blessed is the name of the Lord!

Prayer of adoration: "Jesus, we adore you, lay our lives before you. How we love you." As we think, O Lord Jesus, of your great love for us which moved you to purchase each of us for your kingdom with your very own blood on the cross, we cannot but raise our voices in praise and adoration to you as King of Kings. While your kingdom is not of this world, dear Jesus, we who are in this world just now give you thanks that you have won us for your kingdom and will bring us safely into it one day, even as we have a glimpse of it here and now through your precious church. Amen.

Prayer of confession: O Lord our God and King, by his death and resurrection your Son Jesus purchased and won me as a member of his great kingdom, though I did not deserve such an honor and all too frequently live as though I belong to a different kingdom. Help me when I fail him, and assist me in more often living as he wants all the members of his kingdom to live. Amen.

Prayer of dedication of gifts and self: King Jesus, we offer before your throne of grace a portion of the worldly goods with which you have blessed us. We offer them to you for use in your kingdom work, and as signs of our gratitude for all you have done for us, particularly as you gave your life for our sins. We pray in your name and for your sake. Amen.

Sermon title: Encountering the truth.

Sermon thesis: Pilate encountered the truth on the day he sat in judgment over Jesus, and found himself to be on trial. By his refusal to treat Jesus fairly, he failed himself miserably. How often do we do the same, as we too ignore God's truth and do what the world or our own desires lead us to instead? Show yourself to be a person who is "of the truth." Hear — and heed — Jesus.

Hymn for the day: *"Christ is the King."* George Kennedy Allen Bell (1883-1958) held a Doctor of Divinity degree from Oxford and was highly regarded as a poet. Ordained to the Church of England, he held a number of posts, the last of which was Dean of Canterbury.

Announcements for next week: (Thanksgiving Day)

Sermon title: Learning to Show the Gratitude We Feel.
Sermon theme: Some people really know when to be grateful.
Sermon summary: Thanksgiving Day is a good time to remember that being grateful, while important, isn't the whole story. We need to remember to express our gratitude as well.

Announcements for next week: (First Sunday in Advent)

Sermon title: There's a New World Coming
Sermon theme: The coming of the new requires the passing away of the old.
Sermon summary: The crumbling of old worlds is frightening, but nothing less is required by the coming of God's Savior. The Kingdom cannot exist along side our personal kingdom. The Kingdom of God calls for a radical commitment from us.

Children's object talk:

Who Judged Jesus?

Objects: Five signs each of red cards saying "guilty" and green ones saying "innocent."
Lesson: Being a judge is not very easy — especially when the one being tried is Jesus.
Outline: 1. Practice deciding guilt or innocence.
2. See Jesus as not guilty, though we need him to die.
3. Be grateful Jesus died and sorry for those who killed him.

GOOD MORNING, KIDS. TODAY I'd like to have five volunteers to be on a jury. Your job will be to hold up signs — either red ones or green ones — if you think people are either guilty or innocent.

Our first accused is Jim. Jim is accused of being a boy. All who agree, raise the red sign for "guilty." Those who disagree, raise the green sign for "innocent." Next is Susan. She is accused of having blue eyes. Look carefully, and raise the sign that indicates either guilt or innocence.

Our final defendant is Jesus. He is accused of being our King and of wanting to help us live happier lives. What do you think? Is Jesus guilty or innocent? Remember, if he is guilty, he will have to die on the cross, but if he's innocent, he goes free and we have no savior. Are you ready to vote? Let's see the cards.

Wrap up the sermon based on the voting, reminding kids that though Jesus is our king and did die for us, he was also innocent of wrongdoing. Also point out that though Pilate condemned Jesus, we should feel sorry for him and the Jewish leaders and even be grateful that God used their weakness to bring salvation to all the world, including ourselves.

The sermon:

Encountering the Truth

Hymns:
Beginning of worship: Ten Thousand Times Ten Thousand
Sermon hymn: Lord of Life and King of Glory
End of worship: For All the Blessings of the Year

Scripture: John 18:33-37

Sermon Text: *"For this I was born, and for this I have come into the world, to bear witness to the truth. Everyone who is of the truth hears my voice."* v. 37

"WHY WAS IT THAT SO FEW UNDERSTOOD JESUS?" the student asked the teacher. "The Pharisees and scribes constantly opposed him. His disciples often seemed confused by his teaching, and still others suggested that he was possessed with demons. Even his own family feared for his mental health."

The teacher replied, "Once there was a wedding couple who brought in the finest fiddlers and banjo players to entertain their guests immediately after the ceremony. The music was so captivating that soon everyone, young and old alike, began to dance. The people flung their bodies first one way and then another. The church was filled with joy.

"The men drove by the church building in their new luxury automobile with the windows rolled up and loud music blaring from their car radio. They could not hear a single sound from outside the automobile. When they saw people jumping around they stopped the car, shaking their heads at the sight. 'What a bunch of weirdos,' the driver said to his companion. 'See how they fling themselves about. I tell you the folks that go to that church are crazy.' "

The teacher paused after finishing his story. "That is the conclusion people draw when they cannot hear the music to which others are dancing." ["The Mad Dancers," from *Stories for the Journey*, by William R. White, Minneapolis: Augsburg, 1988 p. 63]

Jesus is difficult for us to understand, and maybe it is because we don't hear the same music that he hears — yet. St. Paul says something similar when he avers that though now we see as through a mirror dimly, the day will come when we see Jesus face to face.

Until that time, however, we along with every person who has lived or will ever live must face the same dilemma that faced Pontius Pilate: We must answer the question, "Who is Jesus?" And though Pilate's answer eventually sealed Jesus' fate to die on the cross, our own answer is as important for each of us as Pilate's was for the whole world, for "whoever believes in Jesus shall not perish, but have everlasting life." Who is Jesus? The time will come when you decide what your answer is to that question. It may as well be now.

Pilate did not have a particularly good time as procurator of Palestine. Some of his key decisions were bad mistakes, made mostly because he just didn't care to get to know the people he was supposed to govern. The first foolish thing he did was to try to force the Jews to accept the presence of small busts of the Emperor on the standards his soldiers carried. He was forced to back down when he realized that the Jewish leaders were willing to die rather than give in. He, on the other hand, wasn't willing to kill them. So he lost round one.

Pilate's next problem came when he used money from the Temple treasury to improve Jerusalem's water supply. Certainly, it was a needed public works project. Even the Temple benefited by the new abundance of water the aqueduct brought. Still, the ungrateful populace rioted against him, so that he had to send his soldiers in plain clothes among the crowd. At someone's signal they turned on the mob, stabbing or clubbing many to death. Since he had been sent there to prevent trouble, not cause it, Pilate lost round two by becoming vulnerable to a bad report to the emperor.

The third thing Pilate did wrong was to have some shields made for his soldiers that bore the name of Emperor Tiberius. The Jews protested that since the Emperor claimed to be a god, the shields amounted to having the name of some other god flaunted in God's own city. They appealed to Pilate, who stood firm. So then they sent word to Caesar, and Tiberius ordered Pilate to get rid of the shields. Round three was a definite loss for Pilate.

Then came this Jesus. Who was he anyway? Some said a prophet. Others called him king. The Sanhedrin said he deserved death, and even Pilate's wife sent advice. Clearly Pilate was troubled as he sought some means or other of avoiding a decision. But he couldn't avoid one. Herod sent Jesus back. The crowd had no sympathy after a vicious scourging, and then preferred Barabbas the robber. He would have to pass judgment, and if he set Jesus free, it would be round four and maybe a KO, once word of the Jews' anger reached Tiberius. So Pilate found Jesus guilty of being a king, never knowing how very correct he was. And while he avoided Tiberius' wrath in this case, he made sure his name would be known by millions of Christians as long as time continues to wind down. In order to avoid ignominy, Pilate gained infamy.

But things could have been worse. There is no tradition to tell us either way, but Pilate need not have remained God's enemy for the rest of his life. Having once misjudged Jesus, Pilate had plenty of time to reconsider, repent and come to faith later. He may not have done so. But then again, he may have. And there's nothing we can do about Pilate today. But there is something each of us here today can do about Jesus' claim to bear witness to the truth. We can listen to what he has to say, and we can believe he is the King — of the Jews and of all people.

Jesus stands before you today just as he stood before Pilate long ago, and the question is the very same one. Are you, Jesus, the King of the Jews? More importantly, are you my King too? As with Pilate, we must provide our own answer to the question, for though he is the King, he refuses to be our King against our will. But he also refuses to go away and leave the question unanswered. Each of us, at one time or another, will answer the question for ourselves. If you haven't done so, please give your answer today: "Yes, Jesus. You are my King. Come into my heart; control my life; show me how you want me to live. And do it beginning right now."

Walter H. Mees, Jr.
Palisades Lutheran Church
Culver City, California

NOVEMBER 28, 1991

Thanksgiving Day (U.S.)

Lessons:

Lutheran:	Deut. 8:1-10	Phil. 4:6-20	Luke 17:11-19
Pres/Meth/UCC:	Joel 2:21-27	I Tim. 2:1-7	Matt. 6:25-33

Introductions to the Lessons

Lesson 1

(1) *Deuteronomy 8:1-10* (**Luth**). In his last message to his people before they enter Canaan, Moses commands them to keep God's laws. They are to remember how good God has been to them since leaving Egypt and now he is bringing them to a wonderful land of plenty.

(2) *Joel 2:21-27* (**Pres/Meth/UCC**). Yahweh is in the midst of his people. Therefore, they can rejoice that he will make the fields produce an abundant harvest and they will enjoy plenty and prosperity.

Lesson 2

(1) *Philippians 4:6-20* (**Luth**). Paul urges the Philippian church to include thanksgiving in their prayers. He has learned to be content with material things whether they are plenty or scarce. For the gift the church sent him, he expresses gratitude. He assures them that God is able to supply their every need.

(2) *I Timothy 2:1-7* (**Pres/Meth/UCC**). Prayers of thanksgiving are to be offered for everyone including top governmental officials. The one to be most grateful for is Christ, who saved us by giving himself as a ransom for all.

Gospel

(1) *Luke 17:11-19* (**Luth**). Ten men with the terminal disease of leprosy begged Jesus to heal them. He did, but only one returned to say thanks. This amazed Jesus that so many would be unappreciative. The grateful one was a Samaritan.

(2) *Matthew 6:25-33* (**Pres/Meth?UCC**). In the Sermon on the Mount Jesus taught his disciples that they could live a life free from worry about material things of life. He called attention to how God fed the birds and clothed the flowers. God knows we have physical needs. If we will place him first, he will fill our material wants.

Theme: Some people really know when to be grateful.

Thought for the day: When we read about ten lepers whom Jesus

151

healed, nine of whom did not return to give thanks and one who did, it is very easy for us to give all our attention to the nine who did not return and virtually ignore the one who did. This story of Jesus is a lesson for us about how we ought to live, yet we nearly always turn it into a lesson about how not to live instead. The truly grateful person is the one who knows when and to whom to give thanks. With a little thought, that could be you and I.

Prayer of meditation: Gratitude. Lord, I guess that one word sums up as well as any what you are looking for in your people. Moved by gratitude, I would be more patient with spouse, children or parents. Moved by gratitude, I would do my best at work or school. Moved by gratitude, I would rejoice at every opportunity to worship and serve you. Help me to, more and more, day by day, live in gratitude to you. In Jesus' name I pray. Amen.

Call to worship: "Ho, everyone who thirsts, come to the waters; and he who has no money, come, buy and eat! Seek the Lord while he may be found, call upon him while he is near. He will have mercy and abundantly pardon; he will heal all your diseases, and forgive all your transgressions." Praise the name of the Lord!

Prayer of adoration: "The eyes of all wait upon you, O Lord, and you give them their food in your good time. You open your hand to satisfy the desire of every living thing." Again your people gather, O Lord, to give you thanks for your bountiful goodness which provides food and water in abundance so that all who live might eat and drink enough. We have not, however, managed to share your bounty with all the world's people. The result of our failure is that not all can gather with us this day in thanksgiving to you. Help us show our thanks by sharing more effectively so that everyone who lives will be able soon to praise your glorious name. Amen.

Prayer of confession: Great God and Father of us all, when your Son was approached by ten lepers on that day so long ago, he was able to give them their heart's desire and he did so. Very often, people come to us seeking what we can give, and we in our ignorance or selfishness do not. Forgive us for those times even as you enable us to love others as Jesus loved us. In his name and for his sake. Amen.

Prayer of dedication of gifts and self: O Christ who brought wholeness to the lepers, you have also offered wholeness to our own lives.

As we bring these gifts to your altar, we would be reminded that they are but a token of what you first gave us. Use them to help others and to enable us to share in that great work. We pray in your name and for your sake. Amen.

Sermon title: Learning to Show the Gratitude We Feel

Sermon thesis: Thanksgiving Day is a good time to remember that being grateful, while important, isn't the whole story. We need to remember to express our gratitude. It would be unfair to say that the other nine lepers were not grateful — they were probably just so excited to be healed that they forgot to say thanks in their impatience to have the healing proven by the priests, so as to hurry home to rejoice with their families. We can just imagine each of them answering their loved ones' questions about how they got healed, stopping in perplexity, and confessing, "And I didn't even say 'thank you'!" Those poor unnamed nine have lived in infamy in the pages of Scripture ever since, all for the lack of a thank you!

Hymn for the day: *"Praise and thanksgiving."* This hymn was written to meet the need for harvest thanksgiving hymns that remind us to share our gifts with others. It speaks of showing our gratitude through sharing. (See September 22 above for information on Albert F. Bayly.)

Children's object talk:

Thanksgiving

Objects: Eyeglasses, a picture of a loved one, a small cross.
Lesson: We all have things for which to be thankful, but the most important of all is Jesus.
Outline:1. Explain why you are thankful for first two items.
2. Have kids share things they're grateful for.
3. Explain how the cross reminds you of Jesus, the most important thing we have to be thankful for.

GOOD MORNING, KIDS. TODAY I've brought some things that I'm thankful for. First, there are my eyeglasses. Because my vision is quite poor without them, I am very grateful that God has given people the ability to make eyeglasses that give me good vision. If God hadn't done that, I'd be very limited in the things I could do. Next I have a picture of my son, Robby. Whenever I think of him, I'm so thankful to God and my wife that he was born. We were pretty old when Robby came along, and maybe that has made me extra thankful for him.

Can any of you now tell me why you are thankful this Thanksgiving Day? (Get some suggestions from the kids. Maybe someone will, prompted by the cross you haven't discussed, say something about Jesus. If so, great! If not, wrap up as follows.)

Thanks for sharing all your reasons to give thanks, kids, but did you notice that we missed one? It's this cross I brought. The cross reminds us on Thanksgiving and every day that among all the wonderful reasons for thanking God, Jesus our savior is the best reason of all. Jesus loves us, and for that we give thanks!

The sermon:

Learning to Show the Gratitude We Feel

Hymns:
Beginning of worship: Come, Ye Thankful People Come
Sermon hymn: We Plow the Fields, and Scatter
End of worship: Now Thank We All Our God

Scripture: Luke 17:11-19

Sermon Text: *"Then one of them, when he saw that he was healed, turned back, praising God with a loud voice; and he fell on his face at Jesus' feet, giving him thanks."* vs. 15 and 16

THERE IS A CUTE SCENE IN ONE OF THE VIDEOTAPES that my son likes to watch before going to bed. In it, the youngest child has obviously been learning the use of "magic words." She turns the lesson on everyone else by correcting parents and older siblings alike. "Pass the milk," says one of them. "Pass the milk, what?" prompts the little girl. "Pass the milk, please" responds the one who has been corrected. "Pass the stupid butter," we hear a few lines later. Again comes the prompting from the youngest: "Pass the stupid butter, what?" And the response: "Please pass the stupid butter."

Many of us have come here today as the result of just this sort of early training. Each Thanksgiving Day, it has been our custom to pile into the family car and go off to church where we give God an annual thanks for all God has done for us during the previous year. It wouldn't be Thanksgiving if we didn't go. The turkey wouldn't taste the same, the football games would lose their attraction. Thanksgiving wouldn't be the same. And that's not all bad. We make a ritual out of things that are good to do as a way of not forgetting to do them. How many of us do not have a morning ritual — a certain sequence of things we do each morning? And how often does an interruption mean we forget something, or at least feel as though we had? Ritual is valuable and comfortable for most of us most of the time.

So we make a ritual of saying "please" and "thank you." We make a habit out of churchgoing. T.V. watching, even billpaying. I do it on Saturday night when I write our offering check. Ritual provides continuity, helps us remember, can even be comfortable. But sometimes ritual is forgotten in the excitement of the moment, and for nine of the lepers who met Jesus that day, that I suspect is what happened. Only one out of ten so remembered his manners as to return to Jesus, fall on his face at Jesus' feet, and give heartfelt and sincere thanks. Only one.

But he's the one who is our example today. Have you heard of the man who had formed the habit of writing "thank you" in the lower left corner of the checks he wrote to pay bills? He would write a check to the electric utility or phone company, and while writing "thank you" in the corner, he would think of all the times that month he'd enjoyed turning on lights, cooking his food, and phoning friends. He would write his monthly mortgage check and give thanks for the roof over his head. He would pay his water bill, and while writing "thank you" in the corner, he'd remember that the water tasted bad lately and wonder what harmful chemicals it contained; but he'd also remind himself that only a few short years before, his forebears had to thaw out the well so it would pump in winter and worry about it drying up in summer. Even when he was not that happy writing a check, as when he paid his income tax in April, he made himself write "thank you" on the check as a way of reminding himself to feel grateful for the benefits that our American democracy provides. He had made gratitude a habit.

Possibly, the one leper was such a person who, even when suffering such a dreadful disease, taught himself to be grateful for what he did have. Thus being in practice at saying "thank you," he came back to thank Jesus and be remembered forever as the one in ten who gave thanks. Possibly.

But you know, it doesn't really matter how that Samaritan came to have the presence of mind to pause for a moment of thanks before hurrying to show his loved ones his good fortune. The important thing is that he did so. He remembered to give thanks. And so have we. We have come here today to thank God for all the good things in our lives; to thank God for life itself; to thank God finally for Jesus our Savior. Having done so, and having remembered those less fortunate than ourselves by preparing an offering to be shared with them, we bring that offering as a sign of our continuing gratitude for blessings granted and blessings to come.

And as we do so, let us not be too hard on the other nine. After all, they may also serve as a reminder of the percentage of the time that we forget to say thank you, forget to be grateful. None of us is grateful all the time. Hopefully, we do better than 10%, But whatever our story, may that of the nine and the one be an incentive for us to do better. Maybe we could even have days of Thanksgiving every day of our lives, as we remember how much like those lepers we are. For before Jesus came into our hearts, our lives, like theirs, were over before they had even begun. But with and in him, we live new lives each day in anticipation of the day that our lives will be really new and we are together with him in the life to come.

May the Lord hasten that day; and in the meantime, may we not forget the one leper and the nine, and may we be grateful for Jesus and his love for us.

Walter H. Mees, Jr.
Palisades Lutheran Church
Culver City, California

DECEMBER 1, 1991

First Sunday in Advent

Lessons:

Lutheran:	Jer. 33:14-16	I Thess. 3:9-13	Luke 21:25-36
Roman Catholic:	Jer. 33:14-16	I Thess. 3:12-4:2	Luke 21:25-28, 34-36
Episcopal:	Zech. 14:4-9	I Thess. 3:9-13	Luke 21:25-31
Pres/Meth/UCC:	Jer. 33:14-16	I Thess. 3:9-13	Luke 21:25-36

Introductions to the Lessons

Lesson 1

(1) *Jeremiah 33:14-16* (**Luth/Pres/Meth/UCC**) In fulfillment of Jeremiah's prediction, the nation and Temple were destroyed in 586 B.C. and the people were taken as slaves to Babylon. In the midst of this calamity, a promise is made to the Exiles that the Lord will produce a son of David who will by his just reign bring back Israel's glory and prosperity.

(2) *Zechariah 14:4-9* (**Epis**) The nations will plunder Jerusalem and the nation. The people will be scattered. Then the Lord will come and be king over all the earth. When he comes the nation will enjoy continuous daylight and warmth.

Lesson 2

(1) *I Thessalonians 3:9-13* (**Luth/Epis/Pres/Meth/UCC**) Paul is looking forward to Christ's second coming. Until he comes, Paul prays that the church will increase in love and live in holiness.

Gospel

Luke 21:25-36 (**Luth/Pres/Meth/UCC**) *21:25-31* (**Epis**) When world conditions are at their worst, Christ promises to return. As we know summer is coming when a tree yields its leaves, so we will know by these conditions that Christ's advent is near. Followers of Christ are urged to watch and pray in preparation for his coming.

Theme: The coming of the new requires the passing away of the old.

Thought for the day: We turn our eyes toward Bethlehem, hoping and praying for a new outbreak of love and peace among us, but it can never happen until we are willing to place our lives in God's hands that we might be reshaped, remolded, and fashioned into a new and different creation.

Prayer of meditation: From the moment of his birth, O God, he divided the people of the earth: those who could see the possibilities and those who could only cling to the past. Let us be more like the shepherds, angels, and kings who savored the richness of a new life with God and less like Herod who could only measure his own personal cost. Help us to choose well — to choose not what has been but what may be under God's ever-new reign. Amen.

Call to worship: "In the beginning was the Word, and the Word was with God, and the Word was God. He was in the beginning with God. . . What has come into being in him was life, and the life was the light of all people. The light shines in the darkness, and the darkness did not overcome it." (John 1:1-5)

Prayer of adoration: Already we can hear the distant song breaking out, O God: he comes! When we are too busy and self-absorbed for our lives to connect with those of others, he comes. When we are full of despair and have had all confidence in our value as people shaken, he comes. When we are lonely, lost, or in search of some purpose for our days, he comes. He comes in judgment and in love, to bind and to loose, to cut down and to raise up. He comes, he comes. And we would receive him. Amen.

Prayer of confession: How curious it is, O God, that you should come to people who have sought so much to go it on our own. We fancy ourselves to be self-made, independent, and able to meet our every need. We have clung to these illusions though our resources have failed us time and time again. We have scheduled a frantic pace to our days and rushed to maintain our momentum while never slowing to hear that still, small voice. And yet you do come, breaking our hearts and lives open and healing our broken spirits. Give us the will to call upon you in our need. Give us the words we long to speak. Come, our loving God, come! Amen.

Prayer of dedication of gifts and self: Our God, soon we shall present our gifts to family and friends. These are days for gathering gifts for those we love. Let our love not be narrow or confined, however, but let our love pour out to our church and its ministries, to those for whom we know their needs if not their faces, and for the causes which have breadth and meaning. Accept these gifts in that spirit, that our love might be more and more an expression of your great love in Christ Jesus, our Lord. Amen.

Sermon title: There's a New World Coming

Sermon thesis: The crumbling of old worlds is frightening, but nothing less is required by the coming of God's Savior. The Kingdom cannot exist along side all our personal kingdoms. The Kingdom of God calls for a radical commitment from us.

Hymn for the day: *"The day is surely drawing near."* This hymn, which first appeared as an anonymous German hymn about 1565, is based on the Latin hymn "Dies irae, dies Illa," an extended hymn about the last judgment. Bartholomaus Ringwaldt (1522-*c.* 1600), a German pastor who served for some 30 years at Langfeld near Sonnenburg, Brandenburg, revised the hymn and published it in 1586. The hymn had much use during the Thirty Years' War (1618-1648) when many were convinced the Last Day was at hand.

Announcements for next week:

  Sermon title: A Faithful Waiting

  Sermon theme: Faithful waiting requires preparation

  Sermon summary: Being called to wait in faith means doing neither more nor less than we are called to do. Faithful waiting requires a proper balance of preparation and trust.

Children's object talk:

Signs Of Christmas

Objects: Advent Wreath

Lesson: The Advent Wreath is the church's sign of Jesus' coming.

Outline: 1. There are many signs that Christmas will soon be here.
2. The church puts out its own signs.
3. The candles of the Advent Wreath are lighted as signs of Jesus' coming.

CHRISTMAS DAY IS NOT FAR OFF. Did you know that? Of course you did. And how is it that you knew Christmas is coming? You know because of all the signs that tell us. The stores are already decorated with tinsel and colorful displays. The newspaper is full of advertisements about toys and clothes that are on sale. And I was at the mall this weekend and I saw that Santa Claus had come to town to start meeting with all of the good boys and girls who have lists of things they want for Christmas. So we know Christmas is coming — there are lots of signs.

Having signs to let us know what is going to happen is a good idea, and so the church has put up some of its own signs. We have decorated the church with garlands and candles, and we have a tree with special decorations on it. But one of my favorite signs that Christmas is coming is the Advent Wreath that is sitting right over there. How many candles are on the wreath? There are five, four around the circle and a large white one in the middle. Do you know how the wreath reminds us that Christmas is coming? Well, there are four Sundays before Christmas, and we light one of the purple candles each Sunday. This morning, we lighted the first candle, and next week we will light two of them and leave two unlighted so we will remember that we have two Sundays left before Christmas. And we will light the other candles on the next two Sundays so that the wreath is sort of like a calendar for us. The more candles we have burning, the closer it is to Christmas. The large white candle in the middle is the one we will light on Christmas Eve.

The wreath is a sign, a very special sign, that reminds us that soon it will be time for us to celebrate Jesus' birth, and when you come into the sanctuary in the next few weeks, remember that Christmas is getting closer and closer.

The sermon:

There's A New World Coming

Hymns:
> Beginning of worship: Watchman, Tell Us of the Night
> Sermon hymn: Let All Mortal Flesh Keep Silence
> End of worship: Lift Up Your Heads, Ye Mighty Gates

Scripture: Luke 21:25-36

Sermon text: *"Now when these things begin to take place, stand up and raise your heads, because your redemption is drawing near."* v. 28

THERE'S A NEW WORLD COMING . . . that is the stuff of Advent. These weeks which lead up to the manger are full of anticipation of the birth of a Savior, the beginning of a new order, ever fresh hope in what is to come. There is an electricity in the air that grows stronger every day as Christmas nears. It is partly the commercial aspects of Christmas that have the children (and the child in all of us) looking forward with eagerness to that special morning, but none of us are so cynical to suppose that the anticipation is only materialistic. No, Advent is about spiritual anticipation mostly. And if there is an electricity growing out there in the shopping malls, there is something even stronger happening inside these doors and especially inside our hearts. Christmas is coming. There's a new world coming.

Which is the bad news, of course. Because if there is a new world coming, then the old song follows, "This one's coming to an end." And that is the focus this morning as we worship on this first Sunday of the Advent season. The scripture lessons assigned to this early portion of Advent are not about shepherds and angels and tiny babes. Instead the Gospel reading assigned to this Sunday is that frightening selection out of Luke about signs and unraveling mysteries and especially about the end of the current age. And it is not an innocent and peaceful scene but is instead a grim and even terrifying threat that looms over the reader. There's a new world coming; this one's coming to an end.

Starting the road to the Bethlehem manger with such a grim first step is a good reminder of what we glean from every page of the Gospel: "Unless a grain of wheat falls to the earth and dies . . ." Or in our everyday talk we know that there can be no growth without pain, that grasping something new means releasing something old, or in the case of Christmas, that new birth means the end of an old style of life. It is a part of the Gospel message, and we have heard it often enough, and we rather believe it . . . but when it comes time to deal with this hard reality, we struggle. Even when the old ways are inadequate, and even though they may not be working for us, they are at the very least familiar. The new that is ahead, as promising as it might be, is not known and it is a tough trade of the familiar for that which is unknown.

Yet, is that not the way of any new structure to our lives? I remember the weeks prior to the birth of our daughter. As my wife's pregnancy progressed, she found that she was having more and more trouble sleeping. When she asked her doctor about this, he shrugged it off saying that it was normal and concluded that it was nature's way of getting mothers ready for the years of wakeful nights that come with a child in the home. He was right — nights in which we could get eight hours of sleep seem to be only a vague memory of a former life. The coming of the new means a passing away of the old.

161

And so it is with the proclamation of the coming Kingdom of God. This text, so full of political overtones and global conflicts, speaks to the marriage of the religious and the secular in our world. To have a vision of a peaceable Kingdom, if we have any real expectation that such a Kingdom shall ever come to pass, requires that we cling less and less to the status quo which we have come to know so well. As citizens of one of the world's superpowers, we are forced to wrestle with how the nations of the world can ever live in peace and harmony without our willingness to cede our clear "advantage" of military superiority. If we know that the old way has not been working and if we would welcome a new way for the people of the earth to live together, the risks of such a movement do seem severe. Nothing less than trust is required among nations whose relationships have been marked by everything but trust.

Still, it is not impossible. In recent years the Wall has come down which had kept old enemies at bay for decades. In the middle of this chaotic turn of events, new possibilities cried out for a reordering of the affairs of nations. The same might be said for every hotspot in the globe. The same turmoil which can be so terrifying holds the seeds of a new way of life if people can only risk a release of the past.

While the world's political struggles are a part of the text's message, of course, they are not the only ground for understanding the text. We know something of the hold that the past has upon us in personal and intimate ways. Forgiveness is really a release of old worlds and it is not an easy matter. Old hurts linger and fester and are not easily forgotten. Ancient slights live on and prevent the healing newness to enter our lives. Good pastors and able therapists will agree, I think, that sometimes the only authentic setting in which healing can occur is in the cathartic terror in which old hurts and angers are faced and then released.

Advent is a time of new possibilities. We do not proclaim the birth of a Savior who has come into this world to give it a stamp of imprimatur. The Christ whose coming we herald comes to redeem the world and to call us into new life under the reign of God. If we understand this, we will surely be shaken and terrified.

The call, however, is for us to raise our heads, let go of the past, and understand that our redemption is drawing ever nearer.

Gary L. Walling
Heights Christian Church
Shaker Heights, Ohio

DECEMBER 8, 1991

Second Sunday in Advent

Lessons:

Lutheran:	Mal. 3:1-4	Phil. 1:3-11	Luke 3:1-6
Roman Catholic:	Bar. 5:1-9	Phil. 1:4-6, 8-11	Luke 3:1-6
Episcopal:	Bar. 5:1-9	Phil. 1:1-11	Luke 3:1-6
Pres/Meth/UCC:	Mal. 3:1-4	Phil. 1:3-11	Luke 3:1-6

Introductions to the Lessons

Lesson 1

(1) *Malachi 3:1-4* (**Luth/Pres/Meth/UCC**) The Israelites held in Babylon as slaves have returned and the Temple was re-built. Now they look forward to Yahweh's coming to the new Temple. His coming will be preceded by a messenger to prepare the people. He will do this by cleansing the priests and their sacrifices. Christians see this messenger in the person of John the Baptizer who prepared the way for Jesus.

(2) *Baruch 5:1-9* (**Epis**) Israel is urged to take off the garments of sorrow and to rejoice because the Lord will bring his people home from captivity in Babylon. He will bless his people with mercy, righteousness, and peace.

Lesson 2

Philippians 1:3-11 (**Luth/Pres/Meth/UCC**) *1:1-11* (**Epis**) Philippians is Paul's thank-you letter for a gift the church sent him. He expresses his love for them and thanks God for them. While appreciative of their present love, he prays that their love may become more and more mature to the end that when Christ returns they may be pure and blameless.

Gospel

Luke 3:1-6 (**Luth/Epis/Pres/Meth/UCC**) The focus is upon John the Baptizer who calls for a baptism for the forgiveness of sins. His ministry is a fulfillment of the promise in Isaiah 40. His mission in life is to prepare the way for the Messiah.

Theme: Faithful waiting requires preparation.

Thought for the day: Like St. Francis, it is always a good prayer that we will have the strength and faith to do those things that are in our power, the trust to lay aside those things which are beyond our abilities, and the wisdom to know which is which.

Prayer of meditation: Teach us, our God, how to make some fruitful use of our waiting lest it be idle and aimless. Remind us that you have other children in our world for whom these days are like any other: consumed in the pursuit of food or shelter, fleeing from the ravages of war, or suffering under the strains of disease. Make us instruments of your care, your peace, your comfort, in ways that give meaning to our waiting. Let us be servants of your children who are in need in these days that we might someday hear the words, "Well done, good and faithful servants." Amen.

Call to worship: "There was a man sent from God whose name was John. He came as a witness to testify to the light, so that all might believe through him. He himself was not the light, but he came to testify to the light. The true light, which enlightens everyone, was coming into the world." (John 1:6-9)

Prayer of adoration: These are days for adoration, our God. Our hearts know it. Our spirits know it and cry out for the voice and harmony that would make a song of the joy and love that comes into our lives anew. Let the joy of these days be infectious — in our lives and through us into the lives of others. In the name of him who was born in a manger, we pray. Amen.

Prayer of confession: O God, we look at ourselves and we see it. There is darkness in our lives, enmity in our relationships with others, and too little trust in our dealings with you. Sin we have known with too much familiarity, and we have continued on our wayward paths without searching for new and better directions. And now we confess to you what you already know: our souls ache and our hearts have been pierced. In this time of your coming, enter into the wastelands we have created. Make the paths we travel straight and level the ground of our being. And give us eyes to see the salvation you lay before us. In the name of the Bethlehem Babe we pray. Amen.

Prayer of dedication of gifts and self: O God, the giver of every good and perfect gift, these are days of plenty for us: trees laden with gifts, kitchens filled with fresh baked goods, and dinner tables weighted under platters of holiday food. Our homes play host to family and dear friends, and our churches take on a special life and vitality. Help us to remember that there are those in our community and world whose needs and wants are as great as our abundance. Receive the gifts we bring — such a small portion of what we possess — and use them for the sake of others. And use us as well in the ministry of our church, in the proclamation of peace and love, and in the caring for every child of the earth claimed by Christ as a brother and sister. Amen.

Sermon title: A Faithful Waiting

Sermon thesis: Being called to wait in faith means doing neither more nor less than we are called to do. Faithful waiting requires a proper balance of preparation and trust.

Hymn for the day: *"On Jordan's banks."* The distinguished scholar and Latin author, Charles Coffin (1676-1749), was born in northern France. Except for a few years as rector of the University of Paris, he spent most of his life as a member of the faculty of the College of Beauvais. His collected poems filled two volumes. The hymn speaks of joyful waiting and preparation for the coming of Christ.

Announcements for next week:

Sermon title: What Joy is This?

Sermon theme: God has a passion about the way we live.

Sermon summary: Advent carries themes of warning and judgment, but rightly heard, even these are cause for joy. To believe in God's anger and judgment is to believe in God's ultimate commitment to creation.

Children's object talk:

Preparations Have To Be Made

Objects: A box with slips of paper inside
Lesson: Before our guests arrive, we have to get ready.
Outline:

      1. We make preparations when people come to visit us.

      2. Christmas is a time when we celebrate Jesus' coming.

      3. Advent is a time to get ready.

I HAVE A BOX WITH ME TODAY and I want each of you to draw out a slip of paper. Each of the papers has a job written down on it. Now, tell me the job that is marked on your slip of paper (putting clean sheets on the guest bed, putting towels in the guest bath, vacuuming the house, going to the grocery store, cooking and baking, etc.).

If your family was going to do all of these things, what do you think would be about to happen? At my house if we were doing all of these things at the same time, it would mean one thing: somebody was coming to visit us. Maybe it would be grandma and grandpa or a special friend, but somebody important would be on their way to town. And we would want everything to be just right for their visit.

A long time ago, somebody went around the country telling everybody to get ready because Jesus was going to come. His name was John the Baptist and he tried to get people ready. Of course, he was not so much interested in vacuuming the manger and cooking some big meals. He knew what would really make Jesus feel welcome. He told the people that if they really wanted to be ready when God's Son came, they should be honest with one another and share food and clothing with people who needed it. He was trying to tell them to be nice and to care about one another because that is what would make Jesus really feel welcome.

And that is what we will do today if we want to be ready for Christmas — to try to get ready for Jesus by being nicer to each other and being honest and sharing more. If we can do those kinds of things, I think Jesus will feel right at home with us.

The sermon: Hurry Up + Wait

A Faithful Waiting

Hymns:
> Beginning of worship: O Come, O Come, Immanuel
> Sermon hymn: On Jordan's Bank, the Baptist's Cry
> End of worship: Savior of the Nations, Come

Scripture: Luke 3:1-6

Sermon text: *"The voice of one crying in the wilderness: 'Prepare the way of the Lord.' "* v. 4

ADVENT IS A TIME FOR WAITING, and the truth of the matter is that we are ill-suited to the task. If we could do something — create a task force or tackle the job ourselves — it would not be so painful, but to sit around and watch the second hand on the clock make its anguishingly slow jog around and around the track is enough to drive us crazy. We are take-charge people, and all our lives we have been told that we can do anything if we put our minds and energies to it. So waiting is not our long suit.

That point is worth considering as we take up our second Advent text this morning. Again, we find ourselves looking ahead to what is around the corner, to that which is veiled and not really known. That is the heart of Advent for us — not what happened once upon a time but what is yet to be. That is why the texts which open the Advent season are not about shepherds and angels and magi-kings, but instead are about signs and portents and thieves that come in the night, about those things that are known only in the mind of God, and about what we must do to ready ourselves. Advent is about the future, God's future, and our waiting for the coming of that Kingdom into our presence.

If the first call of Advent is to wait, it strikes me that we may wait in one of several very different ways. There is a kind of waiting in which time moves on without any sense of progress so that it becomes a passing of time in which there is no expectation. Much of our modern eschatology, our talking about the future, takes on that character of waiting. It is understandable, especially in light of the almost twenty centuries that have passed since the time of Jesus. The early church expected an early return of their Lord — "before the end of the semester" as one of my college professors used to phrase it. In fact, many of the immediate concerns of the apostolic church were centered around such an expectation: what would happen to the believers who were dying in the interim period between Jesus' ascension and his return? Should people avoid marriage since the world would be ending soon? The years passed and the world remained intact and the focus began to change: how would the gospel be passed down as fewer and fewer eyewitnesses to Jesus' ministry remained? There was a shift in the early church's absorption into the matter of the end of the world. Today, when such a radical expectation is proclaimed and dates for the end of the world are proclaimed, these announcements are met with skepticism. Rightly so, I think. Such movements are born out of a fanaticism. Still, we ask where that leaves the rest of us. If we cannot walk with those who purport to read the signs, do we still harbor any expectations of a second coming? And the truth is that many Christians in the closing years of the twentieth century have adopted a life and a faith in which the future lies outside the boundaries of their vision. Life exists only in the moment. Any sense of expectation has been lost in the passing of the years, and so we wait without expectation.

There is another kind of waiting that I see occurring these days. Less common than the first, it is a waiting in which I suppose you could say that people have lost patience . . . lost patience with God. And they have resolved to press ahead on their own, hoping to solve the problems of the world by their own drive and energy. In his fine novel *Dawn*, Elie Wiesel creates two characters who make a pact to "wrest the Messiah from the chains of the future . . . to force God's hand." There is that kind of move in our world today in which some believers move forward in a conviction that the kingdom can be seized and ushered into existence by our own efforts. It is an aggressive approach to waiting, and it is marked with energy and vigor and sometimes an air of panic as people take on the burden of accomplishing a complete reshaping of our world.

There is another way of waiting, I suppose. There is another way of waiting if we can live with the painful understanding that if God has not come, it may well be because we, rather than God, are not ready. I think that Advent is born out of the kind of waiting that recognizes that for God's future to break out upon us, we must be transformed. Advent is a waiting which is a confession that we are not so much the agents of the coming kingdom as we are the obstacles. And if we grasp that, then our waiting takes on the character of opening ourselves to be remade by God, and the present time of our waiting becomes a time of our re-formation. And what is it that we mean by the grace of God at work within us if not this: that we are in the process of becoming a new creation.

John the Baptist appears on the scene with "the voice of one crying in the wilderness." Prepare yourselves for the coming of the Lord, he tells the people. Look inside your hearts and let the crookedness be straightened and let the roughness be made smooth.

You cannot force God's hand. You cannot set the time for the coming of God's Savior. But neither is the only course open to you the one of the aimless marking of time. Ready yourselves. Already, he is coming, so let our lives bear the fruits of his coming.

Gary L. Walling
Heights Christian Church
Shaker Heights, Ohio

DECEMBER 15, 1991

Third Sunday in Advent

Lessons:

Lutheran:	Zeph. 3:14-18a	Phil. 4:4-7 (8-9)	Luke 3:7-18
Roman Catholic:	Zeph. 3:14-18a	Phil. 4:4-7	Luke 3:10-18
Episcopal:	Zeph. 3:14-20	Phil. 4:4-7 (8-9)	Luke 3:7-18
Pres/Meth/UCC:	Zeph. 3:14-20	Phil. 4:4-9	Luke 3:7-18

Introductions to the Lessons

Lesson 1

Zephaniah 3:14-20 (**Epis/Pres/Meth/UCC**); *3:14-18a* (**Luth**) Here are hope and reason for joy by a people in captivity. They are promised release from captivity in Babylon. They have reason to sing and rejoice because God has come to them, is with them, and will defeat their enemies. Yahweh promises to restore their fortunes and bring them home.

Lesson 2

Philippians 4:4-7 (**Luth/Epis**); *4:4-9* (**Pres/Meth/UCC**) The same note of joy is in this pericope as it is in Lesson 1. Christians can rejoice because the coming of Christ is at hand. The joy is in the Lord not necessarily in the economic or health condition of the people. Because the Lord is near, there is no need to worry. Without worry there is peace. Until Christ returns we are to think upon beautiful and commendable things.

Gospel

Luke 3:7-18 (**Luth/Epis/Pres/Meth/UCC**) John the Baptizer was such a popular and fiery preacher that many repented and asked whether he might be the Christ. He destroys that idea by witnessing to Jesus as one mightier than he. John baptizes with water but Jesus will baptize with Spirit.

Theme: God has a passion about the way we live.

Thought for the day: "Rejoice in the Lord always; again I say, rejoice . . . Have no anxiety about anything, but in everything by prayer and supplication with thanksgiving let your requests be made known to God. And the peace of God, which passes all understanding, will keep your hearts and your minds in Christ Jesus." (Philippians 4:4-7)

Prayer of meditation: "Joy to the world, the Lord is come." And let us receive our Savior, O God, with a joy that befits his coming. Let us be glad in the rebirth of hope that renews our tired and despairing world. Let us be glad in the new possibilities of peace which invade the angry and warring nations. Let us be glad in the love which comes to save a lost and aimless creation. "Let heaven and nature sing" and let us join in the happy chorus. In his name we pray. Amen.

Call to worship: "He was in the world . . . He came to what was his own . . . to all who received him, who believed in his name, he gave power to become children of God, who were born, not of blood or of the will of the flesh or of the will of man, but of God." (John 1:10-13)

Prayer of adoration: O God who will not give up on us, as we open the Gospels to read of Christ's birth, remind us that the tidings of great joy were not just given to first century shepherds and kings. The joy is every bit for us as well. And as we hear the story again — the story which is for all times and all people — hear the joy that fills our hearts and receive it back again. Know that your word has not gone unheard. Your joy is even now becoming our joy. Amen.

Prayer of confession: O God, in the coming of your light we discover again how much our lives are shrouded in darkness. We are convicted in the knowledge that we have chosen to reside in the shadows, to withhold from one another the words and actions that might have made for happier lives. Left to our own ways, we would surely be lost, except that you have refused to let it pass that way. You have come to us, judging us where we have fallen to sin and proclaimed a grace that reveals another way: his way. Shine your light upon us, that we might go forth in the light of his life, for we would live in his name and in his presence. Amen.

Prayer of dedication of gifts and self: Our God, your nature is to give, and in these days leading up to Christmas, we know that truth about you especially well. Let us follow the example of others who shared in the Bethlehem birth. Like the angels and shepherds, let us respond with praise and worship. Like the magi from the East, let us give of the riches in our possession. Like Mary and Joseph, let us live in humble trust for what you shall do. And especially like Jesus himself, let us live with such faithfulness that we may place our lives back in your hands. It is in his name that we gather and to his glory that we offer these gifts. Amen.

Sermon title: What Joy is This?

Sermon thesis: Advent carries themes of warning and judgment, but rightly heard, even these are cause for joy. To believe in God's anger and judgment is to believe in God's ultimate commitment to creation.

Hymn for the day: *"Hark, the glad sound".* Philip Doddridge, son of a London oil merchant and one of twenty children, became an Independent minister. In 1727 he was appointed to a parish in Northampton, a parish made up of poor, hard-working people. There he opened an academy for those preparing for the Nonconformist ministry that was attended by young men from all over England and from the Continent. The hymn rejoices in the coming of Christ and describes the New World he will bring with his coming.

Announcements for next week:

Sermon title: A Mother's Song
Sermon theme: We discover what God looks like when we look at Jesus.
Sermon summary: Mary, the mother of Jesus plays a role of humility. Her significance lies not in her own accomplishments but rather in her example of discipleship. In responding to God's call, she points beyond herself to her son. When we look at Mary, we look beyond her and see the Christ.

Children's object talk:

A Time For Giving

Objects: A wrapped present, a can of food, a coat
Lesson: Christmas is a time for giving more than receiving.
Outline: 1. We are expecting lots of presents for Christmas.
2. Christmas will not be complete if we only get things.
3. Christmas is especially about giving.

I DON'T SUPPOSE ANY OF YOU KNOW what this is. Well, you do know and you are right; it is a present. In my living room, we have a tree and there are lots of presents like this one under the tree. Some of them are for me. I know this because I have looked at every one of them about a hundred times and I am pretty excited about what I might be getting.

Still, I keep thinking that Christmas is not just about getting things. As much fun as I have opening my presents on Christmas morning, I think I even have more fun watching other people open the gifts that I have given to them. Christmas is about giving more than receiving.

And that is why the church puts out so many opportunities for us to give around this time of year. Take this present — it is going to go to the children's home across town along with other toys that we are collecting today for those boys and girls. And this can of green beans is one of several hundred food items we collected last week that will go to the city food pantry that is feeding several thousand families this month that do not have enough food. And this coat is going to the Interchurch Council's "Coats For Kids" program so some little boy or girl will be able to stay warm this winter. Christmas is about giving, and that is probably the best way we have of celebrating the birth of Jesus.

The sermon:

What Joy Is This?

Hymns:
Beginning of worship: Joy to the World!
Sermon hymn: Angels We Have Heard on High
End of worship: Good Christian Friends, Rejoice

Scripture: Luke 3:7-18

Sermon text: *"So with many other exhortations, he proclaimed the good news to the people."* v. 18

THERE IS A CERTAIN SOMBERNESS TO ADVENT which is really a bit surprising. What I mean is that when you begin to think of Christmas, you begin to think about angels, shepherds, kings, and a manger baby — all images that bring a smile to your face. When you open your Bible and follow along with the texts that are assigned to these Sundays preceding Christmas, however, it is quite another mood that begins to settle in. The portions of Scripture that have traditionally been a part of the Advent season are about judgment and impending doom and the like . . . such as the text we have just read about the preaching of John, known as the Baptist. You will recall that while John's message is about the coming of a Savior, it is not about a gentle baby in a quiet manger, and it is not about, humble shepherds coming to worship the Messiah, and it is not even

172

about traveling magi whose long journey has been to give gifts to the greatest king. None of that from John to herald the coming of the Christ. Instead, his listeners—in his day and we may suppose in ours—are called a brood of vipers and told how the ax is already laid to the tree. To those listeners and to us, it is not a gentle message.

It is rather like Lent and Easter. I have been warned countless times by wiser ministers and professors than me to resist the temptation to jump over the crucifixion in order to get to resurrection. Easter will come in its own time, but it will never really be understood apart from Good Friday—or so I've been told. And I have come to know that it is true—the good news of resurrection can never be received completely unless we first deal with our own sinfulness, our own willfulness, and our participation in rejecting and crucifying Jesus.

And something of the same relationship exists between Advent and Christmas. Yes, there is that glorious birth—that warm and joyful morning for which we long to reach out. But there is this other message with which we must deal on the way to Bethlehem. And so the prophet John appeared on the scene in the valley of the river Jordan, and he preached to the people:

"You brood of vipers! Who warned you to flee from the wrath to come? . . . Even now the ax is lying at the root of the trees; every tree therefore that does not bear good fruit is cut down and thrown into the fire."

And then he launches into a series of answers to some questions put forth by his listeners about what they should be doing to prepare themselves. And while his answers are not the main focus of my interest this morning, they are interesting. John says that the proper response to the call for repentance is an ethical response . . . if you have extra clothing or food, you must share them; and you must be honest in your dealing with others; and you are not to use the power that you have over others in an unfair or self-serving way.

Then he goes into a rather specific unveiling about the one who is to come as he says:

"I baptize you with water; one who is more powerful than I is coming; I am not worthy to untie the thong of his sandals. He will baptize you with the Holy Spirit and fire."

And he offers one more parting and threatening word:

"His winnowing fork is ready in his hand, to clear his threshing floor and gather the wheat into his granary; but the chaff he will burn with unquenchable fire."

Then the passage ends with a little summary from Luke that is really what I am after this morning. Luke sums up the Baptist's preaching by saying:

"So, with many other exhortations, he proclaimed the good news to the people."

Did you catch it? "The good news." We have gone over it in some detail so I ask you, Is John's preaching what you would call good news? Vipers' brood, ax laid to a tree, baptism with fire, the chaff of the wheat burned—what kind of good news is that?

Our dealing with this question of prophecy and good news has to do with more than this single passage. What is at issue here in a larger sense is how we come to view any prophet. Is the prophet always the one who comes with tattered clothes and wild eyes, yelling and screaming with a fury, much like we typically picture the Baptist? But prophecy is not prediction, and therein lies a very important distinction. Prediction is telling how it is going to be no matter what anyone does, but prophecy is always a bit open-ended. Yet God is going to act in a decisive way, but there is still time. It is really up to you to decide how you will receive God's Messiah. Far from being a prophet of doom, John was also a prophet of hope. The multitudes heard him and instead of shrinking back or running, they embraced his message. He was popular and loved. And why? Because John confirmed their godly hope (Robertson, Bruce *Interpretation*, p. 404, October 1982).

And what does that mean—that the Baptist confirmed the godly hopes of his listeners? Just this, I think. John's message was harsh, but it was a message that God cared . . . that there is some goodness in this world . . . that God takes sides . . . that there is a force for morality that is not indifferent. And our hope in God is really of that character: not so much that there is a God but that it is a God who cares about us. And any of us who have ever had a parent get angry with us can attest to the fact that anger is one facet of love. So John's preaching was received by the multitudes because it confirmed their best hopes about God—that God cared, cared enough even to get angry, and cared enough to do something.

Maybe we will not be able to receive fully the Christmas Babe without the struggle of Advent. If Christmas is about God's love, then maybe the real message of Advent is a story of God's passion. If the Advent texts strike us as a bit hard, then maybe we can see in them something of God's anguish over a world turned crazy. And out of God's anguish comes a passion—a stirring to action.

Bruce Robertson tells an interesting little story about Robert S. McNamara who is best known as John Kennedy's Secretary of Defense but who later served as the president of the World Bank. Upon his retirement, McNamara made a speech in which he noted that in the previous year, Americans had spent more on houseplants than on development in the Third World, and at that point in his address, he began to weep. And for what?

For the government he served in time of war? For the corporate industrial life he served as chief executive? For the church he serves as an elder? He spoke as a man under judgment to others under judgment—as a two-coat type of person. He spoke . . . to (and we live as) a privileged people suffering from "compassion fatigue" (Robertson, p. 405).

I repeat the story to say this: Yes it is a story of judgment to say that we invest more in our foliage than we do in our suffering brothers and sisters. But can it be more than a story of condemnation? If we stand as people under judgment, then can we also receive the judgment as offering hope as well? I think we can, because the story told about McNamara is more than a story of judgment. It is a story of passion, a story of caring, and a story that may yet lead to a change in people's hearts.

Gary L. Walling
Heights Christian Church
Shaker Heights, Ohio

DECEMBER 22, 1991

Fourth Sunday in Advent

Lessons:

Lutheran:	Mic. 5:2-4	Heb. 10:5-10	Luke 1:39-45 (46-55)
Roman Catholic:	Mic. 5:2-5a	Heb. 10:5-10	Luke 1:39-45
Episcopal:	Mic. 5:2-4	Heb. 10:5-10	Luke 1:39-49 (50-56)
Pres/Meth/UCC:	Mic. 5:2-5a	Heb. 10:5-10	Luke 1:39-55

Introductions to the Lessons

Lesson 1

Micah 5:2-4 (**Luth/Epis**); *5:2-5a* (**Pres/Meth/UCC**) In the dark days of the Babylonian captivity, the Jews hoped for a restoration of their nation under a son of David who would be born in Bethlehem as David was. This coming Son of David will feed his people and they will live in peace. Matthew (2:6) sees this passage as a prophesy fulfilled that Jesus, Son of David, would be born in Bethlehem.

Lesson 2

Hebrews 10:5-10 (**Luth/Epis/Pres/Meth/UCC**) Christ did not come into the world to offer sacrifices as the Levitical priests did. He came to do the will of God. What was that will? It was to offer the final and complete sacrifice of himself. In other words, Jesus was born to die for the sins of the world.

Gospel

Luke 1:39-55 (**Luth/Epis/Pres/Meth/UCC**) Mary pregnant with Jesus visits Elizabeth also pregnant with John. Filled with the Spirit Elizabeth hails Mary as blessed among women and recognizes that Mary's baby will be the Christ. In response Mary sang a song known as the Magnificat, a beautiful narrative poem in praise of God.

Theme: We discover what God looks like when we look at Jesus.

Thought for the day: Today we celebrate the giver and the gift. To be truly grateful is to cling less to the gifts we receive and to share more and more the joy which breaks into our lives with the birth of God's Son.

Prayer of meditation: O God, the giver of life and love, let us enter into the fullness of the life and love which you have given and continue to lay before us. You have taken notice of our want, our aimlessness, our need. You have seen us as not even we can see ourselves. Let us be so filled with what you have given that we ourselves will become instruments by which you may continue to give life and love to your children everywhere. Amen.

Call to worship: "And the Word became flesh and lived among us, and we have seen his glory as of a father's only son, full of grace and truth . . . . No one has ever seen God. The only Son, who is close to the Father's heart, He has made him known." (John 1:14, 18)

Prayer of adoration: How is it, our God, that all of creation should sing with joy at the birth of your Son while we would remain mute? How can we not be caught up in the songs of angels, in the praise of all the creatures of the earth, in the joyous devotion of all the peoples of the earth? Receive in this hour the passion of our worship: our hymns and prayers, our searching and proclamations, our dedications of self and possessions. And let our hearts not be calmed when our time here is ended, but let our lives become the sweetest and purest of all our songs of praise. In the name of Christ, our Lord, we pray. Amen.

Prayer of confession: Sometimes, our God, we are too "adult" to enter into the spirit of Christmas. We would rather be the ones to give the gifts because we have not learned how to receive. We are uncomfortable being in someone else's debt. We do not like being beholden to others. Help us to take on some measure of the spirit of children who pass through these days with such expectation and desire. Help us to see how our lives are made complete in your giving to us as you enter our lives through the gift of your Son. And in receiving, let us learn more and more what it means to enter into your joy. Amen.

Prayer of dedication of gifts and self: O God, you have blessed us beyond what we could ever hope to repay, and yet we cannot be content until we have made some response, however much it pales in comparison. If we can never outgive you, we can become imitators of you. So, receive the gifts which we now bring before you. Use them and magnify them so that in their use, we might become like

177

you—lovers of the children of the earth. And let us be as resolute in our blessing of others as you have been in blessing us. We offer these gifts and all of the gifts of our lives in the name of our Lord Jesus. Amen.

Sermon title: A Mother's Song

Sermon thesis: Mary, the mother of Jesus plays a role of humility. Her significance lies not in her own accomplishments but rather in her example of discipleship. In responding to God's call, she points beyond herself to her son. When we look at Mary, we look beyond her and see the Christ.

Hymn for the day: *"From east to west, from shore to shore."* Coelius Sedulius' *Paean Alphabeticus de Christo* is an acrostic, a poem about the life of Christ written twenty-three stanzas, each beginning with one of the letters of the alphabet. A hymn, created of the first seven stanzas of the poem was used extensively through the centuries as a Christmas hymn. Very little is known of Sedulius' life. He was probably born in Rome and lived during the early fifth century. Two of his letters indicate that he was converted to Christianity late in life. Stanza 3 sings of "A maiden, in her lowly place . . . " A continuation of the hymn, translated with a first line, "When Christ's appearing was made known," also can be found in modern hymnals.

Announcements for Christmas Eve:
Sermon title: What Child is This? The Light of the World!
Sermon theme: The light of Jesus is never extinguished.
Sermon summary: Light battles darkness. There is a cost to be paid in the battle. Jesus paid the price so that no darkness would be able to overcome his light. Those who deeply know their need for such light will be seeking him in his season.

Announcements for Christmas Day:
Sermon title: How Close is God?
Sermon theme: When we are afraid, God is close.
Sermon summary: For a while we can escape the need to know and experience the closeness of God. But a time will come when absolutely nothing is more important. The Christmas story is the story, and the only story, that can ultimately satisfy our longing to know that God is as close as our breath.

Announcements for next week:
Sermon title: A Gift of God to Parents
Sermon theme: Christian parents must surrender their children to God.
Sermon summary: God presents parents with many opportunities to learn the discipline of surrendering our children to God. Those events can and do cause parents enormous anxiety and pain. Nonetheless, we must teach our children ultimately to be obedient to God.

Children's object talk:

Like Father, Like Son

Objects: Several photographs
Lesson: We know what God is like because we know what Jesus is like.
Outline: 1. Children will look something like their parents.
2. Children learn to act like their parents.
3. God looks and acts like God's Son, Jesus.

I SORT OF HAVE A PUZZLE for you this morning. Actually, what I have are some photographs of some people – some mothers and fathers and their children. Can you tell me which children go with which parents? (Spend a few moments matching the sets of photographs.)

I think you did very well. I thought you would, because we all have learned that we kind of look like our mothers and fathers – not exactly, because everyone is different, but still there are traits that run through families. For example, I am tall, and my father is a tall man. And Terri, you have blond hair just like your mother. And most of you have heard someone tell you sometime that you have your mother's eyes or that you have your father's hands.

And it is not just that we look like our parents. We also learn to act like them! Sometimes, we will talk like our mothers and fathers or walk like them. Or maybe we learn to like the same things – tennis or working on computers. Sometimes they teach us to do the things that they think are very important – like telling the truth.

Well, what I really want to talk about this morning is not so much how you look like your parents but who Jesus looks like. I think one of the very important things about Jesus being born is that since he is God's Son, we learn something about what God is like. Of course, we don't really know what God looks like – that is not what I mean. But we do get an idea about what God thinks is important because we believe that Jesus acts like God. And if we want to know what God is like, we just have to read about Jesus. We know that he loved people and cared about people who were sick and hungry and hurting. And that is what God is like. God is like a father or mother who teaches their child to act like them – to love people like they love people.

The sermon:

A Mother's Song

Hymns:
Beginning of worship: O Come, All Ye Faithful
Sermon hymn: Lo, How a Rose E'er Blooming
End of worship: Hark, the Herald Angels Sing

Scripture: Luke 1:39-55

Sermon text: *"Blessed are you among women, and blessed is the fruit of your womb."* v. 42

WHEN A CHILD IS BORN, there is one overriding question which supercedes all other matters of interest. It is not necessarily the first question raised, but you know it is the most important one. I know this from personal experience.

My daughter was born on a Monday at 5:13 in the evening. By 5:15 p.m., the doctor had asked us whether the baby girl had a name and we had asked the doctor whether she was healthy. The answers to these two questions satisfied everyone in the room and with the preliminaries out of the way, we were able over the course of the next few hours to move to the most important question: "Who does Kristen look like?" Now to anyone who has seen the child in question — anyone, that is, with the barest capacity towards discernment — will be able to give the obvious answer: she looks like me! That knowledge was clear to me as well from the first moment I laid eyes on this child who is such a transparency of her father. There were a few folks who gathered around in the days and weeks that followed who offered some comments such as, "She has her mother's hands" or "Those are certainly Linda's eyes." Not that I needed any support, but I did place into evidence a snapshot that was taken of me when I was a few months old; and I may have mentioned the similarities in appearance to a few dozen people including my mother-in-law. As a general rule, she is not a meddler, but we did receive by return mail a photograph taken of my wife at two months of age which did have a suspicious resemblance to Kristen.

Having shared this story with you, I find it wise to turn now to the text which is a part of Luke's version of the birth of Jesus. Luke, you see, is the feminist gospel writer — he tells the story from Mary's point of view. She is the recipient of every visitation and poor Joseph is left to be a part of the background scenery along with the innkeeper and the animals in the stable. (Matthew, the traditionalist, gives the male perspective on our story, but that will have to be held for a different time.)

Speaking of Mary, the truth is that we do not have very much information about her. Of course, she has taken on a very large role through the centuries in the Roman Catholic church, where she has been accorded sainthood and made the object of prayer and devotion. But within Protestant circles, Mary has seldom found the spotlight.

In the biblical witness, information about Mary is quite limited, especially if one looks outside the infancy narratives in the opening chapters of Matthew and Luke. She is mentioned a couple of times — at the Cana wedding and at the cross in John's gospel, in the upper room and at Pentecost in Acts, and in a fleeting reference in Paul's Galatian letter — but little information is given about her in any of these passages. Likewise, she is mentioned only a few times in the portions of the synoptic gospels which tell of Jesus' ministry, and in the Gospel of Mark, these passages do not offer an especially flattering portrait. Early in the second Gospel, Jesus' family hears that he is out of his mind, and so his mother and brothers arrive to take charge of him. Jesus disavows them and points to those around him saying that his family is made up of the people who do God's will (3:31-35). Later when Jesus remarks that a prophet is always held in honor except in his own land, he adds and except "among his kinsmen and family." The slap is of particular note since it follows a listing of his family which includes the name of his mother. So, for Mark, Jesus' mother appears in a light which is quite different than that in which she is usually viewed.

The very interesting thing is that the later synoptic gospels, Matthew and Luke, see her in a different light — each softens the stories in his own way. My interest this morning lies in what Luke does. In the first passage, Jesus' family arrives but there is no hint that they are coming to take custody of him, and when Jesus remarks that his mother and brothers are those who hear and act upon the word of God, the biting irony is missing — Jesus' family would seem to be among the ones whose example is praised (8:19-21). At the point in Luke's gospel where Jesus says that a prophet is without honor in his own land, he removes the reference to family and kinsmen (4:24). And Luke has one very important addition to the portrait which he paints of Mary. As Jesus moves through a crowd, a woman shouts a blessing on the woman who gave him birth, and he counters, "No, happy are those who hear the word of God and keep it" (11:27-28).

Now the point of pulling together all of these scriptures, of course, is not to try to play a game of Bible sword drill with you. Rather, what I want to do is to pull together an image of Mary; and if we cannot do that, then at least to try to come to an understanding of how Luke saw her. My sense is that in the context of Jesus' adulthood, Luke sees Mary not in a negative light, but neither does he see her in a romantically sentimental way. What Luke sees and attempts to honor is a woman who is praiseworthy not for her motherhood but for her faithfulness in hearing and acting upon the word of God. Sentimental attachments give way to her example of faithfulness.

And that is exactly what you find in our scripture lesson this morning. You see this first in the text's theme shift — Elizabeth sings praise of Mary, but Mary's praises move toward God: "Tell out, my soul, the greatness of the Lord, rejoice, rejoice, my spirit, in God my Saviour." And on go the words to Mary's glorious song in praise of a God whose name is holy . . . whose mercy is sure . . . who has put down the mighty and the arrogant . . . who has lifted the humble ones and satisfied the hungry. Elizabeth would sing of Mary, but Mary sings about God.

Then, you see it in an oblique way in a change of wording. If you were to examine our passage in the New Revised Standard Version or in most other translations, you would find the word "blessed" used four times, three by Elizabeth and one by Mary, though all are used in reference to Mary. Technically, however, the word which is given four times as "blessed" actually comes from two different Greek words. When Elizabeth is speaking of Mary's pregnancy — God's *blessing* is on you above all women, and God's *blessing* is on the fruit of your womb — the word means blessing in the sense of being praised. The blessing is a condition that has come from another — God has blessed Mary, or praised Mary in selecting her to be the mother of this child. Though it is difficult to catch this nuance in translation, the subject of this blessing is not Mary but God. The two references which follow are about Mary, however — about the result of her having been called by God — and so the word that is used this time means blessing in the sense of being happy or fortunate. Elizabeth says, Happy is she who has had faith that the Lord's promise would be fulfilled, and Mary responds, For, from this day forth, all generations will count me fortunate. Mary is blessed in receiving God's action, but her joy and happiness and most blessed satisfaction comes upon hearing that word and responding to it.

And so, in some rather obvious and some rather discreet ways, Luke puts together a portrait of Mary which presents her as one who is worthy of praise — not for biological reasons but rather for spiritual ones — she heard and she acted. In that way, Mary stands in the Gospel of Luke as a model for us — as a model of discipleship. You look at Mary and you see Jesus even as you look at Jesus and see God. What Mary does is to point beyond herself. If that all-important question is asked, "Who will this child look like?" the answer given is that he will look like God.

That is the overarching truth of Christmas: that this birth goes beyond one mother, beyond one family, and beyond one nation. Finally, it is not Mary's story at all; it is God's story. Luke understands that, and I think we may yet come to understand it also.

Gary L. Walling
Heights Christian Church
Shaker Heights, Ohio

DECEMBER 24, 1991

Christmas Eve

Lessons:

Lutheran:	Is. 9:2-7	Titus 2:11-14	Luke 2:1-20
Roman Catholic:	Is. 9:2-7	Titus 2:11-14	Luke 2:1-24
Episcopal:	Is. 9:2-4, 6-7	Titus 2:11-14	Luke 2:1-14 (15-20)
Pres/Meth/UCC:	Is. 9:2-7	Titus 2:11-14	Luke 2:1-20

Introductions to the Lessons

Lesson 1

Isaiah 9:2-7 (**Luth/Epis/Pres/Meth/UCC**) In the time of Isaiah Israel was a land of darkness caused by disobedience to Yahweh. But, the darkness turned to light and sorrow became rejoicing. This change was caused by the birth of the Messiah whose names depict his nature and whose government of justice and righteousness results in peace. For Christians this took place when Jesus was born.

Lesson 2

Titus 2:11-14 (**Luth/Epis/Pres/Meth/UCC**) In this letter Paul is urging Titus to teach sound doctrine to the church in Crete. Then he focuses upon the chief doctrine: the Incarnation. Referring to the Nativity, Paul says that in Jesus the grace of God appeared for the salvation of the world. The meaning of Jesus' birth is in his death which redeemed us from sin.

Gospel

Luke 2:1-20 (**Luth/Epis/Pres/Meth/UCC**) In obedience to a Roman order for a census, Joseph and Mary go to Bethlehem to register. While there, the baby Jesus was born. His birth was announced to shepherds by an angel, and a choir of angels sang praise to God for his birth. The shepherds went to the manger and saw the child. Then they returned praising God for their experience.

Theme: The light of Jesus is never extinguished.

Thought for the day: Walk outside in the night, when the sky is black and the stars are a million points of light. Contemplate the immensity of light generated by all of them. They are an exquisite gift of God. But, their power is emptiness when compared to even the slightest ray of the light of Jesus shining into our hearts.

Prayer of meditation: My God of light, as I prepare for worship, my eyes are closed to the light around me, but my soul is open to the light within me. I look deep within, and I find you where you have been all the time, doing what you always do. You are loving me, holding me, healing me. You are seeking to be born in my life. Sitting in this sanctuary, and feeling your presence in the sanctuary within, I feel safe. I am willing to be open in this coming hour of worship. I am willing that the truth be spoken to me. I am willing to be enlightened, concerning the darkness of the world and the darkness of my own life. Amen.

Call to worship: There are, in our lives, moments of victory and moments of defeat. Today we are invited to experience the victory. Literally, we — you and I — are invited to come with the most faithful parts of ourselves, joyfully celebrating the triumph of God. We sing together, "O Come, All Ye Faithful."

Prayer of adoration: We come to adore you, our God. It is especially at this season of the year that we remember that adoration is an appropriate feeling to have for God. As we would adore the innocent child in the manger, you invite us, our God, to look upon you gently, kindly. We pray for a softer experience of God to balance the harsh images that were often planted in our souls at a very early age. We pray that our experience of God will be shaped by the vision of Mary's baby, helpless and dependent. As you tenderly hold us in your hands, our God, we would tenderly hold you in our hearts. Amen.

Prayer of confession: We confess, our God of compassion and forgiveness, the Christmas madness that has possessed us during this holy season. In one way or other, we have been captives of a spirit that is not holy. Time has been a problem rather than a blessing. The need to give has provoked feelings of crisis instead of opportunity. Children have been seen as harassing the season instead of hallowing the season. And the world, oh yes, the world that Jesus came to save, well, the world has been pretty much on its own. If the homeless are dependent on our light shining, they are pretty much in darkness. We suspect, if we dare even to think about it, that you look with significant disfavor upon many of our priorities. We are only beginning to be able to apply our Christian faith to our lives. We are utterly dependent, our God, on your mercy. Amen.

Prayer of dedication of gifts and self: Our God, giver of every good and perfect gift, we are thankful for the light of Jesus Christ that shines so brightly into our lives this most holy of nights. We offer these gifts that that light might shine through us as a beacon of hope to neighbors near and far. As so many were drawn to Christ by the Bethlehem Star, so may your lost children everywhere see your church drawing them to their spiritual home. As well as our gifts, we give our lives, that the whole world may, in seeing our good works, give all glory to our God who is in heaven. Amen.

Sermon title: What Child is This? The Light of the World!

Sermon thesis: Light battles darkness. There is a cost to be paid in the battle. Jesus paid the price so that no darkness would be able to overcome his light. Those who deeply know their need for such light will be seeking him in this season.

Hymn for the day: *"While shepherds watched their flocks."* This text is a very literal paraphrase of the biblical narrative. First published in the supplement to the *New Version of the Psalms by Dr. Brady and Mr. Tate,* 1700, it was one of six hymns allowed to be used in the worship service besides the canticles and Psalm paraphrases. (For some two hundred years the church of England, following the convictions of John Calvin, allowed only the singing of Scripture paraphrases — mostly Psalm paraphrases — in worship.) Nahum Tate (1652-1715), son of an Irish clergyman, made his living primarily by writing for the stage. In collaboration with Nicholas Brady he prepared the *New Version* of Psalms paraphrases, which was authorized by the king to be used in all the churches.

Children's object talk:

Christmas Eve

Objects: A lighted candle; a light switch
Lesson: Jesus is the light of the world. When he is with us in our hearts we do not need to be afraid of the dark.
Outline: 1. Light the candle and tell them that Jesus is the light of the world.
    2. Tell a story about being afraid of the dark.
    3. With Jesus in our hearts, we never need to be afraid of the dark.
LET'S LIGHT THIS CANDLE. What's different about our church tonight? That's right, we have many bright candles in the church. Do you know why? That's right, it is Christmas Eve, the birthday of Jesus. And one of the names we call Jesus is, "the light of the

world." There is darkness in the world. Jesus brings light to the darkness so that people who follow him will not stumble and fall. When I was a child, we lived in a very large and old house. There were no lights in the stairways. When I had to go upstairs at night, I would place my hand on the wall and feel my way to the top of the stairs. How do you think I was feeling? That's right, I was pretty nervous, but I wasn't scared. Not yet. Then I would walk quickly past the empty space that was the entrance to my brother Jim's room. My hand would reach out for the wall which guided me around the corner and into my room. I knew exactly where the light switch was. I would reach up for that switch. And, you know what? I will show you what. Would someone like to turn on this switch? It doesn't work. My light switch didn't work either. Now I was scared! I would turn around to run back down the stairs. And if I went too fast I would hit my head on the wall. Or I would trip and fall down.

Unlike the light switch, Jesus always works. His light never goes out. With Jesus in our hearts we can see where we are going and are a lot less likely to stumble and fall. Jesus came into the world to bring light for whose life? That's right, for you and me, Jamie, Peter, Sally, Carrie, all of us — we do not need to be afraid.

The sermon:

What Child is This? The Light of the World

Hymns:
> Beginning of worship: O Come, All Ye Faithful
> Sermon hymn: Light of the World, We Hail Thee
> End of worship: Joy to the World, The Lord is Come

Scripture: John 1:1-5

Sermon text: *"The light shines in the darkness. And the darkness has not overcome it."* v. 5

THERE IS NO MORE UNIVERSAL SYMBOL for the battle between good and evil than the image of light penetrating into and conquering the darkness. The American Indians had a legend. Near the beginning of time the animals in the forest held a council to decide if they should have light in the midst of an all-dark world. Two animal characters offered opposing points of view.

First, Bear adamantly growled, "We must have darkness!" This put an end to most discussion since Bear, by virtue of his size and gruffness, carried a lot of weight in the council of animals. But young Chipmunk, undaunted by Bear's power, bravely sang out, "Let there be light." And again and again Chipmunk sang, "Let there be light, Let there be light." Frightened but not overwhelmed by Bear's fierce power, Chipmunk sang until the sun actually spread its gleam throughout the forest world.

But opposing the forces of darkness is not done without risk. The story ends with Bear menacingly walking toward Chipmunk, who quickly runs into a tree for safety but ends up with Bear-clawed stripes on his back as a permanent reminder of the conflict between light and darkness.

The chipmunk is wounded — stripes on his back — as the price paid for singing "Let there be light." (*Weavings*, Nov./Dec. '86, p. 30) Maybe that reminds you of the price Jesus paid for being the light. You may recall the words of the prophet Isaiah:

"Surely he has borne our griefs, and carried our sorrows: yet we did esteem him stricken, smitten of God and afflicted. But he was wounded for our transgressions, he was bruised for our iniquities; the chastisement of our peace was upon him; and by his stripes we are healed." (Isaiah 53:4-5)

No matter the cost, the claim of Jesus to be the light of the world is bold and absolute. "I am the light of the world," Jesus proclaims in John 8:12; not the moon or the sun; not the power plants that provide megawatts of electricity; not even the candles and lights that brighten Christmas Eve.

If you read the eighth chapter of John carefully, you will discover that Jesus made this claim at a very special time and in a very special place. The time was the Feast of Tabernacles, a feast that celebrated the passage of the people of Israel through the darkness of the wilderness. It was a time to remember the light, the pillar of fire, that guided them through that dark and threatening forty years in the desert. During the feast thousands of Israelites would crowd into the inner Temple court. They were surrounded by absolute and unremitting darkness. In that darkness they were to remember what it is like to live without the guiding light of God. And then, suddenly, four youth would carry into the court a giant candelabra. The piercing light of that candelabra was said to illuminate every street and court and square in the city of Jerusalem. (Barclay, *Jesus As They Knew Him*, p. 266)

In that place and in that time Jesus claimed to be the light of the world. He is the light that penetrates every street and court and square of every city the world over. He is the light that penetrates the darkness of every life. He is the light that conquers darkness world-wide. He is the light that drives darkness from every life.

One of the most amazing features of any light is that by itself no amount of darkness can conquer any amount of light. Darkness alone has no power over light. If the only light in this sanctuary was the Christ candle in the center of the Advent wreath, and if the walls of the church could be taken down to reveal nothing but unending darkness as far as the eye could see, that darkness would have absolutely no effect on the light of the solitary Christ candle. There are, as we all well know, other forces that can extinguish light. Hate can snuff out, for a time, love. Despair can, for a time, diminish faith. Sorrow can, for awhile, overwhelm joy. Violence can, in a season, defeat peace. But nothing, nothing in all creation, can overcome the light of the world. Nothing can overcome Jesus. Nothing can ultimately separate us from his light and love. In Christ the beacon of faith can always be relit, peace can always be re-created from the rubble of war, the possibility of a new and radiating joy always lives, and love can be re-discovered amidst the tragedies of our lives.

Those who will seek the Christ Child in this Christmas season, those who will be willing to follow a star to a Bethlehem stable on this most holy of nights, will include those who are seeking light for the darkness of their lives. The seekers after light will include those who have allowed the light of Christ to illuminate their inner worlds and know that they need a Savior who is willing to bear our griefs, carry our sorrows, be wounded for our transgressions, and suffer the stripes that we deserved in order to bring healing light to our lives.

"What child is this who laid to rest on Mary's lap is sleeping?" This child is the light of the world — the light of our lives.

Thanks be to God!

Kenneth C. Whitt
Mountview Baptist Church
Columbus, Ohio

DECEMBER 25, 1991

Christmas Day

Lessons:

Lutheran:	Is. 62:10-12	Titus 3:4-7	Luke 2:1-20
Roman Catholic:	Is. 62:11-12	Titus 3:4-7	Luke 2:15-20
Episcopal:	Is. 62:6-7, 10-12	Titus 3:4-7	Luke 2:(1-14) 15-20
Pres/Meth/UCC:	Is. 62:6-7, 10-12	Titus 3:4-7	Luke 2:1-18

Introductions to the Lessons

Lesson 1

Isaiah 62:10-12 (**Luth**); *62:6-7, 10-12* (**Epis/Pres/Meth/UCC**) The Babylonian captivity is over and Jerusalem with the Temple has been rebuilt. Now those in Jerusalem are ordered to go through the gates and prepare the way for the remaining exiles to return to Jerusalem. Then Jerusalem will be renowned and the people will be known as a holy people, redeemed of the Lord.

Lesson 2

Titus 3:4-7 (**Luth/Epis/Pres/Meth/UCC**) With the birth of Jesus, the goodness and mercy of God appeared. He saved us not because of our good works but because of his mercy. Through our baptism we received the Holy Spirit. Now we have the hope of eternal life.

Gospel

Luke 2:1-20 (**Luth/Epis**); *2:1-18* (**Pres/Meth/UCC**) See Luke 2:1-20 for Christmas Eve.

Theme: When we are afraid, God is close.

Thought for the day: It is easy for most of us to remember a time when we were alone and afraid. We can also remember times when, because of the presence of another person, we felt confident. Try to hold on to both of those feelings, like they are two balloons. Feel God, on Christmas Day, blowing air into the balloon of confidence. Hold on to this balloon. Let the other go!

Prayer of meditation: My God of hope and help, when that night of magic ended, Mary and Joseph awoke to find themselves parents of a newborn baby, in a world where fresh and innocent creatures faced great dangers. The world has not changed much. I too see, and sometimes feel, the hostility of the world. I know how risky it is to give birth to a gentle new idea or feeling or fragile part of myself. I hesitate to seek new birth in my life. The old and familiar seems so much safer. As I worship, my God, may the courage of Mary and Joseph to face their unknown future also be my courage. May the stories and songs and symbols of Christmas fill my life with hope. Amen.

Call to worship: To yourself, name a fear that you carry with you even on Christmas Day. That fear, whatever it is, is one of the fears the angels were talking about when they said, "Be not afraid." And the good news they delivered, that is for you, too! It is good news of great joy — and it is being delivered, even now, to all of God's people.

Prayer of adoration: How can we tell you thank you, our God? How can we express the glory you deserve for all you have given on this Christmas Day? Shall we sing hymns of praise until we can sing no more? Shall we worship with enthusiasm and sensitivity for all that the incarnation means to our lives? Can the magnificence of this sanctuary and the striking flowers and banners and the resounding notes of the organ adequately express our praise? Or, what about a softly, shyly whispered, "We love you"? Can you hear even the unspoken words of our hearts? With all that we have and with all that we are, we praise you and thank you for a love so amazing that it sent Jesus to be the savior of our lives. Amen.

Prayer of confession: Today would be a good day to leave the prayer of confession out of our worship. After all, our God, look who is at church today. We are! The rest of the folk are too caught up in their materialistic Christmas to give you even an hour. On the day you gave your Son, we give you sixty minutes. It is enough to give one pause. But if we pause too long, we see through our self-deception. We see the minuteness of our devotion up against the immensity of God's gift. And we see ourselves as part of the whole human family that can never measure up to God's generosity. Forgive us for our grandiose thoughts of holiness. Only you, our great God, are holy. Teach us humility. Amen.

Prayer of dedication of gifts and self: We humbly offer our gifts, our God. We offer them with hope. They are an expression of the faith we have experienced in our lives, that, indeed, we do not need to be afraid. And they are an expression of our hope that with God's help we can make a difference in the world. We can pass on the Christmas spirit. We can share the gift of God's love. God holds us tightly so that we can loosen our grip on possessions. God empowers all our activity so that we can loosen our grip on our time. And so with joy, and with thanksgiving, we return to God our gifts of treasure and our gifts of ourselves. Amen.

Sermon title: How Close Is God?

Sermon thesis: For awhile we can escape the need to know, and experience, the closeness of God. But a time will come when absolutely nothing is more important. The Christmas story is the story, and the only story, that can ultimately satisfy our longing to know that God is as close as our breath.

Hymn for the day: *"Hark! the herald angels sing"* Originally beginning "Hark, how all the welkin rings Glory to the King of kings" (1739), this hymn by Charles Wesley was altered to its present opening lines fourteen years later in George Whitefield's *Collection of Hymns.* (See October 27 above for remarks on Charles Wesley.)

Children's object talk:

Listen to the Angels

Objects: Toy farm animals, toy shepherds, wise men, Mary and Joseph
Lesson: To tell how close God was to the people.
Outline: 1. The Jews were subject to Roman authority.
          2. God wanted to show the people how close he really was to them.
          3. The angels explained how important the baby was.
A VERY LONG TIME AGO the people of Israel had almost forgotten that there was a God. Many thought he was very far away because the Roman soldiers were all around. The people were afraid. They did not know where God was.

So God decided to do something to show how close he was to the people. What do you think God decided to do? That's right, he sent the Baby Jesus. But before he could send the Baby Jesus God had to get a lot of things ready. For example, God wanted some animals to be there so he chose one special cow. Can I have the cow to put in the manger scene? And God chose some special sheep and a camel. And God wanted some people to be there so God chose some shepherds and some wise men. And, of course, God needed a mommy and a daddy, Joseph and Mary. Now everyone is at the manger. Are we ready for the baby? No, we are not. We still need someone to tell everyone about the Baby Jesus. Somebody has got to explain how important the baby is. Who could do that? That's right, we need an angel, or a whole choir of angels. Who did I give the angels to? No one? We have to have an angel. Would anyone be willing to stand up here and be the angel? Would you like to say what the angels said? You can just repeat it after me; "Behold/I bring you good news/of great joy/which is for/all the people. For to you/is born this day/a Savior/who is Christ/the Lord."

Thank you, angels! And thank you, God, that you loved us so much that you came to earth to show us how close to us you are all of the time. When we are afraid that God is far away, let's remember Mary and Joseph holding the Baby Jesus. God is that close.

The sermon:

How Close Is God?

Hymns:
Beginning of worship: Angels We Have Heard on High
Sermon hymn: Tell It On The Mountain
End of worship: How Great Our Joy!

Scripture: Luke 2: 1-20

Sermon text: *"But the angel said to them, 'Do not be afraid. I bring you good news of great joy that will be for all the people.' "* v. 10

(The preacher is challenged to learn the text and share the story from memory, in turn challenging the congregation to hear the story as if for the first time.)
HOW FAR AWAY IS GOD? HOW CLOSE IS GOD? It is possible for people to "get by" in this world without asking such questions as these. As long as internal and external events proceed according to my plan; as long as I can fend off the awareness that one day I will die; as long as I can keep at bay all forms of fear; as long as I can ignore the fate of the less fortunate, blaming the hungry

and the poor for their own trouble; for that long I can "get by" in this world without asking, how far away is God? How close is God?

But as soon as anything breaks through my delusional reality; as soon as an inner darkness or an outer tragedy crushes my plans; as soon as death threatens me; as soon as I see the truth about human suffering; I will be forced to ask, how far away is God? How close is God? I will be forced to ask these questions because in my pain I will feel that God is very, very, very far away and I will want God to be very, very, very close. I will want to know, in my soul, that God is, here and now, Immanuel, with me, with us, with all of creation.

A couple of months ago my house was very quiet at 6:00 a.m. on a weekday morning. All the children were still asleep but I had been up for about an hour reading and in prayer. Suddenly the silence was pierced by a cry, "Daddy!" I got up and went into my five-year-old daughter Lauren's room. She was wide awake. As soon as I sat down beside her she lamented, "Daddy, I had a bad dream." "Do you want to tell me about it?" I asked her. "No."

So, I sat with her in silence, holding a hand and offering comfort. And I prayed. And I remembered that my bad dreams at age four almost always meant "monsters." And so I said, "I bet there was a monster in your dream." "Yeah, and he put me in a tree, and wouldn't let me down," Lauren volunteered. "I tried to escape but the monster was at the bottom of the tree. Then he covered his eyes. But there were others there, too. I couldn't get away."

"I remember dreams like that when I was five years old," I told her. "In my dreams the monster would chase me up the road past my house and into my friend David's barn. I would not be able to get out." After a few more moments of silence, I said to her, "Lauren, the next time one of those monsters puts you up in a tree just close your eyes and say, 'God, I need help.' I bet when you open your eyes the monster will be gone." Continuing the discussion about God, I asked, "Lauren, do you know how far away God is?" She spread out her hands and said, "Far, far away." "Lauren, do you know how close God is?" She held up a finger and a thumb, "Very, very close." "Do you want to hear a story about how close God is?" "Yes," she nodded her head energetically. And so I began:

"A long time ago the King, his name was Caesar, decided that he had to count all the people. This was the first time that all the people were counted while a man named Quirinius was the governor of Syria. And everyone had to travel to the city where they were born, to be counted. And Joseph — Do you know who Joseph was? 'Yes, he was Jesus' father. . ."

And I told her the whole story, until the shepherds were safely back on their hillside, taking care of the sheep and telling God just how awesome he was. Lauren never asked me if this was a true story. That's a question adults think they need to ask. Children know with their hearts whether a story is true or not. She knows how close God is to her.

It is possible to "get by," for awhile, without asking the questions, How far away is God? How close is God? But one day, some day, absolutely nothing will matter more than knowing in the deepest place of your heart that God is as close to you as your breath, that God is as close to you as a baby at his mother's breast.

In first century Palestine the lives of the people were filled with fear. They were afraid of disease, especially leprosy. They were afraid of poverty. They were afraid of the Roman oppressors. They were afraid of the religious authorities. But mostly they were afraid of the principalities and powers. The prime spiritual question of that era in the Middle East was, "Are the angels friend or foe?" (Matthew Fox, *The Coming of the Cosmic Christ*, p. 1).

The angels represented the spiritual forces of creation. The people wanted to know, "Are these spiritual forces for us or against us?" By acting in ways that help men and women, the angels prove that with the coming of Jesus the spiritual forces of creation are now on our side. We do not need to be afraid.

In one form or other, the question, "Are the angels friend or foe?" is also our question. "Am I safe in this universe?" "Does God love me?" "Can I really believe that nothing, absolutely nothing, can separate me from God?" Theological speculations are inadequate to answer these questions. The question, "Does God love me?" can only be answered by a story, and a singular story at that. That story begins, "In those days a decree went out from Caesar Augustus. . ."

The child within you already knows that this story is true. The monsters are retreating as the Light of the world advances. And you and I are held safe in the hands of God.

Kenneth C. Whitt
Mountview Baptist Church
Columbus, Ohio

DECEMBER 29, 1991

First Sunday after Christmas (Holy Name)

Lessons:

Lutheran:	Jer. 31:10-13	Heb. 2:10-18	Luke 2:41-52
Roman Catholic:	Sir. 3:3-7, 14-17a	Col. 3:12-21	Luke 2:22-40
Episcopal:	Is. 61:10-62:3	Gal. 3:23-35; 4:4-7	John 1:1-18
Pres/Meth/UCC:	1 Sam. 2:18-20, 26	Col. 3:12-17	Luke 2:41-52

Introductions to the Lessons

Lesson 1

(1) *Jeremiah 31:10-13* (**Luth**) Jeremiah sees beyond the destruction of Israel and the Babylonian captivity of the people to the time when Yahweh will like a shepherd bring his people back to Jerusalem. Then there will be singing and dancing, for their mourning will be turned to joy.

(2) *Isaiah 61:10-62:3* (**Epis**) The nation of Israel has had some bad times: destruction of Jerusalem and the Temple, and the people captive in a foreign country. Though the exiles have returned, the nation is struggling to rebuild. The prophet swears he will not stop pleading with Yahweh until he vindicates Israel and makes it once more great in the eyes of the world.

(3) *I Samuel 2:18-20, 26* (**Pres/Meth/UCC**) Samuel was the answer to his mother's prayer. She dedicated him to the Lord for service under the high priest, Eli, at Shiloh. Each year Samuel's parents came to see him and his mother made him a robe. As he grew up, he grew spiritually as well.

Lesson 2

(1) *Hebrews 2:10-18* (**Luth**) Jesus was born as the Messiah, the Son of God. He came from God and was of God. The author of Hebrews reminds us that Jesus was also human in that he suffered as a human, died as a human, and like all humans he was tempted. Because of this his death was to eliminate our death and his temptations enabled him to know our frame.

(2) *Galatians 3:23-35; 4:4-7* (**Epis**) Before Christ came into the world, we were slaves of the Law. At the right time Christ was born as a human to redeem those under the Law. Consequently, we are no longer slaves of the Law but free children of God because of his grace.

(3) *Colossians 3:12-17* (**Pres/Meth/UCC**) As Christ was born, we Christians have

been born anew in Christ. This new life is expressed in the quality of our lives. Love is the highest virtue. The peace and word of Christ dwell in us so that everything we do is done in the name of Christ.

Gospel

(1) *Luke 2:41-52* (**Luth/Pres/Meth/UCC**) At age 12 Jesus is found by his parents in the Temple having discussions with the learned scholars. Obediently he returns to Nazareth with his parents. During the coming years he experienced a fourfold growth.

(2) *John 1:1-18* (**Epis**) Before Jesus was born, he was with God the Father. He was the Word of God who became human at Christmas. As the Word he participated in the creation of the universe and became the light of the world. John the Baptizer was sent to be a witness to the light. When the Word became human, his truth and grace were seen. Those who believe in Christ the Word were given power to become children of God.

Theme: Christian parents must surrender their children to God.

Thought for the day: There are thousands of occasions for worry in the life of all parents. For every danger we are able to protect our children from, a multitude of others lurk around the next corner. We either worry or we trust. We either control or we surrender.

Prayer of meditation: Gracious God, you are the most perfect and adoring parent. You allow me to strike out on my own at just the right moment. You allow me to fall, but only so far. At all moments I can be certain of your presence and love. I may be free, but I am not forgotten. I make many mistakes, but I am always forgiven. I seek in this time of worship the wisdom and insight to pass on to all others entrusted to my care these qualities of love. May the word of the Lord, spoken, sung or heard in the silence of my heart, convict me of the times when I have dominated in ways I would not want to be dominated; the times I have judged in ways I would not want to be judged. Amen.

Call to worship: A child cries out when lost. He runs, only to get himself farther away from help. She panics, and fear draws her into even greater danger. We are all like children who are lost. Let us stay put for this hour of worship, and let help come to us. Let us wait for the knowledge that we are safe and protected in the hands of God.

Prayer of adoration: Our God, who brings all things to life, we have our lives in and through you. In this hour we gaze upon your face, as an infant focuses on the loving face of his mother. And what we see there is what the fortunate child sees: gentle, adoring love, tempered with wisdom. We see hope there also, hope that returns our gaze and tells us that our lives are treasures and that we will be protected as we pour out this treasure upon the world. Our God of comfort and closeness, we are humbled by your goodness and grateful beyond words for your love. Amen.

Prayer of confession: From the point of view of children, we have wanted, our God, power that we were not yet ready to manage. We have wanted to understand events that are beyond understanding. We have wanted to possess what could not be possessed. From the point of view of adults, we have withheld from others, including children, the rights that were theirs. We have controlled when we should have liberated. We have laughed at them when we should have cried with them. We have searched high and low and far and wide for the one who could understand and set us free. We have demanded that another human being meet our need. And we have failed even to tell you, our heavenly Father, the deepest longings of our souls. Forgive the fumbling ways we seek intimacy. Amen.

Prayer of dedication of gifts and self: In the gifts we give we participate in the recreation of the family of God. We seek to recreate that family in our church, that this may be a place of unconditional acceptance and hope. We pray that our church may truly be a sanctuary for families of all kinds, where individuals and couples and children and young and old can know that it is safe just "to be" for a moment. We seek, in the mission that goes forth from this place, to recreate family in our homes and neighborhoods and schools and places of employment and in our community and in our world. We give our lives to the mission of being family in a world filled with all manner of brokenness and disconnection. God, continue to help us grow in wholeness and empower our connections with you and with those we love that we might, with strength and courage, continue the work of recreating and being family. Amen.

Sermon title: A Gift of God to Parents

Sermon thesis: God presents parents with many opportunities to learn the discipline of surrendering our children to God. These events can, and do, cause parents enormous anxiety and pain. Nonetheless, we must teach our children ultimately to be obedient to God.

Hymn for the day: *"Angels, from the realms of glory."* This hymn, one of James Montgomery's most popular, appeared in the *Sheffield Iris,* December 24, 1816. More on Montgomery can be found at May 3 below.

Announcements for next week:

Sermon title: The Witness

Sermon theme: The importance of the witness who tells of Jesus.

Sermon summary: We often think of personal religious experiences as critical to salvation, which they are. But the focus of the Gospel of John is on the critical importance of the witness. Without the witness, most notably John the Baptist, there is no encounter with Christ. We all must find reliable witnesses, and we must become reliable witnesses to others.

Children's object talk:

We Have A Father Together

Objects: A hammer, a pen, a chef's cap, a calculator, and/or other objects that symbolize what a father does.

Lesson: We have a heavenly Father and we need to do what he tells us to do.

Outline: 1. Establish that we have a Father together.

2. Talk about what fathers do.

3. Decide if we should do what fathers say or what our heavenly Father says.

LET'S BEGIN BY REPEATING AFTER ME. "I have a father." "You have a father." "We have a Father together." Now, say it again. Now, what does it mean to say, "We have a Father together." That's right. We all have the same heavenly Father. Sometimes our individual fathers go away, but the Father we have together is always there.

Let's talk about what fathers do. What does the father do who uses this hammer? Right, he builds houses. (Continue with other objects.) What else do fathers do, besides working? That's right, they drive the car. Yes, they do play. Good, fathers hug us. One other thing fathers do is tell us what to do. What does your father tell you to do? Fathers sometimes have to tell us to keep quiet. And they sometimes yell at us to clean our rooms. That's true too, they give us an allowance.

Now, remember how we said that God is our heavenly Father? Well, as all good fathers, God also tells us what to do. What does God tell us to do? God tells us to love each other. God tells us to follow the commandments.

O.K., here is the problem. I want you to really think on this one. I am a father. Someday I am going to tell my daughter Stacey to do something and she is going to tell me that she believes God wants her to do something else. Who should Stacey follow? Me, her father? Or, God, her heavenly Father? I hope I will be wise enough to respect my daughter when she says she has to do what God says.

The sermon:

A Gift Of God To Parents

Hymns:
Beginning of worship: Love Divine, All Loves Excelling
Sermon hymn: Who Is This Boy?
End of worship: Give of Your Best to the Master

Scripture: Luke 2:41-52

Sermon text: *"Son, why have you treated us like this? Your father and I have been anxiously searching for you."* v. 48

VIEWED FROM THE PERSPECTIVE of Jesus, the closing verses of the second chapter of Luke tell a tale of adventure and self discovery. This was something Jesus had to do, no matter that Mary and Joseph could not understand. It might easily be proposed that this story is a gift of God to children seeking independence. But, viewed from the perspective of Mary and Joseph, these same verses tell a story of soul-piercing anxiety. Despite this pain, it is my proposal that the entire second chapter of Luke is, "A Gift of God to Parents." Let us begin with a story.

"Daughter, why have you treated us like this?" We were standing on the porch of Marge and Joe's home. The pain could not have been more severe had their daughter, Julie, thrust a real sword through their hearts. Just days before, Joe had called. "She is taking our grandchildren away!" he had protested. "I'll be right over," I said. Marge and Joe, as fine a Christian couple as you would ever hope to meet, were finally able, with deep hurt and severe embarrassment, to share their story. Their only daughter, Julie, was a nurse. Her husband, Bob, was pastor. And they were indeed taking the children away. They had been called to Central America, to build a church and a medical clinic. They would be gone at least two years.

There could be no visits home during that time. Julie had explained everything so carefully, so persuasively. And Marge and Joe already understood about things like, "Call." But, their daughter? Their grandchildren? Central America?

And so we stood on the porch for a final goodbye. There were hugs and tears all around. Marge and Joe had agreed to act supportive and even to be excited for the sake of the children. But it was all a terribly thin veneer. Saying goodbye to each child, they acted brave. Inside they were dying. I prayed, God help us! But Joe, unable to wait for divine help, finally pulled Julie aside and quietly spoke, "Can't you see that this is killing your mother and me?" And Julie pulled away, gathered up Bobby, Sarah, and Peter, and her husband Bob, and exited through the tears, saying to Bob, "They do not understand. They just do not understand!"

If the second chapter of the Gospel of Luke helps us to understand, maybe we could see it as "A Gift of God to Parents." Illuminating the story of our lives, the Gospel story may prepare us for the time when the circumstances of life force us to walk in Marge and Joe's footsteps. Look briefly with me at an outline of chapter two.

First, in verses 1-20, there is the ever inspiring, deeply moving Christmas story, complete with angels and shepherds and hymns of glory to announce a child's birth. Certainly, it is easy to understand this part of the story as, "A Gift of God to Parents." Would that every parent could experience the birth of their children as holy and glorious events!

Second, there is a series of encounters with those who give understanding to Mary and Joseph, in verses 21-38. This too is, "A Gift of God to Parents." Which of us does not wish for insight into our children? But this insight comes with a price. Some have said that "ignorance is bliss." Such bliss will not be Mary's and Joseph's lot. As Simeon says to Mary, "And a sword will pierce your own soul too." These parents know they will suffer. But what kind of suffering? We do not have to wait long to find out.

For, third, we find out what it will mean to have a sword pierce the heart of Mary in verses 41-50. I believe that, in this event from ordinary life, in searching for and finding their lost son, God is preparing Mary and Joseph so they will be able to understand and accept the price they must pay when their son is obedient to God.

Christian parents carry an awesome burden. It is our task to teach our children to be obedient to God's call in their lives. But are we conscious of the price we might have to pay if we are completely successful in this endeavor? I believe God seeks to prepare us by confronting us with ordinary events in our lives that guide us towards surrendering our children into God's hands. Our children have talents and gifts different from the ones we might have sought for them. They don't seem to be headed for the destinations we had planned. They have different tastes and even different values. I remember two Christian parents who had a fit when their son began to date an Hispanic girl. He said he was just doing what he had been taught at church. They told him, "Stop talking back!" I can remember having to deal with a very angry parent, after I had invited her daughter to go on a mission encounter trip to Appalachia. "Sherry is too young," she protested. "She could get hurt. She cannot handle it." We all know who could not handle it. Sherry did just fine. Mother is still learning to cope. These are only the beginnings. I believe that the words of Simeon, "A sword will pierce your own soul too," are a gift of God, a warning and a preparation, to all parents who have the courage to teach their children to be obedient to God. And the story of Jesus in the Temple is a gift, for there will be times when, despite all warnings and preparations, we will not understand and will protest, "Son, daughter, why have you treated us like this?" Keep the second chapter of the Gospel of Luke in your heart, and as soon as you have spoken the words of protest towards your child, you will remember the story. And remembering, you may understand.

I would give a cautionary note, suggested by verse 51. "Then he went down to Nazareth with them and was obedient to them." The independent action of Jesus in this story takes place within a context of respect for parental authority and a relationship of mutual love. This is not always the case in our lives. The hearts of parents are pierced by the actions of their children a thousand times a thousand times, and we can only wish it were always because the children were being obedient to God. Most of the time disobedience is grounded in far more mundane issues, like self-will and sinfulness, the absence of relationships grounded in mutual love, and sometimes just plain stupidity. These also can cause a sword to pierce the souls of parents.

The second chapter of the Gospel of Luke is, "A Gift of God to Parents." It celebrates with us, it warns us and it teaches us. As parents, our souls will be pierced with sorrow and anxiety and fear on behalf of our children. Let us do everything in our power — and not everything is in our power — to make sure that the wounds we feel are caused by the obedience of our children to God. We are to guide and protect our children on their journeys. But we must not take their journeys away from them.

Kenneth C. Whitt
Mountview Baptist Church
Columbus, Ohio

JANUARY 5, 1992

Second Sunday after Christmas

Lessons:

Lutheran:	Is. 61:10-62:3	Eph. 1:3-6, 15-18	John 1:1-18
Roman Catholic:	Sir. 24:1-2, 8-12	Eph, 1:3-6, 15-18	John 1:1-18
Episcopal:	Jer. 31:7-14	Eph. 1:3-6, 15-19a	Matt. 2:13-15, 19-23
Pres/Meth/UCC:	Jer. 31:7-14	Eph. 1:3-6, 15-18	John 1:1-18

Introductions to the Lessons

Lesson 1

(1) *Isaiah 61:10-62:3* (**Luth**) Please see Lesson 1, Christmas I, Epis.

(2) *Jeremiah 31:7-14* (**Epis/Pres/Meth/UCC**) Please see Lesson 1, Christmas I, Luth.

Lesson 2

Ephesians 1:3-6, 15-18 (**Luth/Epis/Pres/Meth/UCC**) God has blessed the church in Ephesus with spiritual blessings, with his choice of them to be holy, and with a destiny to be his children. Paul is aware of their faith in Christ, their love for each other, and their hope of a glorious inheritance. He prays that God will give them a spirit of wisdom and revelation.

Gospel

(1) *John 1:1-18* (**Luth/Pres/Meth/UCC**) Please see Gospel, Christmas I, Epis.

(2) *Matthew 2:13-15, 19-23* (**Epis**) The Wise Men came and left the holy family in Bethlehem. Then an angel warned Joseph of Herod's intention to kill the child Jesus. Joseph took mother and child to Egypt and remained there until Herod's death. Again, an angel told Joseph to return to Palestine. Again Joseph obeyed and took his family to Nazareth.

Theme: The importance of the witness who tells of Jesus.

Thought for the day: I will never forget her. Her hair was as white as snow. Her name was Mrs. Sunny. And her job was to tell wild second graders like me about Jesus. And tell us she did! Her hands danced across the flannel-graph; Her lips sang the words of the story. And she introduced me to the one friend who has never left my side.

Prayer of meditation: In the moments before worship, allow my mind, my God, to wander through the memories of my life. And let me stop for a moment on the witnesses who have, with the clearest voices, told me the stories of Jesus. I seek to honor these witnesses with my attention, and to thank them for what they have given. I seek to remember the special flavors of faith they gave the stories, because of their unique personalities and experiences. These witnesses, like John the Baptist, each have a name. And these names are holy in my life. Amen.

Call to worship: Listen; to the silence; to the music; to the words of scripture and to the words of women and men. Listen to all that gives witness to the movement of God and the presence of the Holy Spirit in our midst. In this hour, distinguish carefully between the mundane and the holy voices. By an act of will, turn your ear to hear God.

Prayer of adoration: Thank you, God. You sent a witness to me. And he told me of your love. He told me with such conviction that I could not dismiss your claim upon my life. It could have been so different. I could have failed to listen. Then I would have never known that all of the old and lonely and angry and bitter ways were unnecessary. None could have a greater debt to pay you than I. There is beauty in my life today, and hope and peace and purpose. You gave them all to me. Thank you, God. Maybe there are more poetic and powerful ways to say it, but thank you, God, for your love. And thank you for sending the witness. Amen.

Prayer of confession: There is no way to speak a complete list of the ways I shut my eyes and my ears and my heart. I have my own particular ways of not paying attention when you speak, my God. And I have my own particular list of messages that I will not hear. I have facts and figures to toss at anyone who tells me I must care for the needy. I have a book full of rationalizations and explanations that account for my failures to change and grow. And I will just walk away if anyone gets too close to the truth. There is no witness you can send who can break through my intention to live my life my own way. But oh, my God! Please, my God! Keep trying! Amen.

Prayer of dedication of gifts and self: Our God of ultimate generosity, these gifts are the symbol and the substance of our decisions to be witnesses for you. We direct the good news of your saving love to each person gathered in this place. We open the doors and windows of this building and let the message flow across our community and state. We give our witness legs and wheels and wings that it may be carried across the country and into all of the world. We pray that the good news may never be derailed or sunk for want of our support. We pray for every person whom these gifts support in their efforts to be witnesses for Jesus Christ. And we pray for all the people who will hear, that minds, hearts and souls may be open to receive the holy word that can make all the difference in their lives. And we pray that we too, in every part of our lives, may be those witnesses through whom others learn of Jesus. Amen.

Sermon title: The Witness

Sermon thesis: We often think of personal religious experience as critical to salvation, which it is. But the focus of the Gospel of John is on the critical importance of the witness. Without the witness, most notably John the Baptist, there is no encounter with Christ. We must all find reliable witnesses, and we must become reliable witnesses to others.

Hymn for the day: *"Let all mortal flesh keep silence."* This beautiful hymn is from the Liturgy of St. James, where it was sung as the bread and wine were brought to the table. Celebrated on St. James's Day, October 23, the liturgy is believed to have originated with St. James the Less, first bishop of Jerusalem. It was translated from the Greek by Gerard Moultrie (1829-1885), a priest of the Church of England. The hymn progresses from Jesus' lowly birth to his resounding adoration. It is nearly always sung to the tune PICARDY, a seventeenth-century French folksong about the rich man and Lazarus.

Announcements for Epiphany, January 6

Sermon title: From the East
Sermon theme: Our search for meaning leads to Jesus.
Sermon summary: Matthew seeks from the beginning of his gospel to show the child of Mary as the Christ Messiah, around which revolves the life of the Jewish people. He expands this circle to include both "foreigners" and the cosmos itself. Thus, he invites us to see that all creation is centered in Jesus.

Announcements for next week:

Sermon title: Belonging
Sermon theme: Jesus' baptism is a sign of his belonging, to God and to God's people.

Sermon summary: In his baptism, Jesus hears the words from second Isaiah promising success to the suffering servant of God. When a person knows they are positively viewed by God, they are much more likely to accomplish good things under pressure than if their negatives are constantly paraded before them.

Children's object talk:

A Witness Who Tells The Truth

Objects: An easily described object, like a red, white and blue soccer ball, wrapped in a box.

Lesson: We can each be a witness who tells the truth about Jesus.

Outline: 1. Moses and the ninth commandment, (for Lutherans it's eighth) "Thou shalt not bear false witness."

2. In secret, two children unwrap the box. One has been instructed to bear false witness, the other to bear true witness. Decide who told the truth.

3. Tell them of Jesus' commandment, "You shall bear witness," (John 15:27). No truth is more important to tell than this truth.

WHO IS MOSES? That's right, he did bring the Israelites across the desert. He heard God speak from a burning bush. One other thing Moses did was to receive the Ten Commandments from God. Does anyone know what the ninth commandment is? Very good! "Thou shalt not bear false witness against thy neighbor." (Exodus 20:16) Let's see if I can show you what a false witness is. Behind the pulpit I have a box wrapped like a Christmas present. There is something in the box. John and Sarah, (Choose the children and explain the story to them before the service.) I would like you to go behind the pulpit and open the box together. One of them is going to tell us what is in the box and one of them is going to try to trick us.

(John and Sarah return and "bear witness" to what was in the box.) Boys and Girls, who was telling us the truth? How do you know? How could we find out what is really in the box? That's right. We could send someone else that we trust to look. And they could then "bear witness" to what is in the box.

Jesus gave us another commandment, "You shall bear witness." He meant that we are all to tell the truth. But, what truth did Jesus mean we are to tell? In this case Jesus meant we are all to tell the truth about who Jesus is. We are to "bear witness," to tell others, about Jesus. What do you think we should tell them? Excellent, that Jesus loves us. Jesus is God's Son and we can tell people that. There are a lot of other good answers. We can each be the witness who tells the truth.

The sermon:

The Witness

Hymns:
>Beginning of worship: Of the Father's Love Begotten
>Sermon hymn: Christ Was Born in a Distant Land
>End of worship: I Love to Tell the Story

Scripture: John 1:1-18

Sermon text: *"There was a man sent from God, whose name was John. He came for testimony, to bear witness to the light, that all might believe through him."* vs. 6-7

IN THE BIBLICAL ACCOUNTS OF THE INCARNATION, WHO BEARS WITNESS TO JESUS? In Matthew, Mark and Luke there are shepherds and kings, an old man and an old woman, angels and even animals. But these are not the witnesses in the Gospel of John's account of the incarnation. Here we find, in chapter one, only one witness, a man sent from God whose name was John. As you listen to John 1:1-18, hear the rhythmic flow between proclamation about Jesus and witness to Jesus.

READ JOHN 1:1-18

The evangelist has, in this poetry, established a theme that he will continue to develop throughout the Gospel. That theme is the critical importance of the witness. We know who Jesus is because of the witness, who is John. We know the witness is reliable because he was sent by God. Whenever truth is proclaimed in the Gospel of John, it is attested to by a witness which might be a person, a sign or miracle or God directly. Listen to this series of phrases from John. " . . . the Father who sent me has himself borne witness . . . " (5:37); I bear witness to myself (8:18); "The works that I do . . . they bear witness to me." (10:25) And then, listen carefully, because we shall return to this point. " . . . you also shall bear witness . . . " (15:27). The problem John had to contend with in his church was opposition to the truth. Pagans, Christians teaching false doctrine, and some Jews who continued to oppose the church all had to be battled. The light had to continue to oppose darkness. The truth had to be ever vigilant against distortions and lies. And that is why, of course, such attention is placed on the authority of the witness. There has to be a witness who knows and can tell the truth if there is to be salvation for any of God's people. Without the witness, there can be no faith. The witness creates a connection between Jesus, who is the Light, and anyone still living in darkness. For example, notice the use of the word "we," in the middle of John 1:14: " . . . we have beheld his glory, glory as of the only Son from the Father." Who is this "we?" The "we" is John's church. Because of the witness of Christians who have come before them, John's people have " . . . beheld his glory, glory as of the only Son of the Father." John claims for his people that they, sixty years or so after the resurrection, have seen Jesus, because they have seen him through the eyes of witnesses. It was like they were really there. John's church was saved by Jesus, because they saw Jesus, in all his glory, through the eyes of witnesses.

And what of those who see through the eyes of witnesses, who saw Jesus through the eyes of other witnesses, who saw through the eyes of previous witnesses, who saw Jesus in all his glory through the eyes of still other witnesses, who saw him through the eyes of other witnesses . . . I trust you get the point. Those people who see the glory of Jesus through the eyes of witnesses through almost two thousand years of Christian history, those people whose salvation depends on the testimony of witnesses, are you and I.

The proclamation of the people of John's church is also our proclamation: "We have beheld his glory, glory as of the only Son of the Father . . . And from his fullness have we all received, grace upon grace."

It may be apparent how important it is, then, that we have a practice of listening to and learning from reliable witnesses. Christians, and the Church, can, according to John, reflect the full glory of Jesus only if their lives are grounded in the witness of others who saw Jesus. In turn, the Christian and the Church must bear witness to what they have received. Given the depth of John's emphasis on the importance of the witness, might we not be concerned about how little emphasis there is on "witnessing" among Christians today? The freedom to tell the stories of our meetings with Jesus used to be a great strength in many Christian communities. Given some of the distortions that become all too common, it is not hard to see why giving witness has become a lost art. But it cannot remain lost! The power of the witness to bring others to a saving relationship with Jesus Christ is astounding. On many occasions I have prepared a wonderful class or a great sermon — but it was the spontaneous sharing of a Christian witness that won a soul for Jesus. If the Gospel of John is correct, then careful, prayerful, focused witnessing to Jesus is essential in any and every church that hopes to be the light of Jesus Christ to the darkness of the world.

There is another kind of witness to whom we need to listen. Of course we need to listen to our theologians and our scholars and our preachers and our teachers. And, there are saints of the church who are particularly authoritative witnesses. But in addition, from among the communion of saints stretching through the ages, each Christian can choose a witness, or two, or many, to whom you listen regularly in order to be sure you are seeing Jesus in all of his glory. One witness who has been given to me is Oswald Chambers, a Scottish pastor, preacher, teacher from the beginning of this century. One reason Chambers is good for me, besides the fact that he is spiritually profound and a deep lover of Jesus, is that he comes at Christianity from a different tradition than mine. He is conservative — extremely conservative some might say. And he writes in a slightly different dialect of English. All of this serves to help me to see and to know Jesus in new ways. Literally, day after day, I find myself feeling that I have received from Christ's fullness by way of Chambers' witness.

Oswald Chambers gives witness to the Christ who was first witnessed to by John, who was sent by God. All of that is why I can believe! The fullness of God's love for you and me was passed down witness to witness through decades and generations and centuries of Christian Church history. And look! Do you see it? This light and life and love, Jesus, full of grace and truth, has now come to make his home in our lives and our church. And God the Father is making you into the witness. Do you remember when Jesus said in John 15:27, "You shall bear witness." That word was spoken to

210

the apostles. It was also spoken to John's Church. And it is still the Word of the Lord to us today. You are the witness. I am the witness. We are the witness together. That is how God is acting in our world today to bring the saving light of Jesus to the people, the community, the nation and the world. Do not fail to see — do not fail to be — the witness.

Kenneth C. Whitt
Mountview Baptist Church
Columbus, Ohio

211

JANUARY 6, 1992

The Epiphany of Our Lord

Lessons:

Lutheran:	Is. 60:1-6	Eph. 3:2-12	Matt. 2:1-12
Roman Catholic:	Is. 60:1-6	Eph. 3:2-3, 5-6	Matt. 2:1-12
Episcopal:	Is. 60:1-6, 9	Eph. 3:1-12	Matt. 2:1-12
Pres/Meth/UCC:	Is. 60:1-6	Eph. 3:1-12	Matt. 2:1-12

Introductions to the Lessons

Lesson 1

Isaiah 60:1-6 (**Luth/Pres/Meth/UCC**); *60:1-6, 9* (**Epis**) Epiphany is the festival and season of light. It is associated with the five-pointed star. A star can be seen only in the darkness. Israel at the time of this writing is in the darkness of the dispersion of her people. Now the light of God is seen and the scattered people will be returned and the glory of God will appear in their midst.

Lesson 2

Ephesians 3:2-12 (**Luth**); *3:1-12* (**Epis/Pres/Meth/UCC**) Paul has a secret. It was hidden for centuries. It was revealed to him that the Gospel is for Gentiles as well as for Jews. This makes Christianity a universal religion, for Christ died for all human beings. By the grace of God he was called to proclaim this good news to the Gentiles.

Gospel

Matthew 2:1-12 (**Luth/Epis/Pres/Meth/UCC**) Led by a star, learned men from the East came to worship the king whose star they saw. Since the baby was a child of a king, they naturally went to Jerusalem, the capitol city, where they learned that the Scriptures named Bethlehem as the birthplace. Again, the star led them to the holy family where they worshiped the Christchild with gifts.

Theme: Humankind's search for meaning leads to Jesus.

Thought for the day: A great poet once said of Jesus, "He is the still point of a turning world." Into the swirl of human activity with jealousies such as Herod's, exhaustion such as Mary's, and hope such as that of the Magi, Christ comes like a star of peace, around which all these, like planets, revolve.

Prayer of meditation: Lord, each day I search for that which is of value: a good buy, a fine report, a new idea, a smile or two. Through these things I seek to know that life is good, that it is of worth. Reveal yourself to me on this day, and all others, in such a way that I might see that it is you who make all else worthwhile. Then help me to share the joy I have found in my search with others.

Call to worship:
Leader: We have seen his star in the east:
  People: O come, let us worship him!
Leader: Let us see his light in our lives:
  People: O come, let us worship him!

Prayer of adoration: How awesome is your wisdom, Lord! How humbly you have come! For not with blare of trumpet, or army on the march, or garish press release have you arrived, but with the lonesome cry of our humanity on your infant lips. You have conquered our hopeless hearts with the promise of a child. How awesome is your wisdom, Lord! Let all who would be wise, all who would be strong, all who would be loved, bow before your manger throne of grace! Amen.

Prayer of confession: Lord, we find it hard to be humble. We find it hard to let our vulnerability show, as you did when you came to us as a helpless child. We prefer to let others make the first move, while we lie in wait, like Herod, waiting to pounce on their mistakes. We seek praise, but we are loath to give it, and we are surprised when love eludes us! Forgive us, Lord, our arrogance. Help us to become like the truly wise, seeking the best in others, bowing humbly before their uniqueness while not forgetting our own. As your children reach for us, let us reach for them. Let your love so shine upon us that the shadows of jealousy and indifference may trouble us no more. Amen.

Prayer of dedication of gifts and self: With the wise men who first offered you their gifts of gold and spice, we offer you the best of what we have. We do so with their joy and thanksgiving, and we pray that you will use these gifts to build your Church. As we return to our homes, by another way, the way of compassion, we ask that you use us, too, in that great redemptive work. Lord, open your gifts; but open also our hearts, for your pleasure and your mission.

Sermon title: From the East

213

Sermon thesis: Matthew seeks from the beginning of his Gospel to show the child of Mary as the Christ/Messiah, around which revolves the life of the Jewish people. He expands this circle to include both "foreigners" and the cosmos itself. Thus, he invites us to see that all creation is centered in Jesus.

Hymn for the day: *"Jesus shall reign where'er the sun."* The great English Dissenting minister and hymn writer, Isaac Watts (1674-1748), holds an important place in the transition from the exclusive use of Psalm paraphrases in worship to the singing of hymns. This hymn was the second part of Psalm 72, "Christ's kingdom among the Gentiles," in Watts's *Psalms of David,* 1719. It is an excellent hymn to reflect the Epiphany message that Christ is for all nations.

Announcements for next week:

Sermon title: Belonging

Sermon theme: Jesus' baptism is a sign of his belonging to God and to God's people.

Sermon summary: In his baptism, Jesus hears the words from second Isaiah promising success to the suffering servant of God. When a person knows they are positively viewed by God, they are much more likely to accomplish good things under pressure than if their negatives are constantly paraded before them.

Children's object talk:

The Most Important Thing In Church

Objects: Model of a church building (perhaps your own) with various furnishings and a small figurine of the Christ Child from the Christmas creche.

Lesson: The most important thing in church is Jesus.

Outline: 1. Define the word "important."

2. There are many important things in church.

3. Jesus is the most important.

I HAVE A BIG WORD TO TEACH YOU TODAY. The word is "important." It means something, or someone, that you really want to have or keep. You have some important things in your lives: Mom and Dad, maybe a pet, or a special toy. Sometimes we say that some things or some person is more important. That is, we really, really, really, really want to have or keep them, even if it means giving up something else. For example, you might think it is more important to play with your pet dog than to go to a movie.

I have here a model of our church. There are many important things in our church. Like the altar — or the organ — or the pulpit — or the pastor — (take these objects out of the model in succession). But what is the most important thing or person to have in church?

I bet I know: JESUS! (pull out Christ figure).

Today we read about the wise men who visited Jesus after he was born. They were really smart guys. Do you know why they were so smart? They realized Jesus was the most important thing in their lives. More important than gold, or frankincense and myrrh, which are pretty important things. We're pretty smart, too, because we know what they knew: many things are important to our church, but the most important is Jesus.

The sermon:

From the East

Hymns:

Beginning of worship: Bright and Glorious is the Sky
Sermon hymn: In Christ There Is No East or West
End of worship: As With Gladness Men of Old

Scripture: Matthew 2:1-12

Sermon text: *Wise men came from the East saying, "Where is he born King of the Jews?"* v. 2

THE WONDERFUL STORY of the wise men at the birth of Jesus, which only the Gospel of Matthew records, is a tightly compacted tale replete with a host of Old Testament references, some obvious, some less so. This gospel is so steeped in Old Testament background that we can hardly read a sentence without detecting some allusion to an episode in Hebrew/Jewish history. A quotation here, a code word or two there, and there is triggered in the faithful mind the ancient memories and promises, which Matthew is wont to link to Jesus, the Christ. For example, the notion of the traveling star is less a record of an actual celestial occurrence than it is more a reference to the 24th chapter of Numbers, in which Baalam, a foreign prophet, predicts great things for the nation of Israel by likening its appearance to a "star rising out of Jacob." In Matthew, the remem-berer of that story is thus invited to transfer hope for a bright future from trust in the nation to trust in Jesus.

The story is a workout for the memory — but such a delightful exercise! The setting is the birth of a child. Guests gather to view the new arrival and celebrate the event. We have all seen or participated in such an event, and our attention is thus focused by this narrative. The wise ones behave pretty much the way we would expect good neighbors to behave when the newborn and mother return home. "Where is he/she?" "Can I see him/her?" "Here, I brought just a little something in honor of the day . . . " These are some of the phrases we would use in a similar situation, which have their counterparts in Matthew's tale of the wise ones.

Inexorably, we are drawn into the story, which is made all the more fascinating by the anonymity of the characters. Nothing is known about these wise ones. Current thinking holds that they were astrologers, but this may be a bit condescending. They could easily have been astronomers, part of the long and brilliant tradition of Middle Eastern celestial observation. We do not know. All we can glean are a few facts: they came "from the East;" they professed intelligence (except when asking Herod for directions); and they possessed grace, as witnessed by their offering of gifts. That is all. The very dearth of information about them has captured the imaginations of countless generations. They have been given names, homes, itineraries. They have been written into songs and screenplays. One could suppose that the lack of data given has been interpreted by many as tacit permission to read into the story emotions, thoughts and actions peculiar to other times, other situations. It is so easy, without fixed biographies, to fit our own into the characters and thus approach Jesus at this central point of history, his humble birth in Bethlehem, which at the time was largely ignored by people like us. We "outsiders in time" can thus vicariously experience that wonderful moment.

This may be exactly what Matthew intended to happen. Again, there are clues which might lead us to believe this. Very few of the people encountered by Jesus in Matthew are named. In most cases, they are simply described by a condition. There is a concern for outsiders, sinners in and out of the family of Judaism. And there is a curious collapsing of the boundaries between past, present and future. All of which suggests a blurring of the distinction between you and I in our time and those who look for Jesus in Matthew's Gospel.

Scholars have noted the possible connection between the rising of the star at the beginning of the Gospel and the rising of Jesus at the end of it. The wise ones are seen as representative of all those who have heard about the resurrection and want to know the story behind it. So, predictably, they come to hear the story from the beginning, and Matthew has so fashioned the narrative to allow anyone to do so.

It was to the East of Eden that Adam and Eve were banished after the fall. It was to the East of Eden that Cain was made to live after he had slain his brother Abel. And it is in the East of Eden, figuratively speaking, that all of us dwell who daily must deal with humanity's penchant for self-destruction and our own participation in that unholy guest. The East is a land of shadows, of Herodian intrigue, of frenzied and pointless activity where humans are but numbers and the neighbor is someone to push aside on our way to the top of God knows what. It is from the East that the wise ones come. And it is from East of Eden, from the periphery of true life, that we are called alongside of them to view the Savior of the world, to bow humbly down before the magnificence of the work he has done and the potential for that same work in and through us. To have the eye-opening experience of worshiping the one who will teach us to watch the birds and the flowers, who will remind us of how much we are worth to God, and to rise, thrilled just to be there, and to return "by another way" to our life, determined not to live in the East ever again.

In his book, *The Fires of Spring,* James Michener makes the remark that "the journey men make is to find themselves. Nothing else matters much." The Gospel of Matthew's use of the wise ones meeting Jesus would suggest an amendment — if your journey leads not to Christ, nothing else matters. The fat salary, the high status, the great power possessed by the mighty all pale in comparison to standing in front of this Child, who reaches for us in love. Matthew bids all those who are attracted by the bright star of Jesus' resurrection to stay and find out how he got there, to journey with him on the compassionate path of preaching, teaching and healing, and thus find out what life is really for.

The phrase is timeworn, and perhaps trite, but true: wise men, and women, still seek him.

Kenn A. Nilsen
Lutheran Church Staff
Port Murray, New Jersey

JANUARY 12, 1992

First Sunday after the Epiphany
Baptism of Our Lord

Lessons:

Lutheran:	Is. 42:1-7	Acts 10:34-38	Luke 3:15-17, 21-22
Roman Catholic:	Is. 42:1-4, 6-7	Acts 10:34-38	Luke 3:15-16, 21-22
Episcopal:	Is. 42:1-9	Acts 10:34-38	Luke 3:15-16, 21-22
Pres/Meth/UCC:	Is. 61:1-4	Acts 8:14-17	Luke 3:15-17, 21-22

Introductions to the Lessons

Lesson 1

(1) *Isaiah 42:1-7* (**Luth**); *42:1-9* (**Epis**) This is one of the Servant Songs in Isaiah. In this song the Servant of God is described as chosen by God and endowed with his Spirit. His government is one of justice and he will be a light of freedom to the nations. Christians find that Jesus fulfills this description.

(2) *Isaiah 61:1-4* (**Pres/Meth/UCC**) This was the text of Jesus' first sermon in Nazareth. In fulfillment of the prophecy, Jesus was anointed by the Spirit at his baptism and his ministry was to proclaim liberty and to comfort the afflicted.

Lesson 2

(1) *Acts 10:34-38* (**Luth/Epis**) Peter points to Jesus' baptism when he was anointed with the power of the Holy Spirit. This was the beginning of his ministry of doing good and healing the oppressed.

(2) *Acts 8:14-17* (**Pres/Meth/UCC**) The Christian converts in Samaria were baptized but did not receive the Spirit. The church sent Peter and John to them. When they laid their hands upon the people, they received the Holy Spirit.

Gospel

Luke 3:15-17, 21-22 (**Luth/Epis/Pres/Meth/UCC**) According to Luke, Jesus' baptism by John in the Jordan river was a prayer experience. In this experience the heavens were opened, the Spirit came to him, and God's voice of acceptance and approval was heard.

Theme: Jesus' baptism is a sign of his belonging, to God and to God's people.

Thought for the day: Humans were made to belong. How empty is the self-sufficient life, how rich the life tied to others in friendship! The Baptism of Jesus is a sign of friendship with God, and a willingness to be friends with all the human family.

Prayer of meditation: Of all the fears that plague me, Lord, the thought of rejection is the worst. The idea that I might be unacceptable weighs terribly on me. Help me to remember my baptism today, as I hear of the Baptism of Jesus. Show me once again the joy of my acceptance, that you have also spoken to me as a beloved daughter/son. Amen.

Call to worship:
Leader: The Lord has called us to righteous purpose;
  People: He has taken us by the hand.
Leader: He formed us to be a light to all people;
  People: O come, Let us worship the Lord!

Prayer of adoration: You could have stayed apart from us, Lord. You could have allowed us to wallow in the muck and mire of our human sin, of seeing our neighbors as enemies. Yet you chose to live among us and show us a better way. This you did, and still do, out of your great love. All praise to you for coming among us, serving among us, saving among us. All praise to you for allowing us the chance to be in your likeness once again. Amen.

Prayer of confession: Lord, we have not fulfilled your intention that we live in harmony and peace. We are all too willing to focus on the differences that divide us, rather than the similarities which unite us. We cast each other in categories of race, status and power, and we fail to see the fellow earth traveler simply trying to find his or her way. Forgive us, Lord; and bring us together around the remembrance of baptism, the great unifying sign of all those who seek to be your righteous ones, regardless of color, background, or influence. Amen.

Prayer of dedication of gifts and self: Lord Jesus, in your baptism you offered yourself for the work of God. Your life is totally dedicated to doing good. With these gifts we, too, offer ourselves as signs and symbols of your presence in our world. Renew in us a sense of belonging to you, rather than owning you, and so free us for the tasks of accomplishing good things.

Sermon title: Belonging

Sermon thesis: In his baptism, Jesus hears the words from second Isaiah promising success to the suffering servant of God. When a person knows they are positively viewed by God, they are much more likely to accomplish good things under pressure than if their negatives are constantly paraded before them.

Hymn for the day: *"To Jordan came the Christ, our Lord"/"When Jesus went to Jordan's stream."* Martin Luther (1483-1546) was born in Eisleben, Germany and ordained a priest in 1507. While on the faculty at Wittenberg University he became aware of some of the corruptions in the church of his time. From there the story of the Reformation is well known. A musician himself, Luther encouraged congregational hymn singing and wrote a number of fine hymns. This hymn on the Baptism of Christ was one of Luther's hymns on parts of the Catechism.

Announcements for next week:

    Sermon title: The Difference Jesus Makes

    Sermon theme: Jesus makes a difference in our daily living.

    Sermon summary: This text calls us to the joy of faith. Our spiritual life can go flat, grow dull. Jesus' first miracle can remind us of the joy and gladness which may characterize our relationship with him.

Children's object talk:

A Sign of Love

Objects: Street signs, building signs, etc.

Lesson: Baptism is a sign of God's love.

Outline: 1. Signs help us understand.

         2. Some signs are actions.

         3. Baptism is an action sign of love.

I HAVE HERE SOME SIGNS that I found around town. Some of you can't read yet, but these signs have words on them which tell us what to do. For example, this sign says, "PARKING." That means you can park your car in that spot, if you want to. Signs help us understand things.

Now, some signs aren't printed on a board like these are. Sometimes we make a sign with our fingers, like this: (make the O.K. sign with thumb and forefinger). This sign means, "All right! You did good!" So an action sign like this one also helps you understand things, in this case, that you did well.

Today we will hear about the baptism of Jesus. You know a little bit about baptism: someone puts water on another person's head and says some prayers. That is a sign, just like the O.K. sign I showed you. It means, "I am happy with you." You will hear God saying that about Jesus when he is baptized.

It may sound funny, that putting water on somebody's head is a sign meaning, "I am happy with you," or "I love you," but that is what it means when we do it with prayers to Jesus. Just as these funny letters on a board help us to understand, and the funny way I hold my fingers helps you understand, in the same way putting water on someone with a prayer is a way of understanding that God loves that person, and you do, too.

The sermon:

Belonging

Hymns:
Beginning of worship: On Jordan's Banks the Baptist's Cry
Sermon hymn: To Jordan Came the Christ, Our Lord
End of worship: Spirit of God, Unleashed on Earth

Scripture: Luke 3:15-17, 21-22

Sermon text: *"The people were on the edge of expectation. . ."* v. 15

A FEW YEARS AGO there was discussion among church leaders and teachers from the various Christian denominations about the basics of the faith. The result was a little book entitled, Baptism, Ordination and Ministry. Happily, it represented a real effort to address the different denominational perspectives on these topics. Sadly, unity of thinking on the three remains elusive.

Baptism received extended treatment, yet consensus was not reached. This should not surprise us. The gospels which record the Baptism of Jesus, such a watershed event for us all, differ in what is emphasized about it. Matthew records a thirst for righteousness. Mark remembers the initiation into a time of testing. John is obscure. From what we read in the first chapter of that gospel, we cannot be sure that Jesus was even baptized at all! In Luke, Jesus' baptism brings to mind the anointing of kings, and the people's mobilization for mission. Different perspectives exist even in the gospels.

Luke's recording of the event is interesting, because of the royal themes. The expectation of the people for a messiah, the juxtaposition of this with the sordid behavior of the pretender king Herod, and the recitation of Psalm 2 and Isaiah 42, both of which are laden with royal overtones, all lead to understanding that a new monarch has just been inaugurated.

The concept of the king as God's son, crystallized in Psalm 2, was an old one in Hebrew/Jewish history. It was assumed that God had laid a blessing, and responsibility, on a particular person that made for a close, personal relationship akin to that which occurred in well adjusted families between parent and child. The blessing was the recognition of the specialness of the person; the responsibility was to act, not as power hungry despot, but loving servant leader of God's people.

If we accept this, and further accept Jesus' conferring this status onto his followers at the close of Luke's gospel, then we who are baptized are party to these promises of specialness and responsibility. Let us focus for the moment on the former notion.

Mister Rogers, of television fame, has been the butt of many jokes regarding his gentle, soft spoken approach on his show. But there is much to commend on the program. Almost every episode finds him at one point singing a song about each child being special. It may be that his background as a pastor in the Church shows at such times! Even old curmudgeons would have to admit that being called "special" is a good thing for children to hear. It conveys a sense of worth and belonging.

Adults could stand to hear it now and again, too. it is a good thing to hear that one is special, that in some sort of intangible way you belong. The Japanese take great pains to convey this idea in their businesses to the workers. Worker loyalty is built by reminding people that their opinions and options do count, and that the whole corporation would be diminished by their absence. It is no small accident that the Japanese have one of the most materially productive societies in the world.

I wonder what effect the words of Psalm 2 and Isaiah 42 had on Jesus? I wonder how they sound to you? Because these words of divine pleasure are meant also of sons and daughters who bear the name of Christ. We know how criticism, even rightly intended, can sting. Holding criticism, and accepting wholeheartedly the overt or implied negative assessment of self, can lead to a sense of alienation even among the very mature, when fed a steady diet of it. Certainly Jesus experienced criticism, alienation and ostracism, and we will never be able to escape these things entirely. But isn't it nice to know that by baptism into Christ, the words, "This is my child—I am very pleased with him/her" are meant for us, too? Remember them during the tough times of life. They are meant to add a spring to your step and courage to your heart.

We are not what we do. We are who we are: beloved sons and daughters of God. He is pleased with us. How difficult to believe, but how essential to believe if we are ever to shake off the cruel loneliness and despondency that prevent us from fulfilling our mission of care for others. The Lord has given us a profound compliment by calling us his own in baptism. This satisfies our deepest needs for belonging, a longing to be treasured and loved just for being alive. It makes all the difference in the world for how we then act towards others.

Theologians will continue to differ about the meaning of baptism. May the debate be fruitful. In the meantime, remember that as a baptized child of God, you serve and are loved by somebody special, Jesus Christ, with whom God is pleased. As the Lord is with you, as well.

Kenn A. Nilsen
Lutheran Church Staff
Port Murray, New Jersey

JANUARY 19, 1992

Second Sunday after the Epiphany

Lessons:

Lutheran:	Is. 62:1-5	I Cor. 12:1-11	John 2:1-11
Roman Catholic:	Is. 62:1-5	I Cor. 12:4-11	John 2:1-12
Episcopal:	Is. 62:1-5	I Cor. 12:1-11	John 2:1-11
Pres/Meth/UCC:	Is. 62:1-5	I Cor. 12:1-11	John 2:1-11

Introductions to the Lessons

Lesson 1

Isaiah 62:1-5 (**Luth/Epis/Pres/Meth/UCC**) The prophet Isaiah uses the metaphor of marriage to describe the coming relationship between Yahweh and Israel. As a bride gets a new name, so will Israel. Yahweh will marry Israel because he delights in Israel just as a bridegroom delights in his bride. The land will no longer be forsaken or desolate, for the Lord will marry the country as his own bride.

Lesson 2

I Corinthians 12:1-11 (**Luth/Epis/Pres/Meth/UCC**) Today we begin a series of seven readings from I Corinthians, chapters 11 through 15. This first of the readings deals with the gifts of the Holy Spirit. Perhaps the greatest gift of the Spirit is to enable one to say that Jesus is Lord. In addition, there are nine other gifts of the one, same Spirit. Each Christian has a gift of the Spirit for the good of all.

Gospel

John 2:1-11 (**Luth/Epis/Pres/Meth/UCC**) Epiphany is the season when we see God's glory manifested in Jesus. Last Sunday at Jesus' baptism we saw the glory of God in the Spirit and voice of God that related to Jesus. Today we go to Cana and witness his first miracle, the changing of water into wine. By the manifestation of his glory in his power, faith resulted in the disciples.

Theme: Jesus Makes a Difference In Our Daily Living.

Thought for the day: Jesus' first miracle in Cana shows his practical concern — relieving a host's embarrassment at running out of wine. Faith has its practical side and is not simply other-worldly. The surprising miracle of turning water into wine also reminds us of the sheer joy of the Kingdom. Being a Christian is a happy experience, not one which makes us some kind of dour sourpuss.

Prayer of meditation: Father, as I approach the holy task of leading my people in divine worship and proclaiming the good news of the Gospel grant me these visions: Help me to see you, our loving Father. May I envision your concern for our every need, small and great, and rejoice in your providential care. Grant a glimpse of your joy at our worship and adoration.

Show me as well the diverse group to whom I am about to preach — with varied interests, levels of spiritual maturity and needs. Make this service and message for them. I lift my people to you in prayer just now.

Grant me a vision of the holy catholic church gathered in worship throughout the world, and the Church Triumphant praising you in heaven. Give me a sense of oneness with all the redeemed, the recipients of your divine grace. Make this truly a service of corporate worship in your holy presence. In Christ's name I pray. Amen.

Call to worship: This is the day the Lord has made. This is the Lord's Day. We will rejoice and be glad in it.

Prayer of adoration: God of all seasons, winter's cold and summer's heat, we worship and adore you. We are grateful for the dependable return of the seasons and for the beautiful balance in nature. The earth is yours in all its complexity and fullness — and we are yours as well. Accept our tribute of praise. Show us what time it is in our lives and enable us to live each season of life to your glory. We rejoice in the benefits of each time of life and are grateful for your presence in joy, in sorrow and in the routine times. We lift our hearts heavenward in gratitude and praise. You have all knowledge and all power. You know us and love us still. Thanks be to God. Amen.

Prayer of confession: Father, as we gain a glimpse of your glory, we see our own unworthiness. May the light which reveals your presence also heal the malady of our sinfulness. We adore your perfection and sense our own imperfection. We envision your great knowledge and confess our ignorance. We sense your limitless love and know how narrow is our compassion. Father, forgive.

We confess the duality of our own nature. We are made in your likeness, capable of great good and noble motives. But we are also aware of that dark side of us which has unworthy thoughts and would drag us down to shameful attitudes and actions. Father, make us strong, and along side every temptation provide an escape hatch. Then move us to use it, lest we dishonor you and those whom you love. This we pray in Jesus' strong name. Amen.

Prayer of dedication of gifts and self: Dear Lord, you are the author of all good gifts. We acknowledge you as the source of all we have and are. In gratitude we return to your service a worthy portion of that with which you have blessed us.

As we worship you with the gifts of our hands, we also dedicate ourselves to you, body and soul. Help us to make you Lord of all, lest you become not Lord at all in our life. Bless the gifts we bring and us as givers, we pray, for Christ and the world's sake. Amen.

Sermon title: The Difference Jesus Makes

Sermon thesis: The purpose of this message is to call us to the joy of faith. Our spiritual life can go flat, grow dull. Jesus' first miracle can remind us of the joy and gladness which may characterize our relationship with him.

Hymn for the day: *"In thee is gladness."* This hymn begins with the music, with a tune written by the Italian priest, Giovanni Giacomo Gastoldi (c. 1556-c. 1622). Johann Lindemann (1549-1631), son of a burgess of Gotha in Thuringia, Germany, graduated from the University of Jena and served for nearly 60 years as Kantor at Gotha. "In dir ist Freude" was one of two hymns Lindemann wrote for tunes by Gastoldi. The hymn reminds us that regardless of our life's circumstances our joy originates in our Redeemer.

Announcements for next week:

Sermon title: Home Town Boy
Sermon theme: Jesus' surprising message in his home town still takes us by surprise.
Sermon summary: Jesus came to his home town with an exciting and surprising message. It and he met with rejection. His sermon based on the text from Isaiah is no less shocking today—and may meet with the same rejection.

Children's object talk:

The Right Time

Objects: variety of watches, clocks, hour glass, etc.
Outline: 1. There are many ways to measure time.
2. Time is loaned to us by God.
3. Follow his guidance in your usage of time.

HOW DO YOU THINK the people in Bible days knew about time? They used the sun and moon. For many years the sun dial was used. Do you know how it works? They read the time according to how the shadow fell on the dial. We can measure time with striking of clocks, running of sand, calendars, watches or various clocks. We count time with months, years and centuries.

Time is life. All days are waiting to be developed. They can be full of sunshine, good work or nasty remarks, wasting the day feeling miserable.

Jesus says we should make wise use of God's gifts, and time is one of them. Each day is loaned to us by God. How will you use it? Live one day at a time to the best of your ability. All these days added together will make a life fulfilled.

Pray that God will guide you in the use of your time. Some things must wait until you are older and more mature while others must be acted upon now. When we are growing up we tend to want *everything* NOW. But God teaches us that many things are worth the wait, so be patient. Your time will come.

Use the present to the fullest in the way that pleases God.

The sermon:

The Difference Jesus Makes

Hymns:
Beginning of worship: Jesus Calls Us; O'er The Tumult
Sermon hymn: All Praise to You, O Lord
End of worship: Jesus, Priceless Treasure

Scripture: John 2:1-11

Sermon text: *"Do whatever he says."*

JOHN'S GOSPEL RECORDS seven of Jesus' miracles. This is not meant to be an exhaustive list of the Master's miracles. However, it is a typical selection and the number seven suggests completeness. One commentator called this account "the frontispiece of the Gospel" (John Arthur Gossip).

Jesus' first miracle occurred early in his ministry in Cana of Galilee, a scant three miles from his hometown of Nazareth. It was at a social occasion, a wedding dinner party in the home of his mother's friend, or perhaps relative. Jesus attended along with his family and five of his recently called disciples.

An embarrassing situation arose — the wine ran out. Hospitality is a virtue in the Near East. Mary went to her older son, confident of his help. She told the servants to "do whatever he says." Jesus must have felt uneasy that his hand was being forced when his "hour" of self disclosure had not yet come.

There were six, twenty-gallon stone water jars at the home. These would have been used for ceremonial washing, and for guests to bath their hands between courses — giant finger bowls. At Jesus' word the jars were filled with water. When the toastmaster drew some of it he found superb wine. Jesus made wine, good wine and lots of it — 120 gallons for the wedding reception. The toastmaster commended the groom for saving the best wine until last. Jesus' miracle was done "off stage." Not everyone present was aware of what had happened. The story bears the marks of an eye witness account, and is found only in the fourth Gospel.

What does this miracle mean? C.S. Lewis contended that God makes wine every year, with water, soil, sunlight and bacteria. Jesus simply speeded up the process.

The result of the miracle was that Jesus' disciples witnessed it and believed in him. A secondary result was that a practical need was met: an adequate wine supply for the wedding feast.

In recording the account of this miracle John had a deeper purpose. This was a sign, an act with symbolic and spiritual significance. Its purpose was to encourage belief, to show us that Jesus really is the Son of God with miracle-working power.

Other meanings are drawn from the story. The number seven stood for completeness to the Hebrews. The imperfect number of six jars could symbolize the inadequacy of Jewish law. It shows us our need but provides no means of atonement. The Law can reveal our sinfulness but does not provide salvation.

The wine in this account also stands for the enduring joy and gladness of the Gospel. There was an abundance of wine — enough for everyone.

Jesus turned water into wine at his word, as the Cosmic Christ turned chaos into order at the creation. At his word the world was made and at his word our sins are forgiven. Here we have a sign of the Kingdom of God and its great joy.

The miracle at Cana was a foreshadowing of the Lord's Supper (of which we have no account in John's Gospel). In communion we take the wine of remembrance, which stands for his blood. It is also the wine of anticipation, "until I drink it new with you in the Kingdom."

There are two obvious applications of this event to our lives. The first is to remind us that religion is practical. It is as concerned about the dinner table as about the Lord's table, about world hunger as about world communion; as concerned with our daily bread as the forgiveness of our sins. Christ is Lord of the pots and pans as he is Lord of the altar. He cares about our physical and emotional needs as well as our spiritual needs. This is "practical theology."

The second note sounded here concerns the Kingdom joy. We are not meant to be sour saints in stained glass windows. Rather we are to soil our hands in practical service to others. When we encounter Christ and are claimed by his love we are "surprised by joy." When he comes into a life burdens are lifted, sins are forgiven and guilt is gone. Joy comes. Without Christ, life can be dull and drab, lacking meaning and purpose. Life in Christ can be exhilarating and filled with a new vitality and deep joy, despite circumstances. In a word, when Jesus comes into your life it is like turning water into wine.

A man who was an alcoholic was converted. His former friends taunted him saying, "You don't believe that story about Jesus turning water into wine?" He replied, "I don't know about water into wine but at my house he turned beer into bread."

Alton H. McEachern
Lovejoy United Methodist Church
Hampton, Georgia

229

JANUARY 26, 1992

Third Sunday after the Epiphany

Lessons:

Lutheran:	Is. 61:1-6	I Cor. 12:12-21, 26-27	Luke 4:14-21
Roman Catholic:	Neh. 8:2-4a, 5-6, 8-10	I Cor. 12:12-30	Luke 1:1-4, 4:14-21
Episcopal:	Neh. 8:2-10	I Cor. 12:12-27	Luke 4:14-21
Pres/Meth/UCC:	Neh. 8:1-4a, 5-6, 8-10	I Cor. 12:12-30	Luke 4:14-21

Introductions to the Lessons

Lesson 1

(1) *Isaiah 61:1-6* (**Luth**) Please see Lesson 1, Epiphany I (**Pres/Meth/UCC**)

(2) *Nehemiah 8:2-10* (**Epis**); *8:1-4a, 5-6, 8-10* (**Pres/Meth/UCC**) The Exiles have returned from Babylon. Jerusalem and its walls were rebuilt under Governor Nehemiah. The people were summoned to an assembly to hear the Mosaic law read by the priest, Ezra. They stood for the reading of it lasting from early morning until noon. The Levites interpreted the read law that the people would understand it.

Lesson 2

I Corinthians 12:12-30 (**Pres/Meth/UCC**); *12:12-21, 26-27* (**Luth**); *12:12-27* (**Epis**) Paul continues his explanation of the Spirit and his gifts. While each person has a gift, one is not more important than another. Paul uses the analogy of a human body. Each organ with a different function is necessary for the good of the whole. Christians are members of the body of Christ. Each is different but equally essential.

Gospel

Luke 4:14-21 (**Luth/Epis/Pres/Meth/UCC**) For the next six Sundays we will be hearing passages from the 4th through the 6th chapters of Luke. Jesus was baptized and ordained to the ministry. This was followed by a 40 day temptation when he decided how he was going to fulfill his mission. Now he begins his public ministry in the synagogue of his hometown, Nazareth. He was asked to read the Scripture lesson for the day.

Theme: Jesus' surprising message in his home town still takes us by surprise.

Thought for the day: What is our view of the church and the nature of its ministry? It is often at odds with Jesus' teachings. Like our Master we are to be servant people showing his passion for justice and his compassion for those who are socially, economically and religiously outcasts. He has given us a tough model and one we are not anxious to follow.

Prayer of meditation: Father, I shall soon stand before a portion of the people of God to lead them in worship — ascribing supreme worth to you. I am keenly aware of the glory and wonder of the Gospel I proclaim. And equally conscious that I bear this treasure in an earthen vessel. I am not worthy — but Christ is. May he be lifted up in my words, actions and attitudes until we all go away with a fresh awareness of your greatness and power — and the assurance of divine pardon and grace.

Father, as we glimpse you in your glory and ourselves as sinners, show us one thing more. Enable us to envision the world around us: where a third of the population own the name of Jesus, where millions are lost in spiritual darkness. Enable us to feel the hurt of those who are ill, confused or oppressed. Let us go out of this service with renewed commitment to Christ, to the church and to the world, that we may serve worthily in Christ's name. Amen.

Call to worship: Thanks be to God who has brought us to this hour of worship and praise, comfort and joy.

Prayer of adoration: Great is the Lord, and greatly to be praised. We worship you as Spirit, at all places at all times, permeating creation with your divine presence. We welcome you as Light, revealing sin and evil while healing repentant sinners. We honor you, God of love, who knows no limits and reaches out to us despite our unworthiness.

We praise you Father, Son and Holy Spirit, the Source and Author of creation, redemption and new birth. Along with the redeemed of every generation, angels and archangels we praise and adore you, we worship and honor you.

Great is the Lord, and greatly to be praised. Amen.

Prayer of confession: O Lord, when we look into your Word we see you high and lifted up and join in praise. But we also see our own reflections and know our deep need of forgiveness and spiritual renewal. We have at times given the dark side of our nature ascendancy. We've been proud and selfish, insensitive to the hurts of others and uncaring. Father forgive us, cleanse us, and give us grace to live differently.

May we experience divine pardon and receive the assurance of forgiveness. Then enable us to forgive those who have sinned against us. We love because we are loved. We forgive because we have been forgiven. Now grant us one more grace: the ability to forgive ourselves, to be free of the shadow of guilt and sel- incrimination — free at last in Christ. Amen.

Prayer of dedication of gifts and self: All we have and are is due to your grace and bounty. There are no self-made people. We have nothing we have not received. We owe so much to so many, and especially to you.

Father, we acknowledge your ownership of all and ask that you make us faithful stewards of all with which you have entrusted us.

Just now, we worship you with our gifts, representing our time and effort, returned in gratitude to the Giver. Along with our gifts accept us as well, through Jesus Christ our Lord. Amen.

Sermon title: Home Town Boy

Sermon thesis: Jesus came to his home town with an exciting and surprising message. It and he met with rejection. His sermon based on the text from Isaiah is no less shocking today — and may meet with the same reception.

Hymn for the day: *"Hark, the glad sound"* (see December 15 above).

Announcements for next week:

   Sermon title: Tale of Two Cities
   Sermon theme: Opening ourselves to God, present in our lives.
   Sermon summary: Nazareth heard Jesus only as Joseph's son. Capernuam heard Jesus' teaching and were amazed at his authority. Jesus healed no one in Nazareth and healed many in Capernuam. How do we hear Jesus?

Children's object talk:

Bad News/Good News

Objects: Newspaper (with holes cut out)
Lesson: Share the Good News.

Outline: 1. Look for good in bad news.
2. Be a happy Good News reporter.
3. Share Good News through deeds.

I BROUGHT MY NEWSPAPER with me today, but you know what I did first? I cut out all the bad news. When you read the paper or watch TV news you often think you've had all the bad news you can stand. But sometimes bad news depends upon how you want to tell it or hear it. Some news may be bad for *you* and good to *me*. (Give example: score of a ball game where you were fans for different teams.)

A woman met her husband at the door one evening knowing he would be tired from a long day's work. She said, "You know you have six wonderful children?" He said, "Sure." She said, "You'll be happy to know that five of them did not break an arm today."

So many good things happen around us every day that we should be as happy to tell others about it as we are to tell the bad news.

As Christians — children of good — we have a whole book of Good News to share with everyone we meet. It is the GOSPEL which means GOOD NEWS. Often you can share the Good News with a smile to a new classmate or stranger, a helping hand to someone in need, a word of thank you or encouragement to someone who is not feeling so good about themselves.

When you do hear bad news this week — also remember all the good news and good that is happening in your life — and thank God for it all.

The sermon:

Home Town Boy

Hymns:
Beginning of worship: Hail to the Lord's Anointed
Sermon hymn: "Come, Follow Me," the Savior spoke
End of worship: Lord, Keep Us Steadfast in your Word

Scripture: Luke 4:14-21

Sermon text: *"So he came to Nazareth, where he had been brought up."*

JESUS HAD JUST EXPERIENCED his greatest exhilaration and deepest depression to date. His baptism by John the Baptist was a time of affirmation. He identified with humankind, setting us an example and was endued for his Messianic mission by the empowering Spirit. His heavenly Father spoke approval: "You are my beloved Son in whom I am well pleased."

This spiritually exhilarating experience was followed immediately by his lonely temptations in the wilderness. Jesus was tempted to use his power to satisfy his own hunger. The tempter then suggested he attract a following with sensationalism — "jump from the pinnacle of the Temple." Finally the devil offered him the kingdoms of the world if Jesus would worship him. Jesus wrestled with and refused each temptation and Satan left him alone, for awhile.

His self-searching complete for the moment, the Master heads home for Galilee empowered by the Spirit. He was conscious of being the promised Messiah (Anointed One of God). Jesus went into Galilee, speaking in their synagogues. His popularity soared, "all men sang his praises" (v. 15). Now he returns to Nazareth where he grew up, and as was his custom he attends the Sabbath service at his home synagogue. Jesus will share the Good News with his own people.

Imagine how significant this day was for Jesus, and the anticipation with which his neighbors came to worship that morning. Messianic excitement had been kindled by the preaching of John the Baptist. Oh, to see the Romans thrown out and the Kingdom of God established with Jerusalem as its capital! The young rabbi Jesus was putting Nazareth on the map. What would he have to say?

The synagogue president and elders had invited Jesus to preach. There was a prescribed reading from the five books of the Law followed by a passage from the prophets, chosen by the guest preacher. Jesus read from the scroll of Isaiah in Hebrew and then translated the passage into Aramaic. As the scroll was returned to its sacred cabinet Jesus took his seat to preach, and "the eyes of all were fixed on him." (v. 20)

Notice how Luke makes the point that Jesus regularly attended public worship. We may argue that we can worship as well at the lake or on the golf course. Perhaps we could but we rarely do. In public worship we can experience God's focused presence. It provides a connection with the best traditions of the church across the centuries. And in worship with other believers our own spiritual fires are more likely to be kindled. There is something special about our entering the Lord's presence together. In worship as in other areas, Jesus set us an example.

Jesus took his seat to preach. His single sentence sermon was a startling claim: "Today" he said, "in your very hearing this text has come true" or "Today, this text which you have just heard has come true." (v. 21) This is a startling claim, even as we read it today. No one but Jesus could begin a sermon in that way. Here he was publicly claiming to be the Messiah, the one who would fulfill Isaiah's prophetic text. The Master's hearers were at first surprised at his application of the scripture text. Then as his message sank in, their wonder turned to anger and the worshipers became a mob. But that is the rest of the story, and the subject of next week's sermon.

Now let us turn to examine Isaiah's text about the Suffering Servant. Let's see what Jesus was claiming for himself, how he understood the nature of his Messianic ministry. Jesus obviously saw his role not in the light of popular expectations. He would be no military and political leader whose objective was to throw off the yoke of Roman rule. He settled that when he said no to Satan during the wilderness temptations, and he would refuse that role later when the crowd tried to make him king.

Jesus taught that the Kingdom of God is within you, transcending political barriers. Today the church carries out its mission in all types of socio-economic systems and under every form of government. Further, the Master saw Isaiah's vision of a Suffering Servant as his role model, not that of a conquering ruler. This is a lesson still hard to grasp. Rather than having a government-established and formed church we are called to a ministry of servanthood. Instead of being princes of the church, ministers are to fulfill the role of servants. Jesus exemplified this by washing his disciples' feet. We too belong to the order of the towel — stooping to serve, not lording it over others.

Jesus read from Isaiah 61:1-2 and 58:6. He preached good news for those who were spiritually bankrupt. Empowered by the spirit of the Lord, the Suffering Servant had divine anointing (v. 18). He was set apart and dedicated for this ministry to others.

Notice those to whom the Isaiah figure, and Jesus, directed their ministry: the poor, prisoners and the blind. The result of the preaching of the Gospel and the establishment of the Kingdom is that "the broken victims go free." He came to announce the Lord's favor —

the desperate were not forgotten and their plight would have relief. Jesus' approach was to announce this good news to those who were socially, religiously and economically the "have nots." Here is a passion for justice and divine compassion for those who suffer need. Such a message is relevant to the Third World nations and to many in our own country. Jesus heals the broken-hearted whether they are poor or rich, and the Gospel is for all.

Jesus did not explain suffering, that is mystery still. But he graced it with his presence and caring. He transforms our sadness by walking with us through it. The reference to the blind may be applied both physically and morally. He opens our sight to the presence and need of others. "I can see clearly now."

Eternity begins now and Jesus is God in the present tense. "Today is the day of salvation." With his birth, life, death and resurrection the Messianic Age has dawned. Salvation is here and now. Eternal life begins not at the moment of death but when we believe in Jesus as Savior and Lord. Jesus said, "Behold, I stand at the door and knock; if anyone hears my voice and opens the door I will come in." (Rev. 3:20)

Alton H. McEachern
Lovejoy United Methodist Church
Hampton, Georgia

February 2, 1992

Fourth Sunday after the Epiphany

Lessons:

Lutheran:	Jer. 1:4-10	I Cor. 12:27-13:13	Luke 4:21-32
Roman Catholic:	Jer. 1:4-5, 17-19	I Cor. 12:31-13:13	Luke 4:21-30
Episcopal:	Jer. 1:4-10	I Cor. 14:12b-20	Luke 4:21-32
Pres/Meth/UCC:	Jer. 1:4-10	I Cor. 13:1-13	Luke 4:21-30

Introductions to the Lessons:

Lesson 1

Jeremiah 1:4-10 (**Luth/Epis/Pres/Meth/UCC**) Jeremiah tells how he became a prophet. Yahweh tells him that he was chosen even before he was born. (Jeremiah lived during the reign of King Josiah about 627 B.C.) When Jeremiah tried to escape the call with the excuse that he was too young, Yahweh promises to put words in his mouth, words that would both judge and save the nations.

Lesson 2

(1) *I Corinthians 12:27-13:13* (**Luth**); *13:1-13* (**Pres/Meth/UCC**) The Holy Spirit provides many gifts to the church, but the greatest of these is love. It is so great that without love all other gifts add up to nothing. This is no ordinary love; it is agape love, the kind of love God is and has. This love is greater than faith and hope.

(2) *I Corinthians 14:12b-20* (**Epis**) Speaking in tongues is one of the gifts of the Holy Spirit. Like all gifts, Paul says it should be used only to build up the church. Speaking in tongues without the use of the mind does not edify the church. Therefore, Paul says he would rather speak five words with his mind than 10,000 words in an unknown tongue.

Gospel

Luke 4:21-32 (**Luth/Epis**); *4:21-30* (**Pres/Meth/UCC**) Jesus' first sermon ended in a riot. At first the hometown people liked his reading of the Scripture, but when he preached that Gentiles were more receptive than Jews, they repudiated him and tried to kill him. Then he went to Capernaum where he received a better reception.

Theme: Opening ourselves to God, present in our lives

Thought for the day: Psalm 139:7-8 (NIV) Where can I go from your Spirit? Where can I flee from your presence? If I go up to the heavens you are there; if I make my bed in the depths, you are there.

Prayer of meditation: Gracious God, you are with us even when we are unaware of your presence. You have been with us from the beginning, for you formed us in our mothers' wombs. Help us to see you, to know you, to experience your presence with us today. Help us to hear with joy what you would say to us in this time of worship. All this we ask in the name of our Lord and Savior Jesus Christ. Amen.

Call to worship: Jesus said that where two or more are gathered in his name, he is in the midst. Jesus is here. Let us worship the risen Christ present with us.

Prayer of adoration: Oh Lord, you who created all things and called them good, we thank you for the wonder of this universe and world. We thank you for the beauty of nature found in the fragrance and delicate color of a rose. We thank you for the mystery of life we encounter again with each child born. We thank you that you care for the universe and the pathways of stars, yet you also care for us and know us, every part of us, even the number of hairs on our head. This is too wonderful for us to comprehend. Receive our thankful hearts, we pray. Amen.

Prayer of confession: Gracious God, you call us to love you with all our heart, and soul, and mind. Often we are distracted by the cares of the day and forget you. Forgive us. Lord God, you call us to love our neighbors, to work for their well-being. Yet we question who is our neighbor and we dismiss our responsibility toward some people. Forgive us. We slight and cut down the people whom you love. Forgive us. We are deaf to the cries of the hungry, the children without adequate medical help. Forgive us. Help us to live more simply so others can simply live. Help us to find the time and resources to respond to our neighbors in need. Search us, O God, and know our hearts; test us and know our anxious thoughts. See if there is any offensive way in us and lead us in the way of life everlasting. Amen.

Prayer of dedication: All things come from you, O Lord. All that we have is yours. We bring to you our time, our talents, our energy and ask you to use us and direct us. We bring to you these tithes and offerings and ask that you bless these gifts using them to build up your kingdom here on earth. Amen.

Sermon title: Tale of Two Cities

February 2, 1992

Sermon thesis: Nazareth heard Jesus only as Joseph's son. Capernaum heard Jesus' teaching and were amazed at his authority. Jesus healed no one in Nazareth and healed many in Capernaum. How do we hear Jesus?

Hymn for the day: "O Christ the healer" Frederick Pratt Green (b. 1903), a native of Liverpool, England, served for 45 years as a minister of the Wesleyan Methodist Church. He began to write poetry at the age of 40, and did not begin writing hymns until he was over 60 years of age. This hymn of prayer for health asks for healing of the world's disease of conflict as well as for individual physical healing.

Announcements for next week:

Sermon title: Asking the Ridiculous
Sermon theme: Obedience to Christ brings deeper faith.
Sermon summary: Our journey of faith involves hearing and experiencing God before God calls us, before God asks us to do something ridiculous which if we comply releases God's grace and power.

Children's object talk:

Block to Help

Lesson: To give help, the other has to receive it; to receive help we need to ask and be open to receive.
Outline: 1. Remember times when you tried to give help.
2. Remember times when others tried to help you.
3. God cannot help us when we refuse.

HAVE ANY OF YOU EVER SEEN A FRIEND or someone in your family upset or hurting? (pause to let children respond) How do you feel when someone you love is hurting? (pause for response) Have you ever tried to help and the person says, "Go away, leave me alone." (pause for response) What did you do then? (pause for response) Sometimes even when you want to help someone, because they don't want it, you can't help them.

Have any of you ever been so upset that you have gone to your room and closed the door to be alone or gone off for a walk or bicycle ride? (pause for response) Has there ever been a time when you wanted to be alone and friends or one of your brothers or sisters or your Mom or Dad tried to help you and you refused? (pause for response) Sometimes when people try to help us we refuse their help and they cannot help us because we won't allow them to.

You know that God loves us very much. And God wants to be with us helping us. But God cannot help us if we do not allow God

239

to. If we don't turn to God and ask God, we are like those friends we try to help but refuse our help. Remember, God is always with you, and all you need to do is turn to God to receive God's help.

The sermon:

Tale of Two Cities

Hymns:
Beginning of worship: God is Here
Sermon hymn: In Thee is Gladness
End of worship: Hope of the World

Scripture: Luke 4:21-32 (referring also to Luke 4:33-41)

Sermon text: *"They were amazed at his teaching, because his message had authority."*

JESUS, AFTER HE HAD BEEN TEMPTED in the wilderness, returned to his home town of Nazareth. As was the custom, he was asked to read the scripture as part of the Sabbath worship in the synagogue. After reading, the crowd was pleased with his delivery, his tone of voice, and recognized him as Joseph's son. Jesus was a hometown boy. He handled the responsibility of reading in worship about as well as any one of them.

Jesus then began to comment. He knew their hearts. They had heard stories about what had happened with John and wondered about him. They had seen him grow up. They had seen him working in the carpenter's shop. They had brought him articles to repair. They had bought some things he had made. He was Joseph's son. Yet when he began to tell them what they were thinking, when he began to challenge their view of him as one of their own, they got angry. After all, what right did this young man of their village have to speak to them this way? They all knew him, he was Joseph's son. What was this about being a prophet? They had seen him grow up. What was this about going elsewhere? Wasn't he coming back home?

In the accounts of this encounter in Matthew and Mark, the crowd recounts all of the family which lived in the town, "Is not his mother called Mary? And are not his brothers James and Joseph and Simon and Judas? And are not all his sisters with us? Where did this man get all this? And they took offense." (Matt 13:55-58) They were trying to put Jesus in his place as one of them, not someone special. Many of them had played with him growing up, all the games boys play. They were placing him in his human family they knew his father, his mother and his sisters and brothers. They were making him be just like them — having a family, having a job in the community, drinking water from the same well, worshiping in the same synagogue, going to the same community festivals. After all they knew him, he was Joseph's son.

Jesus answers them by saying that a prophet is not without honor except in his own country and in his own house. Matthew notes that, "he did not do many mighty works there because of their unbelief."

They were angry. This was no prophet, this was Joseph's son. They tried to kill him, run him off a high cliff at the edge of town. They were not going to have this young man speak to them like that. Who did he think he was? So Jesus withdrew and went on his way.

The next week found Jesus in a synagogue, again teaching but this time in Capernaum. The people in Capernaum, did not try to put Jesus in a box. They did not try to define him. They listened to him. The people "were amazed at his teaching, because his message had authority." Jesus was someone special, someone who had something to tell them, someone who spoke words from God in a way they had not heard before. Jesus was a prophet. They listened to him, not with preconceived notions, not limiting or defining the message.

"They were amazed at his teaching, because his message had authority." They heard him and allowed the message to enter into their lives for "his message had authority." They were open to Jesus, they allowed Jesus to be who he was, and Jesus reached out to them and touched them and healed them.

In the synagogue was a man possessed by a demon. Jesus commanded the demon to leave and the man was healed. Afterwards, Jesus went to the house of Simon's mother-in-law. (Simon who would later be renamed Peter). She was sick with a fever and Jesus healed her. Many in Capernaum witnessed what Jesus did and told others. "When the sun was setting, the people brought to Jesus all who had various kinds of sickness, and laying his hands on each one, he healed them." (vs. 40)

What a contrast to Nazareth! In Nazareth, Jesus was run out of town, and "he did not do many mighty works there because of their unbelief." While in Capernaum, the people received his teaching and were healed. Jesus was the same, but the response of the people was different. Where the people were closed, Jesus could do nothing. Where the people were open, Jesus brought healing.

I find these accounts troublesome. They seem to say that I can limit what Christ can do. If I define who Christ is and what Christ can do, then I, like the people of Nazareth, am putting Christ in a box. If I am closed, then Christ is limited. If I am open there is no telling what can happen. A few years ago, J.B. Phillips addressed this problem in the book, *Your God is Too Small.* What we think is possible, what we imagine to be the way things are, defines our world. If we decide God won't heal, that God doesn't care about something so small, that God can't really do anything in the world, it's too big — we define and limit God. If Jesus is only a great teacher, then we hear the ethical teachings but do not receive him as Savior and thus limit the healing and transformation he can bring into our lives.

If Jesus is only a personal Lord and Savior, then we have access to God but fail to allow God to bring through us saving, healing, reconciling action into the world, the community in which we live, and to the polluted earth on which we walk.

If Jesus only healed in the time of the apostles, then we fail to seek and receive Christ's healing now. In each of the images of who Jesus is and how Jesus operates in the world today, we limit what Christ can do. We are like the people of Nazareth, and "he did not do many mighty works there because of their unbelief;" and Jesus does not do mighty acts here because of our unbelief. How can we become more like the people of Capernaum? How can we be open to who Jesus is? How can we free Jesus to be all he is, and to do in our lives, in our community, in our world all that he wants to do?

Part of the answer is the humility found in the 13th chapter of I Corinthians. Paul recognizes that "now we know in part." We do not know everything, there is much about God and how God operates in this world that is beyond our knowing. With humility we come before God, not knowing everything, and acknowledging that God is beyond us. God is infinite and we are finite. Paul recognizes that now we see through a mirror dimly, but then we shall see face to face. Now we see a distorted reflection of who God is. Now we can only know God through our experience which filters and quantifies who God is. Please do not get me wrong — we can know something of God, we can experience something of God; but what we know is only part of who God is, what we experience is only one aspect of God — not all that there is. If we come in humility seeking to know more, seeking to experience more, seeking to understand more, then we are open. If we ask that God work in a situation and trust that God will work with love and healing because that is God's character, then we are open. If in our playful imagination we bring people and situations to Jesus so that he can lay his hands on the people and on the situations, then we are open. When we come to Jesus, trusting that he will act, but not prescribing how it will happen, not telling Jesus what he can and cannot do, then we are open.

Marian Y. Adell
United Methodist Church
Madison, New Jersey

February 9, 1992

Fifth Sunday after the Epiphany

Lessons:

Lutheran:	Is. 6:1-8 (9-13)	I Cor. 14:12b-20	Luke 5:1-11
Roman Catholic:	Is. 6:1-2a, 3-8	I Cor. 15:1-11	Luke 5:1-11
Episcopal:	Judges 6:11-24a	I Cor. 15:1-11	Luke 5:1-11
Pres/Meth/UCC:	Is. 6:1-8 (9-13)	I Cor. 15:1-11	Luke 5:1-11

Introductions to the Lessons:

Lesson 1

(1) *Isaiah 6:1-8 (9-13)* (**Luth/Pres/Meth/UCC**) In the year 740 B.C. when King Uzziah of Judah died, Isaiah received his call to be a prophet. He was worshiping in the Temple when he had a vision of the holiness of God. Isaiah confessed his sin, was forgiven, and then responded, "Here am I! Send me."

(2) *Judges 6:11-24a* (**Epis**) The Israelites were oppressed by the Midianites in the time of the Judges. An angel came to Gideon and called upon him to free Israel from their enemy. Gideon begged off saying that he and his clan were the weakest in Israel. But, Yahweh assured him that he would be with him and give him victory over the Midianites.

Lesson 2

(1) *I Corinthians 14:12b-20* (**Luth**) Please see Epiphany IV, Lesson 2, Epis.

(2) *I Corinthians 15:1-11* (**Epis/Pres/Meth/UCC**) What is the Gospel? Paul sums it up: Christ died for our sins, was buried, and rose from the dead. Since this letter was written about 50 A.D., it is the earliest written account of the resurrection. Paul enumerates the times when the risen Christ was seen. He was one of those who saw him even though he at first persecuted the church.

Gospel

Luke 5:1-11 (**Luth/Epis/Pres/Meth/UCC**) Peter becomes a disciple of Jesus. It happened at the Sea of Galilee where Peter and friends were fishing. Since they caught nothing all night, Jesus told Peter to cast out his nets, and behold the net was filled with fish. Peter fell down at Jesus' feet confessing his sin. Then Peter and his partners abandoned their business to follow Jesus full time.

Theme: Obedience to Christ brings deeper faith.

244

Thought for the day: By challenging us, God helps us become who we were created to be. By challenging us, God helps us develop the gifts and talents God has given us.

Prayer of meditation: Jesus, you came to the people of long ago where they were. You came to them in the synagogue where they worshiped, into the homes where they lived, to the places where they worked. Jesus, come to us today as we worship you. Come to us today where we live and work. Help us see you, help us hear you. Help us to let go of all the unimportant things which clutter our lives, so that we are freer to respond to what you ask of us. Amen.

Call to worship: Come let us worship the Lord. Come let us offer God our praise and thanksgiving. Come let us bow down before God who gives us the breath of life. Come let us together be present with the Risen Christ in our midst who heals, renews, refreshes, and restores us for the journey.

Prayer of adoration: Gracious Lord, we pause in these moments to remember all the gifts you give us—for the shelter we have, for the food which nourishes our bodies, for clothing which gives us warmth, for family which gave us life, for friends which give us support and love, for this church, this community of faith which seeks to follow you, for this time of worship where you are present here with us. We thank you; may our hearts be ever grateful. Amen.

Prayer of confession: Jesus, you are ever present with us, but we in our busyness, in our rushing around, push you aside—forgive us. Help us to stop and turn to you in the midst of our daily tasks. Jesus, you call us to work for the good of all people, but when someone hurts us we want to strike out and not work for their good—forgive us. Help us to see the other from your point of view, help us to pray for the other, committing them to your care and keeping. Jesus, you had fellowship and ate with all people, but we sometimes refuse to be with those who are richer or poorer or different in race or creed or language—forgive us. Help us to value your people who are different from us as you value us. All this we ask in the name of our Risen Lord. Amen.

Prayer of dedication of gifts and self: God, you shape us into your body here on earth. We give you our hands to reach out with your love. We give you our feet to carry us into every part of our community with the good news of a love that conquers death, with the good news that you forgive, heal, renew and restore all who come to you. We give you our bodies to be your representatives wherever we are. We bring to you our tithes and offerings to enable others to be your ambassadors. Bless us and these gifts, empowering them to strengthen your kingdom here on earth. All this we ask in the name our Lord and Savior, Jesus Christ. Amen.

Sermon title: Asking the Ridiculous

Sermon thesis: Our journey of faith involves hearing and experiencing God before God calls us to do something we find ridiculous. But if we comply God's grace and power is released.

Hymn for the day: *"O God, thou/my faithful God"* (see September 15 above for comments on this hymn.)

Announcements for next week:

    Sermon title: The Power Came Forth
    Sermon theme: The paradox of the Gospel
    Sermon summary: The heart of this lesson is that only the kingdom of God can bring us fulfillment and happiness. Our riches must be counted as poverty as we seek God's kingdom.

Children's object talk:

Walking Blind

Objects: Material for blindfold
Lesson: We will walk blind with someone we trust.
Outline: 1. Trust walk
           2. Elements of trust
           3. We walk where Jesus leads because we trust him.

HAVE ANY OF YOU EVER BEEN ON A TRUST WALK? (pause for response). A trust walk is where one person is blindfolded and others lead that person. What do you think the others have to do when they lead the blind person? (pause) They have to tell that person when there is an object they might bump into, or when there is a step. They are responsible for that person's well-being and safety. This morning a couple of you will lead me. (Put on blind-fold and have them lead you).

How did you feel leading me? What did others of you see when I was being lead? I trusted you to lead me and keep me safe. But I must confess I was a little nervous. It is more difficult being led

by someone else rather than doing it yourself.
Sometimes we cannot see where Jesus is leading us. Yet because we trust Jesus, we put our hand in his and go where he leads.

The sermon:

Asking the Ridiculous

Hymns:
Beginning of worship: Jesus Calls Us O'er The Tumult
Sermon hymn: Here I am, Lord
End of worship: Forth in Thy Name, O Lord

Scripture: Luke 5:1-11

Sermon Text: *"Do not be afraid; from now on you will catch my people."*

IN TODAY'S LESSON, Jesus has moved from the synagogue to the open fields. Jesus would go anywhere that people would listen to him. John Wesley, who scandalized the Church of England with his field preaching, said, "Our societies were formed from those who were wandering upon the dark mountains, that belonged to no Christian church; but were awakened by the preaching of the Methodists, who had pursued them through the wilderness of this world to the High-ways and the Hedges-to the Markets and the Fairs-to the Hills and Dales-who set up the Standard of the Cross in the Streets and Lanes of the Cities, in the Villages, in the Barns, and Farmer's Kitchens, etc. – and all this done in such a way, and to such an extent, as never had been done before since the Apostolic age." "I love a commodious room," said Wesley, "a soft cushion and a handsome pulpit, but field preaching saves souls." Jesus had moved out of the synagogue to where the people were, where they worked, where they traveled, where they farmed, where they fished. The setting for today's text is by the Lake of Gennesaret, which we know as the Sea of Galilee. The story is so familiar to us that we can easily miss the drama. If this were a play or a movie, the moment of revelation, the high point would be when Simon Peter falls on his knees in front of Jesus and says, "Go away from me, Lord; I am a sinful man." But coming to this point at the beginning is like reading the last chapter of a book. The question is what happened to Simon which led up to this moment?

Simon had had previous contact with Jesus. Jesus in one of his visits to Capernaum had healed Simon's mother-in-law. (Luke 4:38-39) That very morning after a long hard frustrating night's fishing, he had caught nothing. While he was mending his nets and setting them out to dry, he heard Jesus teaching. When Jesus asked to use his boat so that he could better speak to the crowd, Simon went and got his boat for Jesus.

Simon had experienced Jesus' healing in his own family. Simon had heard Jesus preaching. But none of these experiences had brought him to his knees. All that Jesus had asked of Simon had seemed reasonable, nothing out of the ordinary. Simon had probably eaten with Jesus. Simon had possibly provided hospitality for this traveling rabbi. This was no more than he would have done for any other respected rabbi.

Even though Simon was tired, when Jesus asked to use his boat, Simon responded by going back to his boat and taking Jesus out a bit from the shore. But this too was a reasonable request; Jesus could be heard better from the boat on the water.

Jesus got into the boat and finished teaching. Then he said to Simon, "Put out into deep water, and let down the nets for a catch." Simon answered, "Master, we've worked hard all night and haven't caught anything." At this point I would be inclined to say, "I'm tired. I've worked hours for nothing. And now you are asking me to do something that is ridiculous, no reasonable person would do such a thing. It is the wrong time to fish, it's daylight. Everyone knows that this is the wrong time." But Simon didn't say that. Instead he said, "But because you say so, I will let down the nets." Simon called Jesus "Master," a title used not because Jesus was a teacher but because Simon recognized Jesus' authority. Simon recognized that Jesus was more than an ordinary rabbi, more than a good man. Simon had seen Jesus and heard Jesus and responded with "Master." I will do this crazy unreasonable thing you ask, because it is you that asks it. Simon was willing to take a risk, was willing to try something that seemed absurd, because it was Jesus who asked him to do it. As I've said before, Simon knew that Jesus could heal; Simon knew that Jesus spoke with authority unlike any rabbi he had ever heard. So he and his partners let down their nets. An act of obedience, an act based on trusting the one who asked it. Jesus, the

Master, asked them, tired as they were, discouraged as they were, to try one more time, to make one more effort, to try something where they had failed before. But this time they caught such a large number of fish that their nets began to break. They signaled their partners in another boat to come and help them. There were so many fish that both boats began to sink.

It was at this point that Simon, seeing the incomparable bounty and power of Jesus, fell at Jesus' knees and said, "Go away from me, Lord; I am a sinful man!" Simon called Jesus, "Lord", which acknowledged Jesus' power. Simon was confronted with one who not only spoke with the authority of God but who also acted with the power of God. Simon recognized that in the presence of Jesus he was a sinful man, he was not good enough to receive all that Jesus gave him. He was not good enough to be in the presence of the perfect one, the one giving such incredible gifts.

But what was Jesus' reaction? Jesus said, "Do not be afraid." In my imagination I can see Jesus reaching down and putting his hand on Simon's shoulder, "Do not be afraid; from now on you will catch my people." Each of us has heard the good news that Jesus brought. Each of us has had those times when we have experienced God's presence. Each of us has had a sense of God asking us to do something ridiculous, unreasonable. Maybe someone came to mind and we called them on the telephone to say we were thinking of them. When we made that call we learned that they were having trouble and needed the word of encouragement or the assistance we could give. We were amazed that God could use us. Maybe we had the courage to mention to a neighbor or to a fellow worker that we went to church, or that God was important to us, or told them of that time when God had seen us through a really hard time. We had expected to be laughed at, or to be scorned, and surprisingly the other person had listened and began to tell us their story of faith, or had begun to question us about how our faith grew — eager, hungering to hear more. We were amazed that God could use us. Maybe we became active in some community service, using talents we never knew we had. We were amazed that God could use us. We knew how uncomfortable we were. We knew how afraid we were. We know intimately our many failings, yet God used us. A sense of profound humility before God comes over us when we realize, as imperfect as we are God can use us.

Our journey of faith begins when we hear something of God, when

249

we experience something of God, but it can become deeper when God asks us to do something unreasonable, something absurd. At those moments, we have the choice of whether we respond as Simon did: Although I don't think that it will work, or that it is important, because it is you who asks, I will do it.

William Barclay calls this the willingness to attempt what seems hopeless. Barclay writes, "The night was past and that was the time for fishing. All the circumstances were unfavorable, but Peter said, 'Let circumstances be what they may, if you say so, we will try again.' Too often we wait because the time is not opportune. If we wait for a perfect set of circumstances, we will never begin at all. If we want a miracle, we must take Jesus at his word when he bids us attempt the impossible."

Simon uses three titles for Jesus: teacher, master, lord. Each represents a progression of deeper trust and knowledge of who Jesus is. What do you call Jesus? What level of trust do you have?

Jesus calls each of us to take the next step in our journey of faith. What is Jesus calling us as individuals to do? What is Jesus calling us as church, the community of faith, to do? It is only when we attempt to do what seems ridiculous or impossible in faithful response to Jesus that Jesus' power is shown. If Simon had not put his nets into the sea then he would not have known Jesus' power and grace. When we say, "Because you say so, we will do it," we open ourselves up to God's power and grace. When we say, "Because you say so, we will do it," we open ourselves to be used by God as instruments of God's power and grace released into our homes, our places of employment, our community, our world.

May God grant us the ears to hear and the courage and trust to act.

Marian Y. Adell
United Methodist Church
Madison, New Jersey

FEBRUARY 16, 1992

Sixth Sunday after the Epiphany

Lessons:

Lutheran:	Jer. 17:5-8	I Cor. 15:12, 16-20	Luke 6:17-26
Roman Catholic:	Jer. 17:5-8	I Cor. 15:12, 16-20	Luke 6:17, 20-26
Episcopal:	Jer. 17:5-10	I Cor. 15:12-20	Luke 6:17-26
Pres/Meth/UCC:	Jer. 17:5-10	I Cor. 15:12-20	Luke 6:17-26

Introductions to the Lessons:

Lesson 1

Jeremiah 17:5-10 (**Epis/Pres/Meth/UCC**); *17:5-8* (**Luth**). Cursed are those who do not trust God and blessed are those who do. The person who does is like a tree planted by a river, as Psalm 1 says. Whether a person trusts in God or not depends upon the condition of the heart.

Lesson 2

I Corinthians 15:12-20 (**Epis/Pres/Meth/UCC**); *15:12, 16-20* (**Luth**). Last Sunday in this 15th chapter of I Corinthians Paul witnessed to Jesus' resurrection. Now he faces the problem of some saying that there is no resurrection of the dead. If Christ did not rise, then our faith is in vain and we are still in sin. However, the truth is that Christ did rise from the dead.

Gospel

Luke 6:17-26 (**Luth/Epis/Pres/Meth/UCC**). For today and the next two Sundays we will be hearing passages from the Sermon on the Plain which is similar to Matthew's Sermon on the Mount. In this first section we have both beatitudes and curses. Each "blessed" is balanced with a "woe." Jesus addressed the message to the disciples to give them the ethics of the Kingdom.

Theme: The Paradox of the Gospel.

Thought for the day: First impressions are often wrong. I once had a good friend tell me that she did not particularly care for me when we first met. However, she believed that I must be a nice person, since I was preparing for ministry. Whenever I meet someone, no matter the impression I receive, I tell myself that there is something of worth within that person, something I need to see.

Prayer of meditation: O God, this day is a treasure you have given to me. Help me to see the beauty which lies within, and cause me to share the warmth of this day with those I encounter. Amen.

Call to worship: In the midst of great hostility and much suffering, we gather to find respite, wisdom, and strength from our God. May we worship our God with hearts of expectancy.

Prayer of adoration: God of creation, you have given to us our very lives. You have loved us with a perfect love. You have redeemed us as children within your household. We come to your altar with thankful hearts. Feed us on your word, that we too may grow more like our Savior, Jesus Christ. Amen.

Prayer of confession: God of forgiveness, look upon us with mercy. We have all forsaken the covenant of your love because of our selfish greed and arrogant pride. We have each gone our own way, seeking to be free from the tensions of faith. We come to you today as a people in need. Forgive us, and continue to hold us in your arms of love. Renew your covenant within our hearts, and turn our eyes upon you. Teach us to depend upon you for our wisdom. Help us to discipline our lives so that you may be glorified, and your kingdom increased. Amen.

Prayer of dedication of gifts and self: Lord of life, we have received so very much from you. From the beginning you have loved us, and given yourself for us. You have comforted us in times of sorrow. You have inspired us in times of joy. You have walked with us in times of uncertainty. As you have poured yourself out for us, let us give to you, cheerfully and with vision of what you can accomplish. Amen.

Sermon title: The Power Came Forth.

Sermon thesis: The heart of this lesson is that only the kingdom of God can bring us fulfillment and happiness. Our riches must be counted as poverty as we seek God's kingdom.

Hymn for the day: *"Be thou my vision."* The sermon's message that "Our riches must be counted as poverty as we seek God's kingdom" is seen also in this hymn, where we sing "Riches I heed not . . . Thou mine inheritance, now and always." This Irish hymn first appeared in the eighth century. Translated by Mary Byrne (1880-1931), a researcher in Irish for the National Board of Intermediate Education, it was translated into prose, and first published in 1904. A metrical version prepared by E.H. Hull has been variously adapted as a hymn text. The tune with which it has come to be associated is an altered version of the Irish folk melody, "With my love come on the road."

Announcements for next week:

Sermon title: Adjusting Our Vision

Sermon theme: We must rely on God to adjust our spiritual vision in order to accomplish the tasks of the church.

Sermon summary: If we love only those who love us back, then our faith has not affected our vision. Christianity affects our lives by causing us to do things we would not normally do.

Children's object talk:

Unseen Power

Objects: A flashlight and batteries

Lesson: God can make our lives a light to others.

Outline: 1. This flashlight can bring light to our world.

2. The batteries are the source of this power.

3. Jesus is the power behind our lives.

I BROUGHT A FLASHLIGHT to church today. I thought that I might want to brighten up our sanctuary a little. See, when I turn the flashlight on, I can brighten each of your faces. The light from the flashlight can shine on each person who is here with us. From where do you think the power of the flashlight comes? That's right, from the batteries. Let's open the flashlight and see the power source. These batteries are hidden inside the flashlight, and we can't normally see the batteries themselves. We can see the light which the batteries and flashlight can produce.

Did you know that each one of you is like a flashlight? That's right, each one of you can brighten up our world. It has brightened my day to see you at worship this morning. And do you know the power source that lives within you? The Bible tells us that the love of God lives within us and gives us the power to brighten up our world. We brighten up our world when we love people around us.

The sermon:

The Power Came Forth

Hymns:

Beginning of worship: Be Thou My Vision

Sermon hymn: Break Forth, O Beauteous Heavenly Light

End of worship: Guide Me, O Thou Great Jehovah

Scripture: Luke 6:17-26

Sermon Text: *"And he lifted up his eyes on his disciples, and said: Blessed are you poor, for yours is the kingdom of God."* v. 20

A CERTAIN RICH MAN, a disciple, approached the rabbi requesting to learn about how one becomes rightly related to God. The rabbi took the rich man before a window.

"Look out this window," the rabbi instructed. "What do you see?"

"I see the world," the rich man replied.

"What is it like?" the rabbi queried.

"I see people: a single mother working two jobs in order to feed her tiny children, a man struggling with depression, a teenager confused and frightened about the future. And many others who have great need," the rich man replied.

The rabbi then instructed the rich man to turn around and face a mirror in the room.

"What do you see?" the rabbi again asked.

"A mirror," was the response.

"What does it show?"

"I see only myself," the rich man answered.

The rabbi concluded, "There are two kinds of windows we look through. When the window is clear, we see the world with all its suffering and need. When silver is added to the window, we see only ourselves. If you are to be rightly related to God, you must not let your vision of the world be obstructed by the wealth you possess."

Our gospel lesson deals with one's vision of the world through the window of Christian principles. Jesus has just chosen his twelve disciples, and he is about to give their first lesson on the demands of their new faith. As the disciples gather close to Jesus, a multitude of other disciples and a great crowd has gathered to hear the words of Jesus and to be healed. Undoubtedly, the majority of these common people were economically poor and socially oppressed individuals and families. They have flocked to Jesus, the miracle worker, in hopes of changing their situation in life. Surely this man of God can alleviate the pain and suffering, and right the injustices in life that plague them. The text says that at this moment the people sought to touch Jesus because "power came forth from him."

Jesus then speaks paradoxical words to his disciples. "Blessed are you poor, for yours is the kingdom of God." Imagine that. The poor, the hungry, the sad, and the persecuted are the blessed ones. These multitudes who know poverty so well, are the possessors of happiness. How can that be? How can poverty, especially hunger, grief, and oppression bring happiness to the followers of Christ?

How difficult it is for us to grasp the message Jesus spoke so long ago. We feel much more comfortable with Matthew's rendering of the beatitudes, for there it is the "poor in spirit" who are blessed. But Luke unmistakenly refers to the economically poor who are the blessed ones. A few moments later he condemns the rich, who in the midst of great poverty, are filled with food and laughter.

The heart of this lesson is that only the kingdom of God can bring us fulfillment and happiness. Our riches must be counted as poverty as we seek God's kingdom. That is a radical and difficult statement for today's Christianity. It is so much easier for us to enjoy our wealth and ignore the poor.

In a very real sense, the poor are fortunate, for in their economic poverty, they are able to see their spiritual poverty and need for God. The rich, on the other hand, must learn the taste of poverty in order to see their spiritual need.

Jesus condemned those persons of means who could feel spiritually well while ignoring the needs of others. When we realize that only God can truly satisfy our hungering lives, then our possessions, as well as our time, energy, and minds, are seen as avenues of God's grace to others who live around us.

Wealth, power, prestige, and position can be the additive to the windows of life that reflect only our own selfish importance. Once we place acquisition of the kingdom of God as our only goal, then our windows clear, and we can see the great suffering and need around us. Our possessions become agents of God's grace. Yes, as strange as it seems, seeing our own poverty is the beginning of happiness in the kingdom.

Stan C. Pigue
St. John's United Methodist Church
Danville, Virginia

FEBRUARY 23, 1992

Seventh Sunday after the Epiphany

Lessons:

Lutheran:	Gen. 45:3-8a, 15	I Cor. 15:35-38a, 42-50	Luke 6:27-38
Roman Catholic:	I Sam. 26:2, 7-9, 12-13, 22-23	I Cor. 15:45-49	Luke 6:27-38
Episcopal:	Gen. 45:3-11, 21-28	I Cor. 15:35-38, 42-50	Luke 6:27-38
Pres/Meth/UCC:	Gen. 45:3-11, 15	I Cor. 15:35-38, 42-50	Luke 6:27-38

Introductions to the Lessons:

Lesson 1

Genesis 45:3-11, 15 (**Pres/Meth/UCC**); *45:3-8a, 15* (**Luth**); *45:3-11, 21-28* (**Epis**). From slavery to top governmental authority! That is the story of Joseph. The time came when his brothers who sold him into slavery had to come to him for food. Joseph identified himself to his brothers, but he did not hold them guilty, for he claimed it was God's will for him to save lives, including his own family, which he brought to Egypt to avoid the famine.

Lesson 2

I Corinthians 15:35-38, 42-50 (**Luth/Epis/Pres/Meth/UCC**). What kind of body does a dead Christian have? Does s/he have a body at all? Paul answers these questions in today's lesson. A Christian is given two bodies: a physical one for this life and a spiritual body for the next life. The first body was made of dust and will return to dust. The second body is spiritual, fit for the spiritual kingdom.

Gospel

Luke 6:27-38 (**Luth/Epis/Pres/Meth/UCC**). In this second selection from the Sermon on the Plain, Jesus continues to describe the quality of life in the Kingdom. His followers are expected to be and to do more than non-believers: give more, love more, be more merciful.

Theme: Adjusting Our Vision.

Thought for the day: Over half of Americans have less than 20/20 eyesight. In order to accomplish everyday tasks, these people wear corrective lenses. Spiritually, all people have less than perfect sight. We must rely on God to correct our spiritual vision so that we accomplish the daily tasks of the church.

Prayer of meditation: O God, as I come before you today, remind me that I am a part of the Body of Christ. Let this time of worship draw me together with the others in this sanctuary, and let us treat one another as brothers and sisters in Christ. Amen.

Call to worship: We who live in spiritual poverty gather this day to share the riches of God's Spirit. May we approach him with the love he gives us to live our lives.

Prayer of adoration: O Lord of life, you have called us here to worship you in spirit and in truth. We have received so many of your kind gifts: forgiveness for the sins we commit, compassion for the pain we endure, hope for the years ahead. May we have the humility to bow before you in thankfulness, and the wisdom to rise in heightened dedication to the task before us. Amen.

Prayer of confession: Gracious Lord, we come before you in this time of worship as broken individuals. Dreams of what we could become frighten us. The demands of our faith tire us. The anger of our hostile world enrages us. We have hidden from your perfect love which can take us through these difficult days. Let your grace embrace us as we seek to reinvest our lives in you. Restore our dreams as visions of hope. Remind us of your demands as joyous service. Replace our anger with an out-flowing of compassion. In all of this, assure us of your abiding presence among us. Amen.

Prayer of dedication of gifts and self: Instill within us, Lord, a sense of stewardship of all you have given us. Our lives are not our own, but are a gift from you. Our possessions are resources for your Kingdom. Our minds are instruments of your grace. Our energy is the pathway of your spirit. Let us be faithful to the responsibility that your generosity demands. Amen.

Sermon title: Adjusting Our Vision.

Sermon thesis: If we love only those who love us back, then our faith has not affected our vision. Christianity affects our lives by causing us to do things we would not normally do.

Hymn for the day: *"Lord of all nations, grant me grace." "*. . . grant me grace," the hymn continues, "to love all people." Olive Wise Spannaus, born in 1916 in St.

Louis, assumed leadership roles in many church and community organizations. In 1972 she was the first woman elected to the Board of Directors of the English District of the Lutheran Church — Missouri Synod. This hymn, which was written for the institute of the Lutheran Human Relations Association of America, 1960, is a prayer that Christ will assist us to love and forgive.

Announcements for next week:

Sermon title: From Mountain Top to Valley
Sermon theme: The Lord sets his face to Jerusalem.
Sermon summary: The great decisions of life come as a culmination of a series of small decisions made along the way. Living life means preparing for tomorrow at the same time life is being lived today.

Children's object talk:

Looking Inside

Objects: A piggy bank filled with coins.
Lesson: God loves all of us, even though we are different.
Outline: 1. My piggy bank looks funny.

2. My bank is valuable to me regardless of its appearance.

3. God loves us all because we are valuable to him.

I BROUGHT A FRIEND of mine to church today (show the piggy bank). He has been a friend of mine since I was a young boy. My parents gave him to me as a present. He is not too pretty on the outside. His skin is ragged and torn, and he is not as clean as he could be. But I love him, anyway. And he is valuable to me. Do you know why? Because of what is inside of him (shake the bank).

We love our friends and families because of who they are on the inside. We all look different from each other on the outside, but we are still family and friends on the inside. The Bible tells us that God loves each of us because we are precious to him. He overlooks our bad points, and he sees the great value each of us has within us. Let's thank God for seeing our good — and let's thank God for our friends and our families.

The sermon:

Adjusting Our Vision

Hymns:

Beginning of worship: The Church of Christ, in Every Age
Sermon hymn: Come, Christians, Join to Sing
End of worship: Take My Life and Let It Be

Scripture: Luke 6:27-38

Sermon text: *"But love your enemies, and do good, and lend, expecting nothing in return; and your reward will be great, and you will be sons of the Most High. . ."* v. 35

WHEN I WAS A BOY, my grandfather took me mushroom hunting. We drove from town, climbed a barbed-wire fence, walked through a forest, and reached a slope of dead elms. My grandfather told me to search the top of the slope while he checked the bottom.

An hour later he came back with two large paper sacks filled with mushrooms. I hadn't found even one. I don't remember the exact conversation that occurred then, but I do remember the essence of it. It went something like this.

"I guess your spot was lucky," I said.

"But they're all around you," my grandfather said.

"All around me? Where?"

"You didn't look hard enough."

"I crossed the slope five times."

"You searched but you didn't really see," my grandfather said. He picked up a long stick and pointed it toward the ground. "Focus your eyes toward the end of the stick."

I did. . .

And I've never forgotten the hot excitement that surged through my stomach. The mushrooms appeared as if by magic. They'd been there all along, of course, so perfectly adapted to their surroundings, their color so much like dead leaves, their shape so much like bits of rotting wood and chunks of ugly rock that they'd been invisible to ignorant eyes. But once my vision adjusted, once my mind re-evaluated the visual impressions it received, I saw mushrooms everywhere, seemingly thousands of them. I'd been standing on them, walking over them, staring at them, and hadn't realized.

The Old Testament tells us of the prophet Hosea. Hosea proclaimed the message of God to the Northern Kingdom just before the Babylonians entered and destroyed that nation. And something in the life of Hosea greatly influenced his message. We are told that Hosea had married a prostitute who had been unfaithful to him on several occasions. The scene is unmistakably clear. Hosea's wife would leave him to return to her previous life of promiscuity and unfaithfulness. Hosea would be overcome with pain over this situation and would, like most of us, want punishment and justice for the wrong. However, when his wife would return, Hosea would find himself filled with compassion for this woman, and he would accept her back into his life.

Hosea compares this experience to the religious life of his country. The Hebrews have been unfaithful to God. They have not observed the relationship that God had established with them. According to Hosea, they had breached the law of God, but Hosea singles out three special qualities that cannot be found anywhere among the Hebrews: faithfulness, loving compassion, and a relationship with God. The people had not neglected going to the Temple on holy days and they had not neglected offering their sacrifices. Instead, they had neglected their relationship with God, and they had become selfish. The prophet pleads to them in the name of God: "I desire loving compassion and not sacrifice, the knowledge of God and not burnt offerings" (Hos 6:6).

Hosea blames this unfaithfulness on two things: selfishness, and forgetting. The nation had become too obsessed with itself — too concerned with what it can get for itself right now, that it has abandoned God for the pleasures of the self. It has forgotten its special function as the called-out ones of God. It has forgotten that it is the instrument through which God planned to bless all nations of the earth.

But Hosea does not stop at this note of condemnation. Instead he brings out the compassion that God has for his people, the great sorrow that God endures because they will have to endure punishment for their sins. God does not forget Israel nor lose the hope of recovering its love again. "What shall I do with you, Ephraim? What shall I do with you, Judah? I would restore the fortunes of my people" (Hos 6:4,11).

Hosea longs for the Hebrews to return in repentance to God and to receive God's forgiveness. And in his urging, he relates the longing that God has for his people to return to their faith. Hosea can do this because he believes that God does indeed love his people. He believes that these people are precious to God.

Our NT lesson presents a lesson of Jesus which tells the same story. He calls his followers to return good for evil, to "love your enemies." How can such love be commanded? For Jesus, love is a way of living and relating to other human beings. We act in creative, helpful and redemptive ways toward people for whom we do not feel attracted —

even those who are hostile and vindictive. The examples Jesus uses are everyday occurrences: someone strikes out to hurt you, someone steals from you, someone curses you. But in response, the Christian is called to do the unexpected – to respond in love.

If we love only those who love us back, then our faith has not affected our vision. Christianity affects our lives by causing us to do things we would not normally do. It helps us to adjust our vision so that we look for opportunities to share God's love with our world. We no longer can just pass by the suffering ones who live in our communities, but we are compelled to reach out and be a part of their lives. Adjusting our vision will lead us to invest our lives in people whether or not they can or will reciprocate. This kind of love is not motivated by beauty and goodness in other people; rather it seeks to bring out beauty and goodness in others.

Those people listening to Jesus on that day were not much different from Hosea's audience. They were people of unfaithfulness, many of them. They were people who were so involved with their own lives that they had forgotten the importance of anything or anyone else. Jesus' enemies would surely have rejoiced over the expression of God's love upon their own family and friends. But they were offended at the thought that God would rejoice over these whom Jesus befriended. Jesus reached out to those that were rejected and hated by their society. And these enemies of Jesus were sure that they themselves were more important to God than any of these friends of Jesus. But Jesus sought to teach his listeners that God cares for all people. Everyone is precious in his sight.

These words of Jesus are words of challenge and invitation.

They are words of invitation because they invite each one of us to be included in the love of God. God loves us, no matter who we are or what we do or have done. God loved the arrogant self-righteous Jews of Jesus' day, and God loved the unfaithful selfish Hebrews of Hosea's day. God loved those who were unloved and neglected by everyone else, and God loved the persons of faith who were dedicated to the task God set before them. God loves us all, and he invites us to share in that love. There are many ways we can do that.

These words are a challenge to us, because they ask us to take another look at ourselves and our faith. We don't like to think of ourselves as being like the Hebrews that Hosea spoke to, or like the Jews that Jesus spoke to. But in some ways we may be much alike.

We may not openly reject or hate people around us. We may not think that we are better than everyone else. We may take pride in ourselves for being a warm and friendly church, a loving and caring church.

I believe that our sin today is not of forgetting the laws of God, or of neglecting our relationship with God on purpose. Our sin today is more the sin of apathy. We don't really ignore people around us, we just don't see them. We need to adjust our vision so that we intentionally share God's love with all.

Stan C. Pigue
St. John's United Methodist Church
Danville, Virginia

MARCH 1, 1992

Last Sunday after the Epiphany (Transfiguration)

Lessons:

Lutheran:	Deut. 34:1-12	2 Cor. 4:3-6	Luke 9:28-36
Roman Catholic:	Is. 6:1-2a, 3-8	I Cor. 15:1-11	Luke 5:1-11
Episcopal:	Ex. 34:29-35	I Cor. 12:27-13:13	Luke 9:28-36
Pres/Meth/UCC:	Ex. 34:29-35	2 Cor. 3:12-4:2	Luke 9:28-36

Introductions to the Lessons:

Lesson 1

(1) *Deuteronomy 34:1-12* (**Luth**) Moses was allowed to see but not enter the Promised Land. The Lord led Moses to the top of Mt. Nebo where he could see the land in the distance. Then at age 120 he died and Yahweh buried him. Moses was a mighty man of God who knew God face to face.

(2) *Exodus 34:29-35* (**Epis/Pres/Meth/UCC**) Moses spent 40 days with Yahweh on the top of Mt. Sinai where he received the Decalogue. When Moses came down to his people, his face still reflected the glory of God to the point that they were afraid to approach him. Consequently, he had to put a veil over his face and removed it only when he communed with Yahweh.

Lesson 2

(1) *II Corinthians 4:3-6* (**Luth**) Unlike Moses' face, the Gospel is not veiled for believers. Christians see the glory of God in the face of Jesus. It is this Christ that Paul proclaims.

(2) *I Corinthians 12:27-13:13* (**Epis**) Please see Lesson 2, Epiphany IV, Lutheran.

(3) *II Corinthians 3:12-4:2* (**Pres/Meth/UCC**) Here Paul contrasts the glory of Moses and the glory of Christ. Because of the veil, Moses' face could not be seen. Believers in the Gospel have the veil removed so that they can see the glory of God in the face of Jesus.

Gospel

Luke 9:28-36 (**Luth/Epis/Pres/Meth/UCC**) Like his baptism, Jesus' transfiguration was a prayer experience. It was a mountain-top experience with his three closest friends. At Caesarea Philippi Jesus learned that his disciples knew he was the Christ. Before fulfilling his life's purpose, he needed confirmation and approval of his Father, the Law (Moses), and the Prophets (Elijah). With this approval, he sets his face toward Jerusalem to die for the sins of the world.

Theme: The Lord sets his face to Jerusalem.

Thought for the day: The decisions I make today provide the foundation for the decisions I will make tomorrow.

Prayer of meditation: Almighty God, who calls me to obedience and thus true life, prepare me to recognize your voice; make me aware that in making smaller decisions I am preparing to make larger decisions. Heavenly Creator, strengthen me so that in living my life today I am indeed preparing for tomorrow. Even as I worship you today, help me understand that living today and preparing for tomorrow is one and the same. I pray in the name of Christ my Lord. Amen.

Call to worship:
Leader: As Moses came down from Mount Sinai,
  People: He did not know his face shone from talking with God.
Leader: The Lord is king, let the people tremble!
  People: He sits enthroned upon the cherubim, let the people quake!
Leader: Extol the Lord our God, and worship at his holy mountain;
  People: for the Lord our God is holy.

Prayer of adoration: Almighty God, creator of all that is, sustainer of all life, the one who loves your children so much you came to us in your Son Jesus the Christ, we acknowledge that you are above all and alone are worthy of worship. Strengthen us that we might accept more completely that you are always with us. We come to worship you, to express our adoration, and to submit ourselves to you in obedience. We pray in the name of Jesus our Lord. Amen.

Prayer of confession: Most merciful God, we your children accept your bidding to come to you in confession and to receive your forgiveness. We confess we do not express our love in service: we allow hunger, oppression, discrimination, strife, and permit the rich to increase in power while the poor become even more powerless. As we confess our sin, forgive us and may we know of your acceptance. We pray in the name of Jesus Christ our Lord. Amen.

Prayer of dedication of gifts and self: Almighty God, because you are the Creator of all, and without you we would have nothing, we give you now but your own — that which is already yours. Along with these material things, we also give you ourselves and pray that you will use us as you will, that we may be tools in your hands. In the name of Christ we pray. Amen.

Sermon title: From Mountain Top to Valley

Sermon thesis: The great decisions of life come as a culmination of a series of small decisions made along the way. Living life means preparing for tomorrow at the same time life is being lived today.

Hymn for the day: *"Swiftly pass the clouds of glory."* Thomas H. Troeger (b. 1945), a Presbyterian minister, is associate professor of preaching and parish ministry at Colgate Rochester Divinity School/Bexley Hall/Crozer Theological Seminary in Rochester, New York. He is the author of numerous articles, reviews and papers, as well as many hymns. Together with Carol Doran he has published *New Hymns for the Lectionary*, 1985. The third stanza of the hymn asks God to "recast our life's intentions To the shape of your designs."

Announcements for Ash Wednesday:

Sermon title: The Journey Begins with a Dirty Face
Sermon theme: Being holy for the Lord.
Sermon summary: Lent is a time of repentance but also one of remembering that we know the outcome as we wear the ashes of last year's palm branches. We remember that to understand best Easter we must walk through the forty days of Lent.

Announcements for next week:

Sermon title: The Greatest Temptation
Sermon theme: Our greatest temptation is to be something that we are not.
Sermon summary: As Jesus began his ministry he was driven into the wilderness to confront who and what he really was. Satan tempted him at his strengths, asking him to go another way than the way God had intended. We too are tempted to be other than what we were created to be. Jesus relied on the strength of the Creator to persevere, and so can we.

Children's object talk:

First Looking, And Then Doing

Objects: Two or three pairs of binoculars or "spy" glasses.
Lesson: We look to the future to know what we must do today.
Outline: 1. Look at the back of the sanctuary from the lowest level and from the highest level possible.
2. From the high level you can see where you want to go.
3. In order to get there, you have to walk on the lower level.

THESE BINOCULARS ARE REALLY NEAT, because when you look through them you can see things that are very far away, things you maybe couldn't see without the binoculars. Those far-away objects seem to be very close when you look at them through these. Just take a look at the people at the back of the church. Do you feel like you could put your hand out and touch them? These binoculars would be handy to use on a hike, wouldn't they? You could look way down the trail and see where you're heading. It's almost like seeing into the future. That might fool you, though. While it's exciting to see where you're going to end up, you'd better not forget to watch the trail right in front of you. Really, you need to look both ways, don't you? You surely need to know what your destination is (where you're heading), but you also need to look carefully where you put your foot for the next step.

This makes me think of our journey through life. It's important how we turn out, what kind of persons we become. That's kind of like looking far away through the binoculars. But how we live each day is also important. That's kind of like watching where you put your foot for the next step.

We find out that the two are almost the same. By living every day, even today, the way God wants us to means we will be living God's way all our lives. Getting to where God wants us to be tomorrow means living the way God wants us to live today.

The sermon:

From Mountain Top To Valley

Hymns:
Beginning of worship: Joyful, Joyful, We Adore Thee
Sermon hymn: Christ is Made the Sure Foundation
End of worship: All Hail the Power of Jesus' Name

Scripture: Luke 9:28-36

Sermon text: *"This is my Son, my Chosen; listen to him!"* vs. 35

A VITAL QUESTION MOST THINKING CHRISTIANS will ask after reading today's Gospel lesson is: "What really happened on the mountain top?" Another is: "What did it mean then?" and/or "What does it mean to me today?"

The committed Christian believes at least two things about Jesus: 1) in meeting Jesus we meet God; if we want to know what God is like, we look to Jesus; 2) the historical Jesus was committed to doing the will of God at any cost and he continually sought the approval of God. In a sense, Jesus sought God's permission for action.

Thus it follows that if we are to seek to be Christian we are to follow the example of Jesus. Anything less is to fail completely in our profession of faith in Jesus as the Christ.

We do not know when Jesus first became aware of who he was. What we do know is that at the time of his baptism Jesus received affirmation of his relationship to God. As he came out of the Jordan River after being baptized, he alone heard the words of God: "You are my beloved Son, with whom I am well pleased." Now, at the Transfiguration depicted in today's Gospel lesson, others (Peter, James, and John) heard God say, "This is my Son, my Chosen; listen to him."

God confirmed Jesus at his baptism; God acknowledged Jesus at the Transfiguration!

In order to understand the significance of the Transfiguration, the appearance of Jesus with Moses and Elijah described in this morning's Gospel lesson, we must remember where we are in relationship to Christ's earthly ministry.

Jesus has been preaching and healing. He has been baptized and faced the temptations as to how to carry out his ministry. Jesus has chosen his disciples as his inner band and has taught them and given them work to do.

Then, in an event related shortly before today's reading, a new milestone is reached; it is as though Jesus is testing his disciples. 1) "Who do people say that I am?" and 2) The more important question, "Who do you say that I am?" After this happened, the end of the beginning of Jesus' earthly ministry has come. From now on, from what could be called the beginning of the end of Jesus' earthly ministry, everything points to the crucifixion and, ultimately, the resurrection!

Thus the stage is set for today's dramatic climax. Jesus takes his inner circle, the three disciples apparently most close to him, to the mountain top. There the three witness in some extraordinary way the vindication of the ministry of Jesus!

In an account written down years later, the Gospel writers all describe the Transfiguration as involving the appearance with Jesus of Moses and Elijah, who are symbolic of the law and the prophets. Jesus is the fulfillment of God's efforts for reconciliation with humankind. I am strongly convinced the Transfiguration took place not for Jesus' benefit, but for the sakes of the disciples and of us.

However, we must remember we do not come to this moment in isolation.

We know, and Jesus knew, that the course on which he set himself would lead to death. On that day, when it would seem Jesus made his irrevocable decision to follow the will of God wherever it led, even to the cross, it was as though Jesus could see the cross at Jerusalem (and beyond) all the way from the top of the mountain.

From the mountain top he could see the cross and the empty tomb; Jesus could see the will of God.

To get there, Jesus had to return to the valley and work his way to his goal!

Now, the question remains (as it always does): What does this mean for us today?

If Christianity is to have any bearing on us, the truths of Christianity must speak to us who are in this sanctuary at this moment!

The voice we must hear is that of God through Christ!

The voice we must hear is the voice of God through Christ which tells us we have a mission to perform; we are a part of God's people and we are called to be faithful.

Christ was called to the cross; we are called to be equally faithful! We are called to look at the Transfiguration of the Lord through the eyes of Jesus. We are also called to look at the Transfiguration of the Lord through the mind of God and of Peter, James, and John.

We are called upon to be faithful to God through Jesus the Christ!

We are called upon by God to understand that we have a purpose in life; that this congregation has a vital role to play!

Just as at the Transfiguration Jesus was looking to the future built on the past, so we are called upon to look to the future in the name of God. The past is of help to us; it is a foundation upon which we are called to construct the future in the name of God.

We are also called upon, just as was Jesus, to realize that although we can see glory from the mountain top, a great deal of work must be done as we walk through the valley.

Miles Walter Jackson
United Methodist Church
Bow, Washington

MARCH 4, 1992

Ash Wednesday

Lessons:

Lutheran:	Joel 2:12-19	2 Cor. 5:20b-6:2	Matt. 6:1-6, 16-21
Roman Catholic:	Joel 2:12-18	2 Cor. 5:20-6:2	Matt. 6:1-6, 16-18
Episcopal:	Joel 2:1-2, 12-17	2 Cor. 5:20b-6:10	Matt. 6:1-6, 16-21
Pres/Meth/UCC:	Joel 2:1-2, 12-17a	2 Cor. 5:20b-6:10	Matt. 6:1-6, 16-21

Introductions to the Lessons:

Lesson 1

Joel 2:12-19 (**Luth**); *2:1-2, 12-17* (**Epis/Pres/Meth/UCC**) Sound the alarm! A day of doom is coming. Therefore, repent and return to the Lord with fasting and weeping. If you do, your gracious God will have mercy and bless you.

Lesson 2

II Corinthians 5:20b-6:10 (**Epis/Pres/Meth/UCC**); *5:20b-6:2* (**Luth**) Ash Wednesday is the first day of Lent, a time to be reconciled to God by faith in Christ. Through Paul God is making this appeal to be reconciled. Accept his salvation today. Do not receive the grace of God in vain.

Gospel

Matthew 6:1-6, 16-21 (**Luth/Epis/Pres/Meth/UCC**) In this section from the Sermon on the Mount, Jesus deals with the practice of piety in giving, praying, and fasting. None of this is to be done for "show" but to be done secretly. By doing these things privately and sincerely, we store up spiritual treasure in heaven.

Theme: Being Holy for the Lord

Thought for the day: Seek to be Holy for the Lord, not for others.

Prayer of meditation: Almighty God, who calls me to obedience and thus true life, help me remember a smudge of ash is a reminder to me of my having made a commitment to serve you and not an expression of being "holier than thou."

Call to worship:
Leader: Come into God's courts and cry: "Have mercy on me!"
People: Have mercy on me, most holy Lord.
Leader: Let us confess our transgressions.
People: My sin is ever before me.
Leader: Come, let us begin our forty-day journey.
People: Let us accept the ashes of repentance and praise the Lord!

Prayer of adoration: Most holy God, who loves us s a heavenly parent, we worship you and offer you our adoration as a gift. With the psalmist, we ask: "What are humans that you are mindful of us?" that you gave your only Son to be our Redeemer. For life, for salvation, for opportunity to serve, we praise you and adore you, Almighty God. In the name of Jesus we pray. Amen.

Prayer of confession: Most merciful God, as we begin this forty-day journey to the resurrection, we are mindful of our transgression against your law and your love. We confess it was because of our human sin that Jesus had to make the walk to the cross of shame and death. Forgive us, Almighty God, and strengthen us that we might accept your forgiveness, your love, your peace. We pray in the name of Jesus Christ our Lord. Amen.

Prayer of dedication of gifts and self: With these gifts we present ourselves, Almighty God, and pray that you will use our gifts and our service in the fulfillment of your will. We pray in the name of Christ. Amen.

Sermon title: The Journey Begins with a Dirty Face

Sermon thesis: Lent is a time of repentance but also one of remembering that we know the outcome; as we wear the ashes (either literally or figuratively) of last year's palm branches, we remember that to understand Easter best we must walk through the forty days of Lent.

Hymn for the day: *"Savior, when in dust to you/thee."* This hymn of repentance reviews the life of Christ and its ultimate triumph. First published in 1815 in *The Christian Observer,* it soon entered three American Episcopalian hymn books. The author, Robert Grant (1779-1838), was born in Bengal and educated at Magdalen College, Oxford. Called to the Bar in 1807, he subsequently served for many years as a Member of Parliament. He held a number of other prestigious posts and in 1834, on the occasion of his becoming governor of Bombay, he was knighted.

Children's object talk:

Palm Branches — Ashes — And Getting Ready

Objects: Two or three branches of dried palm leaves from Palm Sunday, 1991.

Lesson: We prepare for the future by remembering (re-experiencing) the past.

Outline: 1. Recall the celebration of last year's Palm/Passion Sunday.
2. Discuss on the children's level the meaning of confession and a desire to live according to God's will.
3. Either burn these branches OR have some pre-prepared ashes to show and explain how these ashes will be used later in the service.

ONE OF THE GREAT WORSHIP SERVICES of the year is Palm Sunday. It is a day when we remember Jesus riding on a donkey into Jerusalem. Last year some of you took part in the first part of the worship service as we all marched into the sanctuary at the very beginning of church. As we marched, we sang and waved the palm branches high over our heads. We tried to understand what it may have been like to have walked with Jesus into the city of Jerusalem long ago.

While this procession was a happy time, it was also the first day of Jesus' last week before his death and also before his coming back to life. During that week, a lot of bad things were done to Jesus. Today is what we call Ash Wednesday; it is the first day of that period of time when we get ready to remember once again all that happened to Jesus that week and also the forgiveness God gives to us because of Jesus.

After while, those who want to will have a bit of ashes put on their forehead as a sign that they are sorry for doing wrong and want to live the way God wants them to. We get the ashes from burning the palm branches from last year's Palm Sunday service. Here are some ashes I prepared earlier by burning some palm branches — they are what we will use in a little bit. When we put on the ashes, we will say words that mean "Remember the Good News Jesus brought, and be glad."

The sermon:

The Journey Begins With A Dirty Face

Hymns:
Beginning of worship: Lord, Who Throughout These Forty Days
Sermon hymn: Amazing Grace
End of worship: Have Thine Own Way, Lord

Scripture: Matthew 6:1-6, 16-21

Sermon text: *"Beware of practicing your piety before others."* vs. 1

ABOUT FIVE YEARS AGO, for the first time in my life I knelt as a lay member of my church imposed ashes on my forehead and pronounced the words: "Repent, and believe the Gospel."

It is nearly impossible for me to relate how I felt at that moment, the emotions involved. For the first time in my ministry, I felt the Ash Wednesday worship service in which I was participating and leading was complete. I understood myself to be a part of the continuing line of splendor consisting of the faithful down through the centuries.

I also confess part of what I experienced was a sense of relief that the service had gone well. For the first time in my thirty-five years of ministry, I had offered members of my congregation the opportunity to receive the imposition of ashes as a token of their confession and of their dedication to serve God through Christ. Also involved was their renewed commitment to prepare for the gift of Easter by living and experiencing the forty days of Lent.

My new relationship to the glory of Easter began with a smudge of ashes on my forehead. Ashes on the forehead had never been part of my personal tradition; for too many years I had kept from myself, and members of my congregations, the sense of commitment and discipline the service of Ash Wednesday could offer.

Today, we begin a forty-day walk in anticipation of celebration of the gift of salvation through God's action in the resurrection. The forty days do not include Sunday because Christians never pretend that Easter has not happened; the Sundays of Lent continue to be "little Easters."

It is significant that this forty-day journey thus begins with a dirty face, the smudge of ashes on our forehead. Traditionally, the ashes come from the burning of the palm branches used the previous year to celebrate Jesus' triumphant entry into Jerusalem. With the imposition of ashes, we identify with the sin of the world, but we also confess our individual sin.

However, our "dirty face" is not only literal and comes from the ashes, our dirty face is also theological. Any Christian understands he/she has fallen short of the glory of God, is sinful and stands in the need of confession.

With the traditional emphasis of the Church on the use of ashes in mind, the Gospel lesson for Ash Wednesday presents us with a seeming contradiction. Throughout the lesson, Jesus is emphasizing the reality that our piety and our confession is to be personal between ourselves and God and is not to be understood as a time to parade our supposed holiness or acts of atonement before others.

The service of Ash Wednesday provides us the understanding that Christianity is both private and public. Although we are in a group at this service, we are in personal privacy before God. If our mind is not on God but rather is concerned with what others may think about the smudge of ashes on our forehead, then we are not worshiping in the way Jesus tells us in today's Gospel lesson.

Today's Gospel lesson helps us to remember who we are as individual Christians and also collectively as the Church, the body of Christ. Just as we do not pretend during Lent that Easter has not happened, neither do we pretend we live in a vacuum. The Church is not the Church in isolation from society; the Church is carrying out its work as the body of Christ when it proclaims to the world the Gospel of our Lord and Savior.

Ash Wednesday provides perfect opportunity for us to reflect on our own individual need to confess our sin before God through Christ, knowing that before God we cannot imagine we are sinless. If we understand we are not sinless then we must realize we need to confess our sin and to receive salvation as God's gift. In a real sense, accepting the smudge of ashes on our foreheads is our confession to God that our spiritual forehead is also dark with sin.

Thus, when we receive the ashes we may be physically in the presence of others, but spiritually we are alone before God. If this is not the case, we are violating the instructions of Jesus in today's lesson.

Ash Wednesday is also a time to acknowledge its (the Church's) failure to live the way of Christ, with the precepts of Christ being the guide for our life and work.

In a very real way, then, as members of the congregation receive the ashes in repentance, they do so not only for themselves but as being a part of the total congregation, the Church. The Church is kneeling in the closet with the door shut; we are not parading our repentance in a "guiltier than thou" procession, we are not looking dismal to the world — but rather we are confessing to our God that we acknowledge our sin. Only in this way can we obtain from God the salvation that only the acknowledged sinner can receive!

At this service we recognize that Jesus is beginning the long walk to Jerusalem, with all that means, and we are promising to walk with him!

Miles Walter Jackson
United Methodist Church
Bow, Washington

MARCH 8, 1992

First Sunday in Lent

Lessons:

Lutheran:	Deut. 26:5-10	Rom. 10:8b-13	Luke 4:1-13
Roman Catholic:	Deut. 26:4-10	Rom. 10:8-13	Luke 4:1-13
Episcopal:	Deut. 26:(1-4) 5-11	Rom. 10:(5-8a) 8b-13	Luke 4:1-13
Pres/Meth/UCC:	Deut. 26:1-11	Rom. 10:8b-13	Luke 4:1-13

Introductions to the Lessons:

Lesson 1

Deuteronomy 26:1-11 (**Epis/Pres/Meth/UCC**); *26:5-10* (**Luth**) When the Israelites arrive in the Promised Land, Moses directed that some of the first yield of the fields shall be brought to a priest as to God. This is to symbolize their past slavery in Egypt, God's providence during the wilderness wanderings, and now their presence in the new land. In gratitude God is to get the first products from the new land as a sacrifice of thanks.

Lesson 2

Romans 10:8b-13 (**Luth/Epis/Pres/Meth/UCC**) What must a person do to be saved? What does it take to be a Christian? Paul gives the answer: hear the Gospel as it is preached, confess that Jesus is Lord, believe in Christ's resurrection. By faith a person is accepted by God, and by witnessing, a person is saved. Heart and mouth respond to God's grace resulting in salvation.

Gospel

Luke 4:1-13 (**Luth/Epis/Pres/Meth/UCC**) Being human Jesus was tempted by Satan just as we are. Jesus was tempted to carry out his call to be the Messiah in ways not in accordance with God's will. He faced three basic temptations and overcame them by quoting the truth in the Scriptures. Satan would have to try again at a later time!

Theme: Our greatest temptation is to be something that we are not.

Thought for the day: The greatest temptation Jesus faced as he began his ministry was to be something other than what God wanted him to be. This is also our greatest temptation.

275

Prayer of meditation: Holy God: you give to each and every one of us special gifts and graces and you call us to serve you with these gifts and graces. Strengthen us so that we might use who and what we are for your glory and be the people that you created us to be.

Call to worship:
Leader: Whoever dwells in the shelter of the Most High,
People: Who abides in the shadow of the Almighty,
Leader: Will say to God, "My refuge and my fortress;"
People: "My God, in whom I trust."
Leader: Let us worship God.

Prayer of adoration: Gracious God: You are above and beyond all that is or will ever be, yet nearer to us than breathing. Gathering together as your people, we worship and adore you, even as we praise your loving kindness to us and to all whom you have created; in the name of Jesus Christ, we pray. Amen.

Prayer of confession: In love you created us, gracious God, with love you redeemed us and with love you sustain us through all the changing experiences of our life. We confess that we sometimes have not answered that love with lives of obedient living. Forgive us; renew us and restore us we pray in the name of the Christ. Amen.

Prayer of dedication of gifts and self: Receive these gifts, O giving God, using them for the good of your people throughout the world. Use us also as concrete expressions of that love to all. Amen.

Sermon title: The Greatest Temptation

Sermon thesis: As Jesus began his ministry he was driven into the wilderness to confront who and what he really was. Satan tempted him at his strengths, asking him to go another way than the way God had intended. We too are tempted to be other than what we were created to be. Jesus relied on the strength of the Creator to persevere; so can we.

Hymn for the day: *"If God himself be for me."* This heroic hymn by Paul Gerhardt has been described as worthy of a place alongside "A mighty fortress." Based on Romans 8, the hymn originally had 15 stanzas. Gerhardt (1607-1676) studied for the ministry at Wittenberg University. The Thirty Years' War (1618-1648) disrupted his schooling and later his finding a parish. He finally settled in Berlin where he came to know two important hymn tune composers, Johann Crüger and Johann Georg Ebeling, with whom he published a number of his hymns. The troubles of the war and the religious disputes of the day were compounded for him by the loss of his wife and four of his children. Yet amidst it all he wrote over 100 hymns, among them some of the finest and most beloved of all Christian hymns. The hymn reminds us that "If God himself be for me I may a host defy."

Announcements for next week:

Sermon title: Facing the Enemy

Sermon theme: As Jesus faced many enemies, so we too face both those outside and those inside us. In both cases God sustains us.

Sermon summary: Our Lord could face the enemy, in his case, Herod Antipas, because he trusted in God, the God who gave him courage even in the face of suffering and death. Each of us must also face various enemies, external and internal, and that same God also gives us courage to stand firm, trusting in his love and grace.

Children's object talk:

Temptation

Objects: Box of candy

Lesson: Jesus was tempted. We are tempted. God can help us.

Outline: 1. Each of us is tempted.

2. Before he could begin his ministry Jesus was tempted.

3. God helped Jesus and he will help us, too.

HAVE YOU EVER REALLY gotten hungry just before dinner? I know that I have. Maybe you're going to have dinner a bit later than usual, but you're hungry now. You go into the kitchen and there on the top shelf you see a big box of candy. Slowly, you climb up to get it and have just gotten it in your hand when in walks your mother. "Billy, what in the world are you doing on that counter?" Now you're caught. No candy for you; you'll have to wait for your dinner. You gave in to temptation. The candy tempted you, even though you knew that you shouldn't touch it.

Before Jesus began his ministry, he was led into the desert and there the devil tempted him, with food and with power, among other things. He could have easily given in to that temptation, but he didn't. Instead he relied on the strength of God to help him.

The main temptation for Jesus was to do what God didn't want him to do; to do things the way someone else (devil) wanted him to do it; to be someone else, not the person God had created him to be.

Have you ever been tempted to be someone else? Oh, not when you are playing, that is fine; but really tempted to change the way you know you are to make someone else happy? That is a real temptation. God created each and every one of us differently, with unique gifts and God wants us to be that special person. God likes us just the way we are, because that is how he created us.

When you are tempted to be someone else; remember that Jesus was, too, and he made it through because he depended on God. You can, too.

The sermon:

The Greatest Temptation

Hymns:
Beginning of worship: Lord, Who Throughout These Forty Days
Sermon hymn: Who Trusts in God
End of worship: A Mighty Fortress

Scripture: Luke 4:1-13

Sermon text: *"And Jesus, full of the Holy Spirit, returned from the Jordan, and was led by the Spirit for forty days in the wilderness. . ."* v. 1, 2a

LENT BEGINS IN THE DESERT! Here for forty days our Lord was tempted by Satan to forego the course of his life that he knew was right and take a new course; one which would change things, which would make him into a different person.

At his baptism Jesus had heard the voice of God: "You are my beloved Son." Now he hears another voice: "If you are the Son of God. . ." Here in this place of barren rock and scrub tree, where the days are blistering and the nights frigid, Jesus comes face to face with temptation. Now his soul is tried to its very limits. Each of the temptations are subtle and strong, speaking to the attractiveness of his ultimate goal; but calling on him to use means which do not belong to God.

Each temptation is part and parcel of the larger temptation which confronts each of us: to be something that we are not; to be untrue to the person we are, the person that God created us to be. Each temptation calls upon Jesus to discard his own identity and give in to someone else's understanding of who and what he is. The Scriptures make clear that such temptations come straight from Satan, that they are evil!

In this familiar story we see ourselves. If we are honest before God, we must admit that the greatest temptation which we face has nothing to do with an extra helping of mashed potatoes, but rather with the siren call to be someone that we are not; to sell ourselves for something which we might fleetingly see as important: fame, power, prestige, money, or what have you.

Have you ever tried to be someone that you weren't because you thought it would advance you in your business or profession? Have you not spoken out on an issue of importance because you were afraid that it would alienate someone who was important to you? Have you trimmed your moral sails because what you stood for was not popular in your group? I dare say that most of us can answer YES to such questions. It is difficult to be your own person. It was difficult for Jesus and it is difficult for us too. We don't want to do anything which will alienate us from those whom we think are important to us. That is human, and that is the greatest of all the temptations: *to be someone that you are not.*

If we succumb to such temptation, we will eventually pay for it. We can only keep up the pretense for so long before we begin to suffer in our souls with guilt, shame, and the deep-seated feeling that we have not only been untrue to our highest ideals, but also to the God who created us to be the unique persons that we are. It is hard to stand firm in the face of such temptations; but it is harder to pay the price later on in guilt, shame, tension and stress: to look at yourself in the mirror and know that you have "sold out."

How can we cope with such temptation? Where can we find strength and courage? This is a lonely time for Jesus in the wilderness; and it is also for us in our own wilderness times. The mystics speak of such times as the dark nights of the souls. Yet really we are not alone. There are resources, but first we are called on to make a choice: "Choose this day whom you will serve." Are we with God or not? No one can make such a decision for us. We cannot pass the buck to someone else. God created us with the freedom to choose and we are called on to exercise that freedom. There is personal responsibility here. Jesus made such a decision. He took that first step; and once that happened there were resources for him to draw on. He used the Scriptures to guide him in his confrontation:

". . . Man does not live by bread alone."
". . . You shall worship the Lord your God."
". . . You shall not tempt the Lord your God."

He drew upon the resources which he had both as a person and even more importantly as a creature of God (just like us). The same is true for us! We are not alone. We can draw upon the power and the love of God. When we call upon God, he is there for us, as he was there for Jesus in the wilderness. We must, though, make a decision to stand; to make a choice; to put on the "whole armour of God."

We can do this in some very practical ways:

1. through personal prayer and meditation
2. through the study of the Scriptures
3. through corporate worship, especially the celebration of the Eucharist
4. by an openness to the power of the Holy Spirit in our lives.

By doing all of these things, we will not be assured of a life free of temptation, but we will be assured that we can, God helping us, stand firm, being the person whom we were created to be.

John N. Cedarleaf
First Congregational UCC
Fairport, New York

MARCH 15, 1992

Second Sunday in Lent

Lessons:

Lutheran:	Jer. 26:8-15	Phil. 3:17-4:1	Luke 13:31-35
Roman Catholic:	Gen. 15:5-12, 17-18	Phil. 3:17-4:1	Luke 9:28-36
Episcopal:	Gen. 15:1-12, 17-18	Phil. 3:17-4:1	Luke 13:(22-30) 31-35
Pres/Meth/UCC:	Gen. 15:1-12, 17-18	Phil. 3:17-4:1	Luke 13:31-35

Introductions to the Lessons:

Lesson 1

(1) *Jeremiah 26:8-15* (**Luth**) Because Jeremiah predicted the destruction of Jerusalem and the Temple by the Babylonians, the people, princes, and priests demanded Jeremiah's execution. In his defense he said that if they would repent this catastrophe would not happen. Moreover, he assured them that the Lord told him what he said.

(2) *Genesis 15:1-12, 17-18* (**Epis/Pres/Meth/UCC**) Abraham and Yahweh enter into a covenant. Yahweh promised Abraham, though at the time childless, that he would have descendants as numerous as the stars and that he would have the land of Canaan. The covenant was formalized with a dinner.

Lesson 2

Philippians 3:17-4:1 (**Luth/Epis/Pres/Meth/UCC**) Paul sets himself up as an example of Christian living for his church to imitate. Some, enemies of the cross, are not following his example. By contrast, true Christians belong to Christ's Kingdom. He exhorts his people to remain faithful to Christ.

Gospel

Luke 13:31-35 (**Luth/Epis/Pres/Meth/UCC**) Jesus is no coward! On his way to Jerusalem, some Pharisees urged him to flee because King Herod was out to kill him. His reply to the Pharisees was that they should tell Herod, "that fox," that he must continue his work. His greater concern is the indifference of the people in Jerusalem to his ministry. His heart cries out, "How often would I have gathered your children . . . but you would not!"

Theme: As Jesus faced many enemies; so we too face both those outside and those inside us. In both cases God sustains us.

281

Thought for the day: Courage in life's struggles is given by God, the God who was with Jesus and is with us too in all that we do.

Prayer of meditation: Strengthening God: sometimes life is a difficult journey, full of thorns along the way. There are enemies to face, internal and external. We would pray that your grace and strength would sustain us in this journey so that we might fulfill your plan for our life; in Jesus' name we pray. Amen.

Call to worship:
Leader: Hear, O God, when I cry aloud,
People: Be gracious to me and answer me!
Leader: You have said, "Seek my face."
People: My heart says to you, "Your face, God, do I seek."
Leader: Teach me your way, O God;
People: And lead me on a level path because of my enemies.
Leader: Wait for God; be strong and let your heart take courage:
People: Yes, wait for God!
Leader: Let us worship God.

Prayer of adoration: Holy God, to worship you is the reason for our life. To be drawn closer to you and to each other is why we are here in this place of sacred memory and present experience today. As we lift our hearts and voices in praise and adoration toward you, might we be lifted up into your presence. We pray in the name of Christ. Amen.

Prayer of confession: Loving and forgiving God: we come before you confessing our sins; those that we commit deliberately and those that we allow to overtake us. Have mercy upon us; forgive us; renew and heal us in the name of Jesus Christ, our Saviour and Lord. Amen.

Prayer of dedication of gifts and self: Take what we offer to you, the giver of all good and perfect gifts, and use them to bring wholeness and healing to all that you have created. Amen.

Sermon title: Facing the Enemy

Sermon thesis: Our Lord could face the enemy, in his case, Herod Antipas, because he trusted in God, the God who gave him courage even in the face of suffering and death. Each of us must also face various enemies, external and internal, and that same God also gives us courage to stand firm, trusting in his love and grace.

Hymn for the day: *"Who trusts in God, a strong abode."* It was fortunate that Joachim Magdeburg found in God a strong abode, for he certainly had none on this earth. Born in Germany around 1525 he studied theology at Wittenberg University. From 1547 until 1583 (after which we know nothing of his story) he met with continual difficulties as a result of the theological battles raging at the time. His single stanza, which has much in common with "A mighty fortress," was published in 1522. Two additional stanzas appeared in a Leipzig hymnal in 1597.

Announcements for next week:

Sermon title: Unless You Repent

Sermon theme: Even though we don't like judgment, God calls upon us to repent, to "turn around" and begin anew, to follow the one we call the Christ.

Sermon summary: The good are not exempt from tragedy and the wicked might indeed prosper. All people are called on to turn their lives around, to repent, and to follow the Christ.

Children's object talk:

Courage

Objects: Fairy tale book about heroes, etc.

Lesson: Jesus faced enemies with courage because God was with him. God gives us courage too.

Outline: 1. What is courage?

2. Jesus faced difficulties with courage.

3. We can face difficulties with courage because God is with us.

DO YOU LIKE TO READ fairy tales? I know that I do. I especially like the ones with dragons, knights, etc. One thing that the knights of old had was courage. Do you know what courage is? It is a big word but it means that we can stand up to scary things. Do you remember in the story of the "Wizard of Oz" the cowardly lion who wanted courage above everything else? All of us want to be courageous, but sometimes it is difficult.

Jesus, in his life, had to face many frightening situations. In today's Gospel lesson old Herod Antipas, whom they called the "fox", wanted to do away with Jesus; but Jesus stood up to him because he knew that God was with him. He was courageous because of God's presence.

In our lives, we will have to face some frightening times. Perhaps even though you are young, you have already faced them. God can be helpful to you; he can give you the courage to stand up.

The sermon:

Facing the Enemy

Hymns:
Beginning of worship: The God of Abraham Praise
Sermon hymn: Jesus, Refuge of the Weary
End of worship: God is My Strong Salvation

Scripture: Luke 13:31-35

Sermon text: *"Go and tell that fox, 'Behold I cast out demons and perform cures today and tomorrow, and the third day I finish my course . . .' "* v. 32

THE HISTORY OF THE CHRISTIAN CHURCH is filled with examples of courage in the face of tremendous odds. Polycarp, an early Christian martyr, when about to be nailed to the stake and burned in Rome said:
"Eighty and six years have I served him, and he hath done me
no wrong; how then can I blaspheme my King who saved me."
Polycarp and countless others throughout the long history of the faith have paid for their loyalty to Jesus Christ with their lives. There are countless other examples both sacred and secular of men and women who have faced the enemy with courage and conviction. As we think of such people we are reminded of a quote from Ernest Hemingway's classic, *A Farewell to Arms:*
"If people bring so much courage to this world the world has
to kill them to break them. So of course it kills them. The world
breaks everyone and afterward many are strong at the broken
places. But those that will not break it kills."
Such was the case of Jesus Christ! The world could not break him, so it killed him, but in the process he displayed courage. He faced the enemy gracefully and courageously. In our Gospel lesson, our Lord is on his way to Jerusalem through the territory of Herod Antipas. Pharisees come to him and warn him to flee, that Herod is after him and will most likely kill him. Jesus' reaction is that wonderful sentence which is our text for the day: "Go and tell that fox . . ." Nothing is about to interrupt his ministry. I have no time for fear. No two bit politician is going to disturb the divine mission that I am on. When Jesus uses the word fox it is meant to be derogatory. Our Lord displays what Ernest Hemingway calls, "grace under

pressure." Most of us are amazed that one could act in such a way. We are awed at the simple human courage that such action takes.

We can learn from Jesus and so many countless others how to face the enemy with courage and conviction and grace.

The late C.S. Lewis spoke many years ago concerning the advisability of fairy tales for children. Answering criticism that fairy tales were unrealistic, and not healthy for young people, he wrote:

"Since it is so likely that they will meet cruel enemies, let them at least have heard of brave knights and heroic courage. Otherwise you are making their destiny not brighter, but darker."

(quoted by Walter Hooper, *Past Watchful Dragons.* p. 26)

Most of us will face no dragons, or evil knights. There will be no niads or dryads or elfs in our lives. Our battles will be fought not on the plains of some fairy tale land but rather within ourselves; and our enemy will not be the evil witch, but rather more likely our own morbid fears about this or that: anxiety, fear, dread. These and countless other enemies will paralyze us, turning us into people who are often unable to function, who live not full of the joy and peace that God intended. How are we to face such enemies? What does our faith teach us about the enemy? Jesus is an example to us in this instance. He stood his ground and in his being personified the words of Deuteronomy 31:6: "Be strong and of good courage . . . for it is the Lord your God who goes with you; he will not fail or forsake you." In his life he made these words come true, as he exhibited a complete trust in the power of God to see him through whatever the future might hold.

Throughout history there have been countless men and women who have felt this same power, often when things seemed the darkest. Anton Boisen, the father of the "Clinical Pastoral Education" movement, spent time in a mental hospital, and in his book, *Out of the Depths,* chronicles his experience. Like the alcoholic who must hit bottom before he or she can begin to rebuild their lives, it is often when we are in the depths that we feel the presence and the power of God, strengthening and sustaining us. Legion are those we can name who have faced sickness courageously because they had a sure and certain faith in the power and the presence of God.

There is a story told of a black pastor who had to undergo serious surgery. Shortly before he went to the operating room an orderly told him that his roommate had died on the operating table. Everyone was panicky and alarmed; but nothing could be done. The operation proceeded and the patient returned to his room. That evening a friend called on him and expressed concern over what had happened. "You probably were terribly alarmed when you heard that your roommate had passed away on the operating table," he said. "Yes, but only for a moment. Then with my eyes closed I saw Marian Anderson with her arms outstretched singing 'He's Got the Whole World in His Hands.' Thus, I went to sleep and thus I awoke after the operation. The whole world is in his hands."

Jesus knew that God had the whole world in his hands, and that knowledge gave him the courage to face not only "the fox" but all that was to come. When we confront our enemies with such a faith then an amazing thing happens — our enemies become manageable. Most of us from time to time make the mistake of overestimating our enemies. Like the spies whom the Israelites sent into the Promised Land, we see giants behind every tree and hill. We have one symptom and we think we have a dozen infirmities. We confront one obstacle and we multiply it ten-fold. We magnify the enemy and at the same time minimize ourselves and our ability to deal with the situation.

Jesus knew that the enemy he faced was nothing compared with the power of God! He knew that when he saw that enemy in the right perspective, when God was magnified, not the enemy, that he would endure. The Psalmist writes: "O magnify the Lord . . ." This puts things in the proper perspective.

When we pray we get such a perspective. Walter Rauschenbusch once said that when he prayed:

"Big things became small and small things became great. The near becomes far and the future near."

When we make God great, then God's power is with us and we are given the power to face the enemy.

John N. Cedarleaf
First Congregational UCC
Fairport, New York

MARCH 22, 1992

Third Sunday in Lent

Lessons:

Lutheran:	Ex. 3:1-8b, 10-15	I Cor. 10:1-13	Luke 13:1-9
Roman Catholic:	Ex. 3:1-8a, 13-15	I Cor. 10:1-6, 10-12	Luke 13:1-9
Episcopal:	Ex. 3:1-15	I Cor. 10:1-13	Luke 13:1-9
Pres/Meth/UCC:	Ex. 3:1-15	I Cor. 10:1-13	Luke 13:1-9

Introductions to the Lessons:

Lesson 1

Exodus 3:1-15 (**Luth/Epis/Pres/Meth/UCC**) Moses fled from Egypt because he killed a man. He became a shepherd for Jethro and one day he led his flock to Mt. Sinai. There he met Yahweh in a burning bush and was given the call to go back to Egypt and lead the Israelites out of bondage to freedom in a new land. When Moses protested that he was not adequate for the task, Yahweh promised to go with him.

Lesson 2

I Corinthians 10:1-13 (**Luth/Epis/Pres/Meth/UCC**) Don't be too sure of your security! Some of Paul's church members felt secure because they had the Word and Sacraments. Paul used the Israelites as an example. God's people, led by Moses, were disobedient and perished. The same can happen to us if we, too, indulge in immorality. However, we have God's promise that when we are tempted, he will provide a means of escape.

Gospel

Luke 13:1-9 (**Luth/Epis/Pres/Meth/UCC**) Is sin the cause of misfortune? Not always, for Jesus gives two examples of disasters and says that the victims were not greater sinners than others. He calls for all to repent lest we perish also. Using a fig tree as an example, he promised to give us one more chance to repent as the fig tree was given another year to produce fruit.

Theme: Even though we don't like judgment, God calls upon us to repent; to "turn around" and begin anew; to follow the one we call the Christ.

Thought for the day: To repent is to turn around and begin to live life in a new way. It is to make a change of principle and practice; to reverse the past; to change. God helps us to do such.

287

Prayer of meditation: God of the old and the new: help us to make needed changes in our lives, no matter how painful those changes might be. Might we be sustained by your grace as we seek to turn our lives around and seek to follow your Son, Jesus Christ our Lord. Amen.

Call to worship:
Leader: Bless God, O my soul;
People: And all that is within me, bless God's holy name!
Leader: Bless God, O my soul,
People: And forget not all God's benefits.
Leader: God does not deal with us according to our sins,
People: Nor repay us according to our iniquities.
Leader: As far as the east is from the west,
People: So far does God remove our transgressions from us.
Leader: Let us worship God.

Prayer of adoration: You, O loving God, seek each and every one of your creatures to worship you with praise and adoration. You indeed are a great God and greatly to be praised. As we your people come together to worship you in this your house, might we be lifted into your presence and there experience your love and light. We pray in the name of Jesus Christ our Savior. Amen.

Prayer of confession: God of light and love, you are great, but we are small. We seek to be more than we were created to be: to be the Creator rather than the creature, to usurp your place in the order of things; and for such insolence we deserve your judgment. Help us, loving Creator, to change, to turn around and become new people, sustained by your love and guided by your grace. We pray in the name of Jesus Christ our Lord. Amen.

Prayer of dedication of gifts and self: All that we have is yours, O God: our talents, our resources, and graces of life. Use them and us to give you glory. Amen.

Sermon title: Unless You Repent

Sermon thesis: The good are not exempt from tragedy and the wicked might indeed prosper. All people are called on to turn their lives around; to repent, and to follow the Christ.

Hymn for the day: *"Lord Christ, when first you came to earth."* The messages of the sermon are clearly reflected in today's hymn. The sermon reminds us that the good are not exempt from tragedy and the wicked might indeed prosper. In the hymn we sing "Lord Christ, when first you came to earth, Upon a cross they bound you . . ." The sermon reminds us that all are called upon to repent. In the hymn we sing ". . . build in us your new creation." Author of the hymn, Walter Russell Bowie (1882-1969), was an Episcopalian priest who served for many years as a professor at Union Theological Seminary in New York City, and later at the Virginia Theological Seminary. This hymn was written in 1928 at the request of Dean Dwelly of Liverpool Cathedral, one of the editors of *Songs of Praise*. Bowie was asked to write an Advent hymn in the mood of the *Dies irae* — an ancient hymn about Judgment Day.

Announcements for next week:

Sermon title: A Forgiving God

Sermon theme: Our God is a God who forgives. This forgiveness is extended to prodigals and elder brothers and sisters alike through the life, death and resurrection of Jesus Christ.

Sermon summary: Like the father of the Prodigal, God's love and forgiveness is unconditional. He seeks and saves those who are lost, coming out to meet us on the way, refusing to let us control the relationship with our petty rules, but taking charge and smothering us with his love given to the world in the cross of our Lord Jesus Christ.

Children's object talk:

Another Chance

Objects: A fig

Lesson: God always gives us a second chance

Outline: 1. What is a fig?

2. Jesus told a story about a fig tree that got a second chance.

3. God gives us a second chance.

DO YOU KNOW what I have here? Yes, that's right — it is a fig. How many of you like figs? I do, especially fig newton cookies; but too many of them are not good for you. The only place you can get figs is in the store, unless you live in a warm climate, and then you could have a fig tree in your garden. In the Middle East where Jesus lived there were lots of fig trees.

Jesus told a story to his disciples about a man and a fig tree. This man had a fig tree in his garden. Every day for a long time he came to get some figs, and he was always disappointed that there were no figs. Finally he told the gardener to cut the tree down because he was tired of always coming for figs and never finding any. The gardener told the man: "Let me try and do something for this tree. I will give it some tender loving care and maybe by next year we will have figs. If not, then I will cut it down." So the fig tree got a second chance.

The Bible tells us to give people one more chance. God gives us many more chances, doesn't he? God is like our parents, always loving us, and giving us just one more chance to be the kind of people that we were created to be.

In the beginning of our Gospel lesson today, the Bible tells us that we should repent; this word means to feel sorry, to ask for forgiveness. God gives us a chance and we are to try to change. When we repent, when we change, when we start over, then the chances come rolling in.

The sermon:

Unless You Repent

Hymns:
Beginning of worship: In the Cross of Christ I Glory
Sermon hymn: There's a Wideness in God's Mercy
End of worship: Guide Me, O Thou Great Jehovah

Scripture: Luke 13:1-9

Sermon text: ". . . *unless you repent you will all likewise perish . . .*"
v. 3

WE DON'T LIKE JUDGMENTAL PEOPLE: those who are always finding fault; looking down their noses; picking apart everything we say or do. All of us know such folk and we try to steer clear of them, for in their negativity they can drag us down. We like positive people!

We feel, too, that our religion should be positive. From the days of Norman Vincent Peale to Robert Schuller, positive thinking has been popular. I am reminded of the pastor of a congregation who doesn't celebrate the Office of Tenebrae because the congregation would have to leave in darkness and that would be depressing! The words of the old song make sense to most of us: "Accentuate the positive, eliminate the negative." After all, didn't Jesus say, "My yoke is easy and my burden is light?" How would we deal today with the preaching of one of the greatest preachers of all time, Jonathon Edwards, who could never be accused of "sweetness and light."

"The God that holds you over the pit of hell, . . . abhors you, and is dreadfully provoked: his wrath towards you burns like fire; he looks upon you as worthy of nothing else, but to be cast into the fire . . ."
Edwards would not have made it on television!

We know, though, that all is not always sweetness and light and, positive thinking. We are fallible and often do not do the things we ought while doing just the things we ought not to do. In our Gospel lesson, Jesus is speaking to a crowd of people when some persons arrive bring him the news that some Galileans had been put to death by Pilate. After telling this story, Luke has our Lord, in a kind of "Can you top this?" manner, tell the story of the accidental death of eighteen residents of Jerusalem killed by the sudden collapse of a tower. These stories do two things:

1. They correct a misunderstanding that tragedy implies sinfulness and the absence of tragedy righteousness; and

2. Drive home the critical nature of human existence.

Our God is not some kind of Ayatollah who strikes down the sinner with a vengeful fury. This is crucial for us to understand; for even in our "enlightened" day we find people making connection between disease, death, and tragedy and human sinfulness.

Read the book of Job to see this really at work, especially Job 8:5-6. Gnawing within us is the idea that illness, poverty, disease, loneliness and death are the punishment for sins known or unknown.

This idea rears its head in one debate concerning AIDS. If such logic is carried out, then are we to understand that all illness is God's punishment? In his novel, *The Bridge of San Luis Rey*, Thornton Wilder tells of a priest and his effort to prove that the reason a bridge collapsed with certain persons on it was to be found in the moral flaws of these persons. Such thinking clouds the real issue addressed here, namely, the obligation of every person to live in penitence and trust before God, without linking our loyalty to God to life's sorrows or joys. The sun does shine on the just and the unjust alike.

The issue is: a turning around. Repentance! There we are again up against that word which we don't like. It signifies that we have something to repent of, and many of us wonder about that. We're pretty good people. Oh, to be sure we have made mistakes, but repentance! That is stuff for hardened criminals, in sentimental Christian literature, not about good folks like us!

Let me try and put this into some kind of perspective. The form of the Greek word used here which is translated as repent means to undergo a change in frame of mind; to make a change of principle and practice, reversal of the past; to repent means to change. Perhaps it is a change necessitated by some form of behavior or way of thinking; but for most of us it is not so dramatic as all that. Rather, Jesus' call for repentance comes to us not when we are almost down and out but rather when we are feeling pretty good about ourselves, pretty confident, pretty comfortable. It is a call to stop and take stock of our lives, to think about who we are and to whom we belong and whom we might wish to follow. Such a call came to Moses, a call to turn around and follow God. Moses said, "I'm retired! Find someone younger, stronger, better able to do the job." But God would not let him alone, and God does not let us alone either. The Christian is not one who is merely religious, who believes certain things and worships God. The Christian is one who has been turned around (sometimes by the shoulders) in his or her tracks and set on a new way of life — a way which seeks to follow the One whom we call Savior: Jesus Christ. Such a turning around is not easy. An old German proverb says: "Every new beginning is hard." Many of you have experienced such new beginnings in your life, new beginnings occasioned sometimes by sorrow, death, divorce, new job, new home, and so on. Yet as you look back, you've seen growth in those experiences when you, like Moses, were spoken to by God.

The calls come then to each and every one of us, not just during Lent, when we more consciously seek to follow him, but throughout all the changing experiences of our lives: the call to *"Stop, turn around and follow me!"*

John N. Cedarleaf
First Congregational UCC
Fairport, New York

MARCH 29, 1992

Fourth Sunday in Lent

Lessons:

Lutheran:	Is. 12:1-6	I Cor. 1:18-31	Luke 15:1-3, 11-32
Roman Catholic:	Josh. 5:9a, 10-12	2 Cor. 5:17-21	Luke 15:1-3, 11-32
Episcopal:	Josh. (4:19-24) 5:9-12	2 Cor. 5:17-21	Luke 15:11-32
Pres/Meth/UCC:	Josh. 5:9-12	2 Cor. 5:16-21	Luke 15:1-3, 11-32

Introductions to the Lessons:

Lesson 1

(1) *Isaiah 12:1-6* (**Luth**) "That day" is the day when Yahweh will gather the dispersed Jews to Jerusalem. The dispersal was understood as the result of God's anger at their wickedness. Now the exiles are home and there is reason to give thanks, celebrate, and praise the Lord of salvation.

(2) *Joshua 5:9-12* (**Epis/Pres/Meth/UCC**) After 40 years of wilderness wanderings, the Israelites under Joshua crossed over the Jordan to the Promised Land. The Abrahamic covenant was renewed by circumcising all who had not been during the wilderness years. The Mosaic covenant was also renewed by the keeping of the Passover. Now the people ate the fruit of the fields, and the coming of manna ceased.

Lesson 2

(1) *I Corinthians 1:18-31* (**Luth**) How important is the cross? For some it is stupidity and for others it is the power of salvation. Jews look for miracles and Greeks want wisdom. For Christians the cross is the power and wisdom of God. For this reason the church preaches the cross.

(2) *II Corinthians 5:16-21* (**Epis/Pres/Meth/UCC**) From a divine point of view, a person in Christ is a new person. S/he is a new person because the person by faith is living in and for Christ. Through Christ sinners have been reconciled to God. This ministry of reconciling the world to God through Christ has been given to the church.

Gospel

Luke 15:1-3, 11-32 (**Luth/Epis/Pres/Meth/UCC**) Should a holy person like Jesus associate with wicked people? Jesus did.

293

Theme: Our God is a God who forgives. This forgiveness is extended to prodigals and elder brothers (and sisters) alike through the life, death and resurrection of Jesus Christ.

Thought for the day: Both the prodigal and the elder brother were estranged from the father. They wanted to be in control of the relationship: how forgiveness was given and received. But the father would have none of it. He went out to seek the lost son on terms of love and forgiveness, and neither the prodigal nor the elder brother was prepared for such unconditional love.

Prayer of meditation: Forgiving God: you seek and save the least and the lost, even us your sons and daughters who seek to control the terms of the relationship with you. Enable us to receive with gratitude your forgiveness and luxuriate in your love. Amen.

Call to worship:
Leader: I will bless God at all times:
People: God's praise shall continually be in my mouth.
Leader: My soul boasts in God;
People: Let those who are afflicted hear and be glad.
Leader: O magnify God with me.
People: And let us exalt God's name together.
Leader: Let us worship God.

Prayer of adoration: God of light and love. You are the source of all life and breath; of all that is or will ever be. Lift our souls this day into your presence so that we might worship you aright, thankful for all that you have done for each and every one of us. Holy are you, and greatly to be praised: Father, Son, and Holy Spirit. Amen.

Prayer of confession: O God of the prodigal and the elder brother, whose love encompasses all; hear our confession this day. Indeed we have done those things which we should not have done, and have not done those things which we should have done. Restore and renew us, one and all, so that we might worship you in spirit and in truth, through Jesus Christ, our Savior and Lord. Amen.

Prayer of dedication of gifts and self: Extravagant God: you shower us with more than we desire or deserve. All the good gifts around us come from your hand. Receive now these symbols of your goodness to us, and grant that we might be living sacrifices given to your service. Amen.

Sermon title: A Forgiving God

Sermon thesis: Like the father of the prodigal, God's love and forgiveness is unconditional. He seeks and saves those who are lost; coming out to meet us on the way; refusing to let us control the relationship with our petty rules; but taking charge and smothering us with his love given to the world in the cross of our Lord Jesus Christ.

Hymn for the day: *"What wondrous love is this."* Both text and tune of this nineteenth-century American hymn are of unknown origins. The text first appeared in a collection published in Lynchburg, Virginia, in 1811; the tune, in William Walker's *Southern Harmony* of 1843. The hymn is one of several which used the so-called "Captain Kidd meter," found in a ballad about a wild pirate executed in England in 1701. It is a wonderful folk hymn of praise for our redemption, quaintly reminding us (stanza 2) "When I was sinking down beneath God's righteous front, Christ laid aside his crown for my soul."

Announcements for next week:

Sermon title: Are You Talking About Me?

Sermon theme: Did Jesus tell stories that were about us?

Sermon summary: The sermons which are most effective are those which involve us personally, which we sense are directed at us. Likewise, the stories of Jesus which "hit home" were the ones which his listeners realized were about them.

Children's object talk:

Keeping Score

Objects: Golf score card

Lesson: God doesn't keep a scorecard of our wrongs but does forgive us.

Outline: 1. In order to play a game you need to keep score.

2. God doesn't keep a score card of our wrongs.

3. God forgives us.

WHAT DO I HAVE in my hand today? Yes, that's right, a scorecard. Do you know what sport it is for? Right, Billy, golf. Now wait a minute, don't look at it; I am a little bit embarrassed about how poor my score is; but I did have fun playing.

In order to play golf, or baseball, or basketball, or football, you need to keep score, and in order to keep score you need a scorecard. Well, some people think that you need such a scorecard for other things in life, too. Some people keep track of the wrongs that others do to them, so that they can get even with them. Do you think that is a good idea?

Suppose that your parents kept a scorecard on you. Right there on the kitchen wall — a large chart on which they kept track of all the bad things you did! When all the squares were filled in, you had to move out! You wouldn't like that, would you? No, neither would I.

I guess in one sense, God does keep a scorecard. God does know all about us, the good and the bad; but God also wipes off that scorecard and forgives us. He doesn't remember all our sins so that he can get even; that is not the way our God is.

Just like the father in the story of the prodigal son in our Gospel lesson today, God wipes the slate clean, forgives and welcomes us back into his love. Isn't that the kind of God we like, one that doesn't keep score?

The sermon:

A Forgiving God

Hymns:
Beginning of worship: How Firm a Foundation
Sermon hymn: Pardoned Through Redeeming Grace
End of worship: Savior, Like a Shepherd Lead Us

Scripture: Luke 15:1-3, 11-32

Sermon text: *". . . while he was yet at a distance, his father saw him and had compassion, and ran and embraced him and kissed him."* v. 20

IN THE MIDST OF THE LENTEN JOURNEY which has been accompanied by the funeral music of judgment and repentance, we pause and hear a note of joy and forgiveness.

This fourth Sunday in Lent is known as Mid-Lent Refreshment Sunday. Ever since the Middle Ages it has been seen as a pause in the austerity of the season, a day which reminds us of the ultimate purpose of Lent: not sorrow for our sins but the attaining of the glory that is to be revealed.

It is a breaking point in the Lenten pilgrimage. During the first half of the season we have concentrated on repentance, and now in this second half we will focus our attention on the crucifixion of our Lord. It is good to pause and remember that God's love and forgiveness are crucial to it all. The message of the Gospel is that

God's love comes to us in the life, death, and resurrection of Jesus Christ.

With this in mind, let us look at one of the most well known and beloved parables in the New Testament, that of the "Prodigal Son." How often we have read this story! How often we have heard sermons on it; some with interesting twists, as for example the one which took the side of the elder brother and tried to understand his feelings. How many of us can identify with that older brother: loyal, played by the rules, resentful about the fuss being made over this twirp who couldn't manage his money. How often have we, like that older brother, felt taken for granted by our wives and husbands, our children, our bosses, in our churches. Everyone pays attention to the prodigals but passes us by, the salt of the earth folks!

Is not the bitterness of the elder brother also sometimes our bitterness?

"Look at the years I have worked for you like a slave, and I have never disobeyed your orders. What have you given me? Not even a goat for me to have a feast with my friends."

Who gives us "steady Eddys" a party? This elder brother reminds us of the Pharisees and scribes and well he should, for this is the context of the parable. In verses 1-2 the Pharisees criticize Jesus for associating with sinners — prodigals.

This is the context of the story and Jesus tells it not in order to teach some timeless truth but rather to speak about what is happening concretely in his life and ministry.

For the Christian love and forgiveness are never seen apart from the cross! It is through the cross that God accepts us and forgives us.

The prodigal is rebellious, selfish, self-centered, wreaking havoc not only in his life but in the lives of those who love him. Yet it all falls apart for him and he begins the journey home, turning over and over in his mind how he will approach his father: humble himself, be a servant, beg forgiveness, ask to be taken back as a servant. He wants to establish his own conditions for his return home, hard as they might be on himself. He wants to be in charge. The elder brother also wants to be in charge, through maintaining his distance, through a rigid ordering of his life. He seeks to maintain control of the relationship between himself and his father and brother. The father, though, will have none of this. He goes out, first to the younger son, refusing the boy's conditions. He gives him the symbols of sonship and throws a party for him, restoring him to the family circle without conditions. He now extends himself to the elder brother, reminding him that his love and care have always been freely given. The love of the father is a no-questions, no-conditions love which reaches out in acceptance to both sons. It is a love which spends itself freely as it seeks to restore to the family table not only the prodigal who physically went away, but the elder brother who, while home, was spiritually "in a far country." How difficult it is, be we prodigal or elder brother to accept forgiveness.

Have you ever been forgiven by one close to you for an offense committed? Perhaps you approached the person as the prodigal did the father, carefully rehearsing what you would say, how best you would deal with the situation. And then that person went out to you and received you; and you experienced at that moment a crumbling of your defenses and a falling away of your pride, and you knew that you would never again be the same person. There was a cleansing of the spirit and a restoring of the soul!

So it is with God! He takes the initiative, coming to meet us where we are. This God touches our lives and invites us into relationship with him.

John Newton, after a life which would have made the prodigal's look tame, came home to be a priest in the Church of England. Gerald Kennedy tells us: "He could never forget how God saved him from shipwreck, from moral disaster, and from despair." This was the man who wrote these words which describe the experience of forgiveness:

"Amazing grace! How sweet the sound that saved a wretch like me! I once was lost, but now am found, was blind, but now I see."

Indeed, God's grace is amazing! Indeed, God's love is full and complete! Indeed, God's forgiveness is freely given to each of us. God comes to meet us, with arms open, offering forgiveness without condition and love without questions. He invites us one and all to the joyous feast of forgiving love, purchased for all in the cross of our Lord Jesus Christ; the cross of suffering — yes! But the cross also of saving, and forgiving love.

John N. Cedarleaf
First Congregational UCC
Fairport, New York

APRIL 5, 1992

Fifth Sunday in Lent

Lessons:

Lutheran:	Is. 43:16-21	Phil. 3:8-14	Luke 20:9-19
Roman Catholic:	Is. 43:16-21	Phil. 3:8-14	John 8:1-11
Episcopal:	Is. 43:16-21	Phil. 3:8-14	Luke 20:9-19
Pres/Meth/UCC:	Is. 43:16-21	Phil. 3:8-14	John 12:1-8

Introductions to the Lessons:

Lesson 1

Isaiah 43:16-21 (**Luth/Epis/Pres/Meth/UCC**). Here Yahweh through the prophet Isaiah promises a second exodus. The first was out of Egypt; the second is out of Babylon. This is the "new thing" he will do for his people: release from bondage and return to Jerusalem. On their return through 600 miles of desert between Babylon and Jerusalem, Yahweh promises to protect them and provide them with water.

Lesson 2

Philippians 3:8-14 (**Luth/Epis/Pres/Meth/UCC**). What is the goal of a Christian? For Paul it was to gain Christ and to be found in him. To have Christ was to have the righteousness of God. Paul's aim was to be like Christ even in his suffering and death. He had not reached the goal but he was constantly pursuing it.

Gospel

(1) *Luke 20:9-19* (**Luth/Epis**). Jesus uses the indirect method to get across to his enemies that he knows they are plotting his death. His method is a parable about wicked tenants of a vineyard. The tenants reject one servant after another, but when the son of the owner comes, they kill him. Time after time God sent prophets, priests, and kings but they were rejected. At last God sent his Son and they killed him.

(2) *John 12:1-8* (**Pres/Meth/UCC**). Just before his triumphal entry into Jerusalem, Jesus had a dinner date with friends Mary, Martha, and Lazarus. While there Mary pours expensive perfume on Jesus' feet and then wipes them with her hair. Judas objected to this apparent waste of money, but Jesus defended her by explaining she did it to prepare his body for burial. Caused criticism by the religious leaders against Jesus. To answer that criticism Jesus told the parable of the prodigal son. But, really there were two prodigal sons: one at home and one in a distant land.

Theme: Did Jesus tell stories that were about us?

Thought for the day: The crucifixion of Jesus is such a horrible event it is natural for us to assume we would have had no part in rejecting him or putting him to death. Is it true that we would have known better and done better?

Prayer of meditation: Lord God, as we move ever closer to that terrible day on which all that was good and true and loving was put to death on a cross, help us to become aware of the ways we continue to put aside the best you have to offer us. Help us to confess that in rejecting what you say, whom you send, and what you want us to do, we are rejecting you. Amen.

Call to worship:
Leader: He was despised and rejected by men;
People: A man of sorrows, and acquainted with grief;
Leader: And as one from whom men hide their faces
People: He was despised, and we esteemed him not.
Leader: All we like sheep have gone astray;
People: We have turned every one to his own way.
Leader: Let us seek to return to the ways of God as we worship.
(Isaiah 53:3-6a)

Prayer of adoration: Loving God, we marvel at your persistence and your patience in dealing with us. You never give up on us. Your love never lets us go. Your challenges never let us off. We thank you that even when we let you down, you lift us up again with the forgiving hands of mercy and grace. Amen.

Prayer of confession: God of infinite love and indefinable grace, we want to be honest about what we see ourselves to be doing. We ask for your word, but doubt. We ask to know your will, but wander from it. We ask to be given some aspect of your work to do, but we are slow to begin it. We ask you to save our world, but we continue to do little to improve it ourselves. We ask you to show us your way, but we stray from it. Forgive us for resisting what you know is best for us and are so willing to show us in the life and example of your Son, Jesus the Christ, in whose name we pray. Amen.

Prayer of dedication of gifts and self: You have, O God, invested so much in us. You have given us stewardship of your creation and the responsibility for caring for it. You have given us enough to share, and that is what we do just now. Accept these offerings as the symbols of how faithful we can be in making good on your investment in us. Amen.

Sermon title: Are You Talking About Me?

Sermon thesis: The sermons which are most effective are those which involve us personally, which we sense are directed at us. Likewise, the stories of Jesus which "hit home" were the ones which his listeners realized were about them.

Hymn for the day: *"Nature with open volume stands."* Mention of Isaac Watts can be found at January 6 above. This hymn was one of Watts's *Hymns and Spiritual Songs,* 1707. God's love for us can be seen all around us, notes this hymn, but it is most clearly seen and understood in the story of Christ on the cross.

Announcements for next week:

Sermon title: Can You Avoid the Cross?

Sermon theme: We need Holy Week to help us face the cross.

Sermon summary: We wish we could control our lives to the point that there is nothing but joy and celebration and success. We would like to avoid all that causes us pain and suffering. We probably do the same with the final days of our Lord's life if we attend worship on Palm Sunday and Easter Sunday, and absent ourselves from Holy Week services.

Children's object talk:

Are You in the Picture?

Objects: Some family pictures
Lesson: The Bible is about us.
Outline: 1. When Jesus told stories it was like holding up a picture.
2. People had to decide if they were in the story and in the picture.
3. Are we in any of the stories Jesus told?

I HAVE HERE some old family pictures. It's fun to look through them, isn't it? Some of them are from my childhood. Sometimes people store family pictures in their Bibles. Older generations used to keep all sorts of family treasures in their big Bibles.

You probably know that the Bible contains many stories and I am sure you can tell some of them. Maybe you have drawn pictures of those stories in Sunday School class. Jesus didn't take pictures, of course, since there weren't cameras in those days, but when he told stories it was almost as if he was drawing a picture. The people who listened to them probably wondered if he was talking about them. When he talked about someone who did the right thing, like in the story of the Good Samaritan, I would imagine everyone who heard him wanted to believe he or she was that kind of hero who helped other people. And when he talked about people who did the wrong thing, like in the story of the Prodigal Son, I would also guess that anyone who listened hoped they were not like him. It's important that we listen intently to what Jesus said, because we just might discover he was talking about us.

The sermon:

Are You Talking About Me?

Hymns:
Beginning of worship: O Young and Fearless Prophet
Sermon hymn: Dear Master, in Whose Life I See
End of worship: Open My Eyes, That I May See

Scripture: Luke 20:9-19

Sermon Text: *". . . for they perceived that he had told this parable against them."* Luke 20:19

ONE OF THE RESPONSES TO A SERMON that never fails to amaze me goes something like this: "That was a good sermon, Pastor. I only wish my husband had been here today to hear it." The real test of a sermon's effectiveness is whether or not you say in response, "He was talking about me," or if you say, "I need to get a copy of that to give to someone else."

Jesus undoubtedly had the same problem with his listeners. The whole intent of his story-telling means of teaching great truths was to involve his listeners in an active way. He wanted them to see themselves in his story, to identify with the characters. I would imagine that most of the time he was successful, as masterful as he was in making the stories relevant and true-to-life.

It was probably hardest to admit he was talking about his audience when the characters were not heroic, but evil. There is a natural refusal to deal with reality, even when it stares us in the face. We turn away. We rationalize. We look around to see if someone we know isn't really the object. How rarely do we confess that the same traits in those we deplore are found in us!

The parable Jesus told about the vineyard was so obvious in its message, it is no wonder the "scribes and the chief priests" who heard it "perceived that he had told this parable against them." Not just about them, but against them! In Clarence Jordan's *Cotton Patch Version of Luke and Acts,* he paraphrases that verse, "For they knew full well that he had aimed this Comparison at them." They were the target. He had hit them squarely between the eyes. And in the heart!

No wonder Luke tells us they "tried to lay hands on him at that very hour." They did exactly what he told them in his parable they would do: ". . . they said to themselves, 'This is the heir; let us kill him' . . . And they cast him out of the vineyard and killed him."

At this point in his ministry Jesus was keenly aware that his fate was inevitable. He, like the son in his story, would be put to death. But had that been on his mind from the beginning? Many say yes, that it was God's original plan, the necessary outcome of his act of sending his Son. Others say no, that was not what God had in mind at all. There is a crucial hint at this idea in the words he put on the lips of the owner of the vineyard: "Then the owner of the vineyard said, 'What shall I do? I will send my beloved son; it may be they will respect him.' "

Leslie Weatherhead's little classic, *The Will of God,* deals with what he classifies as the three distinctive "wills" of God: the intentional, the circumstantial, and the ultimate will of God. And he suggests,

"Was it God's intention from the beginning that Jesus should go to the Cross? I think the answer to that question must be No. I don't think Jesus thought that at the beginning of his ministry. He came with the *intention* that men should follow him, not kill him. The discipleship of men, not the death of Christ, was the intentional will of God, or, if you like, God's ideal purpose. . ."

"It may be they will respect him." Surely God wanted that kind of respect for his Son, that kind of response — that people would follow him, not kill him.

Yet, God was willing for them to decide. They were free to choose the fate of his Son. It was by their free choice that they said, "Let us kill him."

It's not a pleasant story, is it? Here was the best man that ever lived. He loved everyone. Most everyone loved him. He offered everything that people could ever want. He came to save them, to make them whole, to give them forgiveness and new life. He let them into the secret of life itself, and the key to abundant living was theirs for the taking. Why, then, would anyone reject him, throw him out, and kill him?

That raises some questions for me — and about me. Why would anyone go to a doctor and ask for advice on recovering their good health, and take the prescription and good advice, and then ignore it? Or throw the prescription into a trash can? Why would anyone stay away from church? Why would anyone keep their Bible closed and dust-covered on the coffee table? Why would anyone choose to absent themselves from church school, or Bible study? Why, indeed?

Apathy? Ignorance? Resistance? Indifference? Stupidity? Stubbornness? Which of these character-flaws cause us to reject the best? Which of them led to the crucifixion of Jesus? Which of them are there when we hold up the Bible as a mirror and see ourselves in this story?

Ours is not a problem of intense dislike of Jesus, obviously, it is more a question of indifferently ignoring him. So many of us live our lives in complete indifference to Jesus Christ. And to his teachings and example. His values seldom become our values. Think of what Jesus taught and just how little of it we have ever been able to live out in our lives.

Maybe it's a matter of our being fearful. I suspect that was one of the motives behind the rejection he experienced in his life. The establishment was afraid of him, what he might do to their vested interests. People are still afraid of change, of being challenged. We are afraid of venturing out into untried ways, risking everything to follow someone who demands our ultimate and total loyalty.

What frightened the enemies of Jesus the most may have been the same thing he talked about in his parable. The son of the owner came to collect the owner's share of the fruit and to call the tenants into accountability. Jesus came to remind persons what belonged to God. The leaders of the Jewish faith who heard the parable had exploited the privileges of their position instead of rendering to God the obedience and service he demanded. We do not like to be reminded of our responsibilities. We only want to hear about our privileges. We resent someone who calls us to be accountable for what we have done with what God has entrusted to our hands. We become uncomfortable when anyone preaches about our accountability to God.

Yes, the story is about us. He is talking about us and to us. But there is also the word of grace and hope. The conclusion to the story has not been finally written at all. God says again and again, "I will send my beloved son; it may be they will respect him . . ."

William M. Schwein
Meridian Street United Methodist Church
Indianapolis, Indiana

APRIL 12, 1992

Sunday of the Passion. Palm Sunday.

Lessons:

Lutheran:	Deut. 32:36-39	Phil. 2:5-11	Luke 22:1-23:56
Roman Catholic:	Is. 50:4-7	Phil. 2:6-11	Luke 22:14-23:56
Episcopal:	Is. 45:21-25	Phil. 2:5-11	Luke (22:39-71)
			23:1-49 (50-56)
Pres/Meth/UCC:	Is. 50:4-9a	Phil. 2:5-11	Luke 22:14-23:56

Introductions to the Lessons:

Lesson 1

(1) *Deuteronomy 32:36-39* (**Luth**). In his last song Moses declares that Yahweh will have compassion on his people. When his enemies are defeated, Yahweh will ask where their gods were.There is no god but Yahweh who both kills and enlivens, wounds and heals.

(2) *Isaiah 45:21-25* (**Epis**). The Babylonians have gods that cannot save, but the God of the Israelites is the one and only God who can save. Therefore, all nations need to turn to God to be saved. Only in him is their strength. Only in him will the people triumph.

(3) *Isaiah 50:4-9a* (**Pres/Meth/UCC**). God's Servant does not flinch from suffering. He is certain that God will vindicate and help him against his adversaries.

Lesson 2

Philippians 2:5-11 (**Luth/Epis/Pres/Meth/UCC**). Paul had a practical problem in the Philippian church. There was dissension caused by pride. To solve the problem Paul calls upon them to have a humble mind like Jesus had. His humility was expressed in his becoming human, being a servant, and even dying for us on the cross. Because of his humility, God exalted him with a name that is supreme. At this name the whole world should bow down and worship.

Gospel

Luke 22:1-23:56 (**Luth**); *22:39-23:56* (**Epis**); *22:14-23:56* (**Pres/Meth/UCC**). This Passion-Palm Sunday gospel consists of two chapters from Luke, one of the longest readings in the church year. It is the account of Jesus' passion starting with the Last Supper in the upper room to the burial of Jesus. It is the sad, sad story of Holy Week that begins today.

Theme: We need Holy Week to help us face the cross.

Thought for the day: For too many people, Holy Week has two days in it — Palm/Passion Sunday and Easter. Both are days with celebrative qualities to them. But in between those two days was the real drama of our Lord's sacrifice.

Prayer of meditation: God, as we recall the entrance of our Savior into Jerusalem, grant that we may become so involved in reflecting upon the event that we find ways of welcoming him into our lives even now. Do not let us be satisfied to be spectators, but persuade us to become participants. Give us sincere songs of praise. Amen.

Call to worship:
Leader: In thee, O Lord, do I seek refuge;
People: Let me never be put to shame;
Leader: In thy righteousness deliver me!
People: Be thou a rock of refuge for me,
Leader: A strong fortress to save me!
People: For thy name's sake lead me and guide me.
Leader: Into thy hand I commit my spirit;
People:Thou hast redeemed me, O Lord, faithful God.
(Adapted from Psalm 31:1-5)

Prayer of adoration: Lord God, there are times when we cannot contain our joy or constrain our enthusiasm for the ways you come into our lives. Though we are not given to emotional outbursts, we find ourselves singing with our whole hearts, not just with our lips. We become caught up in the beauty of the music from choir and organ. We even find ourselves adding a whispered "amen" to something said in the sermon. Help us to be more willing to give heart, soul, mind and strength to our experience of worship this day. Amen.

Prayer of confession: Merciful God, forgive us if we make too little of this week which we call Holy. Keep us from shortening it into two days of praise and omit the time between which recalls the passion of our Lord. Do not let us move too quickly from a day of triumphal entry to a day of triumphant victory. Help us to see that in our own lives there are going to be those times of suffering which give added meaning to those times of success. Help us to embrace all of life, even as we seek to understand fully the last week of our Lord's life. Amen.

Prayer of dedication of gifts and self: How do we show you whose side we are on, good Lord? How do we acknowledge our loyalty? How do we affirm our faith and trust in your Son? Maybe this is a beginning: To bring the fruits of our labors and the evidences of our faithfulness to your altar. Dedicate them, and us, to your purposes. Amen.

Sermon title: Can You Avoid the Cross?

Sermon thesis: We wish we could control our lives to the point that there is nothing but joy and celebration and success. We would like to avoid all that causes us pain and suffering. We probably do the same with the final days of our Lord's life if we attend worship on Palm Sunday and Easter Sunday, and absent ourselves from Holy Week services.

Hymn for the day: *"Jesus, I will ponder now."* Between Palm Sunday and Easter lies Holy Week. We remember the events of Holy Week in this hymn by Sigismund von Birken (1626-1681). Son of a pastor, von Birken was born in Bohemia, but three years later was forced to flee and took up residence in Nurnberg. He studied law and theology at the University of Jena and became a private tutor. Because of his considerable poetical gifts he was admitted to the Pegnitz Shepherd and Flower Order. In 1662 he became Chief Shepherd of the Order, to which he imparted a distinctly religious cast.

Announcements for Maundy Thursday:

Sermon title: When He Had Given Thanks

Sermon theme: We are to give thanks in all things, at all times.

Sermon summary: We do not know the blessings Jesus was counting that last night with his disciples, and yet we are told that he began the meal by giving thanks. In his ability to find things for which he was grateful at a time when there seemed to be so much for which he should have been sorrowful, we may discover what it means to be thankful in all circumstances.

Announcements for Good Friday:

Sermon title: In the Place of Death, a Garden

Sermon theme: In the midst of death there is promise for life.

Sermon summary: We cannot overlook the fact that even in the place where Jesus was crucified there were already signs of life. John's account of the crucifixion notes the close proximity of the cross and a garden.

Announcements for next week:

Sermon title: The Women's Witness — An Idle Tale?

Sermon theme: Women in Ministry

Sermon summary: Women in ministry is the will of God. Women were the first ones given the mission of proclaiming the resurrection message. We are called to do the will of God in our day.

Children's object talk:

A Funny-Looking Calendar

Objects: A month's calendar with Sundays only, and no days in between.
Lesson: To learn the importance of Holy Week.
Outline: 1. Holy Week begins on Sunday and ends on Sunday.
2. It tells us about the last days of Jesus.
3. We cannot omit any of the days if we are to understand what happened to Jesus.

I HAVE HERE A NEW CALENDAR I am going to try to sell. You will notice that it only has two days a week on it. We have Sunday — and then we have Sunday. It's no different from the kind of weeks I know you wish you had: Saturday and Sunday only. No week days; no school days. Just week-ends.

But we know we cannot pick out the days we like and omit the other ones. We have to take each day as it comes. Even the bad days.

It is the same when we remember the last week of Jesus' life, which we call Holy Week. Today is the day we usually call "Palm Sunday." In a week we will return to celebrate the day we call Easter. Those are both wonderful days, happy days. It would be great if we could just go from Palm Sunday, when Jesus was welcomed triumphantly into Jerusalem, to Easter, when we celebrate his resurrection. But we can't. Too much happened in between. And Easter will not make much sense to us if we do not remember how he suffered and died for us on the cross — on a day we call Good Friday.

That is not the kind of day we like to think about. We do not like to think about Jesus dying. Like anything that is unpleasant in life, we would just as soon skip over it. But life is not like that. And one of the greatest things about Jesus, what he taught and how he lived, was in the way he wants us to understand and accept the bad times and the good times. He came to show us that God is present on bad days, too. God is with us through the week, every single day of the week, not just Sunday.

The sermon:
Can We Really Avoid The Cross?

Hymns:
Beginning of worship: Hosanna, Loud Hosanna
Sermon hymn: All Glory, Laud, and Honor
End of worship: Jesus, Keep Me Near the Cross

Scripture: Luke 22:1-23:56

Sermon Text: *"And as they led him away, they seized one Simon of Cyrene, who was coming in from the country, and laid on him the cross, to carry it behind Jesus."* Luke 23:26

JOHN UPDIKE wrote a book with the intriguing title, *A Month of Sundays*, about a wayward minister who was forced to spend a "month of seventh days" in retreat and rest. The seventh day was traditionally thought of as the sabbath.

When Jesus Christ was risen from the tomb on Sunday, the early Christians began observing that day — the "first day of the week" — as the Lord's Day. Our sabbath became Sunday. (Admittedly, there is still disagreement about that, primarily through the doctrine of the Seventh Day Adventist Church.)

It is interesting that at the time of Jesus, the day of his triumphal entry into Jerusalem was not noted on a calendar as "Palm Sunday." That, too, became a Christian label for a day that was in reality just another day of the Jewish Passover Feast.

Then there is Good Friday. Luke refers to it as "the day of Preparation." Since the sabbath observance began at sundown Friday, that day was given to getting ready for the day of rest. It's also interesting to note the way Luke concludes that 23rd chapter: "On the sabbath they rested according to the commandment." That was, of course, Saturday.

Confusing, isn't it? Almost as confusing as what happened not so many years ago when many denominations changed this day from "Palm Sunday" to "Palm/Passion Sunday." I don't know when, exactly, that it happened. Somebody must have checked the attendance at most churches this week, and realized that the crowds are there for Palm Sunday and for Easter, but few participate in the other observances through the week. And so we went from a triumphal entry to a triumphant "re-entry;" from shouting "Hosanna" to singing "The Hallelujah Chorus," with no idea what happened in between. Somewhere along the way we realized that what happened on Palm Sunday had less to do with the royalty of Christ and more to do with the loyalty of his followers, and that was the story of the rest of the week.

Holy Week can never be a *week of Sundays!*

These are not two "book-end Sundays," then, with nothing in the middle. That is perhaps the reason our lectionary reading for today has nothing at all to do with the passing parade and palms. It is an account of the Last Supper, the trial, the crucifixion, and the burial, all a part of what we refer to as "the Passion of Christ."

In our scripture reading, we are told the whole story. In some congregations, I understand, the reading is done by several persons, taking turns. It is difficult enough for us to read, not just because of its length, but because of what it tells us about betrayal and persecution and death.

So much happened that week. We are told that one-third of all the material in the gospel accounts of the life of Jesus has to do with what happened during that last week of his life. One-half of the gospel of John have to do with what we call Holy Week. We do ourselves a disservice if we shorten the week into two days, Palm Sunday and Easter. This was our Lord's last week on earth. It also speaks of the kind of weeks you and I have in life.

It reminds us of the inevitability of the cross. I do not suggest that by only observing Palm Sunday and Easter we are deliberately trying to avoid dealing with the cross of Jesus or the crosses in our own lives, but we must admit we would rather talk about parades, and even temporary triumph, and resurrections and final victory, than the cross. When Jesus instructed his disciples and us to "take up our cross daily and follow him," he was talking about a decision. He was not talking about the crosses we *have* to bear because life is difficult. When Simon of Cyrene was commandeered to carry the cross of Jesus, it was "laid on him . . . to carry it behind Jesus." How vivid is that picture!

And yet you and I would like to follow far enough behind that there is no way we would ever have to have a cross "laid on us." I would suspect we have a hard enough time coming to terms with the cross on which Christ died. I read an ad once that offered a box of candy, called an "Easter Greeting Box," containing a large, decorated, milk chocolate cross, surrounded by the candy-maker's finest milk chocolate miniatures in a variety of fillings. The ad sought to entice the reader further by describing this as "A very special way to say 'Easter Greetings!' "

We have already made the cross as attractive as possible: made of gold or silver, painted in bright colors, worn as jewelry about the neck, put on key chains right alongside a rabbit's foot. There was even a prominent college basketball coach who clutched a little cross in his hand during every game.

The cross, however beautiful we would like for it to become, was still a rough and rugged thing upon which Jesus died. It was not gold-plated or mother of pearl. George MacLoud once wrote, "I am recovering the claim that Jesus was not crucified in a cathedral between two candles, but on a cross between two thieves, on the town garbage heap . . ."

There was a southern evangelist who was holding a tent revival. He concluded each evening's service by offering for sale a box of crosses, at 10¢ each. He told his congregation he thought that was pretty cheap, and that every one could afford to have one in his pocket. He suggested how nice it would be to be able to put one's hand in the pocket and grab hold of the cross. But then he issued a warning: they had been mass produced, so as to be sold cheaply. And they were rather roughly cut because they were stamped out rather quickly. He warned the purchasers to file off the rough and jagged edges of the pocket crosses, saying, "It would never do to thrust your hand in your pocket, grab the cross, and draw blood."

That is precisely how most of us feel about taking up a cross. We would hate to think of it ever causing us any pain or suffering. But if there is anything at all to the crucifixion of Jesus, it is that pain and suffering are inevitable. If we are to put ourselves in a position of being more than spectators in life, that surely means the time will come when we learn the Maundy Thursdays and Good Fridays of life are unavoidable.

But, as Jesus demonstrated, they can be conquered!

William M. Schwein
Meridian Street United Methodist Church
Indianapolis, Indiana

APRIL 16, 1992

Maundy Thursday

Lessons:

Lutheran:	Jer. 31:31-34	Heb. 10:15-39	Luke 22:7-20
Roman Catholic:	Ex. 12:1-8, 11-14	I Cor. 11:23-26	John 13:1-15
Episcopal:	Ex. 12:1-14a	I Cor. 11:23-26 (27-32)	Luke 22:14-30
Pres/Meth/UCC:	Jer. 31:31-34	Heb. 10:16-25	Luke 22:7-20

Introductions to the Lessons:

Lesson 1

(1) *Jeremiah 31:31-34* (**Luth/Pres/Meth/UCC**). Please see Lesson 1, Reformation, Lutheran.

(2) *Exodus 12:1-14a* (**Epis**). The Israelites are on the threshold of leaving Egypt. Before leaving Moses and Aaron are instructed to hold the first Passover. Each family was to roast a lamb and its blood was to be put on the doorposts. Seeing the blood the angel of death would pass over those homes. This was to be done in remembrance of their great deliverance from slavery.

Lesson 2

(1) *Hebrews 10:15-39* (**Luth**); *10:16-25* (**Pres/Meth/UCC**). The author of Hebrews interprets the Sacrament of Holy Communion as the fulfillment of the new covenant given through Jeremiah. It is the Christian's passover. The blood belongs to the Lamb of God. Christ is the high priest. We enter into his sanctuary for the atonement of our sins.

(2) *I Corinthians 11:23-26* (**Epis**). Here is the earliest account of the institution of the Lord's Supper. The words are known as the Words of Institution. They are spoken when the bread and wine of the Sacrament are consecrated as the body and blood of Christ. Paul assures us that these words came from Jesus himself.

Gospel

Luke 22:7-20 (**Luth/Pres/Meth/UCC**); *22:14-30* (**Epis**). Jesus sent Peter and John to make preparations for the Passover meal. He gathered his men around a table and gave bread and wine as his body and blood in fulfillment of the new covenant.

Theme: We are to give thanks in all things, at all times.

Thought for the day: It is remarkable that Jesus was able to "give thanks" during his Last Supper. It was not the kind of "Thanksgiving Dinner" most of us believe is the setting for expressing gratitude. Perhaps his attitude can teach us something about finding some blessings to count even in the midst of life's most difficult circumstances.

Prayer of meditation: Lord of all of life, we come to this solemn service confused about both its substance and its significance. We are amazed how Jesus was able to give himself in fellowship with those whom he knew were about to let him down. We marvel at his poise, his serenity, his peace. We are surprised at how gracious he was as a host. As he offered the bread and cup to his disciples as reminders of his life and death, may he offer to us this night the means by which we might evidence his attitude in our lives. Amen.

Call to worship:
Leader: What shall I render to the Lord for all his bounty to me?
People: I will lift up the cup of salvation and call on the name of the Lord.
Leader: I will offer to you the sacrifice of thanksgiving
People: And call on the name of the Lord.
(Psalm 116:12-13, 17)

Prayer of adoration: Your grace is amazing, Lord, and your goodness is abundant. Even in the midst of life's struggles, you provide us with enough evidence of your love that we can find things for which we can be grateful: For your help in working everything for good; for your presence which constantly works for our good; for your power which brings good out of evil; for your peace which puts our minds at rest. Let us be more aware of the reasons we have to be thankful and faithful and fruitful in our lives. Amen.

Prayer of confession: We do not come easily to the table of our Lord. We are fearful. We are timid. We are defensive. We are afraid that we will occupy the places where sat one who betrayed, one who denied, one who fell away. We move as far as we can from your side, O Lord, for we are ashamed that we have not followed you as closely as we should. And yet, we feel you draw us closer to you, not in judgment or condemnation, but in love and mercy and forgiveness. Amen.

Prayer of dedication of gifts and self: Loving Lord, you offered broken bread and the cup of your sacrificial love to your disciples.

We come now to offer not only our broken promises, but also our renewed hopes that we might we more sacrificial in our giving and in our serving. Accept what we bring that we might know your acceptance of our needs and our dreams. Amen.

Sermon title: When He had Given Thanks

Sermon thesis: We do not know the blessings Jesus was counting that last night with his disciples, and yet we are told that he began the meal by giving thanks. In his ability to find things for which he was grateful at a time when there seemed to be so much for which he should have been sorrowful, we may discover what it means to be thankful in all circumstances.

Hymn for the day: *"Praise the Lord, rise up rejoicing."* This hymn by H.C.A. Gaunt, an Anglican clergyman born in 1902, was first published in *Hundred Hymns for Today*, 1969. It is a hymn of thanksgiving for the Eucharist and Christ's Passion. From 1929 to 1937 Gaunt was assistant master at Rugby School, after which he was headmaster of Malvern College until 1953. There followed ten years as chaplain and head of the English department at Winchester College and ten years as sacrist and precentor at Winchester Cathedral until his retirement in 1973.

Children's object talk:

What do you See?

Objects: A large piece of newsprint with a black dot in the center.
Lesson: We should look for the good and not the bad of life.
Outline: 1. Most people look at the bad, not the good.
2. Jesus seemed to see the good in others and in the experiences of his life.
3. We should accentuate the positive in life.

I HAVE A RATHER LARGE SHEET of paper. I want you to take a good look at it, and tell me what you see?

If you said you see only a black dot in the center, I wonder why you did not notice that probably 99% of the sheet was blank! Isn't that just like human nature? I've often heard someone say of a certain circumstance or experience, "It's all in how you look at it." That's true, isn't it? It's important for us to see just how we look at the things that happen to us.

Some people never see the bright side of life. They only see the problems. They never consider what they have; they are only concerned about what they don't have. They are never satisfied or happy. If they have a dime, for instance, they may wonder why they do not have a quarter. If they have one talent, they may worry that they do not have many talents. If they have a good bicycle, they may wish they had the newest and best bicycle.

Jesus was able to see the good things in life, even though there were some things that happened to him which weren't so good. He didn't focus his attention on what he didn't have. He thanked God for what he did have. And he did that when he looked at other people, too. He saw good in everyone. Sometimes it was hard to find, but he knew everyone had something good in them, and that is what he wanted them to see in their lives.

It is all in how you look at it! I once heard a person say, "Other people complain that roses have thorns. I am just happy that thorns have roses!" Look for the good!

The sermon:

When He Had Given Thanks

Hymns:
Beginning of worship: Beneath the Cross of Jesus
Sermon hymn: O Sacred Head, Now Wounded
End of worship: What Wondrous Love Is This

Scripture: Luke 22:7-20

Sermon Text: *"And he took bread, and when he had given thanks he broke it and gave it to them. . ."* Luke 22:19

THERE IS AN ACT OF JESUS which may be overlooked. Admittedly, few of us wash feet on Maundy Thursday. But there is something else he did we seem hesitant to do: To give thanks in the midst of the worst moments of our lives.

That one line is seldom lifted up as a part of our Maundy Thursday observance: ". . . and when he had given thanks." Most of us, hopefully, "say grace" or "return thanks" or "ask the blessing" before our meals. Surely that is what Jesus was doing. His exact words were not recorded. Maybe it was a traditional "blessing" he had learned from his youth. Maybe it was more extemporaneous. Have you ever noticed how some children use the prayer before meals to take inventory of all the things for which they are grateful: the birds, the sunshine, their parents, their toys, their friends? It's often a time to count one's blessings.

If there was something of that in the prayer of Jesus, what do you suppose he counted as his blessings at that moment in his life? So much was being taken from him. Yet, there was undoubtedly so much that remained as a source of strength and peace. For what had he given thanks, would you imagine?

Perhaps Jesus simply recited some psalms of thanksgiving. So many of them are appropriate for that situation. Dozens of expressions of thanksgiving come in the very same psalms that include a statement of utter frustration and futility. The seventh Psalm, for instance, ends with this beautiful hymn of thanksgiving:

"I will give to the Lord the thanks due to his righteousness,
    and I will sing praise to the name of the Lord, the Most High."
But what we often fail to realize is that the context for that thanksgiving was in the midst of a cry for help. The psalmist began his prayer with the cry,

". . . save me from all my pursuers, and deliver me . . . lift thyself up against the fury of my enemies."
Or look again at the twenty-eighth Psalm. The psalmist cries out from a hopeless situation:

"Hear the voice of my supplication, as I cry to thee for help."
But the psalm concludes,

". . . with my song I give thanks to God."
The context of those prayers of thanksgiving was one of tremendous trouble. Yet, through them all runs the theme of thankfulness.

You may not have noticed it, but the same phrase used in Luke's account of the Last Supper is echoed in the book of Acts. Paul "took bread, and giving thanks to God in the presence of all, he broke it and began to eat." That act of thanksgiving took place while Paul was on a voyage to Rome, as a prisoner, and the ship he was on had run aground in a storm. Those present with him were his captors. What a situation in which to take time to give thanks to God! We might have expected as much from Paul, for his letters are full of references to the need to give thanks at all times: "Always and for everything give thanks." "Give thanks in all circumstances; for this is the will of God in Christ Jesus for you."

There are those who have caught that spirit of thanksgiving amidst the most troubling circumstances. I'm sure you have heard that our great hymn, "Now Thank We All Our God," was written by a

German pastor when pestilence and war and plagues and famine had taken their toll, killing 8000 persons, including his own wife and children. The first Thanksgiving Proclamation, October 3, 1863, came in the midst of the Civil War, a time described by an article in "Harper's Weekly," as a "gloomy moment in the history of our country . . . It is a solemn moment. Of our troubles no man can see the end."

A famous preacher once told a couple he was marrying, "You will not always be able to choose the changes and chances that will befall you in the coming years, but you will always be able to choose the spirit in which you will meet them." As we see frequently, one's attitude makes possible gratitude in any situation. Some persons have a difficult time feeling positive. There was a farmer who was an eternal grumbler. One fall he had the best apple crop he had ever had. One of his neighbors stopped by to congratulate him, and said, "Well, Hiram, you sure ought to be happy now. This is the finest crop of apples ever raised around these parts." The pessimistic farmer couldn't even smile. He growled, "Well, I suppose they'll do — but where's the rotten ones for the hogs?"

Do we focus on what we have — or on what we don't have? There is something to be said for meaningful thanksgiving even in adversity, for it causes us to count the blessings that really count. Jesus gave thanks at the Last Supper, undoubtedly, because he knew that there was still the love of his heavenly Father. Jeremy Taylor, a seventeenth century preacher, had seen his home plundered, his family driven out, his worldly blessings brought to nothing. But this is what he said:

"What now? Let me look about me. They have left me the sun and the moon, a loving wife and my friends to pity me, and some to relieve me. They have not taken away my merry countenance and my cheerful spirit and good conscience; they have still left me the providence of God and all the promises of the Gospel, and my religion, and my hopes of heaven, and my charity to them, too. . ."

It just might be that the most genuine thanksgiving comes when things are less comfortable and confident for us. A Scottish preacher some years ago wrote in his memoirs that he was subject to great periods of depression, but that he had found a way out of them. He called it "the duty of thankfulness." He could win a victory over discouragement by considering all for which he was bound to thank God.

There was a poem written by a nine-year-old girl with which I close:

"Thank you, Lord, for letting me be alive today,
I like to try to help in many ways,
thank-you for my family,
We do live quite happily,
We always play together,
Oh! thank-you for the sunshine weather
It's just wonderful to be alive!"

That beautiful song of thanksgiving was found the day after its author died of leukemia.

Let us give thanks in all circumstances. Maybe we can face anything that comes our way "after we have given thanks."

William M. Schwein
Meridian Street United Methodist Church
Indianapolis, Indiana

APRIL 17, 1992

Good Friday

Lessons:

Lutheran:	Is. 52:13-53:12	Heb. 4:14-16, 5:7-9	John 18:1-19:42
Roman Catholic:	Is. 52:13-53:12	Heb. 4:14-16, 5:7-9	John 18:1-19:42
Episcopal:	Is. 52:13-53:12	Heb. 10:1-25	John (18:1-40) 19:1-37
Pres/Meth/UCC:	Is. 52:13-53:12	Heb. 4:14-16, 5:7-9	John 18:1-19:42

Introductions to the Lessons:

Lesson 1

Isaiah 52:13-53:12 (**Luth/Epis/Pres/Meth/UCC**). This is one of the most remarkable, beautiful and beloved chapters in the Bible. Christians see the Savior depicted in these words of Isaiah. Yahweh's servant was abused, despised, and rejected. His suffering and death were for our benefit. Patiently he endured it all that our sins might be forgiven. This was all in accord with God's will.

Lesson 2

(1) *Hebrews 4:14-16, 5:7-9* (**Luth/Pres/Meth/UCC**). Even though Jesus is the Son of God and our high priest, he understands our human condition of weakness. He was tempted as we are but did not sin. Through his suffering he learned to be obedient unto death. To all who obey him he is the source of our salvation.

(2) *Hebrews 10:1-25* (**Epis**). Christ is our supreme high priest. Human priests offered sacrifices for their own sins, but Jesus offered himself as the sacrifice for the sins of the world. A human priest repeatedly offered sacrifices for sin, but Jesus offered himself as the one, permanent sacrifice. It was the final and perfect sacrifice for sin.

Gospel

John 18:1-19:42 (**Luth/Pres/Meth/UCC**); *19:1-37* (**Epis**). These two chapters constitute John's account of the Passion. The story begins with Jesus' betrayal and arrest, continues through the trials and crucifixion, and ends with his burial.

Theme: In the midst of death there is promise for life.

Thought for the day: We are constantly seeking signs of life. In those situations which appear to be lifeless or hopeless, God offers some clues that renewal and new life are always possible.

Prayer of meditation: We gather once again beneath the cross of Jesus, O God. We tremble at the suffering and sacrifice it represents. We marvel at the depths of your love it incarnates. We rejoice that it marks no end of our Lord's life, but only the promise of a new beginning and new life for us. Amen.

Call to worship:
Leader: I will tell of your name to my brethren;
People: In the midst of the congregation I will praise you:
Leader: You who fear the Lord, praise him!
People: And stand in awe of him.
(Psalm 22:22-23)

Prayer of adoration: God of grace and God of glory, we praise you for your love made known to us in the suffering and sacrifice of the Christ. We marvel at the way you are able to bring light and life out of the darkest of days. For always overcoming the evil in our lives with your forgiveness and goodness, we thank you, and we ask that you help us to do the same with others. Amen.

Prayer of confession: Merciful God, we come confessing our sins, deserving your condemnation, and you give us your amazing grace. We have done those things which deny your love and destroy life, and you offer us another chance. We have left undone those things which reflect your love and promote life, and you offer us another chance. Your long-suffering is beyond our comprehension and yet within our reach. Through it we pray our lives may be made new. Amen.

Prayer of dedication of gifts and self: "Were the whole realm of nature mine, that were an offering far too small; love so amazing, so divine, demands my soul, my life, my all." Lord God, your love demands our total response, so much more than we are accustomed to offering you. Let us, now, make a commitment to make available to you and your church more and more of our resources of time and treasure and talent. Amen.

Sermon title: In the Place of Death, a Garden

Sermon thesis: We cannot overlook the fact that even in the place where Jesus was crucified there were already signs of life. John's account of the crucifixion notes the close proximity of the cross and a garden.

Hymn for the day: *"Sing, my tongue, the glorious battle."* Benantius Honorius Clemantianus Fortunatus (530-609) was converted to Christianity at an early age. He later entered the Abbey of St. Croix at Poitiers and for the last ten years of his life was Bishop of Poitiers. His poetic writings range from insignificant rhymes to some of the finest hymns of Christendom. This hymn clearly reflects the theme of today's sermon: In the modst of death there is promise for life.

Children's object talk:

Flowers at a Funeral

Objects: Some fresh flowers or a lily.
Lesson: It helps us accept death if we see signs of life.
Outline: 1. We often see beautiful flowers at funerals.
         2. God wants us to see life, not death.
         3. On Good Friday we can look ahead to Easter.

IF YOU HAVE EVER BEEN SICK, OR IN THE HOSPITAL, I would imagine that someone may have sent you flowers. They cheer us up, and express the good wishes of family and friends. People send flowers when they want to lift the spirits of persons having a bad time.

I don't know if you have ever gone to a funeral, but if you have, you probably saw lots of beautiful flowers. We send flowers to grieving families because they express our sympathy and caring. They also are wonderful reminders of how God brings life from death. If you have ever visited a cemetery, you have probably seen potted plants or bouquets near the grave markers. We need to see signs of life even when we are facing death.

Good Friday is one holy day we do not usually have flowers in church. It was such a terrible day, since Jesus was crucified then, that we feel everything is rather lifeless and hopeless. But that doesn't mean we will never see flowers here again. Tomorrow people will come to the sanctuary and place beautiful lilies for Easter Sunday.

When Jesus was buried on Good Friday, his friends had to wait for him to rise from death on Easter. Our Scripture lesson tells us he was buried near a garden. Maybe God was "sending them flowers" in that garden. God wanted to remind them that there was going to be life again, and not to give up hope. So even when we have to face death, we can look ahead to new life, eternal life.

The sermon:

In the Place of Death, a Garden

Hymns:
   Beginning of worship: In the Cross of Christ I Glory
   Sermon hymn: Never Further Than Thy Cross
   End of worship: Were You There

Scripture: John 18:1-19:42

Sermon Text: *"Now in the place where he was crucified there was a garden . . ."* John 19:41

THERE IS A PART OF THE DEATH AND BURIAL of Jesus that we may have overlooked. Most of our Good Friday services conclude with recalling the crucifixion and Jesus dying on the cross. We seldom make note of the burial of the body. In fact, we may sing only the first two stanzas of that familiar hymn, "Were You There," asking ourselves, "Were you there when they crucified my Lord?" and "Were you there when they nailed him to the tree?" But there is that third question: "Were you there when they laid him in the tomb?"

Joseph of Arimathea and Nicodemus *were* there. They alone came for the body of Jesus to prepare it for burial and to place it in the "new tomb where no one had ever been laid." How hard that last act of devotion and friendship must have been for them!

There is a tender, even tense, moment that comes at the conclusion of what we call "the graveside service" which ends a funeral. Before the casket is lowered into the grave, the grieving family and friends are ushered back to their cars. Some will pause to take a flower or two from the "casket piece." Floral arrangements usually surround the scene. The mood, obviously, is somber and sorrowful. Occasionally a member of the family will linger behind to watch the actual burial. But not often.

That is perhaps the most difficult time of all: the actual burial. Watching the casket being lowered into the ground. It is no wonder that only Joseph and Nicodemus were there to do that with the body of Jesus. Most of the disciples had long since gone home. They would not be heard from again until Easter Sunday.

We do not know, of course, but I would imagine Joseph and Nicodemus had a unique experience in tending to that final gesture

323

of love and loyalty. For John tells us that Jesus was buried "in a garden." Have you ever thought of that? In the place of death, there was a garden. Right there, with the cross and the tomb, there were flowers growing. The signs of life were all around. What a fitting word of encouragement and hope — in the midst of death. It gives us confidence to go on looking for the gardens amidst the places of death.

A minister tells of visiting Israel and spending a brief time touring the Golan Heights. From that point, you may remember, the Syrian tanks had been shelling the fertile plains of Galilee during a war there some years back. The minister said the scars of war were evident everywhere:

"In one such gun emplacement, barbed wire still punctuated the muddy tank tracks. As we stood observing this symbol of the ways to darkness and death, there in the mud and rusting wire grew a fragile white wildflower. The seed of life had survived, pushing back on that brilliant morning the stark symbols of death."

Life may seem like a fragile flower in the midst of all the signs of death about us, but it is always there.

We can focus on the crosses and the tombs of life. Or we can look for those signs of life which are subtle parts of the scenery. There is always the potential for life coming out of death. Even in the most unlikely places. In Thomas Wolfe's novel, *You Can't Go Home Again*, there is an unforgettable word of promise:

"Under the pavements trembling like a pulse, under the buildings trembling like a cry, under the waste of time, under the hoof of the beast above the broken bones of cities, there will be something growing like a flower, something bursting from the earth again, forever deathless, faithful, coming into life again like April."

"In the place where he was crucified there was a garden." We cannot dismiss quickly the horrors of the suffering of Jesus on this day. And yet, we may look forward, beyond the tragedy, to the triumph of Easter. The hints and clues were there. I do not believe that was accidental. I believe it was God's way of keeping those who buried Jesus hopeful that out of death would come life!

Ernest Hemingway wrote something in "A Natural History of the Dead" that is worth remembering whenever we feel buried under our burdens or overcome by our troubles:

"When that persevering traveller, Mungo Park, was at one period of his course fainting in the vast wilderness of an African desert, naked and alone, considering his days as numbered and nothing appearing to remain for him to do but to lie down and die, a small moss-flower of extraordinary beauty caught his eye. Though the whole plant,' says he, 'was no longer than one of my fingers, I could not contemplate the delicate confirmation of its roots, leaves and capsules without admiration. Can that Being who planted, watered and brought to perfection, in this obscure part of the world, a thing which appears of so small importance, look with unconcern upon the situation and suffering of creatures formed after his own image? Surely not. Reflections like these would not allow me to despair; I started up and, disregarding both hunger and fatigue, travelled forward, assured that relief was at hand; and I was not disappointed.

Ours is a God who plants and waters the seeds and signs of hope which are always there even in the midst of the most desperate and deserted situations. He can do that for you. The poet, Sara Teasdale, once wrote,

". . . our soul is a dark, plowed field in the cold rain, a broken field, plowed with pain."

That may be what we feel on the Good Fridays of our lives. But into our lives God plants the seeds of hope and of new life. That is the promise; that is our affirmation: In the place of death, there is a garden.

William M. Schwein
Meridian Street United Methodist Church
Indianapolis, Indiana

APRIL 19, 1992

The Resurrection of our Lord. Easter Day.

Lessons:

Lutheran:	Ex. 15:1-11	I Cor. 15:1-11	Luke 24:1-11
Roman Catholic:	Acts 10:34a, 37-43	Col. 3:1-4	Luke 24:1-12
Episcopal:	Acts 10:34-43	Col. 3:1-4	Luke 24:1-10
Pres/Meth/UCC:	Acts 10:34-43	I Cor. 15:19-26	John 20:1-18

Introductions to the Lessons:

Lesson 1

(1) *Exodus 15:1-11* (**Luth**). On this Easter Sunday we can shout, "What great things God has done!" One of the great things God did for the Jews was their escape from the Egyptians at the Red Sea. This was God's victory in behalf of his people.

(2) *Acts 10:34-43* (**Epis/Pres/Meth/UCC**). In speaking to the Roman centurion and his household, Peter reviews the ministry of Jesus including the resurrection. It was God who raised Jesus from the dead. Peter and others had contact with the risen Lord by eating and drinking with him.

Lesson 2

(1) *I Corinthians 15:1-11* (**Luth**). Please see Lesson 2, Epiphany V (**Epis/Pres/Meth/UCC.**)

(2) *Colossians 3:1-4* (**Epis**). As Jesus was raised from the dead, so is a believer in Christ. Believers are raised to new life, because they had died to their old sinful selves. Being raised with Christ, Christians seek spiritual truths and values and set their minds on things above.

(3) *I Corinthians 15:19-26* (**Pres/Meth/UCC**). Christ's resurrection means victory. The dead in Christ shall rise. Evil powers will be conquered. The last and greatest enemy, death, will be destroyed.

Gospel

Luke 24:1-11 (**Luth/Epis**). Women — Mary Magdalene, Joanna, Mary — were the first to discover the empty tomb and the first to broadcast the news of the resurrection. The news was so good that the disciples could not believe it. To them it was an idle tale.

(2) *John 20:1-18* (**Pres/Meth/UCC**). By herself Mary Magdalene goes before sunrise to the tomb and finds the stone rolled away. She reports this to Peter and John who

race to the tomb and find it empty. The men go home, but Mary Magdalene remains weeping. Jesus comes and reveals himself to her. Excitedly she returns to the disciples and exclaims, "I have seen the Lord."

Theme: Women in ministry.

Thought for the day: "Women have contributed much to the ministry of the church throughout its history. However, their role in this area has never been free from controversy. Today, most church bodies are discussing the place of women in their ministries. Crucial to these discussions . . . are the matters of faithful biblical interpretation." David M. Scholer.

Prayer of meditation: Lord, this past week I have been to the place where they crucified my Jesus. It was at his cross that I realized the depth of my sin and guilt before you. Today as I come to the empty tomb I would pray for victory over sin and death in my life. As I experience the power of the resurrection in this service, make me a dynamic witness to the Risen Christ in my world. This I pray in Jesus' name. Amen.

Call to worship:
Leader: Jesus Christ is risen!
People: He is risen, indeed!
Leader: The hope of the world is to be found in the Good News of our Lord's resurrection.
People: Let all of us — men and women, boys and girls — bear witness to the world that the tomb is empty.
Both: We proclaim to all who will listen, "Jesus Christ is risen!"

Prayer of adoration: O God, who raised Jesus Christ from the dead, we come this morning with hearts filled with praise and thanksgiving. We thank you on this Easter Sunday for Jesus Christ, our Risen Savior. We praise you for our salvation secured for us through the cross and the empty tomb. We worship you as our Creator, Redeemer God. We thank you for the beauty of all creation. We exalt you for your work of restoration in lives shattered by the ravages of sin. We cherish you as the God of our salvation. In the name of Jesus, our Risen Savior, we pray. Amen.

Prayer of confession: O Lord, we all stand before you as men and women in the modern world. We find it hard to believe that a dead man can be raised from his grave. We find it hard to believe that through one person the sins of the world can be cared for. We find it hard to believe that through one man all can be saved through faith. On this resurrection morning we believe; but help our unbelief. Help us discover within your Word the power of resurrection, not only of Jesus Christ, but for ourselves. Help us to become new creatures through the energy of the resurrected Christ within us. In his name we pray, Amen.

Prayer of dedication of gifts and self: O God, giver of every good and perfect gift, we come this morning with our offerings to support the witness of this church in this community. We come also to dedicate our lives to proclaiming the gospel of the resurrected Christ. Use these gifts and our lives for the advancement of Christ's work upon this earth. In his powerful name we pray, Amen.

Sermon title: The Women's Witness: An Idle Tale?

Sermon thesis: Women in ministry is the will of God. Women were the first ones given the mission of proclaiming the resurrection message. We are called to do the will of God in our day.

Hymn for the day: *"Christians, to the Paschal Victim."* Both text and tune of the Latin hymn can be found in an eleventh-century manuscript from Einsiedeln. There it is ascribed to Wipo (d. about 1050), a Burgundian who served as chaplain to two German emperors: Konrad II and his son, Heinrich III. It is closely associated with the development of liturgical drama; the brief conversation within the hymn, beginning, "Speak, Mary," could easily have been part of a drama about that first Easter morning. This important Latin hymn served as the basis for a German vernacular version found in English translation as "Christ the Lord is risen today," which in turn was a model for Luther's "Christ Jesus lay in death's strong bands."

Announcements for next week:

Sermon title: Faith: The Key to Life
Sermon theme: Faith is the way to life.
Sermon summary: Faith provides us a relationship with God, a system of belief, passion for life, and a way to live. Faith is the key to life.

Children's object talk:

The Big Surprise

Objects: A woman in period costume with sweet smelling spices
Lesson: We celebrate Easter because of the witness of the women at the tomb.
Outline: 1. The women were surprised that Jesus' body was gone when they took spices to the tomb.
2. The disciples did not believe the women's story.

3. Later the disciples were surprised when they discovered Jesus was risen and the women were right.

NOTE: If possible, have a woman in period costume tell the story. SOME OF THE women who had been followers of Jesus were feeling very sad because Jesus had died and been buried. They wanted to do something special. When many people had been unkind to them, Jesus had treated these women with respect and care. Most men at that time thought women weren't much good. They refused to pay attention to them. Jesus wasn't like that. Women, as well as men, were his friends.

So the women took some special spices to the place where Jesus was buried. (Allow time for children to smell the spices.) When they got there, the stone had been rolled away. What a big surprise! The women were frightened. They thought someone had stolen the body.

Two messengers came and reminded them that Jesus had told them he would rise from the dead. No one understood him at the time. The women listened to the messengers. Now they understood what Jesus meant. They were quite happy and very excited. They ran to tell the disciples.

When the women began telling the disciples about the empty tomb and the message they had been given, the men refused to believe them. You see, they didn't think women would have an important message like that. They thought the women were making the story up.

Later Jesus came and talked with the men. How surprised they were, for the women had been right.

It's because we know the women were right that we celebrate this wonderful, happy day called Easter.

The sermon:

The Women's Witness: An Idle Tale?

Hymns:
Beginning of worship: All Hail the Power of Jesus' Name
Sermon hymn: The Day of Resurrection
End of worship: Thine Is the Glory

Scripture: Luke 24:1-11

Sermon Text: *"But these words seemed to them an idle tale, and they did not believe them."* v. 11 (NRSV)

TODAY IS RESURRECTION SUNDAY! It is the day we as the Christian community celebrate the resurrection of our Lord Jesus Christ.

If we were faithful to the New Testament witness, every Christian pulpit would have a woman proclaiming the gospel of the resurrection on this Easter morning. In all four Gospels women are the first ones given the mission of proclaiming the resurrection faith. Matthew and Mark both report that a messenger from God told the women to go and tell the disciples that Jesus was risen.

Around the world this day the gospel of the resurrection will be proclaimed mostly by men. Indeed, some denominations refuse to ordain women to ministry believing that to do so is to be unfaithful to our Lord. Some denominations approve but have individual churches that believe it is wrong. And of course, there are churches that may approve of women as ordained ministers but have individual members who disapprove.

However, if we are to take this text seriously, women were the first to proclaim the good news that Jesus was among the living, that he had been raised from the dead by the power of God. It is quite remarkable that all four Gospels report that women were the first to witness to Jesus' resurrection. The idea of resurrection is a pretty fantastic concept. If the New Testament writers had been cooking up this idea, they would never have had women being the first believers in and reporters of the resurrection. Everyone knew that women were not credible witnesses. Even the disciples who knew Jesus and these women did not believe them. They saw their report as an idle tale. They responded to these women proclaimers of the resurrection as most men of their day would have.

In the time of Jesus women were usually considered as inferior and subordinate to men in virtually every facet of life. They were to remain at home, to be good wives and mothers. They were to take no part in public life or education. Josephus, an ancient Jewish historian, wrote: "The woman, says the Law, is in all things inferior to the man. Let her accordingly be submissive. . . ." A common saying of the period was: "Better is the wickedness of a man than a woman who does good."

The fact that women were the first to proclaim the gospel of the resurrection fits with Jesus' agenda for women. Jesus, who came proclaiming the gospel of the Kingdom, had a different view of women than was common for his day. Jesus by his teachings and actions affirmed the worth and value of women as persons. He affirmed their place along with men within God's kingdom. They, too, were to give love and service in behalf of a loving God.

Jesus challenged the putting down of women. In his day the prerogative of divorce belonged almost exclusively with men, and virtually any reason could be used to justify divorce. Jesus tolerated no such male bias. Indeed, he recalled the "one flesh" concept from Genesis 2:24 which affirms mutual partnership and God's intention for marriage. Although women were held accountable in Jesus' time for all sexual sin, Jesus rejected this view with his dramatic indictment of men: ". . . everyone who looks at a woman with lust has already committed adultery with her in his heart" (Matthew 5:28).

Our Lord reached out to women who were rejected. In spite of the laws regarding uncleanness, Jesus allowed a woman with a twelve year menstrual problem to touch him and praised her faith. Jesus allowed a sinful woman to anoint and kiss his feet. Our Lord challenged religious leaders when he said, "Truly I tell you, the tax collectors and the prostitutes are going into the kingdom of God ahead of you" (Matthew 21:31). He also extended salvation directly to women who were known as adulteresses.

In his day respectable, responsible rabbis were not to teach women. Nonetheless, Jesus did teach women, and he included them in his band of committed disciples. He taught Mary and commended her learning to Martha, her sister, who was carrying out the traditional female tasks. It was to a Samaritan woman that our Lord made his most explicit claim that he was the Messiah; he shared with her his basic mission. According to the Gospel of Luke many women were in Jesus' circle of traveling disciples. These same women were present at the crucifixion and burial. And as I have already pointed out, they were the first to know of our Lord's resurrection on Easter morning.

Our Lord affirmed the value of committed discipleship and obedience to the will of God. He made that affirmation over the natural and valued role of mother. According to Luke 8:21 he said: "My mother and my brothers are those who hear the word of God and do it." On another occasion according to Luke 11:28 he said to a woman who had praised his mother: "Blessed rather [than his own mother] are those who hear the word of God and obey it."

The women our Lord assimilated became proclaimers of Jesus as Savior and risen Lord. The woman of Samaria evangelized her town.

Women were the first persons to declare that Jesus was risen from the dead. The resurrection message became central to the gospel proclaimed in the early church.

According to David M. Scholer, Distinguished Professor of New Testament and Early Church History at North Park College and Theological Seminary in Chicago, "Jesus' inclusion of and ministry to and through women within his own life and teaching were a powerful witness to the early church of the partnership of women and men within the membership and ministry."

The question we must deal with is this: Why do we resist within the church today what was clearly the intent and purpose of our Lord Jesus Christ? It seems clear to me that to resist and fight the rightful place of women in the proclamation role of the ministry is to resist God's will for the church.

In *Megatrends 2000* John Naisbitt and Patricia Aburdene state that the 1990s will be the decade of women in leadership. Will that be true for the church of Jesus Christ? It can be and should be. Women in the ministry is the will of God. Indeed, for over two decades now God has been calling many women into ministry. Twenty years ago the number of women in theological schools would have been a small percentage. Today they compose a large percentage; in some seminaries they are the majority. Many of them are bright, able, and willing to serve Jesus Christ and his church with full commitment. What's missing is the openness of many churches to God.

Our culture is moving ahead with women in major leadership roles. It seems that God is working the divine will for women within the larger culture while Christ's church takes up the rear guard and fights and resists.

What's your attitude about women in ministry? Is it your conviction that they only have "an idle tale" to tell? Or do you believe they can be authentic witnesses to the resurrection power of an almighty God? Which will it be?

Myron Chartier
Jan Chartier
American Baptist Churches of Michigan
Kalamazoo, Michigan

APRIL 26, 1992

Second Sunday of Easter

Lessons:

Lutheran:	Acts 5:12, 17-32	Rev. 1:4-18	John 20:19-31
Roman Catholic:	Acts 5:12-16	Rev. 1:9-11a, 12-13, 17-19	John 20:19-31
Episcopal:	Acts 5:12a, 17-22, 25-29	Rev. 1:(1-8) 9-19	John 20:19-31
Pres/Meth/UCC:	Acts 5:27-32	Rev. 1:4-8	John 20:19-31

Introductions to the Lessons:

Lesson 1

Acts 5:12, 17-32 (**Luth**); *5:12a, 17-22, 25-29* (**Epis**); *5:27-32* (**Pres/Meth/UCC**). Since the Old Testament knows nothing about the resurrection, the 1st Lessons for the Easter season are taken from the book of Acts. Easter is more than a one-Sunday festival but is a season. Therefore, the Sundays are called *of* Easter rather than *after* Easter. In this first of the series, the Apostles are commanded by the religious authorities to stop preaching about Jesus. They respond, "We must obey God."

Lesson 2

Revelation 1:4-18 (**Luth**); *1:9-19* (**Epis**); *1:4-8* (**Pres/Meth/UCC**). This is the first in a series of six lessons from the last book of the Bible, Revelation. The author, John, is an exile on the island of Patmos and is given a vision of end times and a message to the seven churches. Today's lesson is a part of the letter. He sees the resurrected, ascended, and eternal Christ.

Gospel

John 20:19-31 (**Luth/Epis/Pres/Meth/UCC**). The gospel lessons for the rest of the Easter season are taken from the book of John. For the remainder of the Easter season God's Word will come to us from Acts, Revelation, and John. In today's lesson, the risen Christ makes two appearances: a visit with the Apostles minus Thomas, and a visit with Thomas present.

Theme: Faith is the key of life.

Thought for the day: Our entire hope of justification and salvation rests on Jesus Christ and on his gospel. Jesus Christ has made known to us the good news of God's merciful action. We do not place our ultimate trust in anything other than the promises of God and the saving work of Jesus Christ.

Prayer of meditation: O Lord, I come to this place to worship and adore you. I come beaten down by the struggles of this week. I seek to be renewed by your marvelous grace. Give me faith to believe in your sovereign care; help my unbelief. I wait upon you for an empowering of faith in my life, O Lord. Through Christ my Savior I pray. Amen.

Call to worship:
Leader: Praise the LORD!
People: Praise the LORD, O my soul!
Leader: I will praise the LORD as long as I live;
People: I will sing praises to my God all my life long.
Psalm 146:1-2 (NRSV)

Prayer of adoration: Our Creator and Redeemer, we come to you this morning through faith in Jesus Christ. We thank you for creating us and making us a part of your human family. We give honor to your saving work through the person of your Son, Jesus Christ. We praise you for adopting us into your faith family through the power of your Spirit. Thank you, God, for the gift of faith which makes possible our relationship with you. Be with us as we strengthen our faith bond with you as we engage in worship this day. For Jesus' sake, Amen.

Prayer of confession: Lord, you have called us to be a people of faith. You have called us to trust you and your promises with our whole being. Sometimes, we find it difficult to be a trusting people, O God. When there are wars and rumors of war, faith in you is difficult. When children are born into this world with AIDS or addicted to drugs, faith in you as a just and merciful God is difficult. When we see thousands of homeless persons and families upon our nation's streets, faith in you wavers. When we experience tough times with our personal and family budgets, when we labor over failing health, our legs of faith wobble, O Lord. Almighty and everlasting God, we often struggle with our trust in you and your promises. Help us with our unbelief. Help us to discern your faithfulness in the past. Use it to strengthen our grip on faith in you for the present and the future. Give us once again the gift of faith. In Jesus' name, Amen.

Prayer of dedication of gifts and self: O gracious God, we bring these gifts of money and of self as an expression of our faith in you and your reconciling work in the world. Use our gifts for the advancement of your saving ways in the world. In the name of your perfect gift to us, even Jesus Christ, Amen.

Sermon title: Faith: The Key to Life.

Sermon thesis: Faith provides us a relationship with God, a system of belief, passion for life, and a way to live. Faith is the key to life.

Hymn for the day: *"We walk by faith."* Henry Alford's hymn, "Come, you thankful people, come" is well-known to all. His hymn "We walk by faith" has enjoyed a rebirth in a number of more recent hymnals. It is clearly inspired by the doubting Thomas story, which is heard each year on the second Sunday of Easter. A native of London, England, Alford (1810-1871) was the son of the rector of Aston Sandford, Buckinghamshire. After graduating with honors from Trinity College, Cambridge, he was ordained and served first as vicar of Wymeswold, Leicestershire, then incumbent at Quebec Chapel in London. In 1857 he became dean of Canterbury. Most important of Alford's many writings was a four-volume commentary of the Greek New Testament, a work which took twenty years to complete and which stood as a standard during the last half of the nineteenth century.

Announcements for next week:

Sermon title: Finding God at Home
Sermon theme: Discovering God in the pain and joy of family life.
Sermon summary: Families can experience God's gracious presence in the pain as well as the joy of family living. As God was present at the crucifixion and at the resurrection, God is present in the hurt and celebration of family living.

Children's object talk:

Keep The Faith

Objects: An advertisement for Disney Theme Parks
Lesson: It is important to have faith even when we have to wait.
Outline: 1. Janelle and Daniel's Dad kept telling them to keep the faith and eventually they would go to Disney World.
2. Finally, Dad had the tickets so the family could go.
3. Jesus told Thomas not to doubt but to believe.

Note: You may want to substitute another attraction closer to home. JANELLE AND HER brother Daniel had wanted to go to Disney World for such a long time. Last Christmas Janelle's best friend had gone with her grandparents. During spring vacation their cousins had gone.

When Janelle and Daniel asked their Dad about going, he would smile and say, "Keep the faith, someday we're going."

One time Daniel asked, "When is 'someday?' There may never be a 'someday.' We need a *'real day'*."

Dad seemed a little irritated, but he still said, "Keep the faith, Daniel!"

Then one day Dad came into the family room with an envelope. His eyes twinkled. He asked Janelle and Daniel to guess what was in it! They couldn't guess!

Dad opened the envelope. In it were enough tickets for the family to go to Orlando, Florida. He also took out travellers checks. Then he said, "Remember, I asked you to keep the faith? I know you have wanted to go for a long time. It's taken awhile for our family to get everything in order. Now we're ready."

Janelle and Daniel were so excited. They could hardly talk.

This story reminds me of something Jesus once said to Thomas, the disciple. Thomas was having trouble believing Jesus was alive because he hadn't seen him yet. Thomas was doubting. When Jesus came to see Thomas, he said, "Thomas, do not doubt. Believe." It's like saying, "Keep the faith."

The sermon:

The Key to Life

Hymns:
   Beginning of worship: Great Is Thy Faithfulness
   Sermon hymn: O Jesus, Joy of Loving Hearts
   End of worship: My Faith Looks Up to Thee

Scripture: John 20:19-31

Sermon Text: *"Jesus said to him, 'Have you believed because you have seen me'? Blessed are those who have not seen and yet have come to believe."* v. 29 (NRSV)

ONE OF MY FAVORITE CONTEMPORARY CHRISTIAN song writers and vocalists is Michael Card. He's written and sings a piece entitled: "That's What Faith Must Be." It goes like this:
   "To hear with my heart
   To see with my soul

To be guided by a hand I cannot hold
That's what faith must be.
To trust in a way that I cannot see
That's what faith must be."
Faith is the key to life. Faith is trusting in the ways of God that
we cannot see. Throughout his Gospel John keeps saying: "Faith leads
to life; unbelief brings on death and ruin."

Jesus' experience with Thomas points to the validity of this truth.
Thomas was not with the others when Jesus appeared to them and
had shown them the nail prints and the side wound. When they
shared their experience with Thomas, he refused to believe it.
Thomas, a cautious man, inclined to be skeptical, wanted not only
to see the nail prints but also to touch them as well as the wound
in Jesus' side.

The next Sunday the disciples were again behind locked doors
in the place where they were staying. Thomas was with them this
time. Jesus, unimpeded by solid walls and doors, again appeared
in their midst and greeted them. Then he offered to meet Thomas'
test, and added an appeal and warning, "Do not doubt but believe."
Thomas faced an opportunity for immeasurable privilege and blessing, but to fail to believe would be a terrible tragedy.

Thomas rose to the occasion. John does not tell us whether he
actually touched Jesus. Apparently he did not need to do so. He
saw and recognized the risen Christ, and the stubborn skeptic, now
convinced, made a climactic confession of faith — this risen Jesus was
his Lord and his God.

Our text for the day gives Thomas a mild rebuke for being unwilling to believe without visible proof of Jesus' resurrection.
However, the purpose of these words in John's Gospel is not so much
to criticize Thomas as to point the way of faith to future generations. The rich blessing of God will rest upon all believers who are
able to make Thomas' confession of faith without requiring visible
proof. Faith is trusting what cannot be seen. Trusting faith is the
key to life with God.

John insists that the key to life is faith. Why is this so?

First, faith connects us to God through Jesus Christ. First and
foremost, faith according to the Bible is a trust-relationship with God.
Faith is a leap over the deep chasm of doubt toward God. By trusting
God Abraham and Sarah left their home in Ur of Chaldea for a new
home. By trusting God Abraham obeyed God's command to sacrifice

his son Isaac, only to regain his son. By faithful obedience Jesus went to the cross to secure our salvation. We come to God through an act of trust in the person and work of Jesus Christ.

Our trust-walk with God puts us in touch with eternity. Faith in God through Jesus Christ is the key to life because it places us in touch with the most important relationship we will ever have in life. Our relationship with God is more important than any person or any thing. Jesus came that our relationship with God might be complete and whole. By trusting Jesus we come to know God at deep and intimate levels. Faith is the key to life because it forms our relationship with God, who is the source of all life.

Second, faith in Jesus Christ provides us a belief system. This belief system orients us to a world view that is grounded in the God who made heaven and earth. This creator God formed humanity as male and female. Human beings were to be the stewards of the earth, acting on behalf of a benevolent God. Human beings were created for the love of God and of each other. However, in their freedom to choose obedience or disobedience humanity chose to walk out of step with God. To help human beings stay in step God called Abraham to form a people. This God made a covenant with Abraham by which the Lord God would bless the nations of the earth through the seed of Abraham. Through Moses God gave Abraham's sons and daughters the law by which to stay in step with God and be blessed.

When the children of Abraham, Isaac, and Jacob failed God, the Holy One called into a being a new people. God sent Jesus Christ to help all humanity to live in relationship with the Eternal One. Those who responded to his call became a part of the family of God. They were to be in mission calling the world to repentance and faith. The belief system of this family provides meaning and direction for life. Faith as a belief system is a key to understanding life.

Third, faith provides emotional zest for living. When one contemplates life without faith in God, depression can take place. A trust relationship with the living God yields to the trustful person a sense of well-being and life. Our Lord did not come to bring death but life to persons. This life is from eternity itself. Its source is not from within our human time frame; indeed, it transcends our human condition. It is from God.

All kinds of people have found zest for life by placing their trust in Jesus Christ. Drug addicts, alcoholics, the emotionally depressed, and many others have found in Christ the joy of life. They not only find a belief system worth their investment, but they also find the emotional power to come to grips with the down-side of their lives. Faith in Jesus Christ is the key to discovering the fullness of one's emotional life. Jesus Christ brings peace and joy to broken, anguished lives.

Fourth, faith provides us an ethical walk. What does the Lord of our faith require of us? Our God in whom we have entrusted our lives and our future requires that we do justice, love kindness, and walk humbly with the Almighty. Faith in Jesus Christ makes us ambassadors of reconciliation, seeking to bring peace and justice to the world in which we live. Faith gets lived out in works of righteousness. We are a people of faith created and redeemed to do good works. As James the Apostle said, "So faith without works is dead." Faith in Jesus Christ is the key to finding the way to live life with our neighbors, with the earth, and with our God. Faith empowers us to live moral, ethical lives as the children of God within the Creator's world.

Each of us is called to a life of faith, to trust in a God that we cannot see. When we do, we discover the key to life. We discover the most important relationship in life, a belief system for guiding us, emotional zest for living, and a way to live life justly and peaceably. Faith in Jesus Christ is the key to your life. Have you placed your trust, your faith in him?

Jan Chartier
Myron Chartier
American Baptist Churches of Michigan
Kalamazoo, Michigan

MAY 3, 1992

Third Sunday of Easter

Lessons:

Lutheran:	Acts 9:1-20	Rev. 5:11-14	John 21:1-14
Roman Catholic:	Acts 5:27b-32, 40b-41	Rev. 5:11-14	John 21:1-19
Episcopal:	Acts 9:1-19a	Rev. 5:6-14	John 21:1-14
Pres/Meth/UCC:	Acts 9:1-20	Rev. 5:11-14	John 21:1-19

Introductions to the Lessons:

Lesson 1

Acts 9:1-20 (**Luth/Pres/Meth/UCC**); *9:1-19a* (**Epis**) The author of the book of Acts was Luke who also was one of Paul's co-workers. Paul must have told him how he changed from a persecutor of the church to an apostle. On the way to Damascus to arrest Christians, Paul had a confrontation with the risen Christ. This led to his baptism, reception of the Holy Spirit, and preaching that Jesus is the Son of God.

Lesson 2

Revelation 5:11-14 (**Luth/Pres/Meth/UCC**); *5:6-14* (**Epis**) Christ, the risen Lamb, is found to be the only one worthy to open the scroll with seven seals. Thousands upon thousands of angels surrounding the throne loudly sing praises to Christ. Every creature in heaven and on earth join in the hymn of praise.

Gospel

John 21:1-14 (**Luth/Epis**); *21:1-19* (**Pres/Meth/UCC**) In this appendix to John's gospel, we are given the risen Christ's third appearance to the disciples. It took place on the shore of the Sea of Galilee where seven of the disciples went fishing. Jesus called to them who had fished all night and caught nothing to let down their nets. There was a miraculous catch and some of the fish were cooked for breakfast. As a result of this Easter breakfast the disciples, including Peter, were re-enlisted as followers.

Theme: Discovering God in the pain and joy of family life.

Thought for the day: "Family life is the arena in which the drama of redemption is played out. It is there that 'two or more gather in his name' each day . . . It is in the family that crosses are embraced every day and lives laid down in loving service. It is there that forgiveness is granted . . . over and over again." National Association of Catholic Diocesan Family Life Ministers

Prayer of meditation: Dear Lord, into your holy presence I come this morning. I come as your child, adopted into your family through the life, death, and resurrection of your Son. As your child and a member of your family, I enter this house of worship seeking your will for my life. Prepare me now, O Lord, to meet you in this hour of worship, and when I depart from this place, may I know your will more clearly and love you more dearly as my divine Parent. Amen.

Call to worship:
Leader: Where is God?
People: God is in creation.
Leader: Where is God?
People: God is in Jesus Christ.
Leader: Where is God?
People: God is present in the church.
Leader: Where is God?
People: God is at home in our hearts.

Prayer of adoration: Thank you, God, for calling each of us into your family of faith. Thank you for Jesus Christ, our elder brother, who came to redeem us into your household. Thank you for your Spirit, who speaks to us moment by moment and lets us know that we, indeed, are your children. Thank you now for this opportunity to worship you as your family bonded together by our common calling in and by our common love for Jesus Christ. For all these things and much more we give you thanks. Amen.

Prayer of confession: O God, we come to you knowing that we are sinners. We understand that we were born into a sinful position. We know that we fail you daily by choosing to live in ways that are often far from your ways. We come knowing that we have often failed those we love the most. We have failed because of our human limitations. We have faltered because we have deliberately broken commitments and obligations that we have accepted. Because of our sin and broken condition, we are burdened with guilt and shame. In this hour of worship help us to experience the power of your forgiveness in our lives. Help us to move from the pain of our sinful condition to the joy of your saving power in our lives. In the name of our forgiving Christ we pray. Amen.

Prayer of dedication of gifts and self: All gifts come from you, O God, for you are the Creator of every good and perfect gift. We come this morning returning a portion of your gifts to us to be used for extending your family in the community, nation, and world. With those gifts we keep for our own, assist us in being reliable stewards of what you have given unto us. In Jesus' name, your great gift to us, we pray. Amen.

Sermon title: Finding God at Home

Sermon thesis: Families can experience God's gracious presence in the pain as well as the joy of family living. As God was present at the crucifixion and at the resurrection, God is present in the hurt and celebration of family living.

Hymn for the day: *"Be known to us in breaking bread."* This hymn is the last two stanzas of a longer hymn beginning "Shepherd of souls, refresh and bless," which can also be found in some hymnals. Author of the hymn, James Montgomery (1771-1854) ranks with Isaac Watts and Charles Wesley in his contribution to English hymnody. Intended by his parents for the Moravian ministry, Montgomery instead entered a literary career in which he made a considerable Christian witness. Besides his hymns, he wrote much poetry which spoke out against slavery. As a printer of a newspaper, the *Sheffield Iris,* he also raised a voice against injustice.

Announcements for next week:

> **Sermon title:** Following Jesus
> **Sermon theme:** Being a disciple of Jesus Christ.
> **Sermon summary:** Being a faithful follower of Jesus Christ emerges from an intimate relationship with our Lord. It is our task to develop a close relationship with our Savior.

Children's object talk:

Taken By Surprise

Objects: The Bible and/or a picture of Jesus with the disciples
Lesson: Jesus was with the disciples and is with us today.
Outline: 1. The disciples were surprised when Jesus appread at the lake.
2. Jesus and the disciples had a wonderful time together.
3. Jesus is with us all the time, wherever we are.

TWO WEEKS AGO was Easter. That was a very joyful day because we celebrated that Jesus is risen. He is alive. That had never happened before, and it's never happened again. God did a special thing.

Jesus' disciples and friends didn't really understand having Jesus with them again. He came to talk with them and teach them when they weren't expecting it.

One night some of the disciples had gone out on the sea to fish. All night they caught nothing. In the morning the disciples were tired and discouraged. They had no fish. Jesus came to the shoreline. He called to them, telling them to put their nets down on the other side of the boat. They did and the net was full of fish. Now they could be sure the person on the shore was Jesus.

The disciples hurried back to the shore. Peter was so excited he swam ahead of those who brought the boat with the net full of fish. They ate breakfast together and talked. It was a wonderful time.

The disciples had not expected to see Jesus by the seaside where they were fishing. But there he was.

Sometimes we are like the disciples. We expect Jesus to be present when we come to church. We may forget that Jesus is also present with us in our homes, on our playgrounds, and in our schools. Jesus is with us when we need him most! We don't need to be taken by surprise by having Jesus with us. What a wonderful gift that is to us.

The sermon:

Finding God at Home

Hymns:
Beginning of worship: Now Thank We All Our God
Sermon hymn: A Christian Home
End of worship: Our Thanks, O God, for Parents

Scripture: John 21:1-14

Sermon text: *"Jesus said to them, 'Come and have breakfast.' Now none of the disciples dared to ask him, 'Who are you?' because they knew it was the Lord."* v. 12

WITHIN THE LAST DECADE AND A half there has been a small but growing movement within the Christian community, both CAtholic and Protestant, called "family spirituality." Several Protestant and Catholic writers have written books to help families discover the presence of God in their midst.

One of these is Ernest Boyer, Jr., who a few years ago wrote a book entitled *A Way in the World: Family Life as Spiritual Discipline.* Of the books written on the topic it is probably the best known. It was a religious book club offering. Recently, it was published in a paperback edition entitled, *Finding God at Home.*

As we continue to bask in the bright light of the resurrection power of Easter morning and as we begin Family Week in the life of our church, I wish to speak to you about the subject of family spirituality. Boyer's book will serve as my sermon title: "Finding God at Home."

The disciples, following the events of Holy Week, were most likely men without a purpose. In their aimlessness Peter proposed a fishing trip and received a unanimous response from the others. The desire to go fishing seemed to be a spontaneous suggestion. Peter had no plan, no settled aim. They embarked on a boat at the Sea of Galilee. They fished all night.

At dawn Jesus appeared on the beach and asked them if they had caught any fish. They hadn't. So Jesus helped them pull off a miracle catch.

Then he said to them, "Come, let's have breakfast together." John records no response to this invitation of Jesus. Rather none of them dared to ask who Jesus was. This seems strange since you ask that question only to those you do not know. Yet in all the post-resurrection appearances people had trouble identifying Jesus.

According to John the disciples knew who it was. They knew it was Jesus, but how did they know? Perhaps in the miracle of the fish catch. That could be it. But it also could have been in the invitation to breakfast. For in the breaking of bread and the eating of fish, they had experienced Jesus many times before. It may have been in the daily routine of eating that they knew Jesus. They may have recognized the way he broke bread, the way he served food, and in the way he himself ate. From these routine, ordinary behaviors they may have been able to identify our Lord.

Family spirituality emphasizes the ordinary, routine events of life as being the places we experience the Divine Presence. The primary emphasis of family spirituality is that we can discover the reality of the living God and the resurrected Christ in the routine events and processes of family living. God is present in the conflicts of families as well as in their prayers. God can be experienced in the playful activities of families as well as in family devotional times. God is as near as the air we breath, the water we drink, the tears we cry, and the laughter we express. God is everywhere in the ordinariness of life to be perceived and experienced.

One of the themes in family spirituality is that families can experience God's gracious presence in the pain as well as in the joy of family living. These two realities, pain and joy, correspond to the crucifixion and the resurrection. As God was present at the cross and at the empty tomb, God is present in the hurt and celebration of family life.

Most likely we have no trouble believing God is present in the joy of family living; however, we may miss or overlook the power of God's graciousness to us in those times. We may be so lethargic to the divine reality that we may miss it in those celebrative moments.

We may have difficulty believing God is present in family pain. Hurt and pain are the crucifixion side of family spirituality. Over the years I have experienced the pain of my own family: difficult, chronic illnesses that have not yielded to the wisdom of the medical profession; the death of loved ones; pained family relationships that don't seem to get resolved. I have also experienced the pain of families I have known in my ministry over the years. Breadwinners have lost their jobs and been unable to find other employment. Others have experienced the turmoil of separation and divorce. Still others have had to deal with drug-addicted family members. Some have seen family members in trouble with the law of the land. Others have lost family members in car or motorcycle accidents. The pain of these kinds of events were quite real in the lives of many people. I'm sure that there are those here today who have experienced one or more of these situations.

Where is God when a family suffers? Why must a family be victimized by pain and hurt? If God is all-loving and all-powerful, why?

There is no final, ultimately satisfactory answer to the questions surrounding human suffering. A most helpful perspective for me has been to understand that our suffering is intimately connected with the crucified God. To make the connection between our sufferings, large or small, and the great story of God's pain and suffering in Jesus upon the cross is an important one. By linking the story of our hurt and pain with the story of the Suffering Servant, we rescue our history from its fatalistic chain and empty meaning. We permit our story of suffering to be converted from a series of random incidents and accidents into an opportunity to explore and reflect upon God's working in our lives. By connecting our pain with God's suffering, we can claim the debilitating and the destructive as part of Eternal Love's redeeming activity in our lives.

Joy and celebration are the resurrection side of family spirituality. The gracious activity of God is experienced in times when family life is filled with joy and laughter. With the birth of a healthy child families experience delight. As family members grow and develop in healthy ways, there is a deep satisfaction that transpires. When teenagers graduate from high school, there is gladness. As they enter and successfully complete college, again there is reason for celebration. When families spend time together doing their favorite activities, there is often a sense of enjoyment. One of those times often takes place around the dining room table, where food and drink are shared and consumed. These all can be occasions when we experience not only the joy of family living but also the joy of the Lord. God is present in our midst as families.

We worship a gracious God. The grace of God is experienced in the crucifixion and resurrection of our Lord. The God of grace is present in both the crucifixion and resurrection sides of family living. May God give us eyes to see the Divine Presence in our families.

Jan Chartier
Myron Chartier
American Baptist Churches of Michigan
Kalamazoo, Michigan

MAY 10, 1992

Fourth Sunday of Easter

Lessons:

Lutheran:	Acts 13:15-16a, 26-33	Rev. 7:9-17	John 10:22-30
Roman Catholic:	Acts 13:14, 43-52	Rev. 7:9, 14b-17	John 10:27-30
Episcopal:	Acts 13:15-16, 26-33 (34-39)	Rev. 7:9-17	John 10:22-30
Pres/Meth/UCC:	Acts 13:15-16, 26-33	Rev. 7:9-17	John 10:22-30

Introductions to the Lessons:

Lesson 1

Acts 13:15-16, 26-33 (**Luth/Epis/Pres/Meth/UCC**) On his first missionary journey Paul is invited to address the synagogue in Antioch of Pisidia. He traces God's dealing with the Hebrews from the Exodus to the time of Jesus. He goes on to tell how Jesus was innocently crucified, but God raised him from the dead and Jesus appeared to his disciples who are now witnesses to his resurrection.

Lesson 2

Revelation 7:9-17 (**Luth/Epis/Pres/Meth/UCC**) John is given a vision of heaven. He sees an innumerable number of people from everywhere dressed in white robes. Together with the angels they worship before the throne of the risen Lamb. Who are these in white robes? They are the believers who washed their robes white in the blood of the Lamb. They serve God without any problem, need, or sorrow.

Gospel

John 10:22-30 (**Luth/Epis/Pres/Meth/UCC**) It was around Christmas time when Jesus was in the Temple for the Feast of Dedication (Hanukkah). The Jews corner him and challenge him to say if he really is the Messiah. He says, "I already told you but you do not believe me." The people who believe him know him and obey his voice. They have eternal security in him, for he and the Father are one.

Theme: Being a disciple of Jesus Christ

Thought for the day:
The Lord is my shepherd, I shall not want.

He makes me lie down in green pastures;
he leads me beside still waters;
he restores my soul.
He leads me in right paths
for his name's sake.
Psalm 23:1-3 (NRSV)

Prayer of meditation: Dear Lord, I come this day seeking to be a follower of your Son, Jesus Christ. There are times when I fail in being loyal to him. In this hour of worship I seek strength to be a faithful disciple of my Lord. Be with me and those about me as we worship you and listen to your voice for words of encouragement and strength. In the name of Jesus. Amen.

Call to worship:
Leader: Come, let us worship the Lord.
People: Who can worship the Lord?
Leader: All those who seek to make the Lord first in their lives.
People: What is required of us as we seek to worship the Creator of the universe?
Leader: The Lord requires us to do justice, to love kindness, and to walk humbly with our God.

Prayer of adoration: O God, you who loves us more dearly than any earthly father or mother ever could, we come praising your name for life. We thank you that you created all life. We appreciate the breath of life that you have placed within each one of us. We praise you for the new life that you have given to us through Jesus Christ, our Savior. On this fourth Sunday of Easter, we thank you for the breath of life that your Son breathed upon all creation the morning he rose from the grave. Bless us this morning with the power to follow you and to be faithful to the life that you have placed within us. In the name of Jesus, who is our life. Amen.

Prayer of confession: O Creator of heaven and earth, O Son of God, Redeemer of the world, O Holy Spirit, Three Persons and one God, have mercy upon us, for each of us has fallen short of your glory. Each of us has badly marred the divine image within us. Forgive us for failing to follow Jesus Christ, the Good Shepherd of our lives. O Triune God, help us to be faithful disciples of Jesus Christ. In your name, we pray. Amen.

Prayer of dedication of gifts and self: Lord, as we dedicate our offerings to you, we come also to commit our lives to your loving service. Like sheep we have heard the shepherd's call and we are ready, willing, and eager to follow the Good Shepherd of life. Our world is filled with many sounds and many voices seeking our attention and our loyalty. Help us always to recognize the voice of Jesus and to faithfully follow him. In the name of the Good Shepherd we pray. Amen.

Sermon title: Following Jesus

Sermon thesis: Being a faithful follower of Jesus Christ emerges from an intimate relationship with our Lord. It is our task to develop a close relationship with our Savior.

Hymn for the day: *"O God of Jacob/Bethel."* This hymn for guidance "through each perplexing path of life," was written by Philip Doddridge to follow his sermon, preached on January 16, 1737, on "Jacob's Vow." (See December 15 above for remarks on Doddridge.)

Announcements for next week:

    Sermon title: Love One Another

    Sermon theme: Everyone is called by our Lord Jesus Christ to love one another.

    Sermon summary: Love is an illusive word. In Jesus Christ we are given a new commandment to love one another. What did he have in mind? How are we to love one another? By his example there are at least four aspects of his love that we should emulate as we to love others.

Children's object talk:

Listening to God's Voice

Objects: A telephone

Lesson: Find time to listen to God.

Outline: 1. Telephones help us talk and listen to people many miles away.

         2. Listening to God's voice is different, yet something like talking on a telephone.

         3. Christians should find time to listen to God's voice.

NOTE: SHOW THE children the telephone. Talk with them about the fact that telephones help us talk to people many miles away. You might want to include an illustration from your own experience. Ask them about their opportunities to talk on the phone. Point out that conversation on a telephone needs to be two way. Sometimes we speak. Sometimes the other person speaks, and it is our time to listen. If we don't listen, we miss what the other person says. Ask them to imagine how they would feel if a friend called up and asked them to come to a birthday party. But they didn't listen and missed the party. That would not be fun at all. In fact we would feel very sad.

Suggest to the children that the Bible teaches that we are to listen for God's voice. Listening to God's voice is something like yet different from talking on the phone. We cannot see God as we listen to God's messages to us.

Three ways God talks to us are through reading the Bible, through other Christian people, and through coming to the church for study and worship. Christians must be careful not to become so busy that they forget to listen to God's voice.

The sermon:

Following Jesus

Hymns:
Beginning of worship: Come, thou Fount
Sermon hymn: Savior, Like a Shepherd Lead Us
End of worship: I Have Decided to Follow Jesus

Scripture: John 10:22-30

Sermon text: *"My sheep hear my voice. I know them, and they follow me."* v. 27 (NRSV)

JESUS SAID, "MY SHEEP HEAR MY voice. I know them, and they follow me." What does it take for us to follow Jesus? According to this text followership or discipleship emerges from our relationship with Jesus.

To understand our relationship with Jesus it will be helpful for us to look at the shepherd/sheep relationship in the Middle East. Jesus often used the picture of the shepherd and the sheep to help us understand our relationship with him. The picture of the shepherd was woven into the thought and language fabric of the Jewish people of his day. The Old Testament is full of the imagery of the shepherd and the sheep. Again and again in the Old Testament God is pictured as the Shepherd of a chosen people. The shepherd psalm begins, "The Lord is my shepherd." (Ps. 23:1).

In the Middle East the relationship between the shepherd and the sheep differs from anything we know in the West. In our part of the world sheep are mainly kept for slaughter. In the Middle East they are kept for their milk and for their wool. Why is this difference important? For the simple reason the Eastern shepherd and sheep are together for as long as eight or nine years. In the West the life span of a sheep is much shorter. Also in the West sheep are often left to themselves. In the Middle East the shepherd stays with his flock.

Because the shepherd and the sheep spend so much time together, a special, intimate relationship develops between them. The nature of this close relationship is picked up by two sentences in our text. The first is, "My sheep hear my voice." The second is, "I know them."

Let's take a look at the first. The sheep hear, recognize, and know the voice of their shepherd. Each shepherd has a peculiar call or cry. The sheep know this call and will answer to no other. The sheep will not respond to the call of a stranger. When a stranger calls, the sheep immediately will pause, toss up their heads, and then scamper off to huddle close to their guardian. The voice of a stranger alarms the flock. The sheep recognize and know the voice of their shepherd, but they do not know and do not respond to the voice of a stranger. The sheep hear the shepherd's voice with understanding and appreciation.

H.V. Morton in his book, *In the Steps of the Master,* gives an account of the sheep recognizing the shepherd's voice. He writes as follows: "Early one morning I saw an extraordinary sight not far from Bethlehem. Two shepherds had evidently spent the night with their flocks in a cave. The sheep were all mixed together and the time had come for the shepherds to go in different directions. One of the shepherds stood some distance from the sheep and began to call. First one, then another, then four or five animals ran towards him; and so on until he had counted his whole flock. In the Middle East the sheep know their shepherd's voice and respond to it; they respond to no other."

A child lost in a crowd can be filled with fear. Wandering through a crowd seeking to find one's mother can be an anxiety producing situation for the child. When the child hears the voice of her mother, an excitement and a calm are instantly generated. To know that one has been found brings joy. To hear the voice of an intimate brings a sense of peace.

Like the lost child recognizing the voice of Mother, we as followers of Jesus Christ recognize the voice of our Savior. Like the sheep mixed up with several flocks recognizing the voice of their shepherd, we as disciples of the Risen One recognize the sound of the Good Shepherd's voice. This recognition of the Savior's voice grows out of our having an intimate relationship with him.

Let's now take a look at the second sentence in our text: "I know them." The sheep not only hear, recognize, and know the shepherd's voice, but the shepherd knows his sheep. The shepherd's intimate knowledge of the sheep is demonstrated by the fact that a shepherd literally has a name for every sheep. Indeed, the sheep come to know their names. The shepherd calls his own sheep by name. The personal name for each sheep shows the intimacy that takes place between the shepherd and his sheep.

This intimate knowledge of the shepherd is further illustrated by the fact that in the Middle East a shepherd plays with his flock. H.B. Tristram writes in his book *Eastern Customs in Bible Lands*, "I once watched a shepherd playing with his flock. He pretended to run away; the sheep pursued and surrounded him. Then he pretended to climb the rocks; the goats ran after him; and finally all the flock formed a circle, gamboling round him." The shepherd comes to know his sheep more intimately through their play together.

Jesus, the Good Shepherd, knows his sheep. And his sheep know him. It is a relationship marked by mutual knowledge. This reciprocal knowledge is not superficial; indeed, it is intimate. It is something like the knowledge between God and Jesus. Jesus knows the Father, and the Father knows the Son. Jesus' disciples know him. Our knowledge of Christ is not a natural possession of ours. Indeed, our faith is a gift of God. Jesus Christ knows us. Our following Jesus is directly linked to our close relationship with him.

Although our faith relationship is a gift of God, it is a relationship that has to be nurtured. Jesus is prepared to know us through and through, but for us to recognize the voice of Jesus we must engage in an active relationship with him. This relationship is nurtured through prayer life, Bible reading and study, participation in a Christian fellowship, and involvement in Christian service. Without these four elements we will be unable to recognize the voice of the Good Shepherd in the cacophony of sounds in our pluralistic culture.

Many voices seek our allegiance. We can only recognize the authentic voice of Jesus if we are in intimate relationship with him.

For us to be faithful followers of our Lord requires for us to be in an intimate relationship with Jesus Christ. We can follow Jesus if there is a mutual relationship between our Savior and us. It is impossible to follow Jesus if we do know him and are not known by him. May God help us in these complex times to know the Shepherd's voice, to be known by the Shepherd, and ultimately to be his faithful followers.

Jan Chartier
Myron Chartier
American Baptist Churches of Michigan
Kalamazoo, Michigan

MAY 17, 1992

Fifth Sunday of Easter

Lessons:

Lutheran:	Acts 13:44-52	Rev. 21:1-5	John 13:31-35
Roman Catholic:	Acts 14:21-27	Rev. 21:1-5a	John 13:31-33a, 34-35
Episcopal:	Acts 13:44-52	Rev. 19:1, 4-9	John 13:31-35
Pres/Meth/UCC:	Acts 14:8-18	Rev. 21:1-6	John 13:31-35

Introductions to the Lessons:

Lesson 1

Acts 13:44-52 (**Luth/Epis**) Paul's sermon at Antioch of Pisidia was so well received that he was invited to preach again the next Sabbath. Because a great crowd came, the Jews became jealous and contradicted what Paul said. As a result, Paul and Barnabas announced that since the Jews rejected the Gospel, they would take it to the Gentiles.

Acts 14:8-18 (**Pres/Meth/UCC**) When Paul and Barnabas learned that the people of Iconium were about to stone them, they fled to Lystra where Paul performed a miracle on a cripple from birth. The people were so impressed that they considered Paul and Barnabas to be gods. They were barely able to keep the people from worshiping them.

Lesson 2

Revelation 21:1-5 (**Luth**); *21:1-6* (**Pres/Meth/UCC**) John sees a new heaven and a new earth. God has made all things new. Earth and sea have disappeared. God has come to be with his people. As a result, there is only joy and peace in the new heaven and earth.

(2) *Revelation 19:1, 4-9* (**Epis**) Heaven is pictured as a place where God is joyfully worshiped. The joy is in the wedding of the Lamb of God and the bride of the church. In heaven Christ and his faithful become one. Blessed are those who are invited to the marriage supper.

Gospel

John 13:31-35 (**Luth/Epis/Pres/Meth/UCC**). The Easter season is coming to a close and the Ascension is approaching. To prepare for this, Jesus said, "Yet a little while I am with you." It will not be long before he will be on the cross. Jesus sees this as a time of glorification. In the light of these events, he gives a new commandment to love one another.

Theme: Everyone is called by our Lord, Jesus Christ, to love one another.

Thought for the day: It is so easy to say to another person, "I love you." What do we really mean when we say those words? Jesus had in mind something very profound, yet ever so simple. When he spoke of loving one another, he showed in his own life that it should be done sacrificially, unselfishly, magnanimously and comprehendingly.

Prayer of meditation: O God, my God, as I go forth to lead others in worship this morning, I am so aware that I must first be led by you. As I contemplate your love for me and all humanity that has been revealed in my Lord, Jesus, the Christ, I know how paltry my love really is. Today let the words that will come from my mouth touch not only my heart and mind but also those who have gathered here to praise your name. I seek only to be your vessel and to render unto you an acceptable service of worship, in the name of Jesus, my Lord. Amen.

Call to worship: "The hour is coming, and now is, when the true worshipers will worship the Father in spirit and truth, for such the Father seeks to worship him. God is spirit, and those who worship him must worship in spirit and truth." (John 4:23-24)

Prayer of adoration: You, O Lord, are the giver and sustainer of life. We, your grateful people, have gathered here to praise your name and seek your blessings. May each one of us feel your presence and know your nearness. We have come to know your love and have experienced that love in the living of life. We know that you do care for each one of us and that although we are unworthy of your many blessings, you do freely love us. Come into our presence. Be in our hearts and minds that these moments spent with you may be precious and uplifting. Guide us not only today but in the week to come that we truly may be your people. Amen.

Prayer of confession: O Giver of life, we acknowledge that over the past few days and weeks we have not said and done all that you would have us say and do. We are quick to seek the praise of others at your expense, and all too often we have not stood strong or tall when we should have. You have created each one of us in your image but how unlike your image we are. We know that we cannot hide from you because you are everywhere and know everything. Our every thought, word and deed you know. We come asking for your forgiveness through no merit of our own but come because your Son has taught us that a humble and contrite heart is our only plea. We know that your love is beyond measure or description and so we ask for your forgiveness. Reshape and remold us once again that we may leave this place not only pardoned but remade. Sincerely we speak these words and ask that you hear also our unspoken words that can be found in our hearts and minds. Send us forth renewed to serve you and all humanity in all that we do and say. All this we ask for own sake and in the name of Jesus Christ, our Lord. Amen.

Prayer of dedication of gifts and self: Lord God, you have been so generous to us, your children. We are greatly blessed and have more of life's earthly treasures than we deserve. As we bring now these gifts to you, we do so as an expression of our appreciation for all that we have. Help us to use them faithfully and with care so that those who are less fortunate than we may know and experience your love and concern. We know that you love a cheerful giver and so gladly we present our gifts and offerings this day as an expression of our devotion and dedication. Bless not only the gifts but the givers as well that both may be a blessing unto you. Amen.

Sermon title: Love One Another

Sermon thesis: Love is an illusive word. In Jesus we are given a new commandment to love one another. What did he have in mind? How are we to love one another? By his example there are at least four aspects of his love that we should emulate as we seek to love others.

Hymn for the day: *"Come down, O Love divine."* Laudi, Italian vernacular hymns of praise and devotion, date from the time of Francis of Assisi (1182-1226). "Come down, O Love divine" was translated from a *lauda* by Bianco of Siena (?-1434) who lived in Venice. The beautiful musical setting for this poem with its unusual meter was written by Ralph Vaughan Williams, one of England's foremost twentieth-century composers.

Announcements for next week:
   Sermon title: Attaining Serenity
   Sermon theme: The peace that Jesus Christ offers is the true serenity in life.
   Sermon summary: Jesus told his disciples that he would give them peace which was different from that which the world could offer. No one can really attain their true potential without the inner strength which serenity can offer. It is serenity that makes possible the art of living. It is the only means by which personal happiness can be attained, personal character built and a personal faith established.

Children's object talk:

What Is Love All About?

Objects: Two different lists or bills, two envelopes and $11.00
Lesson: Love is being helpful.
Outline: 1. Conversation between Betty and Bob.
2. Bob and Betty prepare their lists and bill.
3. Mom and Dad prepare their list and bill enclosing $11.00.
BOB AND BETTY were sitting on the front porch of their home. They were brother and sister. Bob was ten years old and Betty was nine. Bob was complaining to his sister that their allowance wasn't fair. They should get more than fifty cents a week. Betty heartily agreed. It was then that Bob said he had an idea. "Why don't we draw up a bill and charge Mom and Dad for all the good things we do for them around the house?" Betty thought this sounded great.

They went inside the house and soon came back out to the porch with paper and pencil. Bob said, "We always have to clean our bedrooms each week. Let's charge $2.00 each for doing the work." So they put that on their list. Betty said, "We have to set the table for dinner each night, then clear the dirty dishes and put them in the dishwasher. Let's charge $7.00 each per week." So Bob wrote that on his list. Then he said, "I have to sweep the garage and put out the trash barrels. I think that's worth at least $2.00 a week." Betty said, "I have to help Mom with the grocery shopping and then put all the food away. I ought to get $2.00 a week for that, don't you think?" They sat there writing out their list and then copied it over in the form of a bill. They decided that they would place the bill in an envelope and put it beside their father's plate when they set the table for dinner. They couldn't wait for the evening meal.

That evening after grace had been said, their father spotted the envelope, opened it and read it out loud. (Show the children the envelope and open it, reading the following list.)

BILL FOR MOM AND DAD
FROM
BOB AND BETTY

Bob	— Cleaning his bedroom each week.	$ 2.00
Betty	— Cleaning her bedroom each week.	2.00
Bob	— Setting and clearing daily the table for dinner.	
	Putting the dirty dishes in the dishwasher.	7.00

Betty — Setting and clearing daily the table for dinner.	
Putting the dirty dishes in the dishwasher.	7.00
Bob — Putting out the trash barrels and sweeping out the garage	2.00
Betty — Helping Mom with the grocery shopping and putting everything away in the cupboard.	2.00
Total	$22.00

Mom and Dad owe Bob and Betty each $11.00

Dad stopped for a moment and then said, "Your mother and I will have to talk about this after dinner. We will let you know our decision tomorrow at breakfast.

Betty and Bob couldn't wait for morning to come and had a hard time falling asleep. Finally they did, and when they came to the breakfast table there was an envelope at their place. They opened it and read out loud the following. (Show the children the envelope and open it with the following list and also $11.00.)

BILL FOR BOB AND BETTY
FROM
MOM AND DAD

1. Providing a warm, clean and comfortable home.	Nothing
2. Providing food daily and all your clothing.	Nothing
3. Mom washing and ironing Betty and Bob's clothing and preparing 3 meals a day.	Nothing
4. Dad transporting Betty and Bob, as well as their friends, all over town.	Nothing Nothing

We do all this and more because we love *you*.

> (Signed) Love,
> Mom and Dad

Betty and Bob looked at each other and then at the $11.00 in each of their envelopes. (Show the children the $11.00.) Betty said, "I didn't think. Please take back the $11.00." Bob said, "I didn't think either. We just wanted an increase in our allowances, that's all." Mom then spoke up and said, "Your father and I would like to talk with you about an increase in your allowances tonight at dinner." Dad said, "I think we all have learned a lot today, and your mother and I want you to keep the $11.00."

The sermon:

Love One Another

Hymns:
  Beginning of worship: My Song is Love Unknown
  Sermon hymn: Immortal Love, Forever Full
  End of worship: Love Divine, All Loves Excelling

Scripture: John 13:31-35

Sermon text: *"A new commandment I give to you, that you love one another; even as I have loved you, that you also love one another. By this everyone will know that you are my disciples, if you have love for one another."* vs. 34-35

THERE IS A TRUE STORY that is told about an event which happened in the parsonage of the Reverend Samuel Rutherford, who served the Presbyterian Church in Anwoth, Scotland over 200 years ago. One evening a stranger appeared at eventide at the parsonage door and sought lodging. He was received graciously and welcomed in. It was the custom for the minister and his family to have devotions at the end of the day and the stranger was asked to join in the family service. After the pastor read the scripture for the day, each person was asked questions about the Bible. When the time came for the stranger's question, he was asked, "How many commandments are there?" He quickly responded, "Eleven." The minister was surprised and shocked at the man's ignorance and immediately corrected him by saying, "There are only ten commandments." The stranger then replied, "Have you never then read, 'A new commandment I give to you, that you love one another'?" The guest was the renowned Biblical scholar James Ussher, the Archbishop of Armagh.

  The next day was Sunday and the Reverend Rutherford asked the Archbishop to preach to his Presbyterian congregation. He used the text "Love One Another." How fitting this was because the hatred between the Anglicans and Presbyterians in that day was extremely strong. How necessary and important it is for us. too, to hear these very same words of our Lord, "Love one another," as we deal with the many different and varied people with whom we come in contact each day.

  Love, if it is real love, is not just a warm and fuzzy feeling inside which one experiences. Real love is sincerely and genuinely willing the very best for another individual. We don't seek to control them or run their life but honestly wish for them the very best. Our every act and word should emulate this reality. Our Lord, Jesus, the Christ, exemplified this very kind of love for each person with whom he came in contact each day. He wanted his disciples to live in the same way. That was why he spoke to them about a new commandment, "Love one another; even as I have loved you."

However, what was Jesus' love for others like? How did he love? First of all, he loved others sacrificially. There were no limits on his love. If it demanded the ultimate such as laying down his life, he was prepared to do just that. We see this so clearly in his willingness to bear the cross. The Apostle Paul said that real love, true love, "does not insist on its own way." (I Corinthians 13:5b) There is an event that comes to us from the Vietnam War which speaks of this kind of love. While on patrol, three black soldiers suddenly came upon a live hand grenade. Without stopping to think, the corporal in the group threw himself on top of the grenade. It exploded under his body killing him instantly, but his two comrades were saved. Later reporters were questioning the two men and the rest of the platoon as to why someone would do a thing like that. One of the members could remember the corporal saying over and over again, "You gotta care, baby; you gotta care." How much our Lord Jesus cared. If we are going to love, then we too are going to have to care, baby!

Secondly, Jesus loved unselfishly. He never approached loving from the perspective of "what's in it for me?" He did it from the perspective of the other individual. Over and over again his concern for others got him into trouble. Willingly he ate with the tax collector. Gladly he did not condemn the woman caught in adultery.

All too often, when we give our love we do it for selfish reasons. We do it because we want it to make us feel good. The motivating factor is that we are seeking our own gratification. But what kind of love is that? You and I are called upon to love our parents, our children, our spouse, our fellow human beings not because they always act in a lovable way but because we are called upon to be lovers. There isn't one of us who can claim that we are so worthy or have earned God's love. God's love, as is Jesus' love, is freely given without hesitation or reservation. Likewise, we are asked to do the same for those with whom we live. True love is always unselfishly given to another.

Thirdly, Jesus loved magnanimously. How difficult it must have been for him when at the end of his life he was all alone. His disciples fled and forsook him. Throughout his ministry they were constantly misunderstanding his teaching and every move. They were totally insensitive and callous. Yet over and over again he loved them with forgiveness. When asked how many times one should be magnanimous he said, "I do not say to you seven times, but seventy times seven." (Matthew 18:22) In essence, Jesus was saying to do it to infinity. Forgiveness must never know any bounds or limitations. How true this was even when he was on the cross. Jesus was able out of love to say to God, "Father, forgive them; for they know not what they do." (Luke 23:34a)

As we live life with others we need to be magnanimous to them as we would hope they would be to us. Yet our forgiveness must be given regardless of what another might do. Love in order to survive and thrive comes only through magnanimity. God graciously and faithfully, day after day, is forgiving us for so much we do that is wrong. We, in our simple way, as we live life together with others, must be magnanimously loving to all human beings.

Finally, our Lord Jesus loved comprehendingly. He knew his disciples as he knew himself. Their strengths and goodness as well as their failures and shortcomings were well known to him. Jesus saw them as they really were and he consistently and constantly loved them. He loved Peter although he would deny him three times. He loved Thomas although he would doubt Jesus' resurrection until he touched and saw Jesus for himself. And, our Lord loved Judas who would betray him.

You and I can never know another person until we have lived with them and can accept not only their good points but also their foibles. It has been said that "love is blind." If this is true this kind of love can only end in chaos, destruction and disillusionment. Real love, true love, is wide-eyed and open. It sees persons as they really are and loves them in spite of, not because of, themselves. Love does not demand that the other be lovable. One loves because that really is the only way in which to live. Jesus' love for his disciples, for us, and for all humanity was exactly that kind of love. That is why he said to his disciples, "A new commandment I give to you, that you love one another; even as I have loved you, that you also love one another. By this everyone will know that you are my disciples, if you have love for one another." The question which we all need to ask ourselves is, "Are we really one of his disciples? What kind of love do we really have for others?"

Charles P. Calcagni
Congregational Church
Greensboro, Vermont

MAY 24, 1992

Sixth Sunday of Easter

Lessons:

Lutheran:	Acts 14:8-18	Rev. 21:10-14, 22-23	John 14:23-29
Roman Catholic:	Acts 15:1-2, 22-29	Rev. 21:10-14, 22-23	John 14:23-29
Episcopal:	Acts 14:8-18	Rev. 21:22-22:5	John 14:23-29
Pres/Meth/UCC:	Acts 15:1-2, 22-29	Rev. 21:10, 22-27	John 14:23-29

Introductions to the Lessons:

Lesson 1

Acts 14:8-18 (**Luth/Epis**) Please see Lesson 1, Easter V:.

Acts 15:1-2, 22-29 (**Pres/Meth/UCC**) Must one become a Jew in order to be a Christian? This question threatened to split the apostolic church. To decide the issue a conference was held in Jerusalem. The unanimous decision was that we are made Christians by grace alone without any work, ceremony, or tradition.

Lesson 2

Revelation 21:10-14, 22-23 (**Luth**) *21:22-22:5* (**Epis**) *21:10, 22-27* (**Pres/Meth/UCC**) A city without a church? So it is in heaven! An angel took John to a high mountain and showed him the new Jerusalem, the city of God. He saw that the city had no temple, sun, or moon. God was the temple and the light. The gates of heaven will be always open to the righteous who will enjoy the tree of life, eternal light, and see the face of Jesus.

Gospel

John 14:23-29 (**Luth/Epis/Pres/Meth/UCC**) The very thought of leaving Jesus would be traumatic for the disciples. Realizing this, Jesus prepares them for his ascension. He promises to send the Holy Spirit to take his place, to overcome their fear and worry, he promises them his peace. Moreover, he says that if they loved him, they would be glad for him because he is going back to his Father.

Theme: The peace that Jesus, the Christ, offers is the true serenity in life.

Thought for the day: There are many philosophies and theologies which claim that they have the truth about life. The Christian, however, marches to a "different drummer" and that is the Lord, Jesus, the Christ. Jesus extends to each person a way of life which brings peace that comes only through serenity from within the individual. Until we attain that serenity it is impossible for us to develop any great art and, most importantly, the art of living itself.

Prayer of meditation: Dear Lord, you have loved me from the moment of my conception because you are the very source of life itself. I know that you seek for me to do the very best that I am able to do. This day I am about to lead others in worship so that they too may realize how great you are. Bless me now so that the task that lies before me may bring glory to your name. Many are the needs of the people who shall be gathering here this day. May I listen, feel and know of your presence. This I ask in your Son's name. Amen.

Call to worship: "Seek the Lord while he may be found, call upon him while he is near; let the wicked forsake his way, and the unrighteous man his thoughts; let him return to the Lord, that he may have mercy on him, and to our God, for he will abundantly pardon." (Isaiah 55:6-7)

Prayer of adoration: Dear Lord and Father of all humanity, to know you is to love you and to love you is to serve you. We seek in all that we do to acknowledge your love, which is beyond all comprehension. Day after day, in way after way, you have lavished upon us a love that knows no measure. Your love is more constant than the sun and deeper than any ocean. It is higher than the stars of the night sky and wider than our very minds. Come into our presence at this moment and touch the very core of our being so that we may truly worship you in spirit and in truth. All this we ask in the name of Jesus Christ, our Lord. Amen.

Prayer of confession: We, your humble servants, come now seeking, O Father, your forgiveness. We are assured by your Son that we are truly forgiven by you if we are genuinely sorry for the things we have done. How sorry we are. We know that life for us is often difficult and as we live it with others we seek our own way and pursue our own wants and desires. Many days in many ways we have had no other concerns but our own. We have tarnished the image in which you have created us and know that we have not been all that we could be and have not done all that we could do.

The needs of humanity are great and we have withheld from others, as well as from you, the very best that we have to offer. Create in us this day a new and clean heart. Help us to acknowledge that what we have been we do not need to continue to be, and give to us visions of what is good, decent and true in life. Hear us now, Lord God, and know that what we have shared with you this day are true expressions from our hearts. Humbly and contritely we ask for your forgiveness, and promise that when we leave this place of worship we shall seek to do better in all that we do and say from this day forward. Amen.

Prayer of dedication of gifts and self: O gracious Giver of life and all that we possess, we as grateful people bring back to you today what you have so graciously entrusted to us. We know that we have materially prospered because of your generosity to us and that we are in no way worthy to have so much. As we come now to your altar we do not in any way attempt to purchase your love by presenting these gifts and offerings to you. Your love is freely given and in no way can it be bought. Likewise, we freely give because we have been taught through your Son, Jesus, that "it is more blessed to give than receive." In and through his name we present these gifts. Amen.

Sermon title: Attaining Serenity

Sermon thesis: Jesus told his disciples that he would give them peace which was different from that which the world could offer. No one can really attain their true potential without the inner strength which serenity can offer. It is serenity that makes possible the art of living. It is the only means by which personal happiness can be attained, personal character built and a personal faith established.

Hymn for the day: *"Dear Lord and Father."* John Greenleaf Whittier (1807-1892), Quaker poet of Massachusetts, is a name well-known to Americans. Prevented by poverty from attending school beyond the local district school, he worked first on the family farm, then as a shoemaker and a teacher until he had accumulated enough money to attend two sessions at Haverhill Academy. Whittier was writing poetry by the time he was fourteen, having been inspired by the work of Robert Burns, and during his life edited several publications including *The American Manufacturer*, the *Pennsylvania Freeman*, and the *National Era*. The hymn is a prayer for serenity.

Announcements for Ascension:

Sermon title: Preaching Repentance and Forgiveness
Sermon theme: The church is called into being to preach repentance and forgiveness of sins.

Sermon summary: Jesus' call to preach repentance and forgiveness of sins must not be seen in the light of a vengeful or wrathful God or that God legalistically holds every human accountable for one's sins, demanding justice. God graciously and with love awaits simply the repentance of each person and freely out of his loving nature forgives them.

Announcements for next week:

Sermon title: Unity Brings Wholeness
Sermon theme: The church of Jesus Christ will never be the church until unity comes.
Sermon summary: At the heart of Christ's Gospel is the call for his church to be one. It is a call that for centuries has gone unheeded by the church as schism and division have been the "order of the day." These words need to be heard again in our time with clarity and freshness. People of good will must reach out in love to heal the wounds of hatred and division which exist not only in the world but in the church as well.

Children's object talk:

A Growing Faith

Objects: A seed (hopefully an acorn), a drawing of a tree on one side of a large poster and a drawing of a tree with many roots on the other.
Lesson: Our faith helps us to grow like the roots help a tree.
Outline: 1. What faith is not.
2. Faith is like a tree that has many roots.
3. Faith helps us to face the storms of life as the roots help the tree to stand tall when the winds blow.

ONE OF THE REASONS that you go to church school and that your parents and friends come to church is so that one's faith might grow. Faith is a hard thing to explain. The writer of the Letter to the Hebrews said, "Faith is the assurance of things hoped for, the conviction of things not seen." This means that faith is believing in things even when you can't prove them. If we know something, that then isn't faith. Knowing something we call knowledge. Second, faith is never believing in something that is not true. Faith is never opposed to truth or reason. God always wants us to use our minds. Faith never expects us to believe in things that are totally unreasonable or which are untrue. Third, having faith does not mean having no problems, difficulties or heartaches. People who have a great deal of faith also have bad things happen in their lives. Faith does not prevent or stop bad things from happening but it helps us to handle and cope with them when they occur.

I believe that faith is like a tree that grows. Can you tell me how a tree is born? That's right, a tree grows and comes from a tiny seed. (Show them the acorn or a tiny seed.) The seed is put in the ground and in time the tree begins to grow. As the tree begins to grow it gets bigger and bigger. (Show them the picture you have drawn of a tree.) Now, every tree has many roots. The taller the tree the deeper and longer the roots. I believe that faith helps a person to grow the same way that roots help the tree to grow. (Show them the drawing on the other side of a tree with a highly developed root system.) I have been told that the average tree has roots which spread out on all sides and down and that they grow in the ground equal to the height of the tree. Thus if the tree is forty feet high it will have roots that will be forty feet long. The tree lives because the roots give it food and drink. But the roots do something more that help the tree. They make it possible for the tree to survive when storms come and the wind blows. The tree would fall over, but it doesn't because the roots hold it steady. It will swing and sway and stand tall because the roots hold it snugly to the ground. The tree may even bend but it does not snap or break.

Faith acts like that for us. When the storms come and the winds blow, faith, like the roots, holds us secure. We too will bend and swing and sway, but we will not snap or be blown over. We are able to stand tall and secure if our life is rooted deep in a growing faith. There is an old saying that goes, "The lofty oak from a small acorn grows." (Lewis Duncombe) You and I are able to grow to be lofty oaks because at the very root of our life is our faith in God through his Son, Jesus.

The sermon:

Attaining Serenity

Hymns:

Beginning of worship: Our God, Our Help in Ages Past
Sermon hymn: Dear Lord and Father of Mankind
End of worship: Savior, Again to Thy Dear Name

Scripture: John 14:23-29

Sermon text: *"Peace I leave with you; my peace I give to you; not as the world gives do I give to you. Let not your hearts be troubled, neither let them be afraid."* v. 27

I CAN RECALL READING many years ago an address which was given by a man for a special occasion. I don't remember his name, where the address was given or anything about the speech except a single statement that he made. He said, There is no great art in life without serenity.

When I first read this statement I questioned its accuracy. As I have pondered it over the years I have finally come to the conclusion that he was right. I, too, believe that "there is no great art in life without serenity." Think about it—could there be any great music, great painting, great architecture, great sculpture or great literature without the creator having serenity?

I can hear you saying exactly some of the things which over the years I have said and thought. "Now wait a minute, you mean to say that those who made great contributions in their chosen fields of endeavor didn't experience turbulence in their lives, that there weren't upsets and that they weren't often torn apart?" When we look at the life of Chopin, he certainly had a turbulent life. Or remember the lives of Wagner, Beethoven, Shakespeare, Goethe, Rembrandt or Velazquez, Rodin or Saint-Gaudens. If we look at our own day and age, at the lives of Frank Lloyd Wright or Greene and Greene, their lives were anything but tranquil. Yet, I would maintain that each one of them was able to produce in whatever field of endeavor they excelled because deep within them they had a true sense of serenity or tranquility. We can liken their lives to a storm that is out on the ocean. The storm may churn up the whole sea on the surface but underneath there is a calm and a quiet. Further, I have come to the conclusion that the highest art form of all is the art of living. Unless you and I learn this particular form of art from the point of serenity, from the point of inner peace, our lives will be constantly turbulent, not only externally but internally as well. It is almost impossible to live life when we are internally torn apart, isn't it?

Serenity in and of itself is not the end of life which we should be seeking to attain. If that were the case, you and I would seek to be perpetually asleep. Sleep is an important part of life because it brings serenity to our tired minds and bodies at the end of each day. Without sleep we would not be refreshed for the coming of a new day and be ready to meet the challenges that each day holds. I believe that without a background of tranquility there can be no foreground of productivity. We all need to have a sense of inner peace or serenity.

This is what Jesus meant in today's section of scripture. He was offering his disciples an inner peace that was special. As a result their hearts would be neither troubled nor afraid.

I believe that there are at least three by-products which peace or serenity brings. First, it is the basis for our own personal happiness. We will never be happy people if we aren't serene inside. Each one of us has tried different ways and different things, haven't we? Maybe we have said, "If only we had more money in the bank, then we would have serenity." Would we? Each one of us has more money, more worldly goods than 90 percent of the whole world's population. Does this face make us happy? Or we might say, "I'm going to surround myself with beautiful things. I'll buy lovely clothes. I'll acquire the best antiques and put the finest quality rugs on the floor. I'll hang great art on my walls." Does this make us happy? I have been in homes which contain some of the loveliest things that money can buy. The people who lived in those homes often were anything but happy or serene.

Perhaps we say, "The fault is my environment. If my surroundings were beautiful, I then would be happy." Come with me to New England and to my home state of Vermont in the fall. There we will see the beautiful, blazing hillsides with all of the myriad colors. Will this make us serene if we are all torn apart and upset inside? No, it is only external and momentary. It is strange that Vermont has one of the highest rates of suicide in the United States along with all its beauty.

But you might say, "What we really need to be able to find the art of living is a challenge or excitement or thrills." I would agree that we need to be challenged in life but that still doesn't bring happiness. I have dealt with men and women who have sought excitement and thrills in all sorts of places. I would contend that one of the reasons for the massive use of drugs today is precisely for the thrill and excitement of it all. Yet, in no way have drugs, wanton sex or misuse of alcohol ever brought serenity or happiness to one's life.

Without serenity there is no great art and the greatest art is life lived happily. Our Puritan forebears were often dour people. Yet they had peace of mind. They felt comfortable with themselves. They knew who they were in spite of the fact that they had struggled with difficulties. They were like the Apostle Paul who could say, "The peace of God passes all understanding." (Phil. 4:7) They were happy with themselves because they were at peace with God. Only by being at peace with God can the art of life be found and this is what our Lord, Jesus Christ, gives.

Second, serenity not only brings personal happiness but it also builds personal character. Life needs inner resources. When we lack serenity we "botch up" our lives. When we don't have that inner peace we "mess up" as parents, we fail in our marriages, we often lose our jobs and we make a shambles of our personal relations with each other.

One of the great institutions of our day is Alcoholics Anonymous. What is one of the first lessons a member of AA learns? He or she learns what is called *The Serenity Prayer.* You are all familiar with it, I am sure. Hear it again: "God grant me the serenity to accept the things that I cannot change, courage to change the things I can, and the wisdom to know the difference."

What helps to erode serenity? Usually it is egotism and an all consuming sense of self-ambition. Sometimes it comes from the very fact that we hoard ill will in our minds or that we cherish a good grudge. It was cherishing a good grudge that destroyed King Saul. When there is serenity within the self, then there is character. We must not have a sense of jealousy, egotism or envy. Our character is dependent upon our being at peace. Serenity makes it possible for us to be truly creative, loving, understanding and kind. Thus we are able to become all the wonderful things which we really know we can be.

The Quakers believe that serenity of the self comes in quietness and in meditation. This is what builds inner strength and character. John Greenleaf Whittier was a Quaker and wrote the poetry that we sang as our hymn just before today's sermon. What was Whittier saying to us? "Dear Lord and Father of mankind, forgive our feverish ways." He was alluding to our running after this and going after that in search of all the things in life that don't bring peace, happiness or serenity. External change will not do it. It has to come from within the individual and from a character that has been carefully molded and constructed.

Finally, serenity helps to build personal faith. Faith isn't just doing good and being a nice person. These attributes are admirable but that is humanism. Real religions — the great religions — I believe have three basic aspects to them. First they believe in something greater than the human self. We as Judeo-Christians would affirm that that which is greater than humanity is God Almighty. The second thing is a philosophy of life which has meaning and is consistent, logical and reasonable. The third aspect is something that affects personal as well as social conduct and which brings out what is noble in all human beings.

I have often had conversations with many of my colleagues who have left the pastoral ministry. Many have soured on the Church and so they left. Often the reason was because things didn't work out the way they felt that they should. Deep down they lacked a sense of serenity and whom they were serving and whose world this really is. Serenity isn't something which comes raining down from heaven or, like a disease, can be caught. It has to be nurtured. It has to be part of one's genuine faith as it undergirds and becomes a genuine part of you. This kind of faith comes to the fore when the going gets rough. That is how the tough are able to succeed when the going is rough.

This is what Jesus was saying to his disciples in today's scripture. "Peace I leave with you; my peace I give to you; not as the world gives do I give to you. Let not your hearts be troubled, neither let them be afraid." It isn't a matter of going through life with a Pollyanna attitude. It sees life realistically and honestly. It acknowledges that there are problems and difficulties. We all need to roll up our sleeves and get involved in making life better. However, you and I know that there is a God and that our God loves us, supports us, sustains us and is always there. It is for these reasons we are able to be serene. We know that there is a philosophical basis and truth to the teachings of our Lord, Jesus, the Christ. They are consistent and they are right. They show us the only way in which to live. We know that we are called upon to be involved in something bigger and more wonderful than ourselves, for God expects us to make this world a better place in which to live.

Charles P. Calcagni
Congregational Church
Greensboro, Vermont

MAY 28, 1992

Ascension of our Lord

Lessons:

Lutheran:	Acts 1:1-11	Eph. 1:16-23	Luke 24:44-53
Roman Catholic:	Acts 1:1-11	Eph. 1:17-23	Luke 24:46-53
Episcopal:	Acts 1:1-11	Eph. 1:15-23	Luke 24:49-53
Pres/Meth/UCC:	Acts 1:1-11	Eph. 1:15-23	Luke 24:46-53

Introductions to the Lessons:

Lesson 1

Acts 1:1-11 (**Luth/Epis/Pres/Meth/UCC**) Luke opens his second book (Acts) with an account of Jesus' ascension to heaven. He reports that the risen Christ was on earth for 40 days during which he instructed the disciples to remain in Jerusalem and wait for the Holy Spirit who would given them power to witness to him. While they were conferring Jesus ascended in a cloud to his Father in heaven.

Lesson 2

Ephesians 1:16-23 (**Luth**) *Ephesians 1:15-23* (**Epis/Pres/Meth/UCC**) What is the significance of Jesus' ascension? In this pericope Paul explains that God raised Jesus from the dead, took him to heaven where he is seated in authority with his Father. In this position the ascended Christ has all power and authority, and all other powers are subject to him. It is this Christ who is the head of the church.

Gospel

Luke 24:44-53 (**Luth**) *Luke 24:49-53* (**Epis**) *Luke 24:46-53* (**Pres/Meth/UCC**) Luke closes his gospel with the final scene of the risen Jesus with his disciples. He explained the Scriptures to them to show that his death and resurrection were necessary for the salvation of the world. Because of this, the disciples are to give the good news of forgiveness to all nations. In an act of blessing them, he departs to heaven.

Theme: The Church is called into being to preach repentance and forgiveness of sins.

Thought for the day: Jesus commissioned his disciples to preach repentance and forgiveness of sins to the world. As a result of his death on the cross and his resurrection, humanity was freed from

374

the fear of death. Through the years the Church has had this same commission. You and I are his disciples today and we are called upon to do no less than the disciples of old.

Prayer of meditation: Dear God, my Father, it is because of your Son Jesus that I know you love me and all humanity. Your love was so clearly revealed upon the cross and I am eternally grateful to Jesus for this revelation. I swore my allegiance to him when I was ordained and as I go now to preach his Gospel may I be a faithful disciple. He instructed his true followers that he had fulfilled what had been written; that he would suffer and rise from the dead on the third day. May those who have gathered here today hear me proclaim faithfully this faith as well as the forgiveness of all sins. In his name I ask this, that you bless what I am about to say and do. Amen.

Call to worship: "O sing to the Lord a new song; sing to the Lord, all the earth! Sing to the Lord, bless his name; tell of his salvation from day to day. Declare his glory among the nations, his marvelous works among all the peoples! For great is the Lord, and greatly to be praised." (Psalm 96:1-4a)

Prayer of adoration: To you, O Lord, we come this day with grateful hearts and minds. We know that we should love you with all our heart, mind, soul and strength. You have loved us since the beginning of our existence, and we know of this love because of the sacrifice on the cross of our Lord and Savior, Jesus, the Christ. Bring us now into your presence so that we may feel your nearness and experience your love. May we hear the words that call each one of us to repentance and receive once again from your bountiful hand the forgiveness we so need All this we ask in your Son's name. Amen.

Prayer of confession: Dear Lord, we start each day with such high hopes and noble expectations. Yet, as each day comes to a close we know how we have failed to live, not only up to the very best that we could be, but have fallen far short of your image in which we were created. You have given each one of us freedom to choose for ourselves what we will do and say. All too often we have abused this freedom and have not done what we should, not been what we could. We know that the only true way for us to live is to follow faithfully the example of your Son Jesus. We approach you now through no merit of our own, but come in the name of our Lord and Savior. Here in these precious moments we come openly and honestly to seek your love and forgiveness. We repent to you silently knowing that you eagerly await our return and that you seek for us always to be your true sons and daughters. Amen.

Prayer of dedication of gifts and self: To you we give the praise and the glory, O God, for you are the font of all which we have and possess. Each one of us has been and is the recipient of your magnificent bounty. We acknowledge that we are unworthy of all that we have. Yet, we with grateful hearts present these our gifts and offerings as an expression of our love for you and our concern for humankind. Bless not only these gifts but the givers as well, so that they both may help to bring peace and love to a needy world. Amen.

Sermon title: Preaching Repentance and Forgiveness

Sermon thesis: Throughout the ages God has been seeking to reconcile humanity to himself. Unfortunately, the Church at times has clouded the issue and made it difficult for people to accept the teachings of Jesus about a loving God because of varying ideas as to why Jesus had to die. The atonement has been hard to accept for many in every age, as explained by the Church. Jesus' call to preach repentance and forgiveness of sins must not be seen in the light of a vengeful or wrathful God or that God legalistically holds every human accountable for one's sins, demanding justice. God, according to the teachings and parables of Jesus, graciously and with love awaits simply the repentance of each person and freely out of his loving nature forgives them.

Hymn for the day: *"Crown him with many crowns."* This hymn by Matthew Bridges (1800-1894) was published in 1851. Bridges, brought up in the Church of England, later became a Roman Catholic. Some of his life was spent in Canada, near Quebec. In some hymnals this hymn also includes stanzas by Godfrey Thring (1823-1893) from a hymn beginning "Crown him with crowns of gold." The hymn reviews Christ's redeeming work and his triumph.

Children's object talk:

A Note From God

Objects: A small box that is wrapped. A piece of paper inside the box with a note in large printing that says, "I LOVE YOU!"
Lesson: God loves you always and in all ways.
Outline: 1. The other day I had a dream that God spoke to me.

2. God wanted me to give you a gift from him.
3. God loves us all.

THE OTHER NIGHT as I was going to bed, I was thinking about what I would say to you today. As soon as I fell asleep I had a dream. I dreamed that God spoke to me and told me what he wanted me to tell you now. When I awoke I was thankful for the dream I'd had, and I would like to share with you what God said to me.

In the dream he told me, "I want you to tell the boys and girls that I care about them a great deal. I LOVE THEM A LOT." He then asked me to give you a gift from him. I put the gift in a box and wrapped it carefully. I have it here with me now. (Show the children the wrapped box with the note inside that says, I LOVE YOU. Ask them if they have any idea what is in the box. Open the package and show them the note.)

Yes, God loves you very much. He loves your parents, all the adults that are here in the sanctuary and all people everywhere. God loves you and me and all people so much that he gave us his Son, Jesus, so that we might know about his love and how to live. You and I are very fortunate to have a God who is like this. I don't want you ever to forget that God loves you when you are good and even when you are bad. That's why Jesus taught us to call him our Father. God is like the most wonderful father and mother that we could ever have. Aren't we fortunate that he loves us. He loves you, and you, and you, and everyone in the whole world.

The sermon:
Preaching Repentance and Forgiveness

Hymns:
Beginning of worship: All Hail the Power of Jesus' Name
Sermon hymn: Jesus Shall Reign Where'er the Sun
End of worship: Ye Servants of God, Your Master Proclaim

Scripture: Luke 24:44-53

Sermon text: *"Then he opened their minds to understand the scriptures, and said to them, 'Thus it is written, that the Christ should suffer and on the third day rise from the dead, and that repentance and forgiveness of sins should be preached in his name to all the nations.' "* vs. 45-47

THE CHURCH IN EVERY AGE has struggled to find its own identity and know its purpose. I believe that the Gospel of Luke gives us a clue as to what that purpose is. The writer records that at the end of Jesus' ministry, just before his ascension, he said it was to be a reconciling force between humanity and God by "preaching repentance and forgiveness of sins to all the nations." Jesus based this upon the Old Testament instruction and fulfillment of who the Messiah was to be. He not only was to suffer but also die as an integral part of God's divine plan for the redemption of humanity. Jesus' disciples were to remember this fact as part of their faith, not just as something to be believed; but they would also be given power as they called all nations, all people to "repentance and forgiveness of sins." Faith in Jesus as the Christ, the Messiah, was what would reconcile humanity to God.

The Apostle Paul phrased this thought in this way. "God was in Christ reconciling the world to himself, not counting their trespasses against them, and entrusting to us the message of reconciliation." (I Corinthians 5:19) This is the miracle of Christ's redemption in every age, that humanity's estrangement from God as a result of sin is forgiven. Thus we are made one with God once again by Jesus' atoning act of reconciliation known not as atonement but at-one-ment. You and I are reconciled and made one with our Father through the teachings, life, suffering and death of Jesus. It is God's Son who saves us from sin and destruction by bringing us to the true knowledge of God's redemptive love and who gives us eternal life.

Why was it necessary for Jesus to have to suffer and die? I believe it was the only way that humanity could know once and for all about the true love God has for all of us. In his life Jesus was able to show us how we were meant to live and what kind of persons we should be. His every word disclosed the true nature of our heavenly Father. By being willing to suffer and die on the cross he revealed to us how much God cared. It was God in Christ who suffered, was forsaken, was reviled and died. Christ revealed how far the love of God was willing to go, even conquering death, so that we, as humans, would know that we have nothing to fear when our own death comes. Thus you and I know there is something beyond our earthly life and that eternal life is ours, through Christ Jesus, our Lord.

This particular theory of Jesus' atoning act is known as the moral view. For me, it not only is the one that makes the most sense but it is consistent with Jesus' joyous teachings of forgiveness and redemption which is found in all four gospels. God not only is a moral Father but he has enacted moral laws which he expects humanity to follow. This view is consistent with a God who is both a creator and a lover. I believe this is what the writer of John's Gospel had in mind when he wrote, "God so loved the world that he gave his only Son, that whoever believes in him should not perish but have eternal life."(3:16) Because of Jesus' example, we are able to scale the higher heights of life, seeking to become better people. You and I are one with all humans the world over in every age, not only as part of "the family of humanity" but also because we are part of God's true family. God welcomes us back into his family when we acknowledge our failures and shortcomings by repentance, and we know that our sins are forgiven by the infinite love of God.

However, the Church has preached and taught at least two other points of view of reconciliation; and I confess neither makes sense to me, nor do I believe in any way meets humanity's needs. One such theory was first propounded by the great Dutch jurist and theologian Hugo Grotius (1583-1645). This is known as the governmental theory. Grotius is credited with being the father of international law. He argued that the only way for society to avoid anarchy and disorder is by punishing the quilty person whenever a law is broken or violated. This was also true of God's law. Thus God found it was necessary for Jesus to die as God's punishment for the sins which were committed by humanity. It was a warning to all people that it was essential for someone to be punished. The death of Jesus on the cross was necessary in order to satisfy the justice of God and the demands of his holy law. Because of what Jesus did on the cross, God no longer found it requisite to punish humanity for their own sins.

I feel that this is fallacious reasoning because it violates both a sense of justice as well as love. It is true that often in life an innocent person will suffer because of the sins of another. This is not because God's law dictates this end arbitrarily but because we are all part of the human family. Thus the innocent suffer *with* and not *instead* of the sinner. All of humanity is hurt when sin occurs. To say that God chose to inflict the pain, suffering and death upon his innocent, sinless Son on the cross, because God's sense of justice demands some form of retribution, is to render God's justice at a lower level than that of earthly governments. Western law has for centuries maintained that each person will be held responsible for his or her own conduct and action. Thank God that Western law long ago rose above the thought of a scapegoat or substitutionary as a form of punishment and justice. This point of view passes over the very fact that God's nature is not only to rule over but to love his creation. The quality of God's beneficent fatherhood over all of his creation is totally circumvented by this theory.

The second view of atonement or reconciliation is that which is held by Calvinist theologians and the Roman Catholic Church. This theory was first put forth by the Archbishop of Canterbury, Anselm, (1033-1109). He was the father of Scholasticism. It was his contention that God demands satisfaction before humanity's sins could be forgiven and redemption made possible. Only a God-man could provide this form of appeasement. It was true that Jesus had lived a perfect life. However, God requires this of all humans. Thus Jesus had no merit or grace to spare. When Jesus voluntarily took upon himself the sufferings of death, which he was not required to do, he thus made possible for all humanity a great reservoir of merit or grace which could be drawn upon by others to appease God's demands. Anselm contended that every time Mass was celebrated Jesus was recrucified, unleashing and making available more merit or propitiation for sinful humanity. God was further appeased when others such as saints imitated Christ, expanding the reservoir. The Church was the only dispenser of the storehouse of grace and this by an elaborate penitential system.

John Calvin, who lived from 1509-64, and was both a lawyer and theologian, accepted Anselm's basic premise without the penitential system. God, for Calvin, was a wrathful deity. Humanity was estranged from God as a result of their sin. It was Christ who saved humankind from God's punishment by vicariously enduring it for them on the cross. Calvin said of Jesus that he, "bore the weight of the finite anger, was smitten and afflicted, and experienced all the signs of an angry and avenging God." He believed that the ultimate characteristic of God was that of justice, and that he exacted punishment of humans according to their sins. Because Jesus suffered for humanity's sins, God forgave them. However, God was limited to forgiving only those whom he had selected for redemption. The rest of humanity was hopelessly damned to hell. In Christ, God's wrath was vented upon his Son on behalf of God's elect or chosen few.

But how does Anselm's and Calvin's theory measure up against the teachings and parables of Jesus about God's love? The parable of the Prodigal Son, the woman caught in adultery, forgiveness that should be given seventy times seven and the list could go on, answers the question itself. If God were as Calvin and Anselm maintained, the teachings and parables of Jesus would be entirely different. Thank God, they are not.

What the world needed to hear in Jesus' day was that God loved, he forgave and there was eternal life. That was why Jesus instructed his disciples to preach repentance and forgiveness of sins. What does our world need to hear today? Is it not the same as then? We all need to recognize and be reminded of God's love for all humanity; that he forgives and grants life eternal. Isn't this what the Church should be preaching?

Charles P. Calcagni
Congregational Church
Greensboro, Vermont

MAY 31, 1992

Seventh Sunday after Easter

Lessons:

Lutheran:	Acts 16:6-10	Rev. 22:12-17, 20	John 17:20-26
Roman Catholic:	Acts 7:55-8:1a	Rev. 22:12-14, 16-17, 20	John 17:20-26
Episcopal:	Acts 16:16-34	Rev. 22:12-14, 16-17, 20	John 17:20-26
Pres/Meth/UCC:	Acts 16:16-34	Rev. 22:12-14, 16-17, 20	John 17:20-26

Introductions to the Lessons:

Lesson 1

Acts 16:6-10 (**Luth**) Paul worked under the direction of the Holy Spirit. There were cities in Asia Minor where he wanted to preach, but the Holy Spirit forbid him to go there. One night he had a vision of a man from Macedonia asking him to come and help them. This vision convinced Paul that this was God's call to serve there.

Acts 16:16-34 (**Epis/Pres/Meth/UCC**) A miracle by Paul caused him and Silas to be thrown in jail. Paul cast out of a slave girl the power to tell fortunes. This ruined the owners' business. They had Paul and Silas arrested and put in prison where they at midnight sang hymns. After an earthquake the jailor asked how he could be saved.

Lesson 2

Revelation 22:12-17, 20 (**Luth**) *22:12-14, 16-17* (**Epis/Pres/Meth/UCC**) Though we have come to the end of the last book of the Bible, we have not heard the last of the risen Lord. In the concluding verses of Revelation he says that he is coming soon to earth. When he comes there will be the separation of the good and evil. The final appeal to us is to come to him and the church prays, "Come, Lord Jesus."

Gospel

John 17:20-26 (**Luth/Epis/Pres/Meth/UCC**) In his high priestly prayer offered during the Last Supper, Jesus prays for those he will be leaving on earth. He prays that his followers will be one as he and his Father are one. He prays also that they may know his and the Father's love.

Theme: The Church of Jesus, the Christ, will never be the Church until unity comes.

Thought for the day: As you and I seek to serve the Church, it is so easy for each of us to be convinced of our own church's superiority. We fall into this trap by believing that we alone are God's chosen people and that our way of belief and doing things is the only way, the true way and the only one that is correct. How wrong we are. We need to have before us consistently and constantly the prayer of our Lord Jesus regarding unity, as we seek to try to be his true Church.

Prayer of meditation: O God, I would seek on this day the spirit of your presence, so that I might be open to the oneness which you desire for all of your creation. Deep down, I know that you love all human beings because we are all your children. However, it is so easy at times to conclude that my ways and thoughts are superior to those of others. Help me to be contrite, humble, flexible and open to your oneness of spirit and truth so that all that I am about to say and do may help to bring unity and not division, love and not hate, clarity and not confusion. This I ask not for myself but for your dear Church which I so dearly love. Amen.

Call to worship: "The God who made the world and everything in it, being Lord of heaven and earth, made from one every nation of people to live on all the face of the earth, that they should seek him, in the hope that they might feel after him and find him though he is not far from each one of us." Come and let us worship God, seeking the true oneness we all share. (Paraphrased—Acts 17:24, 26, 27)

Prayer of adoration: Dear Lord, you have made all humanity of one blood. In creating you have made us inextricably bound one with another here on earth. We are glad that you love us all equally and in no way do you show any favoritism. Help us to see clearly that oneness so that we may grow in our unity to you, as well as toward one another. As we share life here on earth with each other, may the fact that we are all your children invade our every thought, prevail in our every act and pervade our every word. We know that your love is ever constant and true. This day in worship we seek your inspiration so that we may be forevermore bound in the unity and fellowship of the oneness of your love. Amen.

Prayer of confession: Almighty God, we acknowledge our myriad offenses and sins against you and our fellow human beings. These things have been done in thought and deed. They have been done overtly as well as covertly. We have wasted and neglected opportunities to do good which you in your love have given us. All too often the world's temptations have been alluring and we have sought to fill our lives with worldly pleasures instead of those of heaven. We have lived too much for this world instead of remembering that it is your kingdom of heaven we should be striving to bring here on earth. We know that you are patient with us in our vain attempts and are gracious and merciful to us when we return to you. Forgive us, dear Father, our transgressions, so that by your grace we may work in the days to come to live more worthily as your children. Amen.

Prayer of dedication of gifts and self: O Lord, you have called us to be your servants in a needy world and to share your love with all humanity. We know that you want all of your creation to be united as one. Humbly and in gratitude we bring these gifts to you this day. We pray that you will accept from our hands what in truth is your very own. We want to help bring your kingdom here on earth as it is in heaven. Thus, please bless both the gifts and the givers in this service of your kingdom. All this we ask in the name of your Son who taught that if we would save our life we must lost it. Willingly we lose it this day by symbolically giving to you these offerings. Amen.

Sermon title: Unity Brings Wholeness

Sermon thesis: At the heart of Christ's gospel is the call for his Church to be one. It is a call that for centuries has gone unheeded as schism and division have been the order of the day. These words need to be heard again in our time with clarity and freshness. People of good-will must reach out in love to heal the wounds of hatred and division which exist not only in the world but in the Church as well.

Hymn for the day: *"Lord, who the night you were betrayed (O thou who at thy first Eucharist didst pray)."* This hymn about Jesus' prayer for unity was written in 1881 and sung at an English Church Union Anniversary Service. The author, William Henry Turton (1856-1938), was born in India and commissioned in 1876 in the Royal Engineers. He retired from a military career in 1905, having been decorated on several occasions. Besides a number of hymns, he published a work on marine shells based on his collection which is now housed at the National Museum in Washington, D.C.

Announcements for next week:
Sermon title: Who Convinced You?
Sermon theme: The convincing power of the Holy Spirit.
Sermon summary: It is the Holy Spirit who convinces us of who Jesus is and who we are in relation to him.

Children's object talk:

One Means One

Objects: A shiny red apple and a knife.

Outline: 1. An apple which represents the earth. Cut it into three equal pieces.
2. Cut a third off of one of the pieces.
3. The only way in which an apple can be an apple is to have all the pieces together.

I AM HOLDING here in my hand a shiny red apple. This apple represents our earth and all the people who live on it with us. I am going to cut the apple into three pieces. (Produce the knife and cut the apple into three equal parts.)

In my right hand I have a third of the apple. This represents all the people on earth who call themselves Christians. (Cut a third off this piece. Show the small piece and larger piece to the children.) This larger section represents all the people on earth who are Roman Catholics. This smaller piece is for all those who are Protestants. This third of the apple represents all the people who have other religions and this third is for all those who have no religion.

Now, I don't have an apple, do I, if I remove any of the pieces. (Put the pieces together to form the whole apple. Remove one or several of the pieces and then say) If I remove one or a couple of the pieces I have only part of an apple. Jesus, before he died, offered a prayer to God and asked that his Church and all people be made one. He knew that everyone was important to God and that he loved them. What God and the Church need are people like you and your family and all your friends, and everyone to work each day to make all of the people on earth one. (Put all the pieces together.) Only then will Jesus' prayer be truly answered.

The sermon:

Unity Brings Wholeness

Hymns:
Beginning of worship: Lord, We Thank Thee for our Brothers
Sermon hymn: Christ is Made the Sure Foundation
End of worship: The Church's One Foundation

Scripture: John 17:20-26

Sermon text: *"I do not pray for these only, but also for those who believe in me through their word, that they may all be one; even as thou, Father, art in me, and I in thee, that they also may be in us, so that the world may believe that thou hast sent me. The glory which thou hast given me I have given to them, that they may be one even as we are one, I in them and thou in me, that they may become perfectly one, so that the world may know that thou hast sent me and hast loved them even as thou hast loved me."* vs. 20-23

IF A PERSON IS GOING to strive to be a Christian, then one has to seek to follow and obey the teachings of Jesus, the Christ. This is not an easy task and is one that demands great care and devotion. The Universal Church, which is made up of human beings who follow him, is known as the Body of Christ. The Church is neither an institution nor a building nor a certain form of government. It is Christ's physical and representative body here on earth. It can only become the Church through the oneness of his people, who become his true followers. Oneness is paramount. There is no other way.

All too often the Church has been anything but Jesus' true earthly body. It has become only an example of wanton human desires and divisions and is not a worthy representation of its Lord, who is its head. The historic witness of the Church has been one of separation, petulance, dogmatism, self-righteous behavior and chaos. The Church's "track record" couldn't be worse if it had systematically and methodically tried to be.

Somehow, our Lord Jesus seemed to know that this would happen. On that fateful last night of his earthly life, the Gospel of John records a prayer that Jesus offered. He prayed first for himself, then for his disciples and lastly for the Universal Church. It was this section of the prayer that was read to us as today's Scripture lesson. What a

386

scandal we and those who have gone before us have made of one of our Lord's greatest concerns. Hear Jesus' words again. "I do not pray for these only (he is referring to his disciples) but also for those who believe in me through the word (here he is referring to all the people who would become his followers in succeeding generations) that they may be one." Are any of us, who profess that we are Christians able to say honestly, "We are one with all others"? Is there really any sense of unity in the Church when Christian body after Christian body is willing to argue and fight for the superiority of its own position in all sorts of matters?

How many times the gospels record Jesus' concern for unity among his people. He was using symbolic language when he said, "Abide in me, and I in you. As the branch cannot bear fruit by itself, unless it abides in the vine, neither can you, unless you abide in me. I am the vine, you are the branches. He who abides in me, and I in him, he it is that bears much fruit, for apart from me you can do nothing." (15:4,5) Or, on another occasion he said, "I am the good shepherd; I know my own and my own know me, as the Father knows me and I know the Father; and I lay down my life for the sheep. And I have other sheep, that are not of this fold; I must bring them also, and they will heed my voice. So there shall be one flock, one shepherd." (John 10:14-16)

This same theme can be found in the writings of Paul. His letters were written a number of years before the gospel accounts were committed to writing. In I Corinthians he says, "For while there is jealousy and strife among you, are you not of the flesh and behaving like ordinary men? For when one says, 'I belong to Paul,' and another, 'I belong to Apollos,' are you not merely men? . . . For no other foundations can anyone lay than that which is laid, which is Jesus Christ . . . So let no one boast of men. For all things are yours, whether Paul or Apollos or Cephas or the world or life or death or the present or the future, all are yours; and you are Christ's; and Christ is God's." (3:3,4,11,21-23) And yet one more thought of Paul's found in Romans and I Corinthians: "For just as the body is one and has many members, and all the members of the body, though many, are one body, so it is with Christ. For by one Spirit we were all baptized into one body — Jews or Greeks, slaves or free — all were made to drink of one Spirit . . . Now you are the body of Christ and individually members of it." (I Corinthians 12:12, 13, 27)

Over and over again Jesus speaks of the oneness that he shares with the Father. It is that oneness that makes it possible for us to be one with others if we are his body, the Church. Only when we come to realize and recognize that God is our Father in oneness, then, and then only, are we able to function with humanity as our brothers and sisters in Christ. The unity which Jesus prayed for, lived for and died for comes only in this way.

The oneness, the unity which our Lord wanted and sought did not imply that there would be a lack of diversity. Jesus knew well that each person was different from the other. He also knew that each person had a special contribution to make in life. Everyone was unique and no two persons were the same. God in creation had made them that way. Yet the bond that the Church must have if it is to be the Church not only was to recognize this fact but to allow and encourage in love for this diversity. Jesus was not looking for all people to be the same, to be parrots, robots or puppets on a string. There was room in his Church for unity that was made possible in diversity. Conformity was to come out of love born by the realization that Jesus and God were one. All others who are his followers are to acknowledge that oneness as sons and daughters of a God who loves them. If we truly love God we will then seek to be one with all of God's creation.

Paul made this point very clear when he referred to the fact that the physical body has many members. As each member has different functions and different responsibilities, they are all in their own way part of the body. Likewise the Church has diversity among its members. The conformity which exists in the physical body is that divergent members work together so that the body can function as *one* unit. The diversity which exists among Christians should lead to conformity so that the body of the Church can function as *one* to show to the world the love that God has for his whole creation.

It has been said, "The only way we can ever win the peoples of the world to the teachings of the love of Christ is that we first must set an example to them of how much we love one another within the Christian Church." (Unknown) Our behavior and attitude toward others in and outside the Church, who differ or disagree with us, is not only scandalous but a sham to the teachings of Christ.

I can recall a story that was told to me by a good friend and Jewish scholar, Pinchas Lapide. After the Second World War, he was sent by the government of Israel to Italy to be its ambassador. One day he received an invitation to represent the Jewish world community at a special celebration of commemoration and thanks that was to take place at a monastery for Roman Catholic nuns located in the northern part of Italy. The nuns had been responsible for saving the lives of hundreds of Jews during the war. After the festivities were over, Pinchas was walking with the Mother Superior through the cloisters. She was in her late eighties and her memory wasn't all that it once had been. She turned to him and said, "Would you please help me out? What group of people were we remembering here today at this commemoration?" Kindly Dr. Lapide said, "The Jews. The State of Israel and all Jewish people around the world are thankful to you and the good sisters for saving so many Jewish lives during the past war." She then replied, "Please forgive me because you see, we saved so many peoples' lives over the years. Before the war we hid those who believed in democracy as well as those who were communists. During the war we helped the Jews. After the war we helped the fascists to find safety. I just wanted to know for sure which group of people were here today for the dedication service."

Isn't this the spirit and example that the Church should have? Are we not called to work and live for unity at all times and in all places? Jesus' prayer for oneness, I believe, should remind us that we all share in a oneness with God and that as we live we must be united one with the other in our diversity.

Charles P. Calcagni
Congregational Church
Greensboro, Vermont

JUNE 7, 1992

The Day of Pentecost

Lessons:

Lutheran:	Gen. 11:1-9	Acts 2:1-21	John 15:26-27, 16:4b-11
Roman Catholic:	Acts 2:1-11	I Cor. 12:3b-7, 12-13	John 20:19-27
Episcopal:	Acts 2:1-11	I Cor. 12:4-13	John 20:19-23
Pres/Meth/UCC:	Acts 2:1-21	Rom. 8:14-17	John 14:8-17, 25-27

Introductions to the Lessons:

Lesson 1

(1) *Genesis 11:1-9* (**Luth**). Language is a means of communication and understanding. With one language the ancient people were united in building a tower to make a name for themselves. To make them humble Yahweh confused their language to the point that they had to abandon their building. On Pentecost the Spirit enabled the Apostles to speak in the various languages of those assembled in Jerusalem.

(2) *Acts 2:1-11* (**Epis**); *2:1-21* (**Pres/Meth/UCC**). In obedience to Jesus' directive, the disciples waited in Jerusalem for the Holy Spirit. One day when they were all together, the Spirit came upon them. They were enabled to speak the language of foreigners in Jerusalem at the time. Peter explained they were not drunk with wine, as the people supposed, but filled with the Spirit. The coming of the Spirit was prophecied by Joel: "I will pour out my Spirit."

Lesson 2

(1) *Acts 2:1-21* (**Luth**). Please see above Lesson 1, Pentecost (**Pres/Meth/UCC.**)

(2) *I Corinthians 12:4-13* (**Epis**). The Holy Spirit provides nine different gifts to believers. Each person has a gift. Through these gifts services are rendered for the common good. The one source of these divine gifts is the Spirit. As the human body is one with various members, the Spirit is one with a variety of gifts.

(3) *Romans 8:14-17* (**Pres/Meth/UCC**). To be a true Christian is to have the Holy Spirit. The Spirit enables us to call God our Father. Our certainty that we are God's children is based upon the witness of the Spirit in our hearts.

Gospel

(1) *John 15:26-27, 16:4b-11* (**Luth**). Pentecost is the fulfillment of Jesus' promise that he would send the Holy Spirit. What will the Spirit do for his followers? The Spirit

390

will enable them to witness for Christ. Moreover, the Spirit will correct the world about sin, righteousness, and judgment.

(2) *John 20:19-23* (**Epis**). When the risen Jesus met with the disciples on Easter night, he gave them the Holy Spirit. By the power and authority of the Spirit they were to forgive or not forgive sins.

(3) *John 14:8-17, 25-27* (**Pres/Meth/UCC**). In his final address to his disciples Jesus promises to send in his place an Advocate, the Holy Spirit who is the spirit of truth. As such the Spirit will enlighten and teach the truth about himself and his Father. This promise became a reality on Pentecost.

Theme: The Convincing Power of the Holy Spirit.

Thought for the day: Sometimes the things that happen to us in life which seem bad turn out in reality to promote our highest good.

Prayer of meditation: In the quietness of these moments, God, speak to my heart by your Holy Spirit and cause me to be attentive to your voice. If I begin to hear you now, surely I will also be listening for your word in the prayers and proclamations of my brothers and sisters in Christ Jesus. Speak now so that I may hear. Amen.

Call to worship: Come, let us worship the God who promises us that "suffering produces endurance, and endurance produces character, and character produces hope, and hope does not disappoint us, because God's love has been poured into our hearts through the Holy Spirit which has been given to us" (Rom. 5:3b-5).

Prayer of adoration: Eternal God, our heavenly Father, we praise you for the gift of life and for making our lives abundant through the power of Christ's Spirit alive within us. May we be sensitive to that spiritual presence in our lives today as we unite our voices in hymns of praise and as we are encountered by the truth of your word. Strengthen us to dismiss any thought or action which would hinder our communion with you that our worship may be in spirit and in truth. Amen.

Prayer of confession: It is not easy for us to look closely at ourselves, O God, for there is much within us that we do not like to see. We are tempted to stiffen our defenses by closing our eyes to your truth and turning deaf ears to your word. And we certainly would were it not for your holy presence within us pricking our consciences with the realization of our sin. We confess to you now our hardheartedness and our need for your cleansing mercy and grace. Grant these now, we pray, and convince us of that better way you have planned for all your children. Through Christ our Lord. Amen.

Prayer of dedication of gifts and self: We know, our Father, that you are the God from whom all blessings flow, and we pause now to express to you our gratitude. May our offerings reflect a true spirit of thanksgiving as we bring before you not only our substance but ourselves as well. May both be blessed and used to bring persons to the Savior in whose name we pray. Amen.

Sermon title: Who Convinced You?

Sermon thesis: It is the Holy Spirit who convinces us of who Jesus is and who we are in relation to him.

Hymn for the day: *"O day full of grace."* The basis for this hymn was a pre-Reformation vernacular "day song." An ancient folk hymn, it existed in a number of versions throughout Scandinavia. The earliest source is a manuscript from about 1450 in the Uppsala University Library. It was revised for Protestant use by Hans Thomissön and first appeared in print in Danish in 1569. It appears here in a translation by Gerald Thorson (b. 1921), a professor of English at St. Olaf College in Northfield, Minnesota.

Announcements for next week:

Sermon title: Stay Tuned!

Sermon theme: God progressively reveals himself to us.

Sermon summary: God makes himself known to us progressively. He has followed this pattern in dealing with his people over the ages and also does this with us as individuals as the Holy Spirit enables us to grow in our understanding of God's will.

Children's object talk:

God's Spirit Makes Us Strong

Objects: Sheet of paper, book
Lesson: God's gift of his Spirit makes us strong.
Outline: 1. We have our weaknesses.
        2. God wants us to be strong.
        3. The gift of God's Spirit makes us strong.

THIS MORNING WE are learning about the Holy Spirit. To all who know Jesus as their Savior, God has promised to send his Spirit into their lives to make them strong.

Do you believe I can make this flat sheet of paper stand upright on this table? It doesn't matter how hard I try, it just will not do that. But what if I put the paper inside this book — will it stand up now? Sure it does — because the book has the strength to hold it up.

Our lives are like this piece of paper when we try to make it stand up all by itself. We fail, which is to say what we fail to be that God wants us to be.

God does not want us to remain weak, however. He wants us to be strong to do the things we should. So God gives us a special gift to help us. He gives us himself in the form of his Holy Spirit.

Like this book surrounds the piece of paper and enables it to stand, God's Spirit brings strength to our lives so that we can take our stand for God and be all that he wants us to be.

The sermon:

Who Convinced You?

Hymns:
  Beginning of worship: O Spirit of the Living God
  Sermon hymn: There Is a Balm in Gilead
  End of worship: Spirit of God, Descend Upon My Heart

Scripture: John 15:26-16:11

Sermon Text: *"And when he comes, he will convince the world concerning sin and righteousness and judgment. . ."* v. 8

DO YOU EVER HAVE TO BE CONVINCED? Is persuasion ever required to get you to accept or understand or "buy into" what somebody is telling you?

I suppose some people are gullible enough to believe almost anything—why else would the check-out counter tabloids do such a thriving business? Most of us, however, are not quite so foolish. We have to be convinced before we believe.

Now, with that thought, let's go back to our text. Jesus is with his disciples in the upper room. They have gathered there to share the Passover meal together, a last supper before Jesus suffers the cross.

Jesus tells his followers that he will soon be going away from them and returning to the Father who had sent him. No doubt Jesus was trying to convince them of what he was saying. Other things he had told them had failed to "sink in." This was probably no different.

While speaking of his departure, Jesus tells the disciples something which must have been particularly hard for them to accept. In fact, it is likely they were not convinced at all.

Jesus tells them that his going away is actually for their own good; it is to their advantage. Remember, these men had been with Jesus for three years. They had left everything behind to follow him. They did not know where it would all lead, but they surely had not expected it to come to this. How could Jesus possibly convince them that his going away was the best thing that could ever happen for them?

I don't suppose he did — convince them, that is. Instead, he left them with a promise. He told them that after he was gone, he would send them the Counselor and the Counselor would convince them. When the Counselor arrived, they would understand why his spiritual presence in their lives was even better than Jesus' physical presence among them.

Then it happened: Pentecost. "With the rush of a mighty wind" and "tongues as of fire" the promised Spirit came. This was the Counselor of whom Jesus spoke, the Holy Spirit of God, coming to take up residence in the lives of Jesus' followers.

Wherever they would go, the Spirit would be with them. Whatever they would do for their Lord, the Spirit would empower them. The disciples valued the time they spent with Jesus, they felt strengthened in his presence; but while he walked upon this earth, Jesus could not be physically present with all of his followers all of the time.

This is why his going away, though difficult to understand, was for their good. What Jesus could not do while physically present he could do through a spiritual presence. At Pentecost, Christ's Spirit descended upon his disciples and convinced them of their Lord's words: "Lo, I am with you always. . ."

Again, what was it that convinced those early Christians of Christ's continuing presence among them? It was the gift of the Holy Spirit. What was it that assured them that they could accomplish great things for their Lord? It was the Holy Spirit of God residing within them.

We often speak of the Spirit's ability to guide, strengthen, and comfort us. Let us not forget, however, that God's Spirit also works in our lives to convince us! Indeed, that is precisely what Jesus talks about in the passage before us today. He says the Holy Spirit convinces us of "sin and righteousness and judgment."

The Holy Spirit convinces the world of sin, Jesus explains, "because they do not believe in me. . ." (v. 9). It is as God's Spirit deals with us that we face that fact which we would prefer to forget: We are sinners. Our sin can so corrupt our inner selves that our hearts can become hardened towards the goodness of Jesus.

This, in fact, is the most basic sin of all: the refusal to believe in Jesus Christ. To say "no" to Christ is to join forces with those who nailed him to the cross. Sin reached its horrible climax in the cross of Christ. Sin had so corrupted Christ's accusers they actually believed they were doing God a service in crucifying his Son.

Just a few weeks later, however, at Pentecost, Peter preached before a large crowd that had been gathered by the strange and spectacular sounds of the Spirit's arrival. There were no doubt persons in that crowd who had been part of the angry mob that had turned on Jesus and led him to his death. This time, though, as they heard the Gospel proclaimed, the Holy Spirit convinced them and they were "cut to the heart" (Acts 2:37). God's Spirit broke through their sin and brought them to the Savior.

What made the difference? Surely it was the work of the Holy Spirit which even today, two thousand years later, can cause us to see Jesus suffering on the cross and convince us that it was because of my sin and yours that he died. If you are convinced of your sin and your need of the Savior, that is the Holy Spirit at work in your life.

Next, Jesus said the Holy Spirit convinces us "concerning righteousness, because I go to the Father, and you will see me no more" (v. 10). Jesus set the example of how we should live. He is no longer physically upon this earth, however, and we must rely upon his Spirit to convince us concerning righteousness.

First, we must be convinced of Jesus' righteousness. Either Jesus was who he said he was and who his followers claimed him to be, or he was a notorious liar, a phony, a hoax. The religious leaders of the day said he was a heretic. The government leaders called him an insurrectionist. His followers, however, knew him to be the only truly righteous person this world has ever known (I John 2:1). Only the Holy Spirit can convince us that this man who died on a cross as a common criminal was and is the Righteous One, the Son of God.

And there's more. Not only does the Spirit convince us of Jesus' righteousness, He also persuades us concerning our own. He enables us to understand that true righteousness is the result of being rightly related to God, and that only happens through faith in Jesus Christ.

Our righteousness is not based upon anything that we do, but upon what Christ has done for us on the cross. "For our sake he (the Father) made him (the Son) to be sin who knew no sin, so that in him we might become the righteousness of God" (II Cor. 5:21). It is the Holy Spirit who convinces us of the truth of these words and moves us to trust not in ourselves, but in Christ. In him alone can you and I be righteous in the eyes of God.

So far we have considered Jesus' teaching that the Holy Spirit convinces us concerning sin (v. 9) and righteousness (v. 10). Finally, he says the Spirit convinces us "concerning judgment, because the ruler of this world is judged" (v. 11).

To the authorities who ordered his death, to the soldiers who led him away to be crucified, to the crowds who looked on with scorn, it seemed that Jesus was the one being judged. Not so! It was "the ruler of this world" who was being judged.

Sin and Satan were displayed in all their horridness as Jesus hung upon the cross. That men could take the sinless Son of God, gracious, loving, and kind, and seek to destroy him shows how low we can sink in our sin.

What seemed to be evil's greatest triumph, however, became its most devastating defeat. God raised his Son from the dead; and in so doing made it clear that it is not the opinions and judgments of this world which ultimately matter, but God's. He has the final say; and the Holy Spirit convinces us that it is for God's judgment that we must be prepared.

Have you ever been truly convinced of your need of the Savior and turned to him in repentance and faith? If so, it was the Holy Spirit that brought you to that conviction. That's a part of his work in our lives. The Holy Spirit convinces us concerning sin, to bring us to repentance; and concerning righteousness, that we many no longer trust in our own, but Christ's; and concerning judgment, to bring us to decision.

James R. Thomason
Overbrook Baptist Church
Greenville, South Carolina

JUNE 14, 1992

The Holy Trinity. First Sunday after Pentecost

Lessons:

Lutheran:	Prov. 8:22-31	Rom. 5:1-5	John 16:12-15
Roman Catholic:	Prov. 8:22-31	Rom. 5:1-5	John 16:12-15
Episcopal:	Is. 6:1-8	Rev. 4:1-11	John 16:(5-11) 12-15
Pres/Meth/UCC:	Prov. 8:22-31	Rom. 5:1-5	John 16:12-15

Introductions to the Lessons:

Lesson 1

(1) *Proverbs 8:22-31* (**Luth/Pres/Meth/UCC**). According to this passage from Proverbs, the first thing Yahweh created was wisdom. This was before the creation of the earth. Before the mountains, heavens, and sea were made, wisdom existed. On this Trinity Sunday the focus of this pericope is upon God the Father, the Creator.

(2) *Isaiah 6:1-8* (**Epis**). While at a worship service in the temple, Isaiah has a vision of God the Father. He is one of majesty, glory, and holiness. Above all, he is a God of mercy who touched Isaiah's lips with the coals of forgiveness.

Lesson 2

(1) *Romans 5:1-5* (**Luth/Pres/Meth/UCC**). On this Trinity Sunday, we note the Trinity in this pericope. Paul writes that we have peace with God the Father through God the Son. God's love comes into our hearts through God the Holy Spirit.

(2) *Revelation 4:1-11* (**Epis**). John tells of standing before an open door of heaven. He sees a great throne and the company of heaven praising God with the "Holy, Holy, Holy" which may refer to the Trinity.

Gospel

John 16:12-15 (**Luth/Epis/Pres/Meth/UCC**). In this passage Jesus speaks of the Trinity. God the Holy Spirit, the spirit of truth, will come to the disciples. He will glorify God the Son. Jesus then declares that all that God the Father has given to him, the Spirit will give to the Apostles.

Theme: God progressively reveals himself to us.

Prayer of meditation: Help me to look deeply into my own heart today, Lord, that I may discover those areas which are unbecoming to one of your children. Give me the courage to see myself as I truly am, and give me the grace to become all you would have me to be. Amen.

Call to worship:
Leader: In the beginning, God made the heavens and the earth.
People: Praise the God of creation!
Leader: God was in Christ reconciling the world unto himself.
People: Praise the God of salvation!
Leader: The Spirit of God dwell in you.
People: Praise the God who is present with us now!

Prayer of adoration: We stand amazed in your presence, O God, and marvel at who you are, God in three persons, Father, Son, and Holy Spirit. Thank you for making yourself known to us through the wonder of your creation, the sacrifice of your redemption, and the power of your presence with us now. Amen.

Prayer of confession: Even as we acknowledge your holy presence among us, Lord, we must confess that we have hindered your will and way for us by keeping portions of our lives apart from your influence. You have made yourself known to us, yet we have resisted knowing you too well for fear of what might be required of us. Forgive us for the shallowness of our commitments, the selfishness which causes us to hold ourselves back from true discipleship, and cleanse us from all sin that stands in the way of our communion with you.

Prayer of dedication of gifts and self: Eternal God, Creator and Sustainer of our lives, we know that we have received from you grace upon grace and our blessings are too many to number. We count it a privilege to return unto you a portion of that which you have entrusted to our care. Receive these gifts as statements of our love and devotion unto you. Through Christ our Lord. Amen.

Sermon title: Stay Tuned!

Sermon thesis: God makes himself known to us progressively. He has followed this pattern in dealing with his people over the ages and also does this with us as individuals as the Holy Spirit enables us to grow in our understanding of God's will.

Hymn for the day: *"We all believe in one true God."* A single-stanza medieval hymn based on the creed, dating from the fourteenth century, was the basis for this hymn by Martin Luther (see January 12 above). A later German metrical version of the Creed, written by Tobias Clausnitzer (1619-1684) and translated as "We believe in one true God," can also be found in some American hymn books. Both of the hymns have three stanzas—one for each Person of the Trinity.

Announcements for next week:

Sermon title: Amazing Faith
Sermon theme: The amazing faith of the centurion serves as an example for us.
Sermon summary: Jesus found the faith of the centurion amazing because of the concern he had for his servant, the way his faith led him to take needed action, and the humility he expressed in approaching Jesus for help. The centurion's faith has much to teach us.

Children's object talk:

Growing to be Like Jesus

Objects: Two ,athematics books, one elementary, one advanced
Lesson: God wants us to grow in understanding his will.
Outline: 1. In school, we begin with the simple and move to the more difficult.
2. As Christians, we also begin with the simple and grow to new understanding.
3. God makes himself known so as to help us grow.

HERE ARE TWO BOOKS ON MATHEMATICS. I open the first one and find problems like this: "$4+2=$____" and "$7-3=$____" I open the second book and find problems like this: "$7x-y=32$, therefore $x=$____ and $y=$____." Which book is better for someone in the first grade? Why? That's right—the book on basic addition and subtraction is better because it is simpler. You must learn the material in this book (basic arithmetic) before you are ready to tackle what this other book teaches.

As Christians, we also must grow in our understanding of God's will and way for our lives. We do not know everything about God that we need to know when we first become Christians. There is still much that we need to learn as we grow to be more like Jesus.

God has provided what we need to help us grow. He sent his Son, Jesus, to show us how God wants us to live. He gave us the Bible so that we can read about his way for us. And God gives us his Spirit to help us understand his way and strengthen us to live for him each day.

The sermon:

Stay Tuned!

Hymns:
Beginning of worship: Come, Thou Almighty King
Sermon hymn: We Believe in One True God
End of worship: Take My Life, and Let It Be

Scripture: John 16:12-15

Sermon Text: *"All that the Father has is mine; therefore I said that he (the Holy Spirit) will take what is mine and declare it to you."* v. 15

"STAYED TUNED." If you ever watch television or listen to the radio, you've heard this phrase probably more times than you would like to think. Sometimes it takes other forms: "Don't touch that dial," or "We'll be right back after this important word from our sponsor."

Of course, we all know what's coming: a commercial. And, so, we are faced with a decision. Do we make our way to the kitchen or the bathroom or just reach for the remote control? Whatever we do, though, we can be sure that the station wants us to "stay tuned."

I'll confess that I don't always "stay tuned" when told. There is one announcer, however, who usually holds my attention right through the commercial. His name is Paul Harvey. He's a wonderful storyteller who seems to follow the same pattern each time he comes on the air. He tells just enough about a subject to pique your interest and then he says, "Stay tuned for the rest of the story." And I always do!

Did you know that when we study the Bible, when we consider how God makes himself known to us, and when we seek to live the Christian life, it seems that God is saying to us, "Stay tuned for the rest of the story"?

Listen to the words of Jesus in John 16:12: "I have yet many things to say to you, but you cannot bear them now." Although we do not find these words elsewhere in Scripture, surely they reveal something of the mind of God as he inspired the Biblical writers.

Jesus came to this earth to reveal the Father; but even after three years of being with his disciples, teaching them through word and deed, they still had much to learn. Jesus shared with them only what they could "bear," meaning only what they could understand or put into practice.

But then, God has followed this pattern all along as he has made himself known to us. Christians are often disturbed by certain passages in the Old Testament which fall so far short of the teaching of Jesus. What we need to remember is that God has revealed himself in a "progressive" manner, making himself known only to the extent that humankind was able to receive his message at the particular moment in history when it was given.

An often-cited example of this is the Old Testament decree to annihilate all the inhabitants and resources of a conquered city. The sound reasoning behind this practice was the avoidance of any contamination of heathen religion among God's people. God still desires that we maintain the purity of our faith and practice, even though the idea of destroying those who do not share our faith is repulsive to us. We must remember, however, that we have an advantage. We have received the fullness of God's revelation in Jesus Christ. And he taught us that we are not to destroy those who deny our faith, but to love them and serve them and share with them the good news of the Gospel.

How far God's people have come by "staying tuned in for the rest of the story." That's a principle we see at work throughout the Bible, and we need to keep it in mind as we study God's Word.

So God has revealed himself to us progressively according to humankind's readiness to assimilate his truth. In our text for today, Jesus explains how this revelation has happened and how "the rest of the story" continues to come to us today.

Jesus told his disciples that he had taught them all they could take in, but there was more to come. In verses 13-15, Jesus explained how "the rest of the story" would come to his followers. The Holy Spirit is here identified as the "Spirit of truth." His purpose is to bring people to the God of truth (Is. 65:16) who has made himself known through his Son, who is "the way, the truth, and the life" (Jn. 14:6). The Holy Spirit's concern is the communication of "that truth which makes us free" (Jn. 8:32), and he works in our lives to help us see it, understand it, and apply it.

Jesus explains further how this truth comes to us. The entire Godhead, Father, Son, and Holy Spirit, is involved. The Holy Spirit relates to us only that truth that has come to us by way of the Son, and the Son has received all truth from the Father.

Please try to follow this even if you cannot fully fathom it. We serve one God who has made himself known to us as Father, Son, and Holy Spirit. This is what we mean by the Trinity, God in three persons. And this one God has one body of truth to reveal to us and does so through the cooperative efforts of each distinct person in the Godhead.

Should this sound rather mysterious to you, know that you are not by yourself. The great theological thinkers down through the centuries have grappled with this reality and concluded that there are those things about the infinite God which cannot be fully comprehended by finite minds. The Holy Spirit guides us into some truth which can only be affirmed by faith, not explained by human reason.

Let us not forget, however, that there is much of God's truth that we can understand, and it is the Holy Spirit which makes this plain for us to see. Above all, the Spirit works in our lives to draw us to Jesus, to bring us to repentance and faith in him, and to help us understand and follow his way for our lives.

Jesus Christ is the truth that the Father wants us to receive; thus the Spirit never points us to himself but always to Jesus. In verse fourteen, Jesus says, "He (the Holy Spirit) will glorify me, for he will take what is mine and declare it to you." Just as the Son glorified the Father through his earthly ministry, the Holy Spirit glorifies the Son by bringing us to the point of understanding Christ's claim upon our lives as Savior and Lord.

So, in a way that we cannot fully understand, the eternal God, Father, Son, and Holy Spirit, works to make his truth known to us. And it is this truth of God, rooted in the Father, revealed by the Son, and communicated through the work of the Spirit, that sets us free. When we receive it by faith, God's truth sets us free from sin and death, selfishness and pride; it sets us free to experience the peace and joy of the life abundant.

If you're a Christian today, then this is how God's truth has come to you. He has revealed himself progressively, in stages, as humankind has been ready to receive his truth. And God has employed all that he is, Father, Son and Holy Spirit, in making his truth known.

There is one more thing that Jesus says in our text. Remember, he is speaking to his followers, his disciples; but through them, he also speaks to us. And what does he say? "Stay tuned . . . for the rest of the story."

"You cannot bear it all now, you cannot take everything in at once, so don't think you know all there is to know. There's more to come. Stay tuned!"

This, my friends, is the word of the Lord for us today. The same Spirit who leads us to receive Christ as Savior and Lord takes up residence in our lives to mature us daily in both our understanding and doing of God's truth.

Jesus spoke of our need to be "born again" or "born from above." Birth is the beginning of a process of growth which, if not thwarted, leads to maturity.

We are called to be disciples of God's truth, open and attentive to God's Spirit in our lives as he leads us into new truth. It is unfortunate that some Christians go for years without any new insight into the will of God. Some even fail to realize their need for anything more than what they already have.

If we are sensitive to the Spirit's leading, however, there will be those times of spiritual uneasiness as God tries to break through our preconceived notions and confront us with some new truth. When was the last time that happened in your life and mine? Could it be that some of us have gotten so comfortable in our status-quo religion that we cannot remember the last time we allowed God's Spirit to challenge us about anything?

If that's where we find ourselves today, then we can be certain that we have not "stayed tuned" to God. For as God molds us into the people he wants us to be, he must continually challenge our beliefs, attitudes, and actions. He must challenge our values and motives. He must challenge our apathy and neglect.

When we fail to allow God to challenge us, faith shrivels and the Christian life becomes a bore. The excitement is in the challenge. Joy comes through growing in the truth.

You say you're a Christian, but you haven't been challenged by God's Spirit about anything lately? Then I have a challenge for you. Shake the dust off your faith and get in touch with the Spirit of God within you, and then "Stayed tuned . . . for the rest of the story" that God has for your life!

James R. Thomason
Overbrook Baptist Church
Greenville, South Carolina

JUNE 21, 1992

Lutheran: Second Sunday after Pentecost
Roman Catholic: Ninth Sunday of the Year

Lessons:

Lutheran:	I Kings 8:(22-23, 27-30) 41-43	Gal. 1:1-10	Luke 7:1-10
Roman Catholic:	I Kings 8:41-43	Gal. 1:1-2, 6-10	Luke 7:1-10

Introductions to the Lessons:

Lesson 1

I Kings 8:22-23, 41-43 (**Luth/Epis/Pres/Meth/UCC**). Solomon completed the building of the first Temple in Jerusalem. The time has come for the dedication. King Solomon offers the prayer of dedication. He prays that Yahweh will please answer the prayers not only of the Israelites but of foreigners as well who, having heard of the fame of Yahweh, come to Jerusalem to pray in the Temple.

Lesson 2

Galatians 1:1-10 (**Luth/Epis/Pres/Meth/UCC**). For the next six weeks we will be reading from the book of Galatians written by Paul in Ephesus around 52 A.D. Paul wastes no time to get to the reason for writing. He is upset, angry, and astonished at the churches in Galatia. They are accepting a false gospel preached by false prophets.

Gospel

Luke 7:1-10 (**Luke/Epis/Pres/Meth/UCC**). From today until the end of the church year, the gospel lessons will be taken from Luke, from the Sermon on the Plain to the Passion Story. We begin with a miracle. He healed the slave of a Roman centurion stationed in Capernaum. Jesus declared that the centurion's faith was the greatest he had found in Israel.

Theme: The amazing faith of the centurion serves as an example for us.

Thought for the day: When was the last time that someone was amazed by something in our lives which was a clear result of our faith in God?

Prayer of meditation: I need this time of quiet reflection, Lord, as I prepare to express to you my adoration and praise and as I look to you for strength and grace to live my life according to your plan. Prop up my sagging faith, renew my hope, and help me to love you as I should. Amen.

Call to worship:
Leader: "O taste and see that the Lord is good! Happy is the person who takes refuge in him!"
People: "The Lord redeems the life of his servants; none of those who take refuge in him will be condemned" (Ps. 34:8, 22).

Prayer of adoration: We stand amazed in your presence, O God, and wonder how you could love us as we are. We feel unworthy of your mercies, and surely we are; but it is your love for us in spite of ourselves that draws us to you and causes us to love you more. May we grow in our love for you this day, and may our worship reflect hearts which are filled with praise and adoration for you. In your dear name we pray. Amen.

Prayer of confession: Lord, it is so easy to grow lethargic in our faith and in our witness for you. We go through the motions of Christian living, but the reality of Christlikeness seems far removed from us. We speak glibly of our faith without allowing it to move us to action. Forgive our indifference towards that which should be of most importance. Forgive our failure to do something when our actions are so desperately needed. Forgive us for getting entangled in those enterprises which ultimately count for nothing while neglecting the mission to which you have called us. Forgive us and show to us the better way. Through Jesus Christ our Lord. Amen.

Prayer of dedication of gifts and self: It is because of your great love for us, heavenly Father, that we have received the gift of life and all the resources needed to sustain it. We give to you only that which we have first received from you. Accept our offerings as tokens of our love for you and for the people of this world whom you have called us to serve. In Jesus' name. Amen.

Sermon title: Amazing Faith.

Sermon thesis: Jesus found the faith of the centurion amazing because of the concern he had for his servant, the way his faith led him to take needed action, and the humility he expressed in approaching Jesus for help. The centurion's faith has much to teach us.

405

Hymn for the day: *"A multitude comes* (Full many shall come) *from the east and the west."* Based on the parable of the great banquet found in Luke 14:15-24, this hymn was published in Magnus Brostrup Landstad's *Kirkesalmebog,* 1861. Landstad was one of ten children born to a poor parish pastor who served a church in the extreme north of Norway. Ordained a Lutheran pastor, he served a number of Norwegian parishes. He had a keen interest in the folk lore and songs of Norway and published a large and impressive collection of them in 1853. For many years he worked on the revision of the official Norwegian hymnbook.

Announcements for next week:

Sermon title: The Tale of Two Crowds

Sermon theme: The power of the Gospel to transform lives.

Sermon summary: Like the two crowds in our text that met on the road to Nain, two distinct crowds cross paths in our world today. One crowd is dominated by the certainty of death, while those who know the Savior experience the hope and joy of life everlasting.

Children's object talk:

Amaze Somebody!

Objects: Anything which amazes children: a magic trick, an animated toy, etc.

Lesson: When we try to be like Jesus, our actions surprise people.

Outline: 1. We like to be amazed.

2. Jesus often amazed people.

3. When we become like Jesus, people are amazed.

WATCH THIS! It's amazing, isn't it? Do you like to be amazed? I do, too. It makes life fresh and exciting. You cannot be bored and amazed at the same time.

Jesus often amazed people. He amazed them when he healed the sick and fed the crowd. He also amazed people by loving them and being their friend and treating them kindly. He amazed people by acting so differently from what they had come to expect.

Would you like to amaze people, too? Would you like to make others feel good because they found something you did or said to be amazing? The way to do that is to try to be like Jesus. When we try in every situation to do what Jesus would do or say what Jesus would say, people find our words and actions so different, they are amazed. Try to amaze somebody this week by being like Jesus.

The sermon:

Amazing Faith

Hymns:
Beginning of worship: O God, Our Help in Ages Past
Sermon hymn: How Firm A Foundation
End of worship: My Faith Looks Up To Thee

Scripture: Luke 7:1-10

Sermon Text: *"When Jesus heard this, he was amazed at him, and turning to the crowd following him, he said, 'I tell you, I have not found such great faith even in Israel.'"* v. 9

AMAZED, an adjective meaning "filled with wonder; astounded" (*The Random House College Dictionary*, p. 41). To be amazed can be either good or bad. A child is amazed when he sees his first circus, and we experience a bit of wonder ourselves as we see it afresh through his eyes. It is good to be amazed in this way.

We read about Hurricane Hugo, however, and we are amazed at the terrible destruction wrought by that storm. We would prefer not to be amazed in this way, but amazement happens at the extreme of life, whether good or bad.

In our Scripture passage today we read of a time when Jesus was amazed. It may strike us as amazing that Jesus, being who he was, was ever amazed by anything. In taking on human flesh, however, Jesus also assumed in some ways our limitations. Thus he could experience our thoughts and feelings; and he could at times, like ourselves, be amazed.

The Bible tells us of two instances when Jesus was amazed. One occurs in the sixth chapter of Mark's Gospel where we are told of Jesus returning to his hometown of Nazareth to teach in the synagogue located there. As you may recall, he was not well received; and Mark records that Jesus "was amazed at their lack of faith" (Mark 6:6).

That occasion represents the "down" side of amazement, but the one in the passage before us today is different. It depicts the "up" side, the positive side, of being amazed. Luke tells us of the efforts of a certain centurion to obtain help for his ailing servant, and then records this reaction: "When Jesus heard this, he was *amazed* at him, and turning to the crowd following him, he said, 'I tell you, I have

not found such great faith even in Israel' " (Luke 7:9).
Jesus was amazed at the great faith of the centurion. Let us look
back at the story to discover what it was that made the centurion's
faith so amazing.

Early in the story, we find the centurion's faith *amazing in how
it cares*. This is certainly a quality of faith. In I Peter 5:6 we read,
"Cast all your anxieties on him, for he cares for you." When we place
our trust in God, knowing that he cares deeply for each one of us,
it makes us more caring.

How does this centurion bear witness to the caring nature of his
faith? Notice in verse two that the centurion had "a slave who was
dear to him. . ." The slave was sick, at the point of death, and the
centurion was genuinely concerned for the welfare of his slave.

The word translated "dear" means "to honor, to hold in high
esteem." The caring the centurion extended to his slave was not,
therefore, a mere concern for his property. It was a sympathy, a
caring, for the person.

This was not the customary attitude for a master to have towards
his servant. Slaves were personal property, to be used by their
masters as any other tool of production, and then to be cast aside
when no longer profitable.

In that context, the centurion's concern for his slave was remarkable indeed. Surely Jesus was impressed by this man's caring. It was
a testimony to his faith.

Another evidence of the centurion's faith is found in what his concern for his servant leads him to do. His faith is *amazing in how
it acts*.

Like caring, action is another quality of faith. Faith is not just
a matter of believing, but acting upon one's belief. We are told in
Scripture that it is our actions that prove our faith genuine (Js.
2:14-18).

His servant was at the point of death. He desperately needed someone to act on his behalf. The centurion exercised his faith, he cared
enough to do something, and thus he sought help from Jesus.

This was not an easy thing for the centurion to do. He was a
Gentile, a Roman military officer; and given the relationship between
Jews and Romans, he was not the sort of person one would expect
to approach Jesus for help.

He was well aware of the potential obstacles. Rather than approach Jesus personally, he sent the Jewish elders of Capernaum to

ask for Jesus' assistance. Had he known Jesus better, he would have realized this was unnecessary — he could have gone himself and Jesus would have welcomed him. The thing we need to notice, however, is how the centurion refused to allow these perceived racial or cultural barriers to stand in the way of his need to do something.

How surprising it is — and how refreshing — when faith acts this way, refusing to dwell upon the excuses for why something cannot be done, focusing instead upon the resources available to make it happen. A vibrant faith in God produces a "can do" attitude among the faithful.

The apostle Paul, in exhorting the church at Philippi, said, "I can do all things through him who strengthens me" (Phil. 4:13). He demonstrated for them and for us the kind of faith that trusts in Christ and finds in him the strength to accomplish great things for God. Such was also the faith of the centurion.

Something else which must have astonished Jesus about the centurion was his humility. Did you notice the message he sent to Jesus: "Lord, do not trouble yourself, for I am not worthy to have you come under my roof. . ." (v. 6)? The faith of this centurion is *amazing in how it evaluates.*

This centurion was highly regarded in his community. Even the Jewish elders, who were not known for their appreciation of the Gentiles, spoke well of him and sought to convince Jesus that the centurion was worthy of his help.

The centurion himself, however, seems to have evaluated things differently. He spoke of his own unworthiness. He felt unworthy to have Jesus in his home or to have Jesus come to his aid.

No doubt Jesus recognized in the centurion's sense of unworthiness a mark of true faith. It is not the new Christian that feels most unworthy of Jesus' help, but the one whose faith has had time to mature. It is the Christian who has pondered long the loving and gracious sacrifice of his Lord who feels the greatest sense of unworthiness.

It is a characteristic of our faith journey that the more we learn of our Lord, the more we realize what we have left to learn; and the more we grow like our Master, the more obvious the differences become. It was not some new convert, but the seasoned apostle Paul, who referred to himself as "the chief of sinners!"

The centurion's faith led him to make a surprising evaluation of himself. He felt unworthy of Jesus; and, yet, he did not allow his feelings of unworthiness to keep him from seeking Jesus' help. His evaluation of himself was certainly accurate; but, then, so was his evaluation of Jesus.

"I'm not worthy to come to you or to have you come to me," he said, "but say the word, Lord, and my servant will be healed." That's faith, my friends. Amazing faith! And who would have expected it from this centurion? Even Jesus was amazed.

I wonder. When was the last time Jesus had the joy of being amazed by our faith? Perhaps it was when we managed to get self out of the way enough to truly care for another human being, especially someone we were not expected to care for. Or perhaps it was a time when we refused to make excuses or let obstacles stand in our way; and, as an act of faith, we did what needed to be done. Or maybe it was in a moment of recognizing our own unworthiness before God when we understood Jesus' supreme worthiness to be Lord of our lives and to do for us what we could not possibly do for ourselves.

It's amazing, isn't it? That kind of faith is truly amazing. The centurion had it. Do we?

James R. Thomason
Overbrook Baptist Church
Greenville, South Carolina

JUNE 28, 1992

Lutheran: Third Sunday after Pentecost
Roman Catholic: Tenth Sunday of the Year

Lessons:

Lutheran:	I Kings 17:17-24	Gal. 1:11-24	Luke 7:11-17
Roman Catholic:	I Kings 17:17-24	Gal. 1:11-19	Luke 7:11-17

Introductions to the Lessons:

Lesson 1

I Kings 17:17-24 (**Luth/Epis/Pres/Meth/UCC**) In a time of famine caused by a drought, Yahweh sends Elijah to get food and drink from a widow in Zarephath. Though she and her son are down to their last meal, she shares with Elijah and the food supply is never exhausted. After some time the widow's son gets sick and dies. She goes to Elijah for help and by prayer Elijah brings the son back to life.

Lesson 2

Galatians 1:11-24 (**Luth/Epis/Pres/Meth/UCC**) The Galatian churches are hearing two gospels. One gospel is from humans, a false gospel that demands circumcision as a prerequisite to be a Christian. Paul's gospel is from God, a gospel of grace. Paul received his gospel by revelation of Jesus.

Gospel

Luke 7:11-17 (**Luth/Epis/Pres/Meth/UCC**) Only Luke tells us of the miracle at Nain. Jesus and an accompanying crowd met a funeral procession on the way to the cemetery. Since the widow was burying her only son, Jesus had compassion on her. He stopped the procession, brought the son back to life, and gave him to his mother. It was a miracle motivated by compassion.

Theme: The power of the Gospel to transform lives.

Thought for the day: "Even though I walk through the valley of the shadow of death, I fear no evil; for thou art with me. . ." (Ps. 23:4)

Prayer of meditation: Lord, you have placed before me this opportunity to worship you and to be confronted once again by the power of your presence. May the meditations of my heart be acceptable to you. May my prayers conform to your perfect will for my life. May the hymns I sing be offerings of praise and thanksgiving. May the words of scripture and sermon that I hear be agents of your transforming grace in my life. In the Savior's name, I pray. Amen.

Call to worship: Serve the Lord with gladness: come before his presence with singing. Enter into his gates with thanksgiving, and into his courts with praise: be thankful unto him, and bless his name. For the Lord is good, his mercy is everlasting: and his truth endureth to all generations.

Prayer of adoration: Gracious and loving Father God, we worship you now as not only the one who gives us life, but also as the one who has made life worth living through the gift of your Son, our Savior. We are eternally grateful for your unspeakable gift to us and offer to you our adoration and praise. Guide us by your Holy Spirit that our worship may be worthy of one whose majesty and power is excelled only by his mercy and love. Through Christ Jesus, our Lord, we pray. Amen.

Prayer of confession: God of grace and mercy, our minds are troubled by the awareness of our failures and our hearts are heavy with guilt. You alone can forgive and cleanse and set us free to enjoy the abundant life. Thank you for your offer of forgiveness through your Son and your promise to lift completely the burden of our sins when our repentance is sincere. Lord, hear the confessions we make to you now, and assure us of your pardon. Amen.

Prayer of dedication of gifts and self: What shall we give to you, O God, who has given us everything? We bring our money as a symbol of all the physical blessings we have received from you. We bring our lives and talents to affirm that these also come from your bounty. We bring our selfish desires to ask for your cleansing that we might follow the example of our Lord and Savior, Jesus Christ, in giving to you our best and our all. In his name, we pray. Amen.

Sermon title: A Tale of Two Crowds

Sermon thesis: Like the two crowds in our text that met on the road to Nain, two distinct crowds cross paths in our world today. One crowd is dominated by the certainty of death, while those who know the Savior experience the hope and joy of life everlasting.

Hymn for the day: *"Jesus Christ, my sure defense."* This hymn proclaims, "Jesus, my redeemer, lives; I, too, unto life shall waken." An unknown author wrote this masterpiece of Christian poetry, which was first published in Berlin in 1653. The hymnal in which it appeared was prepared by Christoph Runge and Louise Henriette von Brandenburg as a means of bringing together the Lutheran and Reformed communions. Runge (1619-1681) was the son of a book publisher who followed in his father's profession. Louise Henriette (1627-1667) was the daughter of the Prince of Nassau-Orange and Stadtholder of the United Netherlands. She married Elector Friedrich Wilhelm of Brandenburg.

Announcements for next week:

Sermon title: Measure for Measure

Sermon theme: We give as we value God's gifts.

Sermon summary: Simon the Pharisee, a faithful, religious man, offered hospitality roughly according to the rules of his society. The unnamed woman gave everything she had in response to a recognition that she, too, is a human being. Each measured the gift by what he or she had already been given — although of course neither thought about that point. Our giving, like theirs, reveals what we think of God's generosity to us.

Children's object talk:

No More Tears

Objects: Handkerchief

Lesson: Jesus turns sorrow into joy.

Outline: 1. Some things make us cry.

2. A handkerchief wipes away the tears on the outside.

3. Jesus wipes away the tears on the inside.

DO YOU EVER CRY? Sure you do. Even grownups cry. We all do. Sometimes we cry because something hurts us on the outside — like when we fall down and skin a knee. Other times we cry because somethings hurts on the inside — like when someone we love dies or something happens that disappoints us. These things make us cry, don't they?

Well, look what I've got. It's a handkerchief. These come in real handy when you're crying. You can use a handkerchief to wipe away the tears.

A handkerchief takes care of the problem on the outside, but what about the problem on the inside. A handkerchief can never wipe away the pain we feel in our hearts. For that, we need Jesus. He has promised to be with us in our times of hurt and pain; and, if we ask him to, he will replace the hurt with peace and joy. A handkerchief can wipe away the tears on the outside, but it takes Jesus to wipe away the tears on the inside.

The sermon:

A Tale of Two Crowds

Hymns:
Beginning of worship: We Praise Thee, O God, Our Redeemer
Sermon hymn: Open My Eyes That I May See
End of worship: Where Cross The Crowded Ways of Life

Scripture: Luke 7:11-17

Sermon text: *"Soon afterward he went to a city called Nain, and his disciples and a great crowd went with him."* v. 11.

IT WAS THE BEST OF TIMES, it was the worst of times, it was the age of wisdom, it was the age of foolishness, it was the epoch of belief, it was the epoch of incredulity, it was the season of Light, it was the season of Darkness, it was the spring of hope, it was the winter of despair. . ." So begins Charles Dickens' *A Tale of Two Cities* providing for us an eloquent and vivid portrayal of contrasts. Specifically, Dickens compares and contrasts living conditions in London and Paris during the second half of the eighteenth century. In both places, life was very good for some but very bad for others. The contrasts were striking.

In the seventh chapter of Luke's Gospel, we find another study in contrasts. Here we discover "a tale of two crowds" who seem to have come from two cities, Capernaum and Nain.

Luke 7:1-10 (last week's lesson) tells the story of Jesus healing the centurion's servant, an event which created much excitement; and when Jesus traveled from Capernaum to Nain, a large crowd went with him. As Jesus and his exuberant crowd approach the city limits, they meet another crowd heading in the opposite direction. But unlike Jesus' crowd, this crowd is sorrowful. They are slowly making their way out of the city to the cemetery to bury a widow's only son. In the meeting of these two crowds, we discover contrasts every bit as striking as those described for us in Dickens' novel. And in studying these two crowds and what happens when they converge that day, we are reminded of some important truths regarding our faith.

Look with me first of all at the crowd from Nain. Let's call them the "funeral crowd." They are a picture of sadness and loss. They make their way to the outskirts of town bearing the body of one who had died probably only a few hours earlier.

Reality had hardly had time to grip the mother's heart, but we are impressed with the terrible weight of her pain when the dead man is described as "the only son of his mother, and she was a widow" (v. 12). Don't miss the fact that this was truly a man's world in which this woman lived; and having lost both her husband and her only son, she was left in a particularly vulnerable position. Not only was she overcome by grief but also by her sense of helplessness and aloneness in the world.

For this widow who had now lost her only boy, this was truly, to use the words of Charles Dickens, "the worst times. . . the season of darkness. . . the winter of despair. . ." Heartbroken, she leaves a trail of tears as she travels toward her son's grave, surrounded by people who could offer her neither comfort nor hope.

So many people in our world today are part of this funeral crowd. They may not realize it. Death may not have invaded their circle of family and friends to impress this reality upon them. They may be living the "good life" thinking it will go on forever, but then the unexpected happens and they find themselves trapped in their own "winter of despair." All those who attempt to travel through this world without God eventually join the ranks of the funeral crowd.

But now let's look at the other crowd who was on the road that day. We'll call them the "Jesus crowd" since they were gathered because of their attraction to Jesus. This crowd had evidently traveled with Jesus from Capernaum. Recall again that it was in Capernaum that Jesus healed the centurion's slave who was at the point of death until Jesus interceded. Word of this miracle got around quickly, and a crowd of folks joined with the disciples to follow Jesus.

The "Jesus crowd" was an excited bunch. They had heard Jesus speak and seen him act and knew that he did both with authority. They perceived that he was a prophet, at the very least, and wondered if perhaps he could be the Messiah. Certainly he had touched their lives already, and they followed him joyfully. For them, this was "the best of times. . . the season of Light. . . the spring of hope. . ." Faith filled their lives, they felt close to God, and life was good for the "Jesus crowd."

I think it's safe to say, however, that neither crowd was prepared for what happened when the two groups met on the road that day. No doubt the Jesus crowd began to make their way to the side of the road as they saw the funeral crowd approach. They were prepared to let them pass by — an act of common courtesy and respect in that day just as it is in ours.

Jesus, however, did not move aside as expected. Instead, when he saw the dead man's mother, his heart went out to her. He told her not to cry and then touched her son's coffin. "Young man," he said, "get up." And he did! Not only did he sit up, but he began to talk. Then Jesus gave the young man back to his mother, turning her tears of sorrow into tears of gratitude and great joy.

Notice the reaction of the crowds. At first, they were fearful; but then fear gave way to excitement and praise. And so a funeral procession was transformed into a celebration of life, an affirmation of the greatness of God.

Recently I heard Dr. Tony Campolo speaking on the power of the Christian Gospel to transform lives. He told of going as a young man to a black church to attend the funeral of a friend who was killed suddenly in an accident.

Campolo said the preacher spoke for a few minutes from the pulpit on the Christian understanding of death and eternal life. Then the preacher stepped down from the pulpit and went over and stood by the family. He assured the family of God's presence and grace which would be sufficient for their needs.

Then the preacher went and stood by the body of the young man. He called his name, apologized for not saying some things to him earlier, but went on to affirm the young man's faith and Christian character.

And then the preacher did something Campolo said he would never forget. He looked at the young man's body, called his name again, and said, "Now it's time for us to tell you goodnight. . . so goodnight!" he shouted as he slammed the casket lid shut. Then he added, "But we know God's going to give you a great morning!"

And with those words, the choir began singing "In that great gittin' up morning," and people began shouting and singing and praising God for the victory that is ours in Christ Jesus. In the midst of sadness there was also joy, and once again a funeral became a celebration because of the Good News of Christ.

What a wonderful picture that is of the power of the Gospel to transform lives, to change despair into hope and death into victory. How sad it is that so many persons in our world have yet to experience abundant life and hope through faith in Jesus Christ. And how sad that we who are members of Christ's Church, we who are part of the "Jesus crowd" today, often slip timidly to the side of the road and let the "funeral crowd" pass by without ever telling them of the Savior who still reaches out his hand to overcome the powers of sin and death and to lift people to newness of life.

James R. Thomason
Overbrook Baptist Church
Greenville, South Carolina

JULY 5, 1992

Lutheran: Fourth Sunday after Pentecost
Roman Catholics: Eleventh Sunday of the Year

Lessons:

| Lutheran: | 2 Sam. 11:26-12:10, Gal. 2:11-21 13-15 | Luke 7:36-50 |
| Roman Catholic: | 2 Sam. 12:7-10, 13 Gal. 2:16, 19-21 | Luke 7:36-8:3 |

Introductions to the Lessons:

Lesson 1

II Samuel 11:26-12:10, 13-15 (**Luth**) David committed adultery with Bathsheba. When she notified him of her pregnancy, David had her husband, Uriah, killed. Soon after, he brought her into his palace as his wife. Yahweh sent the prophet Nathan to make David realize his sin. When David confessed, he was assured of forgiveness but the child would die.

Lesson 2

Galatians 2:11-21 (**Luth**) Paul and Peter have a face-to-face confrontation concerning Peter's inconsistent behavior. When he was with Gentiles, he acted like a Gentile. When Jews came to Antioch from Jerusalem, he lived by Jewish rules. Paul challenged Peter to be consistent in living by grace and not by good works.

Gospel

Luke 7:36-50 (**Luth**) An unnamed prostitute crashes a dinner party in a Pharisee's home where Jesus was the honored guest. The woman expresses her gratitude to Jesus by washing his feet with her tears, drying them with her hair, and pouring precious perfume on him. When Simon, the host, objects to Jesus' allowing the woman to touch him, Jesus responds by teaching him that the more one is forgiven, the more one loves.

Theme: We give as we value God's gifts.

Thought for the day: Our gifts to God tell God, us and others how valuable we consider God's gifts to us to be. Let us ask ourselves how our actions show our appreciation for the blessings of life God showers on us daily.

Prayer of meditation: We remember with thanksgiving, O God, that you have called us to be your beloved, precious people. You have made us priests who share the treasure of your forgiveness with one another and tell the world about your love. Accept our heartfelt thanks for all your mercies, but especially for the gift of your faithful love. Amen.

Call to worship: Come, let us draw near to the God who loves us and who daily surrounds our lives with caring and forgiveness. Let us raise our songs of thankfulness and praise to our Maker, Defender, Redeemer and friend.

Prayer of adoration: Ruler of all creation, who knows every living creature and remembers the name of every child of grace within your heart, we give you thanks that we may again come together to praise and glorify your holy name. Be present with us now to share our rejoicing and hear our gratitude. We pray in the name of Jesus Christ, your Son, our Savior. Amen.

Prayer of confession: Merciful and ever-loving God, we come before you remembering that we have not been faithful to you as you have been faithful to us. We have not been generous to you and to others as you have been generous to each of us. We have done wrong and have refused to do what is right. We have thought ourselves and our gifts more worthy, more valuable to you and to your creation than the gifts of others. Most of all we have rated our behavior as more loving, more faithful and more worthy of your approval than the behavior of others. Forgive us for not understanding that you love, respect and value each person. Help us to grow daily in the ability to love and value each other and to find in others' love and affirmation your own loving presence. We ask this in the name of Jesus Christ who died to save us. Amen.

Prayer of dedication of gifts and self: Source of all blessings, we offer to you with joy and thanksgiving these gifts which we have received from you. With them we give you thanks for all the blessings of our lives; shelter and family; jobs and food and clothing; good friends and a supportive community. Receive these gifts as our acts of thanksgiving for all your love toward us, and by your Holy Spirit empower us, through our thankfulness, to share your blessings with all the neighbors you have given us in your creation. Amen.

Sermon title: Measure for Measure

Sermon thesis: Simon the Pharisee, a faithful, religious man, offered hospitality roughly according to the rules of his society. The unnamed woman gave everything she had in response to a recognition that she, too, is a human being. Each measured the gift by what he or she had already been given — although, of course, neither thought about that point. Our giving, like theirs, reveals what we think of God's generosity to us.

Hymn for the day: *"Lord, thee I love with all my heart".* The sermon today discusses our response to God's gifts. Today's hymn (st. 2) recalls that it is God who has given us all that we have and prays that we may respond appropriately. The hymn, based on Psalms 18 and 73, was written about 1567. It has been a favorite of many through the centuries. The author, Martin Schalling, studied at the University of Wittenberg and began his ministry at Regensburg. Although he was a moderate and peace-loving man, Schalling lived in a time of great turmoil and controversy in Protestant Germany. Twice he was removed from his position (the second time placed under house arrest) because of his refusal to comply completely with the religious leanings of the persons in power.

Announcements for next week:

Sermon title: The Best Never Rest

Sermon theme: Christ's suffering and resurrection can give meaning to our daily suffering.

Sermon summary: We can take up our crosses daily because Christ has risen. So we can be strengthened in our suffering by the loving companionship of the one who knew suffering in order to redeem us and give us eternal life. Because he lives, we receive grace to endure and to live with him.

Children's object talk:

Love Changes Things

Objects: Thumbprint pictures transformed into flowers, jack-o-lanterns, small animals and other delights.

Lesson: We can make a difference

Outline: 1. Things that seem unimportant or even messy can become delightful pictures.

2. People change when you love them.

3. Try to reach out to people with trust. Many will become your friends.

WHEN I FIRST saw thumbprint pictures, I was astonished. But I wanted to try them. I didn't want to mess my clothing and was a bit careful the first time I wet my thumb, put it into the paint and placed it on the paper. The first flower I printed was black; it also had black leaves. Then I looked and said, "Flowers aren't black. They are pretty colors and have green leaves."

Soon I had a page with a green frog, a brown rabbit, an orange jack-o-lantern, a red flower with green leaves and three black cats, two sleeping and one sitting up. Following a book with black thumbprint diagrams I found I could fill a blank page with delightful creations. I just had to trust myself and try.

I changed the messy thumbprints with just a few lines drawn with a pen. All of a sudden a messy page of thumbprints was full of wonderful, funny animals. I added a bluebird, a spider, and a furry rabbit ready to sink its teeth into a carrot.

You can also change people with a smile, a friendly "Hello," a hand reaching out. They may seem shy or even turn their backs away. Yet when they turn toward you, you may see a beaming smile where before there was a frown, or a frightened or anxious look.

You can change people if you let them see that you like them. Sometimes it is as easy as making a few strokes of the pen over a messy thumbprint. Try it and see how it works for you.

The sermon:

Measure for Measure

Hymns:
Beginning of worship: Joyful, Joyful We Adore You
Sermon hymn: We Give Thee But Thine Own
End of worship: Thou Whose Almighty Word

Scripture: Luke 7:36-50

Sermon text: *". . . (H)er sins, which are many, are forgiven, for she has loved much; but whoever is forgiven little, loves little."* v. 47.

ONE ARGUMENT often used against weekly Holy Communion is, "After all, we aren't that sinful!" Jesus Christ gives us his very body and blood in loving faithfulness; yet the reason we offer for shying away from the gift, except on rare occasions, is that we really do not need it all that much!

In common with Simon the Pharisee we regard ourselves as good, religious people. We certainly try to live faithfully. Even God would grant us that.

Certainly Simon also tried to live faithfully. We can imagine him burning the oil of a lamp late into the night reading the Torah faithfully as a Jewish man was called to do. We can imagine that he gave the full tithe to the Temple and bought the best sacrifices for the appropriate feasts. We can imagine he attended synagogue regularly to make up the minyan (ten men) needed to begin the worship service.

Simon was a religious man. He knew Jesus would be delighted to accept the invitation to dine at his house. For his part, he was honored and delighted to have the company of this illustrious rabbi whom everyone went to hear when he preached. So he spread a huge and tasty feast. Only the best was good enough for his guest. He could afford to be generous.

The woman, by contrast, could not afford her gift. But she dared to give it — at Simon's house. We can only guess at what she was doing there. What we know is that she felt impelled by some prior contact with Jesus which had astonished her and moved her to lavish generosity. What he had done? Her gift and the love with which she gives it tell us that surely he had treated her as a valued person, perhaps even as a friend, although everyone else considered her not worth the dirt under their feet.

Simon undoubtedly gave to God the full measure of what the Law required in daily Torah reading, in worship attendance and in offerings of money and sacrifices. Simon also gave Jesus, who was his guest, a banquet fit for a famous friend. Yet he had missed the courtesy of giving the guest an opportunity to wash his feet — surely an oversight, for it appears to have been a common custom.

No Torah could tell the woman what gift was an appropriate response to the love and humane regard which she had received from Jesus. She just gave back everything she had to someone who had given her everything in life worth having — human affection, respect and dignity. Her gift showed how much she valued the gift.

In forgiving her sins Jesus revealed to Simon and all others present that he was not only a highly acclaimed preacher. He was also God with us, Immanuel, with power to forgive sins, to change human lives, and to welcome everyone who would give their love and loyalty to him. He could forgive Simon for his lapse in etiquette and the woman for her sins. What he would receive in return would be a measure of how his gift of himself, and his presence, was valued by Simon and by the unnamed woman.

What we give to God, not only in our offerings to the mission of Christ's Church, but also in terms of caring for creation and its resources, probably says a lot about whether we are more like Simon or more like the woman whom her society called a sinner. When we were baptized, we were reborn children of God. How we value that precious gift is revealed daily in our actions. Are we meticulously careful of our dwindling natural resources or are we greedy and careless in wasting earth's bounty? Do we persistently seek justice for others or are we selfishly unwilling to insure that all people everywhere receive the justice that we desire for ourselves? Do we give generously to the mission of the Church, or do we carefully measure what we give to God and even give that gift last if at all?

Where do these and our other actions show that we stand? Are we Simon, inviting God to share the riches which, after all, we worked hard to earn? Or are we the unnamed woman, so astonished at the wonder of the gift of our adoption as children of God that nothing we can ever do can be gift enough to respond.

God has generously given us the greatest gift in the universe. Jesus told his disciples (and therefore each baptized Christian) "No longer do I call you servants. . . but I call you friends."

How can we measure the wonder, the immeasurable value, of that precious gift! What loving response, and what responsible love for the earth, for others and for our Savior Christ, could possibly be fit to offer to such a friend?

LaVonne Althouse
Salem Ev. Lutheran Church
Philadelphia, Pennsylvania

JULY 12, 1992

Lutheran: Fifth Sunday after Pentecost
Roman Catholic: Twelfth Sunday of the Year
Episcopal: Proper 7 (June 21)
Pres/Meth/UCC: Second Sunday after Pentecost (June 21)

Lessons:

Lutheran:	Zech. 12:7-10	Gal. 3:23-29	Luke 9:18-24
Roman Catholic:	Zech. 12:10-11	Gal. 3:26-29	Luke 9:18-24
Episcopal:	Zech. 12:8-10, 13:1	Gal. 3:23-29	Luke 9:18-24
Pres/Meth/UCC:	I Kings 19:9-14	Gal. 3:23-29	Luke 9:18-24

Introductions to the Lessons:

Lesson 1

(1) *Zechariah 12:7-10* (**Luth**); *12:8-10, 13:1* (**Epis**) In Zechariah's time (518 B.C.) the Babylonian exiles have returned to Jerusalem. He encourages them with a message of victory over their national enemies and with a promise that Yahweh will pour out upon them a spirit of compassion and will cleanse them of their sin.

(2) *I Kings 19:9-14* (**Pres/Meth/UCC**) To escape from Queen Jezebel who was out to kill him, Elijah hides in a cave in the wilderness. The Lord asks him what he is doing there. Elijah confesses his depression. In a small voice God reveals himself to Elijah.

Lesson 2

Galatians 3:23-29 (**Luth/Epis/Pres/Meth/UCC**) With faith in Christ there is a whole new ball game! Before faith we were slaves of the Law. By baptism we are now in Christ and live in the freedom of grace. By our faith we are children of God and we are all one in Christ.

Gospel:

Luke 9:18-24 (**Luth/Epis/Pres/Meth/UCC**) Jesus asked his disciples the $64,000 question: "Who am I?" Prompted by the Spirit, Peter confessed that Jesus was the Christ, the Savior, the Messiah. Now Jesus is ready to carry out his messiahship by going to Jerusalem to die. He calls upon his followers to do the same: deny self, take up the cross, and follow him to death.

Theme: Christ's suffering and resurrection can give meaning to our daily suffering.

Thought for the day: Immanuel, God-with-us, was willing to suffer, die and be buried rather than lose us. The resurrection of Jesus Christ and the companionship of the Holy Spirit day by day will give us strength to love God and endure our suffering faithfully as Christ loved us and suffered death for us.

Prayer of meditation: I remember with thanksgiving and wonder how your life was given for me, Lord Jesus Christ. Give me faith to trust that you are risen indeed and that your love will never take me where your grace cannot keep me. Amen.

Call to worship: Come to the living water, poured out by the rock who is our salvation, our Savior Jesus Christ. Let us join together to praise the one who gave himself for us, so that we might live with him, in him and for him forever. Amen.

Prayer of adoration: O God who came to live among us as Jesus the Christ, we return this morning to renew our promise to live with you and in you and for you day by day. We give you thanks for life and all your mercies that give life joy. We come to delight in your presence together and to find strength to love you so that every day we may remain faithful to you, to each other, to your people in all the world, and to all of your creation. We bless and praise your holy name. Amen.

Prayer of confession: O God who loves us far better than we deserve, we confess that we have not trusted your love for us. We have felt isolated, alone, bereft. We have not trusted the presence of your Holy Spirit, nor have we sought for understanding and compassion from the sisters and brothers you have given us. We have sought to be strong in our own power to endure rather than opening our hearts to the power of Jesus' resurrection. We have done what we should not have done and have left undone things that we should have done. We have turned away from your love and the love of others in the Church, the body of Christ, that was available to us. Forgive us for our fearfulness, our foolishness and our pride which isolate us when we most need your healing and saving power. By your grace, draw us back to your healing presence in the company of your holy Church. We pray in the name of Jesus Christ, our Savior. Amen.

Prayer of dedication of gifts and self: God who gives us the gift of power to our lives, we return now to you a token of the gifts you have given us. With them we also pledge again to give our whole lives into your loving care. We ask you to use our gifts and talents, the days of our lives and even the sufferings we endure as channels of your love and as a means by which all the world may come to see and know your love and grace. We pray in the name of Jesus Christ, who died and rose again that we might become willing and able to give our lives to you forever. Amen.

Sermon title: The Best Never Rest

Sermon thesis: We can take up our crosses daily because Christ is risen. So we can be strengthened in our suffering by the loving companionship of the one who knew suffering in order to redeem us and give us eternal life. Because he lives, we receive grace to endure and to live with him.

Hymn for the day: *"Let us ever walk with Jesus".* This hymn, which speaks of cross-bearing in the second stanza, speaks throughout of a life-long companionship with and commitment to Jesus. Based on Luke 18:31-48 and first published in 1653, it was originally intended for Passiontide. (Remarks on the author, Sigismund von Birken, can be found at April 12 above.)

Announcements for next week:

Sermon title: We Learn in the Long Run
Sermon theme: Journeying with Jesus is full of surprises.
Sermon summary: When Jesus was on his way to the cross, following him was a strange, risky and unpredictable business. That may also become true for us as we follow him today. We learn a great deal about being disciples as we follow Jesus to Calvary.

Children's object talk:

Jesus Never Leaves Us

Objects: A medium size cross on a chain
Lesson: You can trust Jesus to stay with you.
Outline: 1. Eleanor was afraid of her illness.
2. She learned to trust Jesus to be with her.
3. You can count on Jesus, too.

ELEANOR SAW BY HER MOTHER'S FACE that what the doctor said scared her mother. But to Eleanor the doctor said, "You are going to get well again. Only it will take a long time. Sometimes you will have to be in the hospital for a while."

When her mother had to leave Eleanor in the hospital and go home for the first time, she gave Eleanor a cross too big for her to wear —

but it was on a chain. "Keep this," said her mother, "and look at it often until I come back tomorrow. Remember when you hold it that Jesus Christ is holding you in his arms just as I would if I were here." When her mother was away, Eleanor would take the cross out of her drawer, hold it, remember what her mother had said, and pray.

The treatment for her illness made Eleanor lose her hair. Other girls and boys in the hospital lost theirs, too. They talked about what they would tell their friends. "I'll say the wind blew it away," said one boy. A girl spoke up. "Guess why I just fired my hairdresser!" she said, laughing. "Look what happens when you don't eat your vegetables," said another child. Eleanor decided she would take off her wig when her friends visited her and tell them, "Don't ever, ever stop taking your vitamins!"

Eleanor wanted more than anything else to go back to her junior high school. "I want to go to the prom. I want to graduate from high school," she said when asked her dearest wish.

Time passed. Eleanor prayed every day and trusted the doctor's promise. Now she is in tenth grade. Her dark brown hair is long and beautiful. She is looking forward to her junior prom.

"Jesus is always with you even if your parents have to go away," she tells everyone who will listen. "I know."

The sermon:

The Best Never Rest

Hymns:
> Beginning of worship: Before the Lord We Bow
> Sermon hymn: O God, Our Help in Ages Past
> End of worship: Praise, My Soul, the King of Heaven

Scripture: Luke 9:18-24

Sermon text: *"Let those who would come after me deny themselves and take up their cross daily and follow me. For whoever would save their lives will loses it; and whoever lose life for my sake, they will save it."* vs. 23, 24.

NOBODY IN OUR SOCIETY wants to carry a cross. At least no one I know. What would it mean for us today if we accepted Jesus' invitation to take up our cross each day and follow him?

Jesus' cross brought him enormous suffering and finally death. Did he intend for his followers to wish their deaths?

Jesus died rather than disobey God or deny God's leading. He died rather than abandon his mission to save us from our sins. He died rather than give up on us. When we see Jesus suffering and dying on the cross we see just how far God will go to reach out to us, to bring us back to a relationship with God. Jesus' death and resurrection assure us that the best never rest.

Jesus shows his faithfulness to us, and God's faithfulness to us, by taking up his cross. In dying he tells us there is no price we are not worth. His resurrection declares that no power of evil in all creation can separate us from the love of God which is shown in Jesus Christ.

For these reasons we can say that the cross is for each of us, above all, the final and clearest sign of God's faithfulness to each baptized Christian and to all of creation. In taking up his cross Jesus Christ declares God's faithfulness for all time and eternity.

What then does it mean for us to take up our cross daily? First of all, it means that each day we pray God's Holy Spirit to give us the power to remain faithful to God no matter what happens to us.

Taking up her cross was not, for Eleanor, being brave while she was sick. Rather it was looking at the cross and remembering that Jesus was always there for her, faithful to her, no matter what she suffered. Whether she lived or whether she died, in her baptism she belonged to Jesus. When she took the cross in her hand, she remembered whose she was. That remembering, and asking for faith to believe, was her act of taking up the cross.

Taking up the cross does not mean enduring persecution rather than give up our faith. Yes, it is true that most of Jesus' twelve apostles and many other Christians did in fact die terrible deaths rather than renounce their Lord and Savior. For them taking up the cross daily was praying each day for strength to follow Jesus faithfully and not worship any other gods.

But the cross they bore was the vow of faithfulness they took to the Lord who had been faithful to them until death. The cross they bore with courage by the power of the Holy Spirit was a sign of the God to whom they belonged, who would never let them go. Neither did they let go of that loving and faithful God.

God does not "send us crosses." God never intended that human beings should suffer and die. Death and sin came into the world through the disobedience of the first woman and the first man. At the tomb of Lazarus Jesus showed us how God responds when we suffer and die. At that tomb Jesus wept. When we suffer and die, God holds us in loving arms and weeps with us. Immanuel, God-with-us, died on the cross and rose again to overcome all suffering and death. That is what it means to bring salvation.

Jesus took up his cross as a sign that God is faithful to human beings, no matter how we may waste the resources of our planet, no matter how much injustice we create and perpetuate, no matter how our unfaithfulness to God and others creates hunger and homelessness and disease.

We agree to take up our cross daily when we refuse to become cynical and despairing, when we refuse to give up on God and therefore on life. We agree to take up our cross daily when we remind ourselves daily that the love of God will never take us where the grace of God cannot keep us. We agree to take up the cross each day when we pray to remain faithful to God no matter what happens to us.

We ask God to deliver us from evil. God did this in the death and resurrection of Jesus. God continues to do this as the Church advocates for justice for all people and the wise use of earth's resources. God will at the end of time deliver us from all evil forever. The best never rest.

Until the final deliverance, however, we pray daily that we may respond to the command of Jesus to take up the cross and follow him. He who has given us the will to pray for the strength to take up the cross will give us power daily to perform this obedient action.

LaVonne Althouse
Salem Ev. Lutheran Church
Philadelphia, Pennsylvania

JULY 19, 1992

Lutheran: Sixth Sunday after Pentecost
Roman Catholic: Thirteenth Sunday of the Year
Episcopal: Proper 8 (June 28)
Pres/Meth/UCC: Third Sunday after Pentecost (June 28)

Lessons:

Lutheran:	I Kings 19:14-21	Gal. 5:1, 13-25	Luke 9:51-62
Roman Catholic:	I Kings 19:16b, 19-21	Gal. 5:1, 13-18	Luke 9:51-62
Episcopal:	I Kings 19:15-16, 19-21	Gal. 5:1, 13-25	Luke 9:51-62
Pres/Meth/UCC:	I Kings 19:15-21	Gal. 5:1, 13-25	Luke 9:51-62

Introductions to the Lessons:

Lesson 1

I Kings 19:14-21 (**Luth**); *19:15-16, 19-21* (**Epis**); *19:15-21* (**Pres/Meth/UCC**) When Jezebel threatened his life, Elijah fell into a state of depression. He felt he was a failure. To overcome his discouragement the Lord fed him through an angel, revealed himself in a still, small voice, and now sends him on a mission to secure a new political leader in Jehu and a new spiritual leader in Elisha.

Lesson 2

Galatians 5:1, 13-25 (**Luth/Epis/Pres/Meth/UCC**) A Christian is the freest of all people, because a person in Christ has been set free from the bondage of the Law with its demands. Nevertheless a Christian is free to live in the Spirit resulting in a ninefold path of virtue.

Gospel

Luke 9:51-62 (**Luth/Epis/Pres/Meth/UCC**) Today's gospel lesson begins a section that is given by Luke only. It consists of Christ's teachings on his way to Jerusalem. In this passage there are two kinds of potential followers. When the people of a Samaritan village through which Jesus was passing refused to welcome Jesus, James and John wanted to wipe them out but Jesus would have none of it. The other group consisted of half-hearted would-be followers, but Jesus demanded total commitment.

Theme: Journeying with Jesus is full of surprises.

Thought for the day: When the unexpected happens, Jesus may be there in the midst of the event teaching us.

Prayer of meditation: Help me surrender my life daily to you, O Lord Jesus Christ, who gave your life for me. Amen.

Call to worship: Come to the fountain of all blessings, the God who daily renews our faith by loving faithfulness that provides for our every need. Come with thankful and joyful hearts and be refreshed. Amen.

Prayer of adoration: God, who claimed us as your children when we were baptized, and who daily renews our faith by your continuing providence, we come before you with thanksgiving and joy. Come now to bless our worship as we delight in each other's company and share your holy presence together. We pray in the name of our Savior, Jesus Christ, and the Holy Spirit. Amen.

Prayer of confession: O God, who is always more ready to forgive than we are to confess, we acknowledge that we have not loved and served you faithfully as you have been faithful to us. We have been too busy with our own burdens and sorrows to care for others who need us and to remember you and your faithfulness. We have neglected what we should have done and have done what we should not have done. We have forgotten your presence, your power and your loving providence. Forgive us for our sins, and help us by the power of your Holy Spirit to live more faithfully. We pray in the name of our Savior, Jesus Christ. Amen.

Prayer of dedication of gifts and self: Blessed are you, Giver of Life. We offer with joy and thanksgiving what you have first given us, our selves, our time and our possessions, signs of your gracious love. Receive these gifts and bless them to your use and us to your daily service. We pray in the name of Jesus Christ. Amen. (*Lutheran Book of Worship*, Augsburg-Fortress Publishing House. Used by permission.)

Sermon title: We Learn in the Long Run

Sermon thesis: When Jesus was on his way to the cross, following him was a strange, risky and unpredictable business. That may also become true for us as we follow him today. We learn a great deal about being disciples as we follow Jesus to Calvary.

Hymn for the day: *" 'Come, follow me,' the Savior spoke"* This hymn of discipleship asks for guidance as we follow Christ throughout our lives. A native of Silesia, Johann Scheffler (1624-1677) studied medicine and eventually became Court Physician to Emperor Ferdinand III. Scheffler's father, of Polish nobility, had been forced to leave his homeland because of his adherence to Lutheranism. Johann, however, became interested in mysticism, and later joined the Roman Catholic Church, adopting the name Angelus Silesius after a Spanish mystic. In 1677 he gave up his profession to be ordained a priest.

Announcements for next week:

Sermon title: Just Do It!

Sermon theme: Calling two by two started early; the church still needs this ministry.

Sermon summary: Jesus sent out seventy people, representing the number of nations in the world, to Gentiles to tell them of God's love. That may have scandalized devout Jews, but those who obeyed found their work blessed. There may be a message here for us today.

Children's object talk:

Journeying with Jesus

Objects: Travel brochures

Outline: 1. You and your parents plan your vacations.

2. Jesus goes on a lifelong journey with us.

3. We learn about that journey as we worship.

HAS YOUR FAMILY ever planned a journey — a trip to the shore or to Disneyland or (name the nearest amusement park) by looking through some brochures like these with you? Did you enjoy reading them and dreaming about the journey before you started out? Did the trip live up to your expectations? (Stop to listen to the children's answers to each question and make informal appropriate comments in response.)

Did anyone ever tell you that life is a journey? Can you believe that? If you have just moved here from another place, you must be wondering what school will be like here this year and how many new friends you will make. If you graduate from elementary school and start middle or junior high school, you are going to a strange new place as surely as if you started out on a trip.

Now, however, there are no brochures to tell you what to expect. The adventure ahead is a mystery. Sometimes that makes us eager. We want to know what's ahead. Sometimes the unknown scares us more than we want to admit. Then what do you do?

We will talk all morning about the time Jesus started out on a journey that had a lot of pain and sorrow before its happy ending on Easter. What happened on Easter? (Children may know the answer, that Jesus was alive after being dead. If not, you will have to remind them.)

Jesus walked through life and death and came out on the other side. Now he comes back to each of us in our lives to walk with us into the unknown future.

He doesn't have brochures to give us to help us get excited about the good things that are coming. But he does promise that no matter what happens, whether it is good or bad, he will be there to help us. He will heal us if we become ill. He will comfort us when we are hurt. He will stay with us if everyone else leaves us. He will provide for us and protect us when we need his help.

We learn how much we can count on Jesus as we read the Bible and worship God with other Christians. Instead of travel brochures, we have the stories we can share with each other of the times Jesus rescued us and helped and comforted us and shared our joys and celebrated with us. Ask your parents and grandparents and adult friends to tell you these stories. Also, listen to the Bible's stories of people who tell what God did for them. All these stories will help you know more about the Jesus you can count on to walk with you, just as the brochures tell you about the trip you will be taking.

The sermon:

We Learn In The Long Run

Hymns:
Beginning of worship: I Know That My Redeemer Lives
Sermon Hymn: Jesus Calls Us; O'er the Tumult
End of worship: O Word of God Incarnate

Scripture: Luke 9:51-62
Sermon text: *Jesus said to them, "No one who puts his hand to the plow and looks back is fit for the kingdom of God."* v. 62

VACATION TIME IS A season of journeys. But the trips we are planning are different from the journey we see Jesus start in today's gospel.

His is a strange and painful and necessary and beneficial journey. Painful because at its end is the cross of Calvary. Necessary and beneficial because it will open eternal life to you and me. Strange because of things he says along the way.

When Samaritans refuse Jesus hospitality, the disciples want to call down fire from heaven to destroy their city as punishment. They remember Elijah called down fire to consume the offering on the altar when the god of Baal's priests had no power to respond. But Jesus says their idea is not the way of the cross. He will repeat this when soldiers come to arrest him and Peter takes a sword and cuts off the ear of one of them. He will heal the ear, tell Peter to stop fighting, heal the wound, and continue to the cross. He will choose what God calls him to do.

Our journeys through life may meet with similar rebukes we do not understand. When the U.S. Supreme Court ruled several years ago that flag-burning was an act of free speech protected by the First Amendment many Americans did not like the decision. Jesus' disciples had difficulty accepting some decisions he made on the way to the cross. He helped them understand why the decisions were right. When we have to turn to our faith and wrestle with decisions, we hope the Holy Spirit will help us to see what is right for us to do in order to be faithful.

Jesus warned one volunteer that if he decided to follow Jesus he would never know where his next meal is coming from nor where he would sleep at night. Again, we are startled. Isn't it true that if you follow God's way, God will always take care of you?

Jesus replies that following the way of the cross means risking that things will not always be O.K. Sometimes there will be hunger and thirst, want, suffering, even death for him and for many in the early years of the church.

It is hard to hear that. But Jesus decided anyone getting on board with him ought to face reality as he or she made the decision.

When we decide to follow Jesus we cannot expect things always and everywhere to come our way. God does provide. But God's people take risks as we follow the way of the Cross.

But why wouldn't Jesus let the man go bury his father first? The oldest son of a Jewish family must perform that rite! Why not let another volunteer say farewell to family, when Elisha said goodbye to his parents before giving up all to follow Elijah?

The urgency Jesus felt as he started to Jerusalem to die is hard for us to fathom. We may not have a lot of understanding or empathy for it. But on our journeys through life each of us will come to those times when we will know it's now or never — when everything else must be dropped to do what this moment requires if we are to do the right thing.

Such moments of decision will never be easy. Family and friends may or may not understand. Albert Schweitzer gave up a flourishing medical practice in civilized Germany to found a hospital in the jungle of Gabon. What woman wants to keep house there? Raise a family? Where will the children go to school?

In the coming weeks we will journey with Jesus on the way to the cross. He will say and do things that surprise us. We will struggle with what they mean for us. But this we will always know: the difficulties with which he wrestles are real.

Sometimes we face similar difficulties in our own lives. When we do, we remember that as we journey with Jesus on his way to the cross, so also he journeys with us through all of our life, including the difficult places. We need to learn all we can about this traveling companion who is with us to help us. As we come to know him, we will learn more about the many wonderful ways we can count on him to sustain us when we are in difficulty, in danger, in trouble.

Worship is a weekly journey on which we learn more about the Lord who accompanies us on our journey through life. To know him better is to know completely how we can count on him when we need him. So let us journey with him and learn all we can.

LaVonne Althouse
Salem Ev. Lutheran Church
Philadelphia, Pennsylvania

JULY 26, 1992

Lutheran: Seventh Sunday after Pentecost
Roman Catholics: Fourteenth Sunday of the Year
Episcopal: Proper 9 (July 5)
Pres/Meth/UCC: Fourth Sunday after Pentecost (July 5)

Lessons:

Lutheran:	Is. 66:10-14	Gal. 6:1-10, 14-16	Luke 10:1-12, 16 (17-20)
Roman Catholic:	Is. 66:10-14	Gal. 6:14-18	Luke 10:1-12, 17-20
Episcopal:	Is. 66:10-16	Gal. 6:(1-10) 14-18	Luke 10:1-12, 16-20
Pres/Meth/UCC:	I Kings 21:1-3, 17-21	Gal. 6:7-18	Luke 10:1-12, 17-20

Introductions to the Lessons:

Lesson 1

(1) *Isaiah 66:10-14* (**Luth**); *66:10-16* (**Epis**) In this last chapter of Isaiah, Jerusalem is personified as a mother. As a mother nurses her baby, the people are nourished. She carries her child and comforts it. In the same way the Lords feeds, cares for, and comforts his people.

(2) *I Kings 21:1-3,17-21* (**Pres/Meth/UCC**) Can a person get away with murder? King Ahab could not. His wife, Jezebel, had Naboth stoned to death for not selling the lot bordering the king's palace. Yahwah sent Elijah to announce to Ahab that disaster and death would come to him.

Lesson 2

Galatians 6:1-10,14-16 (**Luth**); *6:14-18* (**Epis**); *6:7-18* (**Pres/Meth/UCC**) In the closing chapter of Galatians, Paul once again brings up the subject of circumcision as a requirement to be a Christian. It is not a matter of circumcision or no circumcision. It is a matter of faith in Christ, of being a new person in Christ. Again, he assures us that salvation is by grace and not by works.

Gospel

Luke 10:1-12,16-20 (**Luth/Epis**); *10:1-12,17-20* (**Pres/Meth/UCC**) Jesus had more than twelve followers. Here he sends out seventy, two by two, to preach and heal in places he intended to go later. Some of the people will accept them and others will reject them, but it is really Christ who is accepted or rejected. The mission was a great success. Satan and his demons were put to flight.

Theme: Calling two by two started early; the church still needs this ministry.

Thought for the day: Only a few religious groups go out calling two by two to seek new adherents to their faith today. Jesus calls us to ask what we are doing in our day that accomplishes the triumph the seventy enjoyed on their first mission.

Prayer of meditation: Thank you, O Lord, for empowering women and men to tell the gospel story to strangers in many lands, including our own. Help me to support this outreach and show me where to act. Amen.

Call to worship:
> Come, O come, O quickening Spirit,
> God of every race and time,
> Visit us with your salvation;
> Fill us with your grace divine. Amen.

Prayer of adoration: God, who promised to make all nations inheritors of your grace through Abraham, and who fulfilled that promise through the death and resurrection of Jesus Christ, we praise and bless your holy name. Come to renew our lives as we come to renew our covenant with you, promising to tell all whom we meet the story of your love. Amen.

Prayer of confession: God, who loves us and will never let us go, we confess that we have not loved you with our whole hearts. We have been embarrassed to tell others the good news of what you have done for us. We have been unfaithful to you in ways that we know and in ways that we do not fully understand. We are sorry and we are ashamed both of our failures to do well or to do good and for our misdeeds. We ask your forgiveness. By the power of your Holy Spirit, grant that we may become channels of your love to all whom we love and all whom we encounter. We pray in the name of Jesus Christ our Savior. Amen.

Prayer of dedication of gifts and self: Merciful giver of all that we possess, we return these offerings as tokens of the lives we rededicate to your service. Bless what we have given here to be used for your glory, and bless us in our daily lives that we may continually be channels of your love. We pray in Jesus' name. Amen.

Sermon title: Just Do It!

Sermon thesis: Jesus sent out seventy people, representing the number of nations in the world, to Gentiles to tell them of God's love. That may have scandalized devout Jews, but those who obeyed found their work blessed. There may be a message here for us today!

Hymn for the day: *"Hark, the voice of Jesus calling"* On October 18, 1868, Daniel March preached a sermon based on Isaiah 6:8, "Here am I; send me." Finding no hymn appropriate to the text, he wrote this hymn, which was sung from manuscript. March (1816-1909), a native of Millbury, Massachusetts, studied at Yale and was ordained a Presbyterian minister. He later became a Congregationalist and ministered to several congregations of that denomination.

Children's object talk:

Never On Sunday

Objects: Checkerboard and checkers
Outline: 1. We like to share our games and toys with friends.
2. Jesus told his friends to bring others to him.
3. We can share our friend Jesus with other friends.

MARCIE WAS eight when Kevin moved next door with his parents and baby brother Jimmy. Kevin was also eight. They walked to school together. Sometimes Kevin came to her house to play and sometimes she went next door.

One day they watched Marcie's father and uncle play checkers together. Both wanted to learn to play. When Uncle Fred went home, Marcie's father taught them the game. They liked it so much that it was hard for Kevin's mother to coax him to come home at night. They learned the game on Tuesday, and every day after that they spent all day playing checkers.

On Saturday night, Kevin said, "Goodnight, Marcie. I'll be over tomorrow morning to play checkers again."

"No, Kevin, I won't be here. I have to go to Sunday school tomorrow. Then we go to church. Then we have to eat. I can't play checkers tomorrow morning at all!"

"What is church?" asked Kevin.

"It's where we learn about God and Jesus and sing and pray. We have to do it once a week, on Sunday."

"Can you play checkers in church?" asked Kevin.

Marcie looked at her mother. "No," she said. "We'll have to leave the game at home. You can play after we have Sunday dinner."

"But Kevin can come to Sunday school with me," said Marcie. "Tommy and Kathy from the third grade come."

"Tommy goes to your Sunday school?" asked Kevin.

"Kevin will have to ask his mother if he may go with you," warned Marcie's mother.

"I want to go. I want to go. Mom!" called Kevin, running out the door and climbing over the railing that separated the two porches.

Mrs. James came to the door. "Mom, may I go to Sunday school and church with Marcie?" he asked. "Tommy goes there, too!"

Mrs. James looked at Mrs. Perkins. They talked about where the church was, the time for Sunday school, and the time for worship. Mrs. James said she would find out if her husband would bring the family to visit the congregation the next day.

Marcie learned that evening that she could share more than her games with her friend, Kevin. She could also share her friend, Jesus, with him.

The sermon:

Just Do It!

Hymns:

Beginning of worship: Jesus Shall Reign Where'er the Sun
Sermon hymn: I Love to Tell the Story
End of worship: Rise Up, O Saints of God! or O Zion, Haste

Scripture: Luke 10:1-12, 16 (17-20)

Sermon text: *"Whoever hears you hears me, and whoever rejects you rejects me, and whoever rejects me rejects the one who sent me."* v. 16

IN THE GOSPEL LESSON for today Jesus is repeating an action we read about a few weeks ago. He is sending seventy missionaries out two by two this time — he sent only twelve before. Did the twelve successfully recruit these disciples on their earlier visits? Have they now been trained to go out two by two to bring back more disciples for more training? Would you welcome these visitors into your home and gladly hear about Jesus Christ if they came to visit you?

Most of us do not welcome house-to-house callers of any kind. I resist the salespeople. Usually I invite the religious people in warning them that I am a Lutheran pastor, but listening with interest to what they have to say. But from Mormons or from Jehovah's Witnesses, the only callers who come, I have learned no new ways of making door-to-door visits.

You may think such an approach foolhardy. But if you are distressed about house-to-house callers who tell of their faith, remember at least that Jesus was one of the people who initiated the idea! He said, "Whoever rejects you rejects me, and whoever rejects me, rejects the one who sent me." In other words, "Just do it!"

Apparently folk received the seventy well. Some callers had such good experiences that they reported having seen Satan fall like lightning from heaven!

How do you feel about being sent out on such a mission? As Jesus puts it in today's lesson, they were to "heal the sick and say, 'The Kingdom of God has come near to you.' " In other words, "You are cordially invited to join us and learn how the kingdom of heaven is emerging in our very midst!" If Jesus asked you, would you go on such a journey?

If the congregation's evangelism committee members asked you, would you go on such a walk through this neighborhood? If a new person moves into your block, do you drop by to welcome them? Do you invite them to visit your congregation?

There is no precedent among the religious Jewish people of Jesus' day for making such visits either among their own people in the community or to the Gentiles who lived among them. Polite and intellectually curious Gentiles sometimes came to sit at the rear of synagogues to learn about Jewish worship. Roman soldiers were under orders to respect the religion of the peoples in the countries they occupied. Probably it looked well on your military record if you had a reputation of being a God-fearer (inquirer) in Palestine.

Knowing even this little, we can understand that Jesus expected at least some positive reception from the Gentiles. The story says the disciples returned "with joy." If they were half as apprehensive of going out as you or I would be, you know how amazing that report is.

How did Jesus get them to go out in the first place? He said, "Just do it!" To receive them, after all, was to receive him and to reject them was to reject him — and God!

When we hesitate to invite friends to church, does Jesus say to us also, "Just do it!"? After all, could it hurt to ask?

When members of the evangelism committee ask you to visit new neighbors, is Jesus behind them calling you to "Just do it!"? Would Jesus ask us to go out two by two today if he realized how that looks to our society? One wonders, reading the story, where he got seventy volunteer visitors, as well as how he equipped and encouraged and prepared them for such an effort, even once.

Growing congregations, say the church growth experts, are congregations where members regularly invite family members, friends, neighbors, co-workers or others they know to visit and worship with them. We tell the old, old story. We have a story to tell to the nations (that's who the Gentiles were). It is a story of how people move out on God and how God continually tries to move in on us.

You are invited to pray daily that God's reign will continue to come into our world. You are invited to help that reign flourish by inviting others to worship with you and to tell what God has done for you. You are invited to help others discover what God is doing in their lives and to respond with thanksgiving and joy.

Will you begin by praying daily for God's reign to extend to all people? Will you help strengthen that reign by inviting others to worship with you? Remember, Jesus says, "Just do it!"

LaVonne Althouse
Salem Ev. Lutheran Church
Philadelphia, Pennsylvania

PART II

Other Worship Planning Resources

Preaching from the Common Lectionary

Resources
for
Preaching

by David H. Schmidt*

One-volume commentaries to be used throughout the three year cycle include:

James L. Mays, general editor, *Harper's Bible Dictionary*, (Harper & Row, 1988). Published in cooperation with the Society of Biblical Literature, this new one-volume commentary provides good brief information which reflects the current state of scholarship. There are good overview articles as well as comments on each book (including the Apocrypha). A second current one-volume work is Raymond E. Brown et al. *The New Jerome Biblical Commentary*, Revised edition (Paulist Press, 1989). While Roman Catholic in origin, it is a valuable tool for all. About two-thirds of revised edition is new material.

Books for study of the Psalter for all three years:
Overview and Theology

H.J. Kraus, *Theology of the Psalms* (Augsburg, 1986) is a good discussion by a scholar who has also published a major commentary (below). A briefer but insightful work is C. Westermann, *The Living Psalms* (Eerdmans, 1988). It would serve as a fine introductory study.

*David H. Schmidt is Campus Minister at the Wesley Foundation, United Methodist Church, Northern Illinois University in DeKalb, Illinois.

Commentaries

H.J. Kraus, *Psalms 1-59* and *Psalms 60-150* (Augsburg, 1987, 1989) is one of the most detailed works of this century. For those who want a less formidable study, A.A. Anderson, *The Book of Psalms*, The New Century Bible Commentary (Eerdmans, 1972) is a solid, yet inexpensive two volume set that will serve the pastor well. Don't overlook C. Stuhlmueller in the Harper's commentary above.

ORDINARY TIME, Aug. 4 to Nov. 24, 1991

For the study of the Gospel lessons (John five times and Mark eleven times):

Overviews

D. Moody Smith, *John*, Proclamation Commentary, 2nd ed. (Fortress 1986) will provide a good overview for John. A more detailed discussion may be found in Robert Kysar, *The Fourth Evangelist and His Gospel: An Examination of Contemporary Scholarship* (Augsburg, 1975).

Paul Achtemeier, *Mark*, Proclamation Commentary, 2nd rev. ed. (Fortress, 1986) will provide a fine overview for Mark. Werner H. Kelber, *Mark's Story of Jesus* (Fortress, 1979) provides a good sweeping account with many insights.

Commentaries

Raymond E. Brown, *The Gospel According to John*, Anchor Bible 29, 29A (Doubleday, 1966, 1970) is an excellent work for exegetical study. Couple this with the expository effort of Gerald Sloyan, *John*, Interpretation Commentaries (John Knox, 1988) for a solid set of resources. For those who desire more on the Greek, C.K. Barrett, *The Gospel According to St. John*, 2nd rev. ed. (Westminster, 1978) continues to be popular.

For Mark, Lamar Williamson, Jr., *Mark*, Interpretation Commentaries (John Knox, 1983) provides a solid expository study. One could supplement it with Eduard Schweizer, *The Good News According to Mark* (John Knox, 1970) which has a number of helpful insights for the pastor. Or W.L. Lane, *Commentary on the Gospel of Mark*, New International Commentary on the New Testament (Eerdman's 1974) is a solid evangelical study. Ched Myers, *Binding the Strong Man: A Political Reading of Mark's Story of Jesus* (Orbis, 1988) is a socio-literary study that challenges one to rethink Mark even if you disagree with the author.

For the completion of the David saga (four times):
Good expository assistance is now available in Walter Brueggemann, *First and Second Samuel,* Interpretation Commentaries (John Knox, 1990) and Richard D. Nelson, *First and Second Kings,* Interpretation Commentaries (John Knox, 1987). The former is especially helpful. If one wants an exegetical supplement, P.K. McCarter, *II Samuel,* Anchor Bible 9 (Doubleday, 1984) and G.H. Jones, *1 and 2 Kings,* Vol. 2, New Century Bible Commentary (Eerdmans, 1984) are suitable recent studies.

Books for the study of Epistle lessons during this time (Ephesians five times, James four times, Hebrews seven times):
Markus Barth, *Ephesians,* Anchor Bible 34, 34A (Doubleday, 1974) is a detailed study which will provide the pastor with plenty of material. A smaller work that can be a suitable starter is C.L. Mitton, *Ephesians,* The New Century Bible Commentary (Eerdmans, 1976).

James has benefited from several good studies of late. One might begin with James B. Adamson, *James,* The New International Commentary on the New Testament (Eerdmans, 1976) or S. Laws, *A Commentary on the Epistle of James,* Harper's New Testament Commentaries (Harper & Row, 1980). For a scholarly book on the Greek text see Peter Davids, *Commentary on James,* New International Greek Testament Commentary (Eerdmans, 1982). An interesting overview can be found in Elsa Tamez, *The Scandalous Message of James* (Crossroads, 1990).

F.F. Bruce, *The Epistle to the Hebrews,* Rev. ed., The New International Commentary on the New Testament (Eerdmans, 1990) is a solid place to begin for Hebrews. Harold W. Attridge, *Hebrews,* Hermeneia (Fortress, 1989) is a fine study on the Greek text, but the book is designed so others can use it without too much trouble. Ernst Kaesemann, *The Wandering People of God* (Augsburg, 1984) is a well recognized treatise which might be read along with one of the above commentaries.

THE NATIVITY CYCLE AND SUNDAYS AFTER EPIPHANY, C

Books for the study of the Lukan Gospel lessons (seven times, for the three John lessons see above):

Overviews

F.W. Danker, *Luke,* Proclamation Commentary, 2nd rev. ed. (Fortress, 1987) will provide a good discussion to prepare one for the year. C. Talbert, *Reading Luke* (Crossroads, 1982) offers a literary and theological review with stimulating ideas.

Commentaries

A most detailed and helpful set is Joseph Fitzmyer, *The Gospel According to Luke,* Anchor Bible 28, 28A (Doubleday, 1981, 1985). Add to this the new expository work by Fred Craddock, *Luke,* Interpretation Commentaries (John Knox, 1990) for good preaching help. Eduard Schweizer, *The Good News According to Luke* (John Knox, 1987) provides a nice combination of exegetical and pastoral insight. I. Howard Marshall, *The Gospel of Luke,* New International Greek Commentary (Eerdmans, 1978) offers a solid evangelical study of the Greek text.

Studies

Raymond E. Brown, *The Birth of the Messiah* (Doubleday, 1979) is a detailed study of the infancy narratives in Matthew and Luke. Walter E. Pilgrim, *Good News to the Poor* (Augsburg, 1981) offers a provocative sermon starter on issues of wealth and poverty. Likewise J. Massyngbaerde Ford, *My Enemy is My Guest* (Orbis, 1984) stimulates thinking on the issues of non-violence in Luke. Both books invite one to look at the gospel from a new perspective.

Books for the study of the Old Testament texts (Isaiah, six times and Jeremiah, four times):

R. Clements, *Isaiah 1-39,* New Century Bible Commentary (Eerdmans, 1980) and R.N. Whybray, *Isaiah 40-66,* New Century Bible Commentary (Eerdmans, 1975) provide good inexpensive commentaries. A more detailed set would be O. Kaiser, *Isaiah 1-12,* Old Testament Library, 2nd ed. (Westminster, 1983) and *Isaiah 13-39,* Old Testament Library (Westminster, 1974) plus Claus Westermann, *Isaiah 40-66,* Old Testament Library (Westminster, 1969). Wolfgang Roth, *Isaiah,* Knox Preaching Guides (John Knox, 1988) gives a good concise overview.

For Jeremiah Ronald Clements, *Jeremiah,* Interpretation Commentaries (John Knox, 1989) offers a good expository study. John Bright, *Jeremiah,* Anchor Bible 21 (Doubleday, 1965) has a fresh translation and helpful insight. R. Carroll, *Jeremiah: A Commentary,* Old Testament Library (Westminster, 1986) is one of several solid new works to appear in recent years for those wanting more exegetical material.

Books for the study of I Corinthians (six times):
C.K. Barrett, *I Corinthians*, Harper's New Testament Commentaries (Harper and Row, 1968) continues to be a solid help. Gordon D. Fee, *The First Epistle to the Corinthians*, New International Commentary on the New Testament (Eerdmans, 1987) is a good detailed new evangelical study. H. Conzelmann, *I Corinthians*, Hermeneia (Fortress, 1977) is a scholarly work based on the Greek text. C. Talbert, *Reading Corinthians* (Crossroads, 1987) provides a fine literary and theological supplement to any of the above.

THE PASCHAL CYCLE 1992

For study of the gospel lessons, see Luke and John above.
Books for the study of Acts:
W.H. Willimon, *Acts*, Interpretation Commentaries (John Knox, 1988) gives a second expository start for the pastor. E. Haenchen, *The Acts of the Apostles: A Commentary* (Westminster, 1971) is the top scholars' commentary at present. C.S.C. Williams, *The Acts of the Apostles*, Harper's New Testament Commentaries (Now from Hendrickson, 1957) or F.F. Bruce, *The Book of the Acts*, The New International Commentary on the New Testament, rev. ed. (Eerdmans, 1988) provide solid alternatives that may be easier to use.

Books for the study of epistle lessons (Philippians three times, Revelation six times):
Fred Craddock, *Philippians*, Interpretation Commentaries (John Knox, 1985) gives a brief expository starting point. G.F. Hawthorne, *Philippians*, Word Bible Commentaries (Word, 1983) or R.P. Martin, *Philippians*, New Century Bible Commentary (Eerdmans, 1983) will provide a helpful exegetical counterpart.

M. Eugene Boring, *Revelation*, Interpretation Commentary (John Knox, 1989) offers a very good expository treatment. G.R. Beasley-Murray, *The Book of Revelation*, New Century Bible Commentary (Eerdmans, 1974) or E. Schussler Fiorenza, *Invitation to the Book of Revelation* (Doubleday, 1981) provides helpful exegetical material. Couple with these the interesting studies by Ted Grimsrud, *Triumph of the Lamb* (Herald Press, 1987) and Allan A. Boesak, *Comfort and Protest: The Apocalypse from a South African Perspective* (Westminster, 1987) for provocative preaching on Revelation for Today.

ORDINARY TIME, June 21 to July 26, 1992

For the Gospel lessons from Luke, see above.

For Old Testament lessons from I Kings, see above.

For the study of the Epistle (Galatians six times):

Charles Cousar, *Galatians*, Interpretation Commentaries (John Knox, 1982) provides good expository material. Hans Dieter Betz, *Galatians*, Hermeneia (Fortress, 1979) gives a scholarly interpretation on the Greek text, but most can use it. F.F. Bruce, *Commentary on Galatians*, New International Greek New Testament Commentary (Eerdmans, 1982) is a solid evangelical alternative.

FOUR YEAR CHURCH YEAR CALENDAR

	Series B 1990	Series C 1991	Series A 1992	Series B 1993
Advent begins	Dec. 2	Dec. 1	Nov. 29	Nov. 28
Christmas	Dec. 25	Dec. 25	Dec. 25	Dec. 25
	1991	1992	1993	1994
Epiphany	Jan. 6	Jan. 6	Jan. 6	Jan. 6
Ash Wednesday	Feb. 13	March 4	Feb. 24	Feb. 16
Passion Sunday	March 24	April 12	April 4	March 27
Maundy Thursday	March 28	April 16	April 8	March 31
Good Friday	March 29	April 17	April 9	April 1
Easter Day	March 31	April 19	April 11	April 3
Ascension Day	May 9	May 28	May 20	May 12
Pentecost	May 19	June 7	May 30	May 22
Trinity Sunday	May 26	June 14	June 6	May 29
Reformation	Oct. 31	Oct. 31	Oct. 31	Oct. 31
All Saints	Nov. 1	Nov. 1	Nov. 1	Nov. 1

CALENDARS

1991

	JANUARY							FEBRUARY							MARCH							APRIL					
S	M	T	W	T	F	S	S	M	T	W	T	F	S	S	M	T	W	T	F	S	S	M	T	W	T	F	S
		1	2	3	4	5						1	2						1	2		1	2	3	4	5	6
6	7	8	9	10	11	12	3	4	5	6	7	8	9	3	4	5	6	7	8	9	7	8	9	10	11	12	13
13	14	15	16	17	18	19	10	11	12	13	14	15	16	10	11	12	13	14	15	16	14	15	16	17	18	19	20
20	21	22	23	24	25	26	17	18	19	20	21	22	23	17	18	19	20	21	22	23	21	22	23	24	25	26	27
27	28	29	30	31			24	25	26	27	28			24	25	26	27	28	29	30	28	29	30				
														31													

	MAY							JUNE							JULY							AUGUST					
S	M	T	W	T	F	S	S	M	T	W	T	F	S	S	M	T	W	T	F	S	S	M	T	W	T	F	S
			1	2	3	4							1		1	2	3	4	5	6					1	2	3
5	6	7	8	9	10	11	2	3	4	5	6	7	8	7	8	9	10	11	12	13	4	5	6	7	8	9	10
12	13	14	15	16	17	18	9	10	11	12	13	14	15	14	15	16	17	18	19	20	11	12	13	14	15	16	17
19	20	21	22	23	24	25	16	17	18	19	20	21	22	21	22	23	24	25	26	27	18	19	20	21	22	23	24
26	27	28	29	30	31		23	24	25	26	27	28	29	28	29	30	31				25	26	27	28	29	30	31
							30																				

	SEPTEMBER							OCTOBER							NOVEMBER							DECEMBER					
S	M	T	W	T	F	S	S	M	T	W	T	F	S	S	M	T	W	T	F	S	S	M	T	W	T	F	S
1	2	3	4	5	6	7			1	2	3	4	5						1	2	1	2	3	4	5	6	7
8	9	10	11	12	13	14	6	7	8	9	10	11	12	3	4	5	6	7	8	9	8	9	10	11	12	13	14
15	16	17	18	19	20	21	13	14	15	16	17	18	19	10	11	12	13	14	15	16	15	16	17	18	19	20	21
22	23	24	25	26	27	28	20	21	22	23	24	25	26	17	18	19	20	21	22	23	22	23	24	25	26	27	28
29	30						27	28	29	30	31			24	25	26	27	28	29	30	29	30	31				

1992

	JANUARY							FEBRUARY							MARCH							APRIL					
S	M	T	W	T	F	S	S	M	T	W	T	F	S	S	M	T	W	T	F	S	S	M	T	W	T	F	S
			1	2	3	4							1	1	2	3	4	5	6	7				1	2	3	4
5	6	7	8	9	10	11	2	3	4	5	6	7	8	8	9	10	11	12	13	14	5	6	7	8	9	10	11
12	13	14	15	16	17	18	9	10	11	12	13	14	15	15	16	17	18	19	20	21	12	13	14	15	16	17	18
19	20	21	22	23	24	25	16	17	18	19	20	21	22	22	23	24	25	26	27	28	19	20	21	22	23	24	25
26	27	28	29	30	31		23	24	25	26	27	28		29	30	31					26	27	28	29	30		

	MAY							JUNE							JULY							AUGUST					
S	M	T	W	T	F	S	S	M	T	W	T	F	S	S	M	T	W	T	F	S	S	M	T	W	T	F	S
					1	2	1	2	3	4	5	6	7				1	2	3	4							1
3	4	5	6	7	8	9	8	9	10	11	12	13	14	5	6	7	8	9	10	11	2	3	4	5	6	7	8
10	11	12	13	14	15	16	14	15	16	17	18	19	20	12	13	14	15	16	17	18	9	10	11	12	13	14	15
17	18	19	20	21	22	23	21	22	23	24	25	26	27	19	20	21	22	23	24	25	16	17	18	19	20	21	22
24	25	26	27	28	29	30	28	29	30					26	27	28	29	30	31		23	24	25	26	27	28	29
31																					30	31					

	SEPTEMBER							OCTOBER							NOVEMBER							DECEMBER					
S	M	T	W	T	F	S	S	M	T	W	T	F	S	S	M	T	W	T	F	S	S	M	T	W	T	F	S
		1	2	3	4	5					1	2	3	1	2	3	4	5	6	7			1	2	3	4	5
6	7	8	9	10	11	12	4	5	6	7	8	9	10	8	9	10	11	12	13	14	6	7	8	9	10	11	12
13	14	15	16	17	18	19	11	12	13	14	15	16	17	15	16	17	18	19	20	21	13	14	15	16	17	18	19
20	21	22	23	24	25	26	18	19	20	21	22	23	24	22	23	24	25	26	27	28	20	21	22	23	24	25	26
27	28	29	30				25	26	27	28	29	30	31	29	30						27	28	29	30	31		

LECTIONARY LESSONS

(Series B through November 24, 1991; Series C beginning December 1, 1991)

August 4, 1991 – Eleventh Sunday after Pentecost
(Roman Catholic – 18th Sunday of the Year)
(Episcopal – Proper 13; Pres/Meth/UCC – 11th after Pentecost)

Lutheran:	Ex. 16:2-15	Eph. 4:17-24	John 6:24-35
Roman Catholic:	Ex. 16:2-4, 12-15	Eph. 4:17, 20-24	John 6:24-35
Episcopal:	Ex. 16:2-4, 9-15	Eph. 4:17-25	John 6:24-35
Pres/Meth/UCC:	2 Sam. 12:15b-24	Eph. 4:1-6	John 6:24-35

August 11, 1991 – Twelfth Sunday after Pentecost
(Roman Catholic – 19th Sunday of the Year)
(Episcopal – Proper 14; Pres/Meth/UCC – 12th after Pentecost)

Lutheran:	1 Kings 19:4-8	Eph. 4:30-5:2	John 6:41-51
Roman Catholic:	1 Kings 19:4-8	Eph. 4:30-5:2	John 6:41-52
Episcopal:	Deut. 8:1-10	Eph. 4:(25-29) 30-5:2	John 6:37-51
Pres/Meth/UCC:	2 Sam. 18:1, 5, 9-15	Eph. 4:25-5:2	John 6:35, 41-51

August 18, 1991 – Thirteenth Sunday after Pentecost
(Roman Catholic – 20th Sunday of the Year)
(Episcopal – Proper 15; Pres/Meth/UCC – 13th after Pentecost)

Lutheran:	Prov. 9:1-6	Eph. 5:15-20	John 6:51-58
Roman Catholic:	Prov. 9:1-6	Eph 5:15-20	John 6:51-58
Episcopal:	Prov. 9:1-6	Eph 5:15-20	John 6:53-59
Pres/Meth/UCC:	2 Sam. 18:24-33	Eph 5:15-20	John 6:51-58

August 25, 1991 – Fourteenth Sunday after Pentecost
(Roman Catholic – 21st Sunday of the Year)
(Episcopal – Proper 16; Pres/Meth/UCC – 14th after Pentecost)

Lutheran:	Josh. 24:1-2a, 14-18	Eph. 5:21-31	John 6:60-69
Roman Catholic:	Josh. 24:1-2a, 15-17, 18b	Eph. 5:21-32	John 6:60-69
Episcopal:	Josh. 24:1-2a, 14-25	Eph. 5:21-33	John 6:60-69
Pres/Meth/UCC:	2 Sam. 23:1-7	Eph. 5:21-33	John 6:55-69

September 1, 1991 — Fifteenth Sunday after Pentecost
(Roman Catholic — 22nd Sunday of the Year)
(Episcopal — Proper 17; Pres/Meth/UCC — 15th after Pentecost)

Lutheran:	Deut. 4:1-2, 6-8	Eph. 6:10-20	Mark 7:1-8, 14-15, 21-23
Roman Catholic:	Duet. 4:1-2, 6-8	James 1:17-18, 21b-22, 27	Mark 7:1-8, 14-15, 21-23
Episcopal:	Deut. 4:1-9	Eph. 6:10-20	Mark 7:1-8, 14-15, 21-23
Pres/Meth/UCC:	1 Kings 2:1-4, 10-13	Eph. 6:10-21	Mark 7:1-8, 14-15, 21-23

September 8, 1991 — Sixteenth Sunday after Pentecost
(Roman Catholic — 23rd Sunday of the Year)
(Episcopal — Proper 18; Pres/Meth/UCC — 16th after Pentecost)

Lutheran:	Is. 35:4-7a	James 1:17-22, (23-25) 26-27	Mark 7:31-37
Roman Catholic:	Is. 35:4-7a	James 1:2-5	Mark 7:31-37
Episcopal	Is. 35:4-7a	James 2:17-27	Mark 7:31-37
Pres/Meth/UCC:	Prov. 2:1-8	James 1:17-27	Mark 7:31-37

September 15, 1991 — Seventeenth Sunday after Pentecost
(Roman Catholic — 24th Sunday of the Year)
(Episcopal — Proper 19; Pres/Meth/UCC — 17th after Pentecost)

Lutheran:	Is. 50:4-10	James 2:1-5, 8-10, 14-18	Mark 8:27-35
Roman Catholic:	Is. 50:5-9a	James 2:14-18	Mark 8:27-35
Episcopal:	Is. 50:4-9	James 2:1-5, 8-10, 14-18	Mark 8:27-38
Pres/Meth/UCC:	Prov. 22:1-2, 8-9	James 2:1-5, 8-10, 14-17	Mark 8:27-38

September 22, 1991 — Eighteenth Sunday after Pentecost
(Roman Catholic — 25th Sunday of the Year)
(Episcopal — Proper 20; Pres/Meth/UCC — 18th after Pentecost)

Lutheran:	Jer. 11:18-20	James 3:16-4:6	Mark 9:30-37
Roman Catholic:	Wisd. 2:12, 17-20	James 3:16-4:3	Mark 9:30-37
Episcopal:	Wisd. 1:16-2:1, (6-11) 12-22	James 3:16-4:6	Mark 9:30-37
Pres/Meth/UCC:	Job. 28:20-28	James 3:13-18	Mark 9:30-37

September 29, 1991 — Nineteenth Sunday after Pentecost
(Roman Catholic — 26th Sunday of the Year)
(Episcopal — Proper 21; Pres/Meth/UCC — 19th after Pentecost)

Lutheran:	Num. 11:4-6, 10-16, 24-29	James 4:7-12 (13-5:6)	Mark 9:38-50
Roman Catholic:	Num. 11:25-29	James 5:1-6	Mark 9:38-43, 45, 47-48
Episcopal:	Num. 11-4-6, 10-16, 24-29	James 4:7-12 (13-5:6)	Mark 9:38-43, 45, 47-48
Pres/Meth/UCC:	Job 42:1-6	James 4:13-17, 5:7-11	Mark 9:38-50

October 6, 1991 — Twentieth Sunday after Pentecost
(Roman Catholic — 27th Sunday of the Year)
(Episcopal — Proper 22; Pres/Meth/UCC — 20th after Pentecost)

Lutheran:	Gen. 2:18-24	Heb. 2:9-11 (12-18)	Mark 10:2-16
Roman Catholic:	Gen. 2:18-24	Heb. 2:9-11	Mark 10:2-16
Episcopal:	Gen. 2:18-24	Heb. 2:(1-8) 9-18	Mark 10:2-9
Pres/Meth/UCC:	Gen. 2:18-24	Heb. 1:1-4, 2:9-11	Mark 10:2-16

October 13, 1991 — Twenty-first Sunday after Pentecost
(Roman Catholic — 28th Sunday of the Year)
(Episcopal — Proper 23; Pres/Meth/UCC — 21st after Pentecost)

Lutheran:	Amos 5:6-7, 10-15	Heb. 3:1-6	Mark 10:17-27 (28-30)
Roman Catholic:	Wisd. 7:7-11	Heb. 4:12-13	Mark 10:17-30
Episcopal:	Amos 5:6-7, 10-15	Heb. 3:1-6	Mark 10:17-27 (28-31)
Pres/Meth/UCC:	Gen. 3:8-19	Heb. 4:1-3, 9-13	Mark 10:17-30

October 20, 1991 — Twenty-second Sunday after Pentecost
(Roman Catholic — 29th Sunday of the Year)
(Episcopal — Proper 24; Pres/Meth/UCC — 22nd after Pentecost)

Lutheran:	Is. 53:10-12	Heb. 4:9-16	Mark 10:35-45
Roman Catholic:	Is. 53:10-11	Heb. 4:14-16	Mark 10:35-45
Episcopal:	Is. 53:4-12	Heb. 4:12-16	Mark 10:35-45
Pres/Meth/UCC:	Is. 53:7-12	Heb. 4:14-16	Mark 10:35-45

October 27, 1991 – Twenty-third Sunday after Pentecost
(Roman Catholic – 30th Sunday of the Year)
(Episcopal – Proper 25; Pres/Meth/UCC – 23rd after Pentecost)

Lutheran:	Jer. 31:7-9	Heb. 5:1-10	Mark 10:46-52
Roman Catholic:	Jer. 31:7-9	Heb. 5:1-6	Mark 10:46-52
Episcopal:	Is. 59:(1-4) 9-19	Heb. 5:12-6:1, 9-12	Mark 10:46-52
Pres/Meth/UCC:	Jer. 31:7-9	Heb. 5:1-6	Mark 10:46-52

October 27, 1991 – Reformation Sunday

Lutheran:	Jer. 31:31-24	Rom. 3:19-28	John 8:31-36
Pres/Meth/UCC:	Heb. 2:1-4	Rom. 3:21-28	John 8:31-36

November 3, 1991 – Twenty-fourth Sunday after Pentecost
(Roman Catholic – 31st Sunday of the Year)
(Episcopal – Proper 26; Pres/Meth/UCC – 24th after Pentecost)

Lutheran:	Deut. 6:1-9	Heb. 7:23-28	Mark 12:28-34 (35-37)
Roman Catholic:	Deut. 6:2-6	Heb. 7:23-28	Mark 12:28b-34
Episcopal:	Deut. 6:1-9	Heb. 7:23-28	Mark 12:28-34
Pres/Meth/UCC:	Deut. 6:1-9	Heb. 7:23-28	Mark 12:28-34

November 3, 1991 – All Saints' Day

Lutheran:	Is. 26:1-4, 8-9, 12-13, 19-21	Rev. 21:9-11, 22-27 (22:1-5)	Matt. 5:1-12
Roman Catholic:	Rev. 7:2-4, 9-14	I John 3:1-3	Matt. 5:1-12a
Episcopal:	Eccles. 44:1-10, 13-14	Rev. 7:2-4, 9-17	Matt. 5:1-12
Pres/Meth/UCC:	Rev. 21:1-6a	Col. 1:9-14	John 11:32-44

November 10, 1991 – Twenty-fifth Sunday after Pentecost
(Roman Catholic – 32nd Sunday of the Year)
(Episcopal – Proper 27; Pres/Meth/UCC – 25th after Pentecost)

Lutheran:	I Kings 17:8-16	Heb. 9:24-28	Mark 12:41-44
Roman Catholic:	I Kings 17:10-16	Heb. 9:24-28	Mark 12:38-44
Episcopal:	I Kings 17:8-16	Heb. 9:24-28	Mark 12:38-44
Pres/Meth/UCC:	I Kings 17:8-16	Heb. 9:24-28	Mark 12:38-44

November 17, 1991 – Twenty-sixth Sunday after Pentecost
(Roman Catholic – 33rd Sunday of the Year)
(Episcopal – Proper 28; Pres/Meth/UCC – 26th after Pentecost)

Lutheran:	Daniel 12:1-3	Heb. 10:11-18	Mark 13:1-13
Roman Catholic:	Daniel 7:9-14	Heb.10:11-18	Mark 13:24-32
Episcopal:	Daniel 12:1-4a (5-13)	Heb. 10:31-39	Mark 13:14-23
Pres/Meth/UCC:	Daniel 7:9-14	Heb. 10:11-18	Mark 13:24-32

November 24, 1991 – Last Sunday after Pentecost, Christ the King
(The end of Year B in the Lectionary series)

Lutheran:	Dan. 7:13-14	Rev. 1:4b-8	John 18:33-37
Roman Catholic:	Dan. 7:13-14	Rev. 1:5-8	John 18:33b-37
Episcopal:	Dan. 7:9-14	Rev. 1:1-8	John 18:33-37
Pres/Meth/UCC:	Jer. 23:1-6	Rev. 1:4b-8	John 18:33-37

November 28, 1991 – Thanksgiving Day (U.S.)

Lutheran:	Deut. 8:1-10	Phil. 4:6-20	Luke 17:11-19
Pres/Meth/UCC:	Joel 2:21-27	I Tim. 2:1-7	Matt. 6:25-33

December 1, 1991 – First Sunday in Advent
(The beginning of Year C in the Lectionary series)

Lutheran:	Jer. 33:14-16	I Thess. 3:9-13	Luke 21:25-36
Roman Catholic:	Jer. 33:14-16	I Thess. 3:12-4:2	Luke 21:25-28, 34-36
Episcopal:	Zech. 14:4-9	I Thess. 3:9-13	Luke 21:25-31
Pres/Meth/UCC:	Jer. 33:14-16	I Thess. 3:9-13	Luke 21:25-36

December 8, 1991 – Second Sunday in Advent

Lutheran:	Mal. 3:1-4	Phil. 1:3-11	Luke 3:1-6
Roman Catholic:	Bar. 5:1-9	Phil. 1:4-6, 8-11	Luke 3:1-6
Episcopal:	Bar. 5:1-9	Phil. 1:1-11	Luke 3:1-6
Pres/Meth/UCC:	Mal. 3:1-4	Phil. 1:3-11	Luke 3:1-6

December 15, 1991 – Third Sunday in Advent

Lutheran:	Zeph. 3:14-18a	Phil. 4:4-7 (8-9)	Luke 3:7-18
Roman Catholic:	Zeph. 3:14-18a	Phil. 4:4-7	Luke 3:10-18
Episcopal:	Zeph. 3:14-20	Phil. 4:4-7 (8-9)	Luke 3:7-18
Pres/Meth/UCC:	Zeph. 3:14-20	Phil. 4:4-9	Luke 3:7-18

December 22, 1991 — Fourth Sunday in Advent

Lutheran:	Mic. 5:2-4	Heb. 10:5-10	Luke 1:39-45 (46-55)
Roman Catholic:	Mic. 5:2-5a	Heb. 10:5-10	Luke 1:39-45
Episcopal:	Mic. 5:2-4	Heb. 10:5-10	Luke 1:39-49 (50-56)
Pres/Meth/UCC:	Mic. 5:2-5a	Heb. 10:5-10	Luke 1:39-55

December 24, 1991 — Christmas Eve

Lutheran:	Is. 9:2-7	Titus 2:11-14	Luke 2:1-20
Roman Catholic:	Is. 9:2-7	Titus 2:11-14	Luke 2:1-24
Epsicopal:	Is. 9:2-4, 6-7	Titus 2:11-14	Luke 2:1-14 (15-20)
Pres/Meth/UCC:	Is. 9:2-7	Titus 2:11-14	Luke 2:1-20

December 25, 1991 — Christmas Day

Lutheran:	Is. 62:10-12	Titus 3:4-7	Luke 2:1-20
Roman Catholic:	Is 62:11-12	Titus 3:4-7	Luke 2:15-20
Episcopal:	Is. 62:6-7, 10-12	Titus 3:4-7	Luke 2:(1-14) 15-20
Pres/Meth/UCC:	Is. 62:6-7, 10-12	Titus 3:4-7	Luke 2:1-18

December 29, 1991 — First Sunday after Christmas (Holy Name)

Lutheran:	Jer. 31:10-13	Heb. 2:10-18	Luke 2:41-52
Roman Catholic:	Sir. 3:3-7, 14-17a	Col. 3:12-21	Luke 2:22-40
Episcopal:	Is. 61:10-62:3	Gal. 3:23-25; 4:4-7	John 1:1-18
Pres/Meth/UCC:	2 Sam. 2:18-20,26	Col. 3:12-17	Luke 2:41-52

January 5, 1992 — Second Sunday after Christmas

Lutheran:	Is. 61:10-62:3	Eph. 1:3-6, 15-18	John 1:1-18
Roman Catholic:	Sir. 24:1-2, 8-12	Eph. 1:3-6, 15-18	John 1:1-18
Episcopal:	Jer. 31:7-14	Eph. 1:3-6, 15-19a	Matt. 2:13-15, 19-23
Pres/Meth/UCC:	Jer. 31:7-14	Eph. 13-6, 15-18	John 1:1-18

January 6, 1992 — The Epiphany of our Lord

Lutheran:	Is. 60:1-16	Eph. 3:2-12	Matt. 2:1-12
Roman Catholic:	Is. 60:1-6	Eph. 3:2-3, 5-6	Matt. 2:1-12
Episcopal:	Is. 60:1-6, 9	Eph. 3:1-12	Matt. 2:1-12
Pres/Meth/UCC:	Is. 60:1-6	Eph. 3:1-12	Matt. 2:1-12

January 12, 1992 — First Sunday after Epiphany
(The Baptism of our Lord)

Lutheran:	Is. 42:1-7	Acts 10:34-38	Luke 3:15-17, 21-22
Roman Catholic:	Is. 42:1-4, 6-7	Acts 10:34-38	Luke 3:15-16, 21-22
Episcopal:	Is. 42:1-9	Acts 10:34-38	Luke 3:15-16, 21-22
Pres/Meth/UCC:	Is. 61:1-4	Acts 8:14-17	Luke 3:15-17, 21-22

January 19, 1992 – Second Sunday after the Epiphany

Lutheran:	Is. 62:1-5	I Cor. 12:1-11	John 2:1-11
Roman Catholic:	Is. 62:1-5	I Cor. 12:4-11	John 2:1-12
Episcopal:	Is. 62:1-5	I Cor. 12:1-11	John 2:1-11
Pres/Meth/UCC:	Is. 62:1-5	I Cor. 12:1-11	John 2:1-11

January 26, 1992 – Third Sunday after the Epiphany

Lutheran:	Is. 61:1-6	I Cor. 12:12-21, 26-27	Luke 4:14-21
Roman Catholic:	Neh. 8:2-4a, 5-6, 8-10	I Cor. 12:12-30	Luke 1:1-4, 4:14-21
Episcopal:	Neh. 8:2-10	I Cor. 12:12-27	Luke 4:14-21
Pres/Meth/UCC:	Neh. 8:1-4a, 5-6, 8-10	I Cor. 12:12-30	Luke 4:14-21

February 2, 1992 – Fourth Sunday after the Epiphany

Lutheran:	Jer. 1:4-10	I Cor. 12:27-13:13	Luke 4:21-32
Roman Catholic:	Jer. 1:4-5, 17-19	I Cor. 12:31-13:13	Luke 4:21-30
Episcopal:	Jer. 1:4-10	I Cor. 14:12b-20	Luke 4:21-32
Pres/Meth/UCC:	Jer. 1:4-10	I Cor. 13:1-13	Luke 4:21-30

February 9, 1992 – Fifth Sunday after the Epiphany

Lutheran:	Is. 6:1-8 (9-13)	I Cor. 14:12b-20	Luke 5:1-11
Roman Catholic:	Is. 6:1-2a, 3-8	I Cor. 15:1-11	Luke 5:1-11
Episcopal:	Judges 6:11-24a	I Cor. 15:1-11	Luke 5:1-11
Pres/Meth/UCC:	Is. 6:1-8 (9-13)	I Cor. 15:1-11	Luke 5:1-11

February 16, 1992 – Sixth Sunday after the Epiphany

Lutheran:	Jer. 17:5-8	I Cor. 15:12, 16-20	Luke 6:17-26
Roman Catholic:	Jer. 17:5-8	I Cor. 15:12, 16-20	Luke 6:17, 20-26
Episcopal:	Jer. 17:5-10	I Cor. 15:12-20	Luke 6:17-26
Pres/Meth/UCC:	Jer. 17:5-10	I Cor. 15:12-20	Luke 6:17-26

February 23, 1992 – Seventh Sunday after the Epiphany

Lutheran:	Gen. 45:3-8a, 15	I Cor. 15:35-38a, 42-50	Luke 6:27-38
Roman Catholic:	I Sam. 26:2, 7-9, 12-13, 22-23	I Cor. 15:45-49	Luke 6:27-38
Episcopal:	Gen. 45:3-11, 21-28	I Cor. 15:35-38, 42-50	Luke 6:27-38
Pres/Meth/UCC:	Gen. 45:3-11, 15	I Cor. 15:35-38, 42-50	Luke 6:27-38

March 1, 1992 – Last Sunday after the Epiphany
(Transfiguration Sunday)
(Roman Catholic – Eighth Sunday of the Year)

Lutheran:	Deut. 34:1-12	2 Cor. 4:3-6	Luke 9:28-36
Roman Catholic:	Is. 6:1-2a, 3-8	I Cor. 15:1-11	Luke 5:1-11
Episcopal:	Ex. 34:29-35	I Cor. 12:27-13:13	Luke 9:28-36
Pres/Meth/UCC:	Ex. 34:29-35	2 Cor. 3:12-4:2	Luke 9:28-36

March 4, 1992 – Ash Wednesday

Lutheran:	Joel 2:12-19	2 Cor. 5:20b-6:2	Matt. 6:1-6, 16-21
Roman Catholic:	Joel 2:12-18	2 Cor. 5:20-6:2	Matt. 6:1-6, 16-18
Episcopal:	Joel 2:1-2, 12-17	2 Cor. 5:20b-6:10	Matt. 6:1-6, 16-21
Pres/Meth/UCC:	Joel 2:1-2, 12-17a	2 Cor. 5:20b-6:10	Matt. 6:1-6, 16-21

March 8, 1992 – First Sunday in Lent

Lutheran:	Deut. 26:5-10	Rom. 10:8b-13	Luke 4:1-13
Roman Catholic:	Deut. 26:4-10	Rom. 10:8-13	Luke 4:1-13
Episcopal:	Deut. 26:(1-4) 5-11	Rom. 10:(5-8a) 8b-13	Luke 4:1-13
Pres/Meth/UCC:	Deut. 26:1-11	Rom. 10:8b-13	Luke 4:1-13

March 15, 1992 – Second Sunday in Lent

Lutheran:	Jer. 26:8-15	Phil. 3:17-4:1	Luke 13:31-35
Roman Catholic:	Gen. 15:5-12, 17-18	Phil 3:17-4:1	Luke 9:28-36
Episcopal:	Gen. 15:1-12, 17-18	Phil 3:17-4:1	Luke 13:(22-30) 31-35
Pres/Meth/UCC:	Gen. 15:1-12, 17-18	Phil 3:17-4:1	Luke 13:31-35

March 22, 1992 – Third Sunday in Lent

Lutheran:	Ex. 3:1-8b, 10-15	I Cor. 10:1-13	Luke 13:1-9
Roman Catholic:	Ex. 3:1-8a, 13-15	I Cor. 10:1-6, 10-12	Luke 13:1-9
Episcopal:	Ex. 3:1-15	I Cor. 10:1-13	Luke 13:1-9
Pres/Meth/UCC:	Ex. 3:1-15	I Cor. 10:1-13	Luke 13:1-9

March 29, 1992 – Fourth Sunday in Lent

Lutheran:	Is. 12:1-6	I Cor. 1:18-31	Luke 15:1-3, 11-32
Roman Catholic:	Josh. 5:9a, 10-12	2 Cor. 5:17-21	Luke 15:1-3, 11-32
Episcopal:	Josh. (4:19-24) 5:9-12	2 Cor. 5:17-21	Luke 15:11-32
Pres/Meth/UCC:	Josh. 5:9-12	2 Cor. 5:16-21	Luke 15:1-3, 11-32

April 5, 1992 — Fifth Sunday in Lent

Lutheran:	Is. 43:16-21	Phil. 3:8-14	Luke 20:9-19
Roman Catholic:	Is. 43:16-21	Phil. 3:8-14	John 8:1-11
Episcopal:	Is. 43:16-21	Phil. 3:8-14	Luke 20:9-19
Pres/Meth/UCC:	Is. 43:16-21	Phil. 3:8-14	John 12:1-8

April 12, 1992 — Sunday of the Passion (Palm Sunday)

Lutheran:	Deut. 32:36-39	Phil. 2:5-11	Luke 22:1-23:56
Roman Catholic:	Is. 50:4-7	Phil. 2:6-11	Luke 22:14-23:56
Episcopal:	Is. 45:21-25	Phil. 2:5-11	Luke (22:39-71) 23:1-49 (50-56)
Pres/Meth/UCC:	Is. 50:4-9a	Phil. 2:5-11	Luke 22:14-23:56

April 16, 1992 — Maundy Thursday

Lutheran:	Jer. 31:31-34	Heb. 10:15-39	Luke 22:7-20
Roman Catholic:	Ex. 12:1-8, 11-14	I Cor. 11:23-26	John 13:1-15
Episcopal:	Ex. 12:1-14a	I Cor. 11:23-26 (27-32)	Luke 22:14-30
Pres/Meth/UCC:	Jer. 31:31-34	Heb. 10:16-25	Luke 22:7-20

April 17, 1992 — Good Friday

Lutheran:	Is. 52:13-53:12	Heb. 4:14-16, 5:7-9	John 18:1-19:42
Roman Catholic:	Is. 52:13-53:12	Heb. 4:14-16, 5:7-9	John 18:1-19:42
Episcopal:	Is. 52:13-53:12	Heb. 10:1-25	John (18:1-40) 19:1-37
Pres/Meth/UCC:	Is. 52:13-53:12	Heb. 4:14-16, 5:7-9	John 18:1-19:42

April 19, 1992 — The Resurrection of our Lord. Easter Day

Lutheran:	Ex. 15:1-11	I Cor. 15:1-11	Luke 24:1-11
Roman Catholic:	Acts 10:34a, 37-43	Col. 3:1-4	Luke 24:1-12
Episcopal:	Acts 10:34-43	Col. 3:1-4	Luke 24:1-10
Pres/Meth/UCC:	Acts 10:34-43	I Cor. 15:19-26	John 20:1-18

April 26, 1992 — Second Sunday of Easter

Lutheran:	Acts 5:12, 17-32	Rev. 1:4-18	John 20:19-31
Roman Catholic:	Acts 5:12-16	Rev. 1:9-11a, 12-13, 17-19	John 20:19-31
Episcopal:	Acts 5:12a, 17-22, 25-29	Rev. 1:(1-8) 9-19	John 20:19-31
Pres/Meth/UCC:	Acts 5:27-32	Rev. 1:4-8	John 20:19-31

May 3, 1992 — Third Sunday of Easter

Lutheran:	Acts 9:1-20	Rev. 5:11-14	John 21:1-14
Roman Catholic:	Acts 5:27b-32, 40b-41	Rev. 5:11-14	John 21:1-19
Episcopal:	Acts 9:19a	Rev. 5:6-14	John 21:1-14
Pres/Meth/UCC:	Acts 9:1-20	Rev. 5:11-14	John 21:1-19

May 10, 1992 — Fourth Sunday of Easter

Lutheran:	Acts 13:15-16a, 26-33	Rev. 7:9-17	John 10:22-30
Roman Catholic:	Acts 13:14, 43-52	Rev. 7:9, 14b-17	John 10:27-30
Episcopal:	Acts 13:15-16, 26-33 (34-39)	Rev. 7:9-17	John 10:22-30
Pres/Meth/UCC:	Acts 13:15-16, 26-33	Rev. 7:9-17	John 10:22-30

May 17, 1992 — Fifth Sunday of Easter

Lutheran:	Acts 13:44-52	Rev. 21:1-15	John 13:31-35
Roman Catholic:	Acts 14:21-27	Rev. 21:1-5a	John 13:31-33a, 34-35
Episcopal:	Acts 13:44-52	Rev. 19:1, 4-9	John 13:31-35
Pres/Meth/UCC:	Acts 14:8-18	Rev. 21:1-6	John 13:31-35

May 24, 1992 — Sixth Sunday of Easter

Lutheran:	14:8-18	Rev. 21:10-14, 22-23	John 14:23-29
Roman Catholic:	Acts 15:1-2, 22-29	Rev. 21:10-14, 22-23	John 14:23-29
Episcopal:	Acts 14:8-18	Rev. 21:22-22:5	John 14:23-29
Pres/Meth/UCC:	Acts 15:1-2, 22-29	Rev. 21:10, 22-27	John 14:23-29

May 28, 1992 — Ascension of our Lord

Lutheran:	Acts 1:1-11	Eph. 1:16-23	Luke 24:44-53
Roman Catholic:	Acts 1:1-11	Eph. 1:17-23	Luke 24:46-53
Episcopal:	Acts 1:1-11	Eph. 1:15-23	Luke 24:49-53
Pres/Meth/UCC:	Acts 1:1-11	Eph. 1:15-23	Luke 24:46-53

May 31, 1992 — Seventh Sunday of Easter

Lutheran:	Acts 16:6-10	Rev. 22:12-17, 20	John 17:20-26
Roman Catholic:	Acts 7:55-8:1a	Rev. 22:12-14, 16-17 20	John 17:20-26
Episcopal:	Acts 16:16-34	Rev. 22:12-14, 16-17 20	John 17:20-26
Pres/Meth/UCC:	Acts 16:16-34	Rev. 22:12-14, 16-17 20	John 17:20-26

June 7, 1992 – The Day of Pentecost

Lutheran:	Gen. 11:1-9	Acts 2:1-21	John 15:26-27, 16:4b-11
Roman Catholic:	Acts 2:1-11	I Cor. 12:3b-7, 12-13	John 20:19-27
Episcopal:	Acts 2:1-11	I Cor. 12:4-13	John 20:19-23
Pres/Meth/UCC:	Acts 2:1-21	Rom. 8:14-17	John 14:8-17, 25-27

June 14, 1992 – The Holy Trinity
(First Sunday after Pentecost)

Lutheran:	Prov. 8:22-31	Rom. 5:1-5	John 16:12-15
Roman Catholic:	Prov. 8:22-31	Rom. 5:1-5	John 16:12-15
Episcopal:	Is. 6:1-8	Rev. 4:1-11	John 16:(5-11) 12-15
Pres/Meth/UCC:	Prov. 8:22-31	Rom. 5:1-5	John 16:12-15

June 21, 1992 – Second Sunday after Pentecost
(Roman Catholic – 9th Sunday of the Year)

Lutheran:	I Kings 8:(22-23, 27-30) 41-43	Gal. 1:1-10	Luke 7:1-10
Roman Catholic:	I Kings 8:41-43	Gal. 1:1-2, 6-10	Luke 7:1-10

June 28, 1992 – Third Sunday after Pentecost
(Roman Catholic – 10th Sunday of the Year)

Lutheran:	I Kings 17:17-24	Gal. 1:11-24	Luke 7:11-17
Roman Catholic:	I Kings 17:17-24	Gal. 1:11-19	Luke 7:11-17

July 5, 1992 – Fourth Sunday after Pentecost
(Roman Catholic – 11th Sunday of the Year)

Lutheran:	2 Sam. 11:26-12:10, 13-15	Gal. 2:11-21	Luke 7:36-50
Roman Catholic:	2 Sam. 12:7-10, 13	Gal. 2:16, 19-21	Luke 7:36-8:3

July 12, 1992 – Fifth Sunday after Pentecost
(Roman Catholic – 12th Sunday of the Year)
(June 21: Episcopal – Proper 7; Pres/Meth/UCC – 2nd after Pentecost)

Lutheran:	Zech. 12:7-10	Gal. 3:23-29	Luke 9:18-24
Roman Catholic:	Zech. 12:10-11	Gal. 3:26-29	Luke 9:18-24
Episcopal:	Zech. 12:8-10, 13:1	Gal. 3:23-29	Luke 9:18-24
Pres/Meth/UCC:	I Kings 19:9-14	Gal. 3:23-29	Luke 9:18-24

July 19, 1992 — Sixth Sunday after Pentecost
(Roman Catholic — 13th Sunday of the Year
(June 28: Episcopal — Proper 8; Pres/Meth/UCC — 3rd after Pentecost)

Lutheran:	I Kings 19:14-21	Gal. 5:1, 13-25	Luke 9:51-62
Roman Catholic:	I Kings 19:16b, 19-21	Gal. 5:1, 13-18	Luke 9:51-62
Episcopal:	I Kings 19:15-16, 19-21	Gal. 5:1, 13-25	Luke 9:51-62
Pres/Meth/UCC:	I Kings 19:15-21	Gal. 5:1, 13-25	Luke 9:51-62

July 26, 1992 — Seventh Sunday after Pentecost
(Roman Catholic — 14th Sunday of the Year)
(July 5: Episcopal — Proper 9; Pres/Meth/UCC — 4th after Pentecost)

Lutheran:	Is. 66:10-14	Gal. 6:1-10, 14-16	Luke 10:1-12, 16 (17-20)
Roman Catholic:	Is. 66:10-14	Gal. 6:14-18	Luke 10:1-12, 17-20
Episcopal:	Is. 66:10-16	Gal. 6:(1-10) 14-18	Luke 10:1-12, 16-20
Pres/Meth/UCC:	I Kings 21:1-3, 17-21	Gal. 6:7-18	Luke 10:1-12, 17-20

Dear Reader:

Are you a regular subscriber to THE CLERGY JOURNAL?

If not, please write for a sample copy.

We believe this magazine can be of help to you in your important work.

Our magazine is in its sixty-seventh year of helping America's church leaders to be more effective leaders.

We invite you to become one of the many pastors who find inspiration, advice and practical professional aid in our pages.

Why not send in the coupon below today?

The magazine about church administration, preaching, worship, finance, programming . . . practical, timely, popular . . . the clergy magazine that belongs in every congregation and on every pastor's desk.

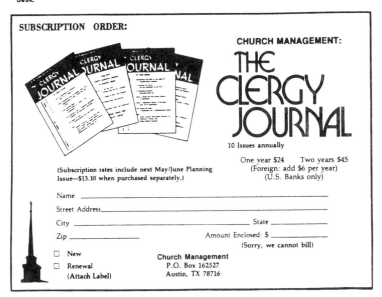

SUBSCRIPTION ORDER:

CHURCH MANAGEMENT:

THE CLERGY JOURNAL

10 Issues annually

One year $24   Two years $45
(Foreign: add $6 per year)
(U.S. Banks only)

(Subscription rates include next May/June Planning Issue—$13.10 when purchased separately.)

Name _____

Street Address_____

City _____ State _____

Zip _____   Amount Enclosed: $ _____
                          (Sorry, we cannot bill)

☐ New
☐ Renewal
   (Attach Label)

Church Management
P.O. Box 162527
Austin, TX 78716

NAMES AND ADDRESSES
OF AUTHORS

Marian Y. Adell
United Methodist Church
15 Woodcliff Dr.
Madison, NJ 07940
February 2, 9, 1992

LaVonne Althouse
Salem Lutheran Church
5227 Castor Ave.
Philadelphia, PA 19124
July 5, 12, 19, 26, 1992

John R. Brokhoff
119 Harborage Court
Clearwater, FL 34630
Introductions to Lessons

Charles P. Calcagni
Oneonta Congregational Church
PO Box 121
Greensboro, VT 05841
May 17, 24, 28, 31, 1992

John N. Cedarleaf
First Congretional UCC
26 East Church St.
Fairport, NY 14450
March 8, 15, 22, 29, 1992

Myron R. and Jan Chartier
American Baptist Churches of Michigan
315 W. Michigan Ave.
Kalamazoo, MI 49002
April 19, 26, May 3, 10, 1992

David deFreese
Immanual Lutheran Church
104 Galvin Road North
Bellevue, NE 68005
September 29, October 6, 13, 20, 1991

Heather Murray Elkins
William Wesley Elkins
Bernardsville United Methodist Church
22 Church St.
Bernardsville, NJ 07924
August 4, 1991

Thomas N. Gard
The Presbyterian Church of Watertown
905 7th Ave NE
Watertown, SD 57201
September 1, 8, 15, 22, 1991

Dale I. Gregoriew
Christ the Servant Lutheran Church
501 Hightrail
Allen, TX 75002
October 27 (2), November 3 (2), 1991

Miles W. Jackson
The United Methodist Church
352 Legg Road
Bow, Washington 98232
March 1, 4, 1992

Greg J. Johanson
Delaware Valley United Methodist Church
Rt 2, Box 343
Branchville, NJ 07826
August 11, 1991

Alton H. McEachern
Lovejoy United Methodist Church
1951 Mount Carmel Rd.
Hampton, GA 30228
January 19, 26, 1992

Walter H. Mees, Jr.
Palisades Lutheran Church
11208 Hayter Ave.
Culver City, CA 90230
November 10, 17, 24, 28, 1991

Kenn Nilsen
Lutheran Church Staff
Rt 1, Box 106
Port Murray, NJ 07865
January 6, 12, 1992

Harold C. Perdue
The United Methodist Church
1701 S. Mays, Suite J-186
Round Rock, TX 78664
August 18, 25, 1991

Stan C. Pigue
St. John's United Methodist Church
Route 2, Box 1400
Danville, VA 24540
February 16, 23, 1992

David H. Schmidt
United Methodist Campus Ministry
633 West Locust St.
DeKalb, IL 60115
Lectionary Preaching Resources

William H. Schwein
Meridian St. United Methodist Church
6625 N. Sherman Dr.
Indianapolis, IN 46220
April 5, 12, 16, 17, 1992

Marilyn Stulken
1601 Circlewood Drive
Racine, WI 53402
Hymn for the Day

James R. Thomason
Overbrook Baptist Church
1705 East North St.
Greenville, SC 29607
June 7, 14, 21, 28, 1992

Richard Austin Thompson
Central Presbyterian Church
200 East 8th St.
Austin, TX 78701
Article on Communication

Gary Walling
Heights Christian Church
17300 Van Aken Blvd.
Shaker Heights, OH 44120
December 1, 8, 15, 22, 1991

Kenneth C. Whitt
Mountview Baptist Church
2140 Fishinger Rd.
Columbus, OH 43221
December 24, 25, 29, 1991
January 5, 1992

ADDITIONAL WORSHIP
PLANNING RESOURCES

Litanies for dedication services are frequently needed by those planning special worship services. For more than thirty years, *The Clergy Journal* has annually published a variety of dedications, litanies and rededication services. All of these have been used in real situations. Many have been published in a book, but others are available only in back issues of the Annual Planning issue.

If you are responsible for planning a special dedication service, you may want to review the following listing from the book *Dedication Services for Every Occasion* (available from Church Management, Inc., $8.95 plus $1.05 postage/handling).

Ground breaking and site dedication
Service for laying a cornerstone
Dedication of a new church building
Dedication of new educational wing
Dedication of stained glass windows
Dedication of new office and study
Dedication of a new church kitchen
Dedication service for a memorial library
Dedication of the church sign
Litany for burning the church mortgage
Litany for the anniversary of building the sanctuary
Rededication of a church building
Litany for closing a sanctuary
Dedication of chancel memorials
Dedication of altar memorial vases
Dedication of a chalice
Dedication of communion ware
Dedication of cross and candlesticks
Litany for dedication of candelabra
Dedication of baptismal font or baptistry
Litany for dedication of new offering plates
Litany for the dedication of candlelighters
Dedication of a pulpit Bible
Organ dedication and celebration
Dedication of a piano
Dedication of a church bell
Dedication of a carillon
Dedication service for handbells
Dedication of hymnals
Dedication of choir robes
Dedication of chair lift or elevator

Dedication of Christian and national flags
Litany for a manse site dedication
Dedication of a parsonage
Dedication of a home

If you do not find the dedication or litany you need in that listing, the following is a list of other such worship resources available in photocopy from Church Management, Inc., P.O. Box 162527, Austin, TX 78716. Send $3.00 and a self-addressed business size stamped envelope.

Ground breaking service in verse
Prayers for use in laying a cornerstone
Litany for the dedication of new church doors
Dedication of a steeple and bell
Cross-lifting ceremony
Dedication of memorial plantings
Dedication of a tower clock
Dedication of appointments and memorials
Office for the blessing of an altar
Dedication of a new Bible stand
Consecration of memorial paraments
Rededication of an organ
Litany for dedication of a sound system
Dedication of flag and flagpole
Litany for the dedication of a stage
Dedication of pulpit chairs
Dedication of a sanctuary piano
Litany for the dedication of organ chimes
Dedication of a funeral pall
Dedication of acolyte robes and stoles
Litany for the dedication of a literature rack
Dedication of a water treatment plant
Litany for the dedication of a community swimming pool
Services of dedication of a community building and flagstaff
Service for the launching of a ship
Litany for the dedication of a hospital
Dedication of a headstone
Dedication of church lawn plantings
Dedication of a welcome card pew rack
Dedication of church office machines
Dedication of a movie projector
A service for the burial of ashes at sea
Dedication of Church World Service clothing
Litany for reception of financial pledges
Dedication of new paraments
Dedication of memorial cloths for Holy Communion

Dedication of church furnishings
Dedication of a church library
Dedication for site development and parking lot
Dedication for a communications center
Dedication of new organ chimes
Dedication prayer for baptismal bowl
Dedication of a parking lot
Dedication of a Tree of Faith
Service for razing a church building
Litany for closing of a sanctuary
Dedication of a kneeling bench and candelabras
Dedication of an amplified lectern
Service for merging two congregations
Groundbreaking service for home for senior citizens
Fiftieth anniversary of a church building
Litany of appreciation for an old church building
Dedication of offering plates
Renewal of marriage vows
A litany for the choir
Service of Holy Communion following a wedding service
Dedication after child is baptized in hospital
Litany of commissioning for director of music
Commissioning service for church school class
Commissioning service for Christian education staff

If you still cannot locate the needed service, please write to Church Management, P.O. Box 162527, Austin, TX 78716 and ask. A service to match your needs may have been received by the editor after this listing was published.

Preaching the Practice

Communications
by Richard Austin Thompson*

The Practice
"**I**n the beginning was the Word. . ."

It's not accident that communications comes first in John's gospel. Nor is it by happenstance that this text echoes the first verse of the first book of the Hebrew Bible. Creation is inseparable from the communications process.

The Necessity
Anthropologists have identified language as that which gives humanity its distinctiveness. Culture and civilization are of a piece with the capacity to receive and send verbal and non-verbal messages.

Frederick the Great is said to have conducted an experiment in which certain infants were not to be spoken to, but were to have had all other needs met. The aim was to find what language came naturally to the little ones. Of course, no speech came without speaking. Moreover, the children began to perish. Survival itself, apart from a flourishing existence, depends upon that give-and-take.

"The intimacy of communication within a religious fellowship is like that within a marriage, the very substance of which is defined by a shared understanding which transcends audible messages."

In any attempted take-over of a government, the opposition invariably seeks to seize the mass communications systems. For whoever is in charge of the information flow has gone far in controlling the whole.

These examples are the negative way of pointing up the incomparable potency of the word. Positively, the development of com-

471

munications skills is the ticket for those who would rise above limitation. To name a fear is to harness its destructive effects. William James said, "Expression deepens impression." To learn to express oneself is to bring a new self into being.

As this is true for the society at large and individuals, so is it particularly the case for persons of faith in the religious community. There are dimensions and principles of communications which are common to all enterprises, but which come with special significance in a spiritual corporation.

The Dimensions

Human communication takes written and spoken, verbal and non-verbal, private and public forms. While a newsletter, for instance, may seem a relatively insignificant part of a local congregation, it does, in fact, play a role of disproportionate importance in the total life of the group.

To shut-ins, for instance, the newsletter may be the only regular tie that they have with the faith community. A letter from the clergy person may serve as their spiritual "lifeline," if they lack access to public worship. That letter also provides the means for the minister periodically to convey an overall vision or direction, in a form which reaches everyone in the group concurrently. Therefore, a regular, carefully prepared communique from the leader of the fellowship serves a variety of essential functions.

"There is simplicity in all good communication."

I find it incongruous that seminaries usually make a point of providing instruction on the musical aspect of church life, but omit guidance in the use of graphics. The layout, design, and eye-appeal of a publication does as much to communicate as the content.

Likewise is non-verbal communication even more powerful in its subliminal effects than the spoken word. When concluding a graveside service, for instance, bending to embrace members of the family does far more to signify warmth than simply pronouncing a benediction.

The intimacy of communication within a religious fellowship is like that within a marriage, the very substance of which is defined by a shared understanding which transcends audible messages. That "sixth sense" in counseling applies to the clergy no less than the secular therapist. But to know when and how to use prayer is a peculiarly rich resource for those in a religious calling.

For prayer opens up the feelings in a way which no other discourse is able to achieve. Instead of saying to parishioner that I will be praying for her or him, I ask what it is that she or he would have me pray for in her or his behalf. Thus does the devotional practice serve in the clarification of feelings, and provides the basis for empathetic response. Communication, at this point, passes into communion.

The Principles

Communications Theory has become a discipline in itself. William Schramm, in *The Science of Human Communications*, has identified its pioneers and those secular institutions which specialize in its theoretical development. Theodore Baehr's *Getting the Word Out* is a recently published guide to communication in congregations. In analyzing "The Foundations of Powerful Communication," he defines the why, who, what, and how of the process in a religious context. John Edward Lantz not only wrote *Speaking in the Church*, but has endowed a chair in the field at Yale Divinity School.

"It is the need for faith which gives substance to its meaning and which gives urgency to the means of imparting it plainly."

At the local level, I have found it helpful to be intentional about the way I go about communicating, and to share those understandings and skills with as many in the church as possible. For instance, when instructing youth in a confirmation program, I teach the MAD principles of reading scripture in public, whereby:

M means reading meaningfully,
A for audibly,
D for distinctively.

These guidelines are not limited to the religious setting. But the reading with expression presupposes a conviction which gives color to the tone and variation to the style of speaking. To project so as to be heard, shows that the speaker cares about his listeners. To pronounce the words clearly, rather than slur them, evidences also that one cares about the text, and wants the message to be received.

As this process applies to speaking, so does it in regard to the totality of the communication system within a congregation. As an official board makes the effort to let the people know the what and why of its policies, caring is transmitted. As there is a network of support groups within a parish, the message comes across "loud and clear" that the impersonality of modern organizational life is transcended. As the church demonstrates that it is one of the last places where "housecalls are made," then the signal of God's love for the individual is not slurred.

The necessity, dimensions and principles of effective communication are expressed in the following text/sermon which serves as the application for this particular aspect of parish practice.

The Preaching

Communicating Faith

Habakkuk 1:1-4, 2:1-4

It was while riding on a high-speed train that I thought of this text from Habakkuk. It may seem like a strange connection to make — linking this modern-day conveyance with the teachings of a lesser-known prophet in the remote past. But under those circumstances, that verse leaped to mind: "Write the vision; make it plain. . . so he may run who reads it."

"Prayer, to be sure, involves our speaking. But what is often overlooked is how it is primarily a listening, an openness to what comes from beyond."

To be sure, I wasn't running; but I was moving so fast that the billboards posted in the stations along the way sped by so quickly that all I could do was to catch a glimpse of what was being advertised. And each of those signs had one common characteristic — they were all eye-catching, with large print and few words. All were designed so that those whizzing by would get the point. For there is simplicity in all good communication. That truth is the reason we find this element included in this text.

But what is the message, the vision which would be made plain? The answer is contained in this verse:

Behold, he whose soul is not upright in him shall fail,
but the righteous shall live by his faith.

The Talmud, the later Jewish interpretation of the Old Testament, considered this teaching so simple and complete that it declared all 613 commandments of Moses had been reduced to this one — "The righteous shall live by his faith." The Apostle Paul built his whole doctrine of justification by faith around this text. Martin Luther followed suit many centuries later.

But if faith is the content of the vision, and simplicity the means of conveying it, we still are left with the question of why is such communication necessary. That is, in fact, the key to communicating faith at any time and place. For it is the need for faith which gives substance to its meaning and which gives urgency to the means of imparting it plainly.

Why?

To determine the original motivation we must go back to the beginning of the text, where the prophet plays the role of skeptic as he himself asks God "The Why Question."

Why dost thou make me see wrongs
and look upon trouble?. . . .
For the wicked surround the righteous,
so justice goes forth perverted.

In other words this is another one of those places in the Bible where sensitive souls want to know why evil seems to triumph, and why those who are trying to do the right thing are the ones to suffer. The term "theodicy" has been given to such a challenging of God about life's unfairness.

Whatever we call it, this is the question of questions for most people as far as religion is concerned. It is so perplexing that we find it repeatedly raised in the Bible — in the book of Job, in the Psalms, and certainly in the teachings of Jesus. *Why Do Bad Things*

Happen to Good People? is the way Rabbi Harold Kushner posed the issue in a best-seller of that title.

When it comes to Habakkuk's faith contribution, we would do well to be faithful to the particular form which that concern took for him. It was some 600 years before the time of Christ. Within Judah, justice was being perverted. The Chaldeans, the superpower of the day, were initially perceived as executing judgment upon the unrighteous. Yet their barbarism only compounded the problem, as even more innocent people were being made to suffer. So the prophet's challenge to God persists, until he makes a decision to do more than complain. He says:

> *I will take my stand to watch,*
> *and station myself on the tower,*
> *and look forth to see what he will say to me,*
> *and what I will answer concerning my complaint.*

Receptivity

Before proceeding to the answer that was forthcoming, let us simply recognize how receptivity is the prerequisite to any effective communication. Habakkuk shows an expectant spirit — ready to watch; he positions himself to gain a wider view — the reason for stationing himself on the tower; and is prepared to enter into dialogue with the Lord — wanting first to hear and then to make his own reply.

The Jehovah's Witnesses have taken the image of *The Watchtower* as the title for their publication and for their belief that they have been given the long view so as to be able to foresee the coming end of the world. While no one can identify that tower for certain, we may surmise it to be the pinnacle of the Temple, from which the prophet could rise above immediate impressions and so broaden his horizons. Yet there is no question that his position included prayer, the mood of receptivity and dialogue with the Maker.

Psychologist Robert Ornstein has distinguished between two forms of consciousness — the active mode and the receptive mode. The active is one of logic, control, of talking. The receptive is that of intuition, surrender, and of listening. Prayer, to be sure, involves our speaking. But what is often overlooked is how it is primarily a listening, an openness to what comes from beyond. It is in learning to listen, to receive, that we may gain understanding and power which would not be forthcoming otherwise.

Especially is the tendency great to do little but talk when we have felt ourselves treated unfairly by life, or by God. The temptation is to keep on asking "Why me? Why me, Lord?" While the feeling of perplexity is understandable, the fact is that we have a choice of whether to succumb to self-pity, so that all voices are drowned out but our own.

It's been rightly said that the Lord gave us one mouth and two ears that we may do twice as much listening as talking. It was in the listening posture that Habakkuk did indeed receive the inspiration which led to his insight – the vision which he was told to make so plain that people, even "on the run," could read it.

Wait for the Vision

But before returning to the content of that communique, let us note one other feature of how it comes about – both slowly and quickly. The vision "awaits its time. . . yet hastens to the end." Its coming may seem slow, yet the Lord says to

> . . . *wait for it;*
> *it will surely come, it will not delay.*

If spiritual development seems to come in fits and starts it's because that's the way growth of any kind takes place. It's the way you and I "make haste slowly."

It was just before Thanksgiving – just before the holidays, when the stress level is apt to increase sharply – that a call came from a husband who, in tears, exclaimed that his wife had left him, taking their two young children with her. In the face-to-face conversation which immediately followed, he went ahead to explain how her frustration had been building up over a period of years, occasioned by her description of him as a "cold fish." While her abrupt departure took him by complete surprise, in retrospect he could see what she was talking about. He then recognized how his manner had been so "uptight," so compulsively rigid that he could discern how she would have felt little warmth emanating from him.

But at the time of this confession, he was showing plenty of feeling. The tears, which had been bottled up in him for years, came flowing forth. He wished only that he could have his family back.

But in the weeks to follow, well into December, the family remained apart – he in one state, she and their children at her parents' home in another. While at one level, time seemed to drag for him during this period, something else was happening at another. The way he put it was that the events which had so precipitously transpired had been like a hammer which smashed the brittle exterior of his life, which he compared to porcelain. Yet, to his amazement, a warm, caring person was waiting to make his appearance just below the surface. That inner self had been forming silently in the recesses of his inner being over the years, but had not had the occasion to emerge until the crisis occurred.

Besides himself, the most surprised person to be making the discovery was his wife, who found that, for the first time in their ten year marriage, he was communicating. Once that process had commenced, she was ready to give it another try; and by Christmas they were together again. Those events transpired fifteen years ago. Now that is what the storybooks call "a happy ending."

But what happens when it doesn't turn out happily? Or when one or both parties make fundamental changes, yet when it is too late for the relationship?

That reality, which can be denied only if we are to fly in the face of the facts, is what brings us back to the content of the prophet's vision, the substance of the communication about coping with life's apparently unfair treatment. While Habakkuk says that the insight is slow to come, it will, nonetheless, and sometimes with breath-taking speed. Again:

> *Behold, he whose soul is not upright. . . will fail,*
> *but the righteous shall live by. . . faith.*

The downside of that truth is that those who seem to be getting by with murder, in the end, won't; while the upside is that those with integrity will be sustained. This prophet comes to that realization because he is viewing the scene from a tower, in broad perspective.

So, on a clear day of prayer, you can see forever, discerning how destructive consequences come upon those who don't tell or do the truth. As historian Charles Beard—skeptic though he was—concluded after decades of studying the human story, "the mills of the gods grind slowly, but they grind exceedingly fine," and "the night is darkest before the dawn."

Moreover, the call to ministry will inevitably involve the conviction that "everything works for good. . . to those who are called according to his purpose." As the mother of a brain-damaged child describes rehabilitation, "You can't turn the clock back. But we are slowly winding it up again." If, in fact, time is redeemed by infinite love, there is no end to making new beginnings. Even when your loved one is gone for good, the going can be for good, if there is no separation from the One who loves us ultimately.

So there it is, so plain and simple that even we who run may read—in the name of him who came that we may have life, and have it abundantly.

INDEX OF SERMON TEXTS

Pre-publication Advance Order Form

THE MINISTER'S ANNUAL MANUAL
FOR
PREACHING AND WORSHIP PLANNING
1992-1993

60 complete sermon and
worship planning helps
beginning August 2, 1992
through July 31, 1993

(Available by June 1, 1992)

$19.90

CLIP AND SEND NAME/ADDRESS WITH PAYMENT TO:

CHURCH MANAGEMENT, INC., P.O. Box 162527, Austin, TX 78716.
My check for $19.90, payable to CHURCH MANAGEMENT, INC. is enclosed for
one copy of *The Minister's Annual Manual for Preaching and Worship Planning
1992-1993*

Name _____

Address _____

City/State/Zip _____